Religion in the South
John B. Boles, Series Editor

# Episcopalians
## *and* Race

### Civil War
### to
### Civil Rights

GARDINER H. SHATTUCK JR.

THE UNIVERSITY PRESS OF KENTUCKY

Publication of this volume was made possible in part
by a grant from the National Endowment for the Humanities.

Scholarly publisher for the Commonwealth,
serving Bellarmine College, Berea College, Centre
College of Kentucky, Eastern Kentucky University,
The Filson Club Historical Society, Georgetown College,
Kentucky Historical Society, Kentucky State University,
Morehead State University, Murray State University,
Northern Kentucky University, Transylvania University,
University of Kentucky, University of Louisville,
and Western Kentucky University.

*Editorial and Sales Offices:* The University Press of Kentucky
663 South Limestone Street, Lexington, Kentucky 40508–4008

04 03 02 01 00 5 4 3 2 1

Library of Congress Cataloging-in-Publication Data

Shattuck, Gardiner H.
    Episcopalians and race : Civil War to civil rights / Gardiner H. Shattuck, Jr.
       p.    cm.
    Includes bibliographical references and index.
    ISBN 0-8131-2149-3 (cloth : alk. paper)
    1. Race relations—Religious aspects—Episcopal Church—History—
19th century. 2. Episcopal Church—History—19th century. 3. United
States—Race relations—History—19th century. 4. Race relations—
Religious aspects—Episcopal Church—History—20th century.
5. Episcopal Church—History—20th century. 6. United States—Race
relations—History—19th century. I. Title.
BX5979.S53   2000
261.8'348'00973—dc21                    99-41357

In memory of

my father
Gardiner H. Shattuck
(1911–1994)
and
my seminary classmate
Pauli Murray
(1910–1985)

God . . . hath made of one blood
all nations of men for to dwell on all the face of the earth,
and hath determined . . . the bounds of their habitation.

—Acts 17:24, 26 (KJV)

# Contents

*Illustrations follow pages 90 and 170*

# Acknowledgments

To accomplish a project of this scope would have been impossible without the aid and encouragement of numerous people. First of all, I wish to thank John Booty, the historiographer of the Episcopal Church, and Arthur Walmsley, the retired bishop of Connecticut, for asking me to undertake the research that has led to this book. The initial stages of my work were supported by a sizable grant, presented to Arthur on the occasion of his retirement, by the Church Missions Publishing Company of Connecticut. It had long been Arthur's hope to interview Episcopalians active in the civil rights struggle of the 1960s, and he was given the grant to help support a study of that era. Although the project has evolved considerably since they first contacted me, I am extremely grateful to both Arthur and John for showing confidence in my abilities as a historian and for raising funds that supplemented the original grant. I owe special thanks as well to John Morris, now a retired priest in Atlanta, who was the executive director of the Episcopal Society for Cultural and Racial Unity (ESCRU) between 1960 and 1967. John and his late wife Patsy not only supplied copious information (including manuscripts and photographs) about ESCRU and race relations in the South, but also furnished generous financial assistance and hospitality during the course of my research. Without the immense help that John Booty, Arthur Walmsley, and John Morris offered me, this book could never have been written.

Several other people and institutions provided funding at critical junctures in my research. A substantial grant from the Louisville Institute was valuable in enabling me to undertake the majority of the oral history interviews on which this study is based, and I wish to thank James Lewis, the executive director of the Institute, for all his helpfulness. Two additional grants from the Church Missions Publishing Company, moreover, allowed me to complete the interviewing process. I appreciate the efforts of Jerry Carroon and Jack Spaeth in arranging those grants and assisting me in numerous other ways at diocesan headquarters in Hartford, and I am grateful to Clarence Coleridge, the current bishop of Connecticut, for approving that funding. In addition, the Historical Society of the Episcopal Church, the Evangelical Education Society of the Episcopal Church, the Committee for Clergy Continuing Education of the diocese of Rhode

Island, the Archives of the Episcopal Church, Avery Brooke of Noroton, Connecticut, and Mary Eunice Oliver of San Diego, California, provided key financial support. And I am indebted to the deans of the following schools for making lodging available to me while I did research in their libraries: Dusty McDonald of the Episcopal Theological Seminary of the Southwest; Guy Lytle of the School of Theology, University of the South; and Richard Reid of the Virginia Theological Seminary. I owe a tremendous debt of gratitude to the above organizations and individuals.

Throughout my research, I received important assistance from people at numerous archives and libraries. Greatest thanks go to Mark Duffy and the hard-working staff members of the Archives of the Episcopal Church, especially Jennifer Peters, Sylvia Baker, and Kathleen Burnside, who answered virtually every request and assisted me with unfailing cheerfulness and professionalism over the course of the past seven years. In addition, I appreciate their generosity in waiving royalty fees on the many photographs from the Archives that are published in this book. Julie Randle at Virginia Theological Seminary, Annie Armour at the University of the South, and David Green and the late Katherine Austin at General Theological Seminary carefully guided me as well while I worked in manuscript collections housed in their archives. Several other archivists and librarians gave special attention to my needs, and I am appreciative of their assistance, too: Cynthia Lewis, archivist at the Martin Luther King, Jr., Center for Non-Violent Social Change; Mattie Sink of the Mitchell Memorial Library, Mississippi State University; Nora Murphy, archivist of the diocese of Massachusetts; Kenneth Wills, archivist of the diocese of Mississippi; and Clarence Hunter of the Zenobia Coleman Library, Tougaloo College. A host of other individuals imparted essential information by allowing me to interview them, by sharing portions of their personal papers and libraries, and by responding to questions via telephone and letter. Although there is not space enough to list all of them here, I have noted their important contributions to this project in the endnotes.

I appreciate the helpful suggestions offered by the anonymous scholars who read my manuscript for the University Press of Kentucky and by John Boles, the general editor of the Religion in the South series. All of them have improved this book considerably and have made it more accurate and readable.

I have greatly profited from the insights and ideas of a number of colleagues and fellow scholars who study twentieth-century American religious history. Jim Findlay and Michael Friedland, who are both authors of important works on the involvement of American Christians in social issues in the 1960s, not only have given me a scholarly context in which to write, but have also become supportive friends. Jo Gillespie and Donald Cunnigen generously shared with me portions of their own writings and research about the civil rights activities of Episcopalians. And thanks to this project I have been able to spend many enjoyable hours with Ken and Toni Kesselus, from whom I have learned much about the life and prophetic ministry of John Hines.

Last but by no means least, I want to thank members of my family for their forbearance throughout the seemingly interminable period in which I worked on this project. My daughter Rachel has advanced through adolescence into adulthood and is now embarking on an academic career of her own; my mother, Mary Shattuck, has done her part by praying that she would live long enough to see this book finished. My wife Cynthia not only has endured my preoccupation and absences while researching and writing, but she has also shared her own redoubtable talents as a professional editor on the manuscript. Words cannot express how much I appreciate Cynthia's unflagging support. Finally, I have dedicated this book to the memory of two Episcopal priests who in substantial (though quite different) ways influenced its creation: Pauli Murray, the civil rights pioneer whom I was honored to know as a fellow student at General Seminary; and my father, the "real" Gardiner Shattuck, whose love of the past first quickened my interest in history.

One further note. Working on this book has brought me into contact with scores of people about whom I have written and commented in the pages that follow. Without exception, I found them all extraordinarily gracious and likable, and I want them to know how much I appreciate the ways in which they assisted me personally and helped enrich the experience of producing this book. Having said that, I must confess to feelings of uneasiness about aspects of the story I am telling, because I know that my narrative sometimes differs from the memories and opinions of my informants. I have attempted to be accurate and fair in relating what I have been told, but as a historian I have also had to choose between differing accounts and interpretations of events, highlighting some versions and de-emphasizing others. In recent years there has been significant disagreement among Episcopalians (as well as Americans as a whole) about a number of social issues, including race. This book will neither solve nor end those conflicts but will, I hope, illuminate how and why various controversies have developed and taken place.

# *Introduction*

Ulrich B. Phillips, born in Georgia in 1877, is generally regarded as the preeminent southern historian of his generation. Raised in an environment that revered the values of the slaveholding class, Phillips's greatest contribution to scholarship was his argument that the plantation system represented the key to understanding the antebellum South. The plantation, he maintained, functioned both as an economic institution and as a means of social control, unifying southern society and fostering an enduring relationship between benevolent white masters and childlike black slaves. Phillips's quintessential statement on race is found in the essay, "The Central Theme of Southern History" (1928). The South, he wrote, is "a land with a *unity* despite its diversity, with a people having common joys and common sorrows, and, above all, . . . a common resolve indomitably maintained—that it shall be and remain a white man's country." This belief in white supremacy, whether it was "expressed with the frenzy of a demagogue or maintained with a patrician's quietude," united the region and remained an essential mark of the white southerner. Although Phillips's ideas were thoroughly racist, his reputation was strong enough to shape academic and popular opinion about the meaning of slavery and race in the United States during the period between the two world wars.[1]

Another historian, Grace Elizabeth Hale, has recently reexamined Phillips's theories in an effort to interpret and rethink southern race relations. She links the image of the harmonious "plantation pastorale," which Phillips and other white writers self-consciously constructed, with the development of racial paternalism in the South in the late nineteenth and early twentieth centuries. Upper- and middle-class white southerners, she suggests, longed to recover a closeness they imagined they had enjoyed with African Americans before the Civil War. In order to fulfill this emotional need for "integration" with blacks, they manufactured a romanticized picture of the antebellum period. It was an era free of racial conflict, they said, when masters and slaves interacted on intimate, mutually supportive terms. Hale claims that members of the white elite also used African Americans to help define themselves in comparison with lower-class whites. Unlike so-called "rednecks" or "white trash," "the nice people" or "better class" of whites treated African Americans with a tolerant kindness, and in return (they believed) blacks offered them gestures of deference and respect. Whatever the reality of the situation, this myth of a unified biracial society served as the central paradigm of race relations in the South for several decades. It had a tremendous impact upon southern culture, for it not only reinforced existing social divisions but also circumscribed the autonomy of poor whites as well as African Americans.[2]

This book is organized around the theme of social and racial unity outlined by historians Phillips and Hale, and it analyzes how religious interpretations of this concept influenced race relations among members of the Episcopal Church between the Civil War and the civil rights movement. Throughout much of the roughly hundred-year period this book studies, leading Episcopalians in the South proclaimed their belief that God "hath made of one blood all nations of men" (Acts 17:26 KJV). They insisted, moreover, that no matter how racial differences were treated in the secular realm, all people were equal in the sight of God. But despite their official views on race, church members were often sharply divided about the practical application of those teachings and about the manner in which Americans of different colors were meant to relate to one another. Was it better, for example, if African Americans and whites worshiped in racially distinct parishes or if they worshiped together in the same buildings? And did racial separation, when it was practiced, advance or retard the progress of African Americans toward equality with whites?

"Race" itself is a complicated and contested term. Since my narrative focuses primarily on the church in the South, the word signifies (at least for the purposes of this book) the relationship between white and black Americans. Although some scholars debate whether "race" actually exists or whether it is right to confine discussions of it only to African Americans, I will have to ignore those deeper hermeneutical questions. Because of the obvious virulence of white racism and because of its profound, long-term effects upon African Americans, the position of black people within society was viewed as the most critical racial question facing church people in the United States throughout the era I am studying. And while Episcopal leaders sometimes categorized Native Americans,

Asian Americans, Hispanic Americans, and other ethnic groups as "racial minorities," black Episcopalians constituted the largest nonwhite group in the denomination, especially in southern and urban dioceses, in the mid-twentieth century. More scholarly work certainly needs to be done on Native American missions and on the church's response to the internment of Japanese Americans during World War II, but those are the subjects of books other than this one. On the other hand, my book is *not* a history of black Episcopalians per se, but relies upon contributions and insights on that subject provided by scholars such as Harold Lewis and J. Carleton Hayden. My interest is principally in the ideas of church leaders (predominantly white) about their relationship with African Americans.[3]

My narrative is divided into three main sections. Each of these examines the racial paradigm under which Americans generally, and Episcopalians in particular, operated within a given time frame: segregation (from the late 1860s through the early 1950s); integration (from the release of the *Brown* decision in 1954 through the Selma-Montgomery march in 1965); and what I call "fragmentation" (the breakup of the civil rights coalition in the late 1960s and early 1970s). This book concludes with an epilogue that carries the story of Episcopalians and race forward to the controversy surrounding the location of the denomination's 1991 General Convention—a troubling instance of history repeating itself.

In his classic study of race relations, *An American Dilemma* (1944), Gunnar Myrdal argued that the inability of whites to reconcile their belief in human equality with the actual experiences of black citizens in the United States was an ongoing source of confusion, frustration, and shame. Although Myrdal's perspective had its own limitations, his ideas about the ironies of American race relations might be applied as much to the Episcopal Church as to the nation as a whole. Thanks to traditional Anglican establishmentarian ideas, which encouraged the desire to become a "national church" incorporating all non-Roman Catholic Christians, Episcopalians in the early twentieth century assumed that their denomination had a key role to play in the unification of American society. This belief carried special weight during the civil rights era when clergy and lay people labored in often heroic ways to effect social and racial harmony in the United States. But despite the undeniable legal advances of the 1960s, the meanings of "race" and "unity" remain problematic for Episcopalians even at the end of the millennium.[4]

White leaders in the Episcopal Church have generally understood unity—the unity of humankind, created by God, redeemed (as the Nicene Creed says) by "one Lord Jesus Christ," and gathered by the Holy Spirit

in the church—as a salutary theological concept. Yet in spite of the undeniable religious truth of that ideal, it has also been misapplied and used
to repress divergent voices and concerns within the church. Thus, the
quest for ecclesiastical and social unity has had negative as well as positive consequences for African Americans and, akin to the myth of the
harmonious, biracial plantation of the Old South, has tended to promote
the invisibility (to use Ralph Ellison's famous metaphor) of black people
within decision-making areas in the Episcopal Church.

# Part I

# Segregation

A colored priest of my acquaintance recently related to me, with tears in his eyes, how his reverend Father in God, the Bishop who had ordained him, had met him on the cars on his way to the diocesan convention and warned him, not unkindly, not to take a seat in the body of the convention with the white clergy. To avoid disturbance of their godly placidity he would of course please sit back and somewhat apart. I do not imagine that that clergyman had very much heart for the Christly (!) deliberations of that convention.

—Anna Julia Cooper,
*A Voice from the South*

# 1

# *Racial Paternalism and Christian Mission after the Civil War*

As W.E.B. Du Bois observed in his path-breaking history of the Reconstruction era, news of the signing of the Emancipation Proclamation evoked exuberant expressions of religious feeling among African Americans in the South. Beginning on January 1, 1863, Union army camps became both bases of military operations and havens for thousands of jubilant runaways. Du Bois wrote: "To most of the four million black folk emancipated by civil war, God was real. They knew Him. They had met Him personally in many a wild orgy of religious frenzy, or in the black stillness of the night. His plan for them was clear; they were to suffer and be degraded, and then afterwards by Divine edict, raised to manhood and power; and so . . . He made them free. It was all foolish, bizarre, and tawdry. Gangs of dirty Negroes howling and dancing; . . . and yet to these black folk it was the Apocalypse." The Emancipation Proclamation contained similar religious meaning for opponents of slavery in the North, and those who had been active in the abolitionist movement gave thanks to God that their nation was at last purging itself of its most detestable sin. During the final two years of the Civil War, they watched with gratification as Federal troops radically altered southern society. Northern abolitionists and black southerners together not only believed in the justice of the Union war effort, but also saw a divine hand in the struggle to set a captive people free.[1]

The reaction of African Americans on Pawley's Island in South Carolina was typical of what Du Bois described when news of emancipation reached the slave quarters in 1865. Hearing that Lee had surrendered at Appomattox, freed people proclaimed that their prayers had been answered and that the great day of Jubilee had at last arrived. But while African Americans were praising God for their deliverance, Alexander Glennie, the Episcopal rector of nearby All Saints' Church (Waccamaw), felt that God had entirely deserted him. Glennie had served successfully on Pawley's Island for over thirty years. When he started his ministry, All Saints' contained only ten black communicants, but his diligent evangelistic efforts increased that figure to nearly three hundred by 1862. Indeed, Episcopalians throughout South Carolina were highly successful in gathering African Americans into their churches, and at the outbreak of the Civil War there were almost as many black communicants as white ones in the state. The rice planters of the Carolina lowcountry gladly supported this mission, for though the white clergy taught that all people were equal in God's sight, they also stressed the need for slaves to remain obedient to their masters. The collapse of the Confederate government, however, brought Glennie's work to an abrupt halt. In mid-1865, he reported that most of his black parishioners no longer attended biracial Episcopal services but had instead joined congregations led by African American preachers. Believing his ministry had been repudiated virtually overnight, the disillusioned Glennie resigned his position in 1866, leaving All Saints' parish without stable clerical leadership for more than a decade.[2]

The mass departure of black church members that Alexander Glennie witnessed on Pawley's Island was observed throughout the South between 1865 and 1870. Thousands of African Americans abandoned their membership in the Episcopal Church and other white-controlled denominations, while the African Methodist Episcopal Church, the African Methodist Episcopal Zion Church, and black Baptist churches experienced astounding growth. Although white Episcopalians seemed genuinely amazed at what Joseph Wilmer, the bishop of Louisiana, called "the strange defection of this people from our fold," they should not have been surprised, for Africans Americans simply recognized the implications of the gospel that white clergy had preached to them. Since the antebellum mission to slaves made paternalism and social control indispensable adjuncts to the Christian faith, African Americans saw that the creation of independent Baptist and Methodist churches represented their best opportunity to achieve freedom from the values of their former masters, now condemned by God for having gone to war to uphold the wicked institution of slavery. Having been relegated to galleries and treated as mere observers in biracial churches prior to their emancipation, ex-slaves welcomed the chance to escape the restrictive hand of whites like Glennie by organizing their own congregations and ordaining pastors who under-stood their true spiritual needs.[3]

Against this backdrop of ecclesiastical collapse in the South, del-egates to the denomination's General Convention—the triennial decision-making body of the denomination—assembled in Philadelphia in October 1865. Despite the severity of the exodus of black southerners, the first task the convention addressed was perceived to be even more pressing: healing the division that had occurred between white Episcopalians dur-ing the Civil War. Episcopal leaders had been generally unmoved by abo-litionist rhetoric and—unlike the Presbyterians, Methodists, and Baptists—had maintained a unified church during the bitter national con-troversy over slavery in the 1830s and 1840s. Abhorring ecclesiastical schism more than the suffering of people held in bondage, white Episco-palians had argued that slavery was a purely political question and, as such, beyond the church's concern. Friendships formed at schools and at summer resorts in the North also continued to unite bishops and leading clergy across sectional lines. The secession of eleven states from the Union and the outbreak of war, however, had placed Episcopalians in the South in an untenable position. As a consequence, they organized a new de-nomination, the Protestant Episcopal Church in the Confederate States of America, which operated as a completely independent body during the war. They not only adopted their own constitution, canons, and prayer book, but also authorized the consecration of Richard Hooker Wilmer as bishop of Alabama. Since Wilmer was consecrated without receiving the approval of dioceses in states still loyal to the Union, that action repre-sented a potentially serious violation of Episcopal canon law.

Despite this provocation, most Episcopal leaders in the North re-mained true to their prewar views and desired unity and reconciliation with the southern dioceses once peace arrived. Thomas Atkinson, the bishop of North Carolina, and Henry Lay, the bishop of Arkansas, an-swered the entreaties of Presiding Bishop John Henry Hopkins of Ver-mont, a noted proslavery advocate, to forget wartime animosities and return to the Episcopal Church in the United States. Thanks in large measure to Hopkins's resolute indifference to the moral and political fac-tors that had caused the Civil War, Atkinson and Lay recognized his sin-cerity and accepted his invitation to join their colleagues in the House of Bishops at the convention in Philadelphia. From the perspective of these men, the meeting went extremely well. Despite the efforts of a few die-hard northerners in the House of Deputies to pass a resolution of thanks-giving for Union victory, the convention followed Hopkins's lead, choosing only to adopt a statement thanking God for the return of peace and for the restoration of unity within the *church*. The church also acted favorably on Bishop Wilmer of Alabama. Although Wilmer himself remained hesitant about reunion and even directed congregations in his diocese not to pray for the president of the United States, the convention recognized the legality of his consecration. Finally, Atkinson and Lay were well received by their fellow bishops, and they soon encouraged other white Episcopalians to regard the wartime division as only temporary and rejoin the denomination they left in 1861.[4]

While healing this split in the ranks of the denomination's white membership, the General Convention of 1865 also established the Protestant Episcopal Freedman's Commission and gave it a mandate to win back African Americans who had deserted the Episcopal Church at the time of their emancipation. Since Congress had recently created the Freedmen's Bureau as a federal agency designed to assist former slaves in obtaining basic commodities such as food and clothing, the church adopted a similar strategy to deal with the spiritual needs of black southerners. Like the mission among slaves prior to the war, the Freedman's Commission was dedicated to fostering social stability in the South. Francis Wharton, the secretary of the commission, believed that African Americans constituted an essentially "ignorant and debased race" who threatened the health of American society. He trusted, however, that with the guidance of white church people they could still be "elevated to self-support and self-control." To address these concerns, the commission's organizers introduced a program of practical as well as religious instruction by which they hoped to entice African Americans back into Episcopal parishes. The commission also founded several educational institutions (most notably, St. Augustine's College in Raleigh, North Carolina) to train black Episcopalians as leaders who would cooperate with whites.[5]

The conservative intentions of its white founders notwithstanding, the commission soon met with opposition. Bishops in the southern states where the commission operated distrusted its work, for they thought it detracted from their right to control church affairs within their dioceses. Since it was also a northern-based organization created at a General Convention that most southern Episcopalians did not attend, some church members worried that the name "Freedman's Commission" carried secular overtones and suggested the kind of social radicalism they thought was embodied in the government's Freedmen's Bureau. Would African Americans not be tempted, they asked, to take advantage of the educational opportunities the commission offered without either joining the church or accepting its guidance over their religious affairs? In response to these concerns, the next General Convention (in 1868) adopted nomenclature that was more clearly evangelistic in focus, and the organization's name was changed to the Commission of Home Missions to Colored People.[6]

Despite the lack of support from white Episcopalians in the South, leaders of the commission continued to challenge their denomination to take seriously its responsibilities in providing guidance to the African American community. Unless significant evangelistic action was taken, they insisted, freed slaves would continue to follow the "ignorant and . . . grossly immoral" black preachers who were widening the gulf between the races and carrying African Americans inexorably beyond the reach of white church people. These views were, of course, commonplace among whites after the Civil War. That African American worship consisted of wild and inappropriate revelry, that black preachers were poorly equipped to be ministers, and that their churches were centers for political organizing were all articles of faith in white denominations in the late 1860s. By the early 1870s, however, diminishing concern for the spiritual affairs of black southerners paralleled both the decline in the political importance of African Americans and the waning of the federal Reconstruction program. Meanwhile, interest in the nation's western expansion increased dramatically, and after the Episcopal Church established its Indian Commission in 1871, donations to the missionary work among Native Americans quickly surpassed what was being raised to evangelize black southerners. In its report to the 1877 General Convention, the denomination's Board of Missions conceded that most black people in the South were indifferent to the Episcopal Church and that most white Episcopalians were unconcerned about reversing that trend. As a result, the Commission of Home Missions to Colored People was formally disbanded in 1878, and its duties were assigned to the general care of the Board of Missions instead.[7]

In spite of their unwillingness to cooperate with the national leaders of the Episcopal Church, the majority of bishops and clergy in the South recognized the value to white Episcopalians of keeping a hand in the religious affairs of black people. The trustees at Virginia Theological Seminary in Alexandria, for instance, thought African Americans should receive a theological education, but since they did not want black ministerial students to enroll at their white school, they authorized the collection of funds to establish a racially separate seminary on the grounds of St. Stephen's Church in Petersburg. Giles Cooke, a priest and former officer in the Confederate army, had opened a normal school for ex-slaves at St. Stephen's after the war, and his institution soon became the recipient of Virginia Seminary's largesse. The money from the seminary enabled Cooke to add a theological department in 1878, and from it the Bishop Payne Divinity School—the principal training ground for black clergy in the South—later emerged. Cooke was a racial paternalist who envisioned a relationship between education, evangelism, and social control. He emphasized the importance of saving African Americans from the "heathenish manifestation of wild religious feeling" into which preachers of their own race were carrying them, and he thought his school provided a healthful counterweight to "the leadership of so-called spiritual pastors, who instead of preaching the blessed Gospel of love and peace, substitute . . . the teaching of enmity and strife between the races." Those preachers, he concluded, were worse than "designing politicians" in alienating African Americans from white Episcopal clergy, who were struggling to provide black people with proper religious guidance.[8]

Throughout the 1870s, white Episcopalians in the South wrestled with the question of whether black parishes, composed entirely of African Americans whom they had evangelized, should receive official recognition in their dioceses. Although clergy were generally willing to concede some status to black Episcopalians in exchange for their continued loyalty to the church, lay leaders tended to be indifferent to the denominational affiliation of African Americans. Thus, when St. Mark's Church in Charleston (a parish composed of former slaves) applied in 1875 for admission as a full member of the diocese of South Carolina, Bishop William Howe and most of the clergy argued that the refusal to accept the parish would seriously undermine their efforts to influence and instruct African Americans. The laity, however, insisted that important social barriers between black and white South Carolinians would be weakened if the request from St. Mark's were granted, and they eventually succeeded in blocking that petition. The refusal to admit St. Mark's had the consequences Howe feared, for though that parish remained faithful to the Episcopal Church, six other African American congregations in the state withdrew from the denomination. Dismayed about their inability to achieve recognition as Episcopalians, the five hundred communicants of those congregations joined the newly organized Reformed Episcopal Church in mid-1875.[9]

By the early 1880s prominent white Episcopalians in the South were keenly aware of the dilemma they faced concerning the ecclesiastical status of African Americans. How were they to keep black people accountable to the authority of white clergy (as well as compliant with the overall ascendancy of whites in civil affairs) if they did not also offer them some incentive to remain part of a biracial Episcopal Church? The Methodist Episcopal Church, South had developed a workable solution to a similar predicament white Methodists faced in the aftermath of the Civil War. In order to discourage the church's black membership from transferring allegiance to the northern-oriented African Methodist Episcopal and African Methodist Episcopal Zion denominations, southern Methodists organized a new and separate denomination, the Colored Methodist Episcopal Church, in 1870. In exchange for maintaining cordial relations with the Methodist Episcopal Church, South, Colored Methodists received property from the parent denomination and were allowed to ordain their own pastors and bishops. Although they were still denied equality with whites, those black Methodists at least gained freedom to run their own institutional affairs.[10]

Mindful of the white Methodists' apparent success in balancing autonomy and control, a group of Episcopal bishops, priests, and lay people assembled for a conference at the University of the South in Sewanee, Tennessee, in July 1883. William Green, the bishop of Mississippi, had contacted his colleagues in the southern dioceses and asked them to come to Sewanee for a meeting at which they could discuss the relationship between African Americans in the South and the Episcopal Church. Following several days of debate, the Sewanee conference considered but rejected both the Methodist plan of separate racial jurisdictions and the idea (originally proposed by Bishop Alexander Gregg of Texas) of creating a position of "suffragan" (assistant) bishop in charge of the evangelism of African Americans. The group believed that, because administrative unity was an essential attribute of Episcopal dioceses, it was wrong to consecrate more than one bishop for ministry within a single geographical area. "There can be but one fold and one Chief Shepherd for all the people in any field of Ecclesiastical designation," conference participants argued. In order to maintain this principle of all Episcopalians united under a single (necessarily white) bishop, the Sewanee conference decided that each diocese containing a large number of African Americans should establish a "special Missionary Organization" to which its black members could be assigned. Black Episcopalians would worship apart from whites, but they would still be under the authority of the diocesan bishop. The recommendation seemed suitable to almost everyone present at Sewanee: it acknowledged "the peculiarity of the relations" of white and black southerners but maintained the nominal unity of the denomination by providing a mechanism for keeping African Americans within the Episcopal fold.[11]

The Sewanee conference took place at the beginning of a fateful evolution in race relations in the United States. During the last two decades of the nineteenth century, the Supreme Court gradually abolished the civil rights gained by African Americans in the 1860s and 1870s, while outspoken racists vied with paternalists for political control in the South. Within this context, most Episcopal leaders occupied a middle ground between the few white southerners who genuinely wished to assist African Americans and those who sought only to degrade them. Upper-class southerners like the men who assembled at Sewanee were adept at keeping African Americans "in their place" (in order to protect them from assaults by "lower-class whites," they said), and thus they devised a system that reaffirmed the comfortable old pattern of the antebellum period: African Americans remained in a distinctly subordinate position in the same church with whites. White clergy had control over the affairs of black Episcopalians and denied them the relative freedom they might have enjoyed if separated outright from the Episcopal Church.[12]

Angered by what the Sewanee conference proposed, Alexander Crummell, the senior black Episcopal priest and rector of St. Luke's Church in Washington, D.C., soon brought black Episcopalians together and asked them to make a concerted effort to oppose the plan. Crummell even gained an important, if quixotic, ally in Richard Wilmer of Alabama, who had been the only person present at the Sewanee conference to dissent openly from the majority's position. Wilmer had questioned the Sewanee plan by arguing that it was "inconsistent with true Catholicity" and "contrary to the mind of Christ."[13] His reasoning was based as much on racial prejudice as on theology, however, for he believed that African Americans were incapable of maintaining dignity and decorum in church affairs without the constant supervision of whites. Wilmer wanted black Episcopalians to become a "leaven" raising their people out of moral decay, and he considered any form of racial separation to be dangerous for *whites*. Like a number of white southerners at that time, Wilmer thought the African American population was prone to degenerate morally if it lacked the everyday guidance of whites.[14]

The General Convention assembled in Philadelphia in October 1883 and discussed at length the strategy advanced by the Sewanee conference. The House of Bishops officially endorsed the plan—it was the brainchild of its prominent southern bloc, after all—but the proposal failed to win the necessary approval in the House of Deputies. Despite an expression of appreciation for the efforts of southern Episcopalians in aiding "the poor and ignorant" in their midst, the deputies questioned the value of "drawing lines of classification and distinction between the followers of our common Lord." The deputies insisted that, instead of creating special missionary organizations in the South, the church should continue to make the evangelism of African Americans a high priority at the national level. Restating the position adopted when the Commission on Home Missions to Colored People was terminated in 1878, the House of Deputies affirmed that black southerners still fell under the care of the denomination's Board of Missions.[15]

In the wake of the defeat of the Sewanee plan at the 1883 General Convention, several dioceses in the South acted unilaterally and created not "missionary organizations" but "colored convocations" for their black parishes. By 1889 the dioceses of Virginia and South Carolina, for example, had segregated and effectively disfranchised their African American lay people. Despite the protests of a handful of white leaders, who charged that the Episcopal Church was being transformed into "a race Church," the denomination as a whole had no way to prevent individual dioceses from segregating their black membership. Thus, during the same period in which southern states enacted Jim Crow laws, white Episcopalians in the South circumscribed the freedom of African Americans in the ecclesiastical sphere. Joseph Tucker, a priest from Mississippi who attended the Sewanee conference, spoke for many whites when he argued that northerners should stop interfering in the South and let white southerners, who knew black people the best, settle their own racial affairs. Because the religious, ethical, and material condition of African Americans had declined so precipitously since emancipation, Tucker said, it was absurd to think that African Americans were fit to enjoy equality with whites in the leadership positions of the church.[16]

Like many of the southern bishops who helped devise the Sewanee plan, Thomas Underwood Dudley of Kentucky opposed the absolute separation of African Americans from whites. Dudley, who grew up in Virginia and served as a Confederate officer during the Civil War, sounded a theme common among racial paternalists: the black community needed the sympathetic aid of white southerners to recover from the damaging effects of emancipation. Although he believed that "race-peculiarities" were destined to be erased as the world's people came to see themselves as "descendants of one father, the redeemed children of one God," his views were based on the assumption that African Americans were inferior and could only "be carried up to the superior sphere" by whites.

Dudley was especially disturbed about the situation in churches founded and led by African Americans, and he hoped that white evangelists would work hard to overcome the ephemeral popularity of black preachers—men who were "ignorant of the very first principles of the gospel." Properly instruct African Americans, Dudley urged, or social and religious chaos might be the result.[17]

Although Alexander Crummell and other black Episcopalians could do little to stop white church people in the South (even ostensibly "supportive" ones such as Dudley and Wilmer) from regarding them as inferiors, they organized an association (the Conference of Church Workers among Colored People) designed to lobby for recognition and respect in denominational affairs. Crummell believed in a strong racial ministry, and this attitude set the tone for the Conference of Church Workers (CCW). Like many white clergy of the time, he lamented the fact that so many African Americans had deserted the Episcopal Church after the Civil War. But rather than blaming African Americans in the South for their exodus from the denomination, Crummell knew (from painful personal experience) that the refusal of whites to encourage and accept the leadership of black men and women was the real cause. If the Episcopal Church adopted an evangelistic plan that allowed African Americans to minister to and uplift their own people, Crummell asserted, it would have a providential opportunity to imbue a significant portion of southern society with its theological and social ideals.[18]

Anna Julia Cooper, the widow of an Episcopal priest and a teacher at St. Augustine's College in North Carolina, was an important supporter of Crummell's efforts to foster racial uplift. Cooper, who was born in slavery, emphasized the value of education, religion, and proper conduct in assisting the rise of black women and men in the South. One of six delegates from the United States to the Pan-African Conference in London in 1900, Cooper was an active public speaker and writer. In an address to a convocation of black priests in 1886, she summoned the clergy to the task of saving their people from "the peculiar faults of worship" into which they fell when left on their own. She praised the Episcopal Church for the positive influence it had offered African Americans before the Civil War, but she was concerned that, following emancipation, white Episcopalians had been pathetically slow in recruiting and ordaining black priests. Although white southerners complained that African Americans were no longer interested in the Episcopal Church, they had created the problem themselves. Since most southern bishops advised black ministerial candidates to aspire only to deacon's orders, they not only relegated black men to "a perpetual colored diaconate" but also tacitly encouraged them to seek full ordination in other denominations. African Americans in the Episcopal Church needed priests of their own race, Cooper said, for only black men could be fully trusted to "come in touch with our life and have a fellow feeling for our woes."[19]

As the arguments of Crummell and Cooper suggest, leading black Episcopalians actually agreed with white paternalists about some of the reasons for bringing African Americans into the church: their denomination had the potential to become a stabilizing and uplifting presence within the black community. They disagreed with whites, however, about who should have the primary responsibility for ministering to the black population in the South, and they protested vigorously when the dioceses of Virginia and South Carolina removed African American representation from their annual conventions. If white Episcopalians were as concerned as they claimed to be about the education and conversion of African Americans, why had they continually ignored the contributions of their fellow church members who were black? Black Episcopalians also opposed white southerners on theological grounds. Skin color, they maintained, could not be used to prevent a priest from exercising the authority, judicial as well as sacerdotal, to which ordination entitled him. No matter what some whites happened to believe, Christian theology taught that race had no bearing on the powers a priest received at his ordination, and black *clergy*, at least, should be granted seats in the legislative assemblies of their dioceses.

This protest was presented in the form of a "memorial" from the CCW to the 1889 General Convention. After receiving and debating this document, the House of Bishops and the House of Deputies both recognized the truth of the theological principles articulated by the CCW. The convention acknowledged that, because "God hath made of one blood all nations of men" (Acts 17:26), and because "by one Spirit are we all baptized into one body" (1 Cor. 12:13), racial distinctions had no place in the church. However, because white paternalists had often employed belief in the unity of humankind to justify their exercising control over black church affairs, Crummell's group also sought assurance that white Episcopalians valued African Americans as their equals as well as their wards. On this point the convention rebuffed the black leaders. Although Phillips Brooks, a clerical deputy from Massachusetts, condemned the segregation and disfranchisement of black communicants, the House of Deputies as a whole decided that representation in diocesan conventions was a question over which the national denomination had no say.[20]

Black Episcopalians received another kind of setback a year later, when African American educator Booker T. Washington, the founder of Tuskegee Institute, lambasted black clergy as unfit to be the leaders of his race. Most Episcopal, Congregational, and Presbyterian clergy were generally capable men, Washington conceded, but they were out of touch with their fellow African Americans; the majority of Methodist and Baptist ministers, on the other hand, were simply a disgrace to the gospel. Although these remarks elicited an angry response from various black leaders, Washington immediately received offers of financial support from white philanthropists wishing to aid his efforts to educate his people. Washington's outlook helped set the tone for race relations in the South over the next half century. In his "Atlanta Compromise" speech of 1895, he spoke comforting words to conservative whites, reassuring them that most black people were not interested in being accepted as their social equals. Rather, African Americans were prepared to begin at the bottom of the social order, he said, and they simply wanted a chance to develop the practical skills they needed to make a successful living.[21]

Edgar Gardner Murphy, the rector of St. John's Church in Montgomery, Alabama, was an important white Episcopalian who responded warmly to the social, cultural, and educational ideas Washington advocated. Murphy believed in segregation, but he tempered his conservative racial views with a commitment to the "social gospel" and an ostensible desire to assist the poorer classes. Between 1890 and 1900 four southern states restricted the civil rights of their black citizens, and when Alabama began to revise its voting laws, Murphy took steps to ensure that the question would be settled calmly and judiciously. Like Washington, he thought African Americans should rely upon upper-class whites, who could accomplish the necessary voting "reforms"—disfranchising "unworthy" voters and "protecting" blacks from manipulation by white political bosses—without evoking outbursts of racial violence. In order to foster the results he desired, Murphy helped organize the Southern Society for the Promotion of the Study of Race Conditions and Problems in the South, which met for the first (and only) time in Montgomery in May 1900. Although Murphy sought Washington's support and invited him to speak at the conference, the other organizers excluded African Americans from leadership positions and admitted them only as observers, seated in a segregated gallery.[22]

Most of the speakers who addressed the Montgomery conference were paternalists who favored Washington's program of industrial education as an effective means to control southern blacks. One of the conference sessions considered the religious affairs of African Americans. Both speakers at that gathering (D. Clay Lilly, secretary of the Southern Presbyterian Board of Colored Evangelization, and William Alexander Guerry, Episcopal chaplain at the University of the South) employed traditional arguments about keeping black church members subordinate to white leaders. Guerry, for instance, insisted that emancipation had proved disastrous for African Americans. As soon as slaves were released from bondage, they rejected the benevolent advice of whites and began to follow black preachers, who were "unsafe and dangerous guides" leading their people into vice, immorality, and crime. Guerry praised his own Episcopal Church for refusing to allow African Americans to retreat into "religious isolation" after the Civil War. Although there was a strong impulse simply to let black communicants go (as white Methodists and Baptists had done), white Episcopalians had practiced "Christian brotherhood" and kept African Americans under their tutelage within the same ecclesiastical organization. "The best teacher for the Negro is the Southern white man," Guerry concluded—an ideal that his denomination continued to uphold.[23]

Following the Montgomery conference, Edgar Murphy remained involved in educational planning. In 1901 he resigned his position at St. John's Church in order to become the executive secretary of the newly created Southern Education Board. Although Murphy believed that many of the social problems the South faced in the early twentieth century were related to the inescapable presence of African Americans, he thought a renewal of the paternalistic spirit that he imagined masters had shown their slaves in antebellum times might provide needed guidance to black southerners. Instead of abandoning African Americans to their own devices, he said, white southerners needed to train them and use to full advantage the strongest institutions the South possessed: its churches and its schools. Although short-sighted whites might argue that an educated black person was a threat to the well-being of southern society, the opposite, in fact, was true: only proper instruction and training would draw "the vague, shifting, inchoate masses of an ignorant and unresponsive negro life" under the beneficent sway of "the stronger race."[24]

Most white leaders in the Episcopal Church in the South agreed with Murphy's assessment and saw education as their most effective means to head the black population in the directions they chose. Theodore DuBose Bratton, the bishop of Mississippi, for example, wished to assist African Americans without disturbing traditional patterns of race relations. Familiar with nostalgic tales about the "Old South" that writers such as Joel Chandler Harris and Thomas Nelson Page had popularized,

Bratton evoked comforting images of the way things used to be during the slave regime, when "the master was a shepherd of the plantation flock." In order to restore the "kindly feeling and sympathy" of the past, he called upon white Christians to work closely with African Americans once again—establishing schools where they could learn practical and useful skills.[25]

In February 1906 the Board of Missions of the Episcopal Church fulfilled Bratton's and Murphy's wishes and sponsored an educational venture similar to what those men envisioned. Named the American Church Institute for Negroes (ACIN), this agency was committed to the idea that African Americans in the South were in need of moral and spiritual uplift and that courses geared to a combination of vocational and religious training represented the most effective means to aid this development. The policies of the institute were determined by a board of twelve prominent white Episcopalians. Racial paternalists all, the ACIN board members assumed that sympathetic white people like themselves were capable of restoring "good relations between the races." They also expected that the financial assistance they provided would extend their denomination's influence into the black community, thus fostering both social progress and harmonious race relations. The ACIN supported ten schools, at which young men were taught skills such as farming, carpentry, and tailoring, and young women learned to become cooks, seamstresses, and domestic workers. According to Robert W. Patton, who became the executive director of the organization in 1914, "many ignorant, shiftless, dishonest and seemingly hopeless Negroes are being transformed into decency, respectability, and usefulness" through the auspices of the Episcopal Church.[26]

African Americans were understandably skeptical of what Patton, the ACIN, and white Episcopalians generally were proposing to do on their behalf. No one was more critical than the activist intellectual W.E.B. Du Bois. Several members of Du Bois's family had belonged to the Episcopal Church, and his grandfather had once served as parish treasurer for Alexander Crummell at St. Luke's Church in New Haven, Connecticut. But Du Bois himself did not share those family members' fondness for the denomination. As he noted in his study *The Negro Church*, white Episcopalians had "probably done less for black people than any other aggregation of Christians." When Samuel H. Bishop, an ACIN field agent, asked Du Bois what he thought of the church's new educational organization, he admitted he was distrustful about what the Episcopal Church intended to do. Du Bois could not imagine how a church that had been so slow to recognize the "human manhood and Christian equality" of African Americans could ever overcome its "shameful" record in that regard. The fact is, he wrote Bishop, that "the southern branch of the Church is a moral dead weight and the northern branch of the Church never has had the moral courage to stand against it, and I doubt if it has now."[27]

Following Crummell's death in 1898, George Freeman Bragg Jr., rector of St. James' Church in Baltimore, emerged as the leading figure among black Episcopalians. Bragg was active in the Niagara Movement (a forerunner of the National Association for the Advancement of Colored People), and he recognized that if black Episcopalians were ever to achieve parity with whites, they needed to free themselves from domination by white paternalists. At a meeting the CCW arranged with a group of bishops in the fall of 1903, Bragg reiterated the position that black Episcopalians had raised in their statement to the 1889 General Convention. He reminded the bishops how much African Americans resented being relegated to "colored convocations" where they had no voice in the official affairs of their church. Instead of keeping them in a subordinate position within dioceses in the South, Bragg and the CCW asked, why not let African Americans organize their own independent missionary jurisdictions? Or rather than keeping blacks under the direction of white church leaders who considered their presence in southern dioceses to be offensive, why not release them and place them under the guidance of the church at the national level instead? Such alternative arrangements, Bragg argued, would provide an effective way for self-respecting black men and women to remain loyal to the Episcopal Church.[28]

Bragg's proposal perplexed the southern bishops, and they debated its merits among themselves for several months. Though the plan maintained the separation of black and white church members in southern dioceses—an arrangement of which most white lay people heartily approved—it removed African Americans from the pastoral oversight of white priests and bishops, thus undercutting the paternalistic ideals that most clergy held dear. Fearing a loss of control, the southern bishops eventually rejected Bragg's plan. In response, the CCW addressed a memorial to the 1904 General Convention, requesting that it allow the establishment of "special Missionary Districts for races and languages." When this proposal came up for debate in the House of Bishops, the majority of northern bishops agreed with their southern counterparts and concluded that such a "departure from ancient custom" required further consideration. They formed a small committee to study the question and deferred their final decision for another three years.[29]

William Montgomery Brown, the bishop of Arkansas and a self-educated exponent of social Darwinism, was one of the few white bishops to favor what the CCW suggested. As he wrote in *The Crucial Race Question* (1907), Brown believed that "Negro degeneration" had become such a severe problem since the abolition of slavery that constant vigilance was needed in order to preserve the United States as "an Aryan white man's country." Unlike the paternalists, he thought the best way to keep the nation racially pure was by keeping whites and blacks separated from one another in every possible way. Whereas the majority of his fellow southern bishops opposed the black Episcopalians' proposal because they assumed African Americans could only make progress if provided with the sympathetic guidance of white people, Brown regarded that assumption as deluded and hopelessly sentimental. He invoked, moreover, not benevolent Christian ideals about "the Universal Fatherhood of God and Brotherhood of Man," but the Darwinian notion of an inexorable biological process in which only the strongest race would survive.[30]

Brown's racist beliefs meshed well for a while with the strategy adopted by the CCW. He encouraged African Americans to leave the Episcopal Church and establish a new denomination analogous to the Colored Methodist Episcopal Church. He also offered to participate in the consecration of several black bishops, as long as they were given absolutely no authority in the white Episcopal Church. In 1905 Brown called George Alexander McGuire, the rector of St. Thomas' Church, Philadelphia (the oldest black parish in the Episcopal Church), to serve as his archdeacon for colored work and assist his efforts in strengthening a separate black ministry. McGuire worked with Brown until 1908, but he eventually recognized that Brown's ideas not only were unworkable within the context of the Episcopal Church, but also were motivated by racism. After McGuire resigned and left Arkansas, he moved back to the Northeast. Continuing his commitment to a distinct religious body for African Americans, he became chaplain general of Marcus Garvey's Universal Negro Improvement Association, and in 1921 he founded the African Orthodox Church, which he hoped might evolve one day into a racial branch of the Episcopal Church.[31]

The next General Convention, which met in Richmond, Virginia, in October 1907, focused on the controversial ideas that Bragg, Brown, McGuire, and others had raised. The issues discussed at the convention were so complex, in fact, that four separate constituencies presented views about how the church should deal with ethnicity and race.

1. The report of the suffragan bishop committee: This committee

had been formed at the 1904 General Convention and given a mandate to consider the feasibility of consecrating suffragan bishops for service in dioceses either too geographically large or too ethnically diverse for a single bishop to oversee. The suffragan plan was favored principally by bishops and deputies in growing urban areas in the Northeast and in the missionary regions of the West. By creating suffragan bishops, the committee argued, the church would be able to minister to larger numbers of people without curtailing the authority of the diocesan bishop within his own jurisdiction.[32]

2. The majority report of the committee studying the CCW memorial of 1904: This group believed that the election of black suffragan bishops might be an effective way to address the issue of African American autonomy while maintaining the unity of the denomination. Although suffragan bishops would be available to lead and minister to black church members, they would not be allowed to vote in the House of Bishops and would always remain under the authority of white bishops. Instead of dividing the denomination along racial lines, this report stated, the Episcopal Church should affirm "the ancient ideal of . . . an ecclesiastical order in which men as Christians, and not as members of particular races, may co-operate for their moral and spiritual welfare." Despite such lofty rhetoric, the committee also upbraided black Episcopalians for trying to undermine the power that whites held over them. Since "Anglo-Saxon Churchmen have earned by centuries of toil and suffering the right to leadership in teaching and guarding the faith," the report concluded, black Episcopalians needed to reconcile themselves to their second-class status in the church.[33]

3. The minority report of the CCW memorial committee: Joseph Blount Cheshire Jr. (the bishop of North Carolina) and William Clark (a priest from the diocese of Virginia) agreed with the majority's theological views on racial unity but opposed its position on practical grounds. Cheshire himself had long been known as a paternalist who insisted that the church should not be divided on racial lines. In prior discussions about that subject, he had always distinguished between what he regarded as local, "human arrangements" (that is, racially separate parishes) and the essential unity of the church (the bishop, clergy, and people of a diocese). In recent years, however, his mind had changed, and he now feared that race relations in the United States had become so poor that only drastic measures could improve the situation. He saw the creation of racial missionary districts as a helpful compromise, for they would give African Americans a sense of membership in the Episcopal Church at the

national level without threatening the dominance of white Episcopalians within southern dioceses.[34]

4. The response of the CCW: Bragg and other black Episcopalians adamantly opposed both the first and second proposals. They feared that the creation of suffragan bishops would not help them but would simply continue (under a new guise) old patterns of racial paternalism. Suffragan bishops, after all, could only be elected by white delegates at segregated diocesan conventions, and they would always be under the thumb of white bishops. As long as segregation existed in southern states and dioceses, the CCW argued, "separate but *equal*" racial districts would be the best arrangement for African Americans.[35]

After debating at length the merits of these four positions, the 1907 General Convention affirmed the majority report of the CCW memorial committee and approved in principle the election of suffragan bishops. Although no further action was taken that year, the next General Convention (in 1910) amended the church's constitution, thereby allowing several northern and western dioceses to elect the suffragan bishops they had been requesting. Dioceses in the South, though, were slow to respond to the change. When William Guerry, then the bishop of South Carolina, called for the election of a black suffragan in 1912, his request was soundly rejected by the convention of his diocese. Since no other southern diocese elected a suffragan bishop in the intervening years, the issue resurfaced for debate at the General Conventions of 1913 and 1916 along now familiar ideological lines. Those favoring the suffragan plan tended to be racial paternalists who argued in favor of the unity of humankind, the catholicity of the church, and the superiority of the white race; suffragan bishops under the authority of whites would aid the uplift of the degraded black race, they insisted. Those favoring separate missionary districts, on the other hand, were either African Americans or white Episcopalians who were comfortable with a pragmatic approach to race relations. They accepted the reality of racial prejudice and thought the Episcopal Church could have the greatest impact on the black community by adopting the plan that most black church members favored.[36]

The debate about the legitimacy of separate missionary districts continued for several more decades, but the question of racial suffragans was settled in May 1917 when the diocese of Arkansas (then under the leadership of James Winchester) elected James Solomon Russell, archdeacon for colored work in the diocese of Southern Virginia, as its suffragan bishop. However, when Russell refused to accept his election, Edward Thomas Demby, the archdeacon for colored work in Tennessee, was chosen instead. A few months after Demby's election, Henry Beard Delany, archdeacon for colored work in North Carolina, received the strong backing of Bishop Cheshire and was elected to serve as the suffragan in his diocese. Although both men were consecrated in 1918, even the raising of Demby and Delany to the episcopate continued to highlight the racial dilemmas that Episcopalians faced. The two black bishops never received full support from the CCW, because they were thought to be too closely tied to the denomination's white establishment. George Freeman Bragg did not think any "constructive Negro . . . with respect to real ability" could have been elected bishop at that time, and he believed that Demby and Delany had been selected because whites regarded each man as "a good and safe Negro." W.E.B. Du Bois was even more blunt than Bragg. He dismissed Delany as "a 'handkerchief head' type of Negro" whom white people could easily manipulate.[37]

The consecrations of Demby and Delany coincided with a critical period of transition within southern society. Participation in World War I unleashed a number of social changes, none more significant than the dramatic alteration in race relations in the South. The draft transferred many southern black men away from their rural homes, and wartime prosperity encouraged northern industries to hire black workers. As a result, nearly half a million African Americans left the South and moved to urban areas in the Northeast and Midwest. For these African Americans, the "Great Migration" from the South not only represented an experience akin to emancipation after the Civil War, but it also encouraged the emergence of a new militancy about race. The economic base for black-owned businesses, professions, and religious institutions broadened considerably as the number of residents in areas like Harlem grew rapidly in the early twentieth century. This mass movement and the relative improvement in the economic status of black people, however, angered many white Americans, and following the revival of the Ku Klux Klan in 1915, there was an upsurge in white-on-black violence. Although the Episcopal Church had failed to denounce lynching and mob violence prior to that time, the House of Bishops called for the formation of local committees to foster interracial harmony, and the General Convention of 1919 adopted the first churchwide antilynching resolution. Those statements manifested as much concern for social stability as for racial justice, continuing the theme that upper-class white Episcopalians were the natural protectors of African Americans, but they were at least a step in the right direction.[38]

Though white southerners believed that the migration of African Americans northward had made evangelism in the black community increasingly more difficult for them, they also contributed significantly to their own problems. Four southern dioceses (East Carolina, South Carolina, Upper South Carolina, and Virginia) still relegated black Episcopalians to "colored convocations," thus denying them any representation at diocesan meetings. In Arkansas and North Carolina, Bishops Demby and Delany were given little opportunity to make an impact on church life, and when the latter died in 1928, no one was chosen to fill his post. Exasperated by the failure to improve their position in the church, black church members again pressed the General Convention to create for them a racial missionary district under the authority of a black bishop, but white leaders refused to release black Episcopalians from their oversight. The General Convention of 1934, for example, ruled that the missionary district plan would be "dangerous, if not disastrous" to the unity of the denomination. A special commission appointed to study the role of African Americans in the church insisted that white diocesan bishops were capable of mediating between the two races without favoring the interests of one over the other—the argument being that the episcopate (at least when it was held by a white man) transcended race![39]

By the late 1930s, however, when the impact of the New Deal began to change the racial situation for the better, white church leaders in the South became increasingly more aware of the status of the black people in their midst. The region attracted the concern of a number of outside reform groups—labor unions, northern black organizations, and even the federal government—that offered the hope of social progress, and among southern Protestants a few white reformers, such as Myles Horton (a Presbyterian) and James A. Dombrowski (a Methodist), supported equal rights for African Americans. Strongly influenced by Reinhold Niebuhr's neoorthodox theology and committed to the idea of applying Christian ethical principles to social problems, Dombrowski openly challenged the Jim Crow system and was instrumental in the founding of the Conference of Younger Churchmen of the South (later known as the Fellowship of Southern Churchmen) in 1934. Two white Episcopal priests, Moultrie Guerry, chaplain of the University of the South, and Thomas H. Wright, rector of the parish in Lexington, Virginia, were also among the original organizers of the conference.[40]

These developments were not lost on the Episcopal Church as a whole, and at the 1937 General Convention the denomination created the Joint Commission on Negro Work to oversee and improve its approach to African Americans. With its membership divided intentionally (for the first time) between an equal number of black and white Episcopalians, the group was given the task of considering the perennial question of whether special racial districts should be carved out of dioceses in the South. A year later, the bishops of the province of Sewanee (the fifteen dioceses in the states of Alabama, Florida, Georgia, Kentucky, Louisiana, Mississippi, North Carolina, South Carolina, and Tennessee) also considered the desirability of forming the separate missionary districts for which their African American membership had long been pressing. Although the bishops rejected the idea in 1938, they reversed that decision when they met again in 1939 and voted to bring their proposal, reminiscent of the first "Sewanee plan" of 1883, to the 1940 General Convention. Most of the bishops said they longed for a time when there would be "one fold and one Shepherd" and "children of every race shall kneel side by side before a common altar." However, though the church's theology recognized no theoretical differences between the races, Christians in the South witnessed examples of inequity and inequality every day. The bishops concluded that since white Episcopalians had failed to give African Americans a fair chance, establishing a missionary district with a bishop of its own was the only possible way for them to show confidence in the leadership abilities of black members of their denomination. Despite the charge that the plan represented a form of segregation, the bishops did not think it implied inferiority but was simply a mechanism for including African Americans in the highest legislative councils of the church.[41]

With the support of the CCW, the southern bishops presented their proposal to the General Convention in October 1940. Not all black Episcopalians at the convention, however, favored the racial district scheme. Edward Demby addressed the House of Bishops for the first time since his consecration in 1918 and argued against the plan. The biracial Joint Commission on Negro Work, to which Demby and five other black Episcopalians belonged, also lodged its disapproval, reasoning that "the oneness of the Church . . . and the undivided nature of the Bishop's function and office" were ideals that ought not to be relinquished. The commission insisted, moreover, that the long-standing arrangement of one white bishop exercising authority over all people without regard to race symbolized a "living principle of integration," whereas a black bishop and a white bishop working side-by-side in a diocese was an unacceptable "policy of segregation."[42] Curiously, several southern bishops known as supporters of racial segregation (Albert Sidney Thomas of South Carolina, Charles C.J. Carpenter of Alabama, and R. Bland Mitchell of Arkansas) also agreed with the Joint Commission on Negro Work. A black ministry outside the control of white church people, they thought, would be foolhardy. Bishops of northern dioceses, too, were perplexed by the idea that black Episcopalians wished to have their own church organizations. As Francis Taitt, the bishop of Pennsylvania, humorously observed, African Americans in *his* diocese were as happy as "contented cows" and desired no change in the present unified church system. In the end a coalition of northern bishops with generally liberal views on race and southern bishops who were strongly committed to segregation prevailed, and together they defeated the proposal for racial missionary districts.[43]

When Middleton Barnwell of Georgia, one of the most ardent advocates of the new Sewanee plan, arose to speak to his fellow bishops at the convention, he expressed exasperation both with the discussion and with the decision that had been reached. It was often difficult for some people to understand what it was like to live with racial segregation laws, he said. Those laws mandated, for instance, that at diocesan gatherings in Savannah white and black Episcopalians could not eat together, sit together at meetings, or kneel together at the communion rail. "The present situation is disgraceful," Barnwell said, but southern state laws were not going to be changed in the near future. Until the racial situation in the South improved, Episcopalians "*have* segregation, and we must act in view of that fact." The missionary district plan and racial episcopate that his province proposed was simply an attempt to deal creatively with an unavoidable real-life situation. It provided Episcopalians, white as well as black, with some relief from the consequences of racial discrimination, and whenever integration finally did come, the plan could be quickly terminated. "Until our Black and our White sheep *can* walk along together to the fold," he pleaded, African Americans needed to have a bishop of their own race to whom they could turn. Barnwell's appeal fell on deaf ears, and the majority of bishops, all white except one, maintained that *they* provided African Americans with all the guidance that was needed in spiritual and ecclesiastical affairs.[44]

The contours of this debate reveal Episcopalians' profound confusion about the role that race and racial differences ought to play within the church fellowship. Most of those engaged in discussion tried to approach the subject with genuine good will, but they seemed incapable of understanding how African Americans in the South might have benefited more from being independent of whites than from having regular contact, however benevolent, with them. Furthermore, though virtually all Episcopalians accepted the biblical dictum that "God hath made of one blood all nations of men" (Acts 17:26), the practical application of that principle had brought church people into conflict over race ever since the end of the Civil War. Although vast numbers of African Americans fled the white-dominated Episcopal Church when emancipated in 1865, a few black Episcopalians still remained. Racial prejudice, however, prevented them from being accepted as equals by their white fellow church members. Prominent white clergy stressed the value of unity within church and society but often regarded African Americans through the paternalistic eyes of former slaveholders. The majority of white Episcopalians, for their part, simply wanted to be sure that no blacks held or exercised power in "their" parishes or "their" dioceses. As a result black Episcopalians in the South found themselves tossed back and forth between opposing white viewpoints. Despite their desire to remain loyal to the worship and beliefs of their church, African American leaders realized that, without the respect of whites, unity alone was valueless.

# 2

# Negro Work and the
# Decline of the
# Jim Crow Church

In *The Negro's Church* (1933), African American scholars Benjamin
Mays and Joseph Nicholson collaborated on one of the most influential studies ever published on black religious institutions. The authors, who were ministers in the Northern Baptist and Colored Methodist Episcopal denominations, respectively, spent over a year collecting
data on nearly eight hundred urban and rural churches throughout the
United States. Despite the importance of the statistical information they
gathered, Mays and Nicholson intended their research to fulfill a larger
purpose: they wanted it not only to give social scientists an appreciation
of religion's role as a dominant factor in African American life, but also to
encourage leaders in the mainline Protestant denominations to help "improve the Negro church." Although the book refrained from invoking the
full litany of ills in which other analyses of black religion then indulged,
it did point out a number of areas where change was needed. Clergy in
rural areas, for example, tended to be poorly educated and theologically
unsophisticated. Mays and Nicholson hoped that if enough pressure were
exerted by black reformers like themselves, African American clergy would
eventually adopt a modern, professional approach to the Christian ministry.[1]

The statistics the book presented about the Episcopal Church were
especially grim. Over 50 percent of all urban black churches were Baptist,
17 percent were Methodist, and 16 percent belonged to Holiness groups,
but less than 2 percent were Episcopal. Outside the cities, the situation
was even worse, for less than 1 percent of all rural black churches were
affiliated with the Episcopal Church. Moreover, after the heavy migration

of African Americans northward in the era of World War I, black Episcopal membership had actually decreased in the South. Although this was offset somewhat by rapid growth in the black Episcopal population in the Northeast—over two-thirds of the denomination's thirty-one thousand black communicants were located in northern cities in the early 1920s—the decline in the South greatly disturbed those concerned about the church's mission to African Americans. Theodore Bratton of Mississippi, for instance, expressed disappointment that black congregations in his diocese had lost nearly half of their membership during World War I. And Virginian Robert Patton of the ACIN lamented that his organization was once again faced with the difficult task of trying to convince African Americans that the Episcopal Church was the best place for them to develop morally and spiritually.[2]

In order to meet this challenge, the General Convention's Joint Commission on Negro Work undertook its own investigation of the denomination's black parishes and schools, and its conclusions shed further light on what Mays and Nicholson had discovered. African American institutions in the Episcopal Church, the commission reported, received "insufficient income from Church sources" and consequently were quite weak; they suffered from "a woeful lack of sufficiently trained Priests"; and they employed clergy who were inevitably paid less than priests doing similar work in white parishes. These problems together had produced an environment in which few African Americans "of extraordinary native talent, superior intellectual gifts and ardent missionary zeal" were attracted to serve. Despite these persistent deficiencies and problems, the commission proposed a workable solution: hire a black priest to serve as an "Executive Secretary for Negro Work" on the staff of the National Council (the executive body responsible for decision-making in the church between General Conventions), and empower him to evangelize African Americans, recruit new clergy, and strengthen black parishes in the South.[3]

Although these ideas were not entirely new (the CCW had tried without success to introduce a similar plan at the 1898 General Convention), the time now seemed ripe for the church as a whole to accept them. Several other denominations were also wrestling with questions concerning outreach to African Americans in the South, and their efforts gave support to the hopes of Episcopalians. In the Presbyterian Church in the United States, for example, African American evangelism had become an important concern in the 1930s and 1940s, and urban missionary activity was recognized to be critical for dealing with the black migration from rural areas. Because this work also highlighted deficiencies in the education and preparation of African American clergy in the denomination, many southern Presbyterians assumed that a fresh strategy would be useful in addressing that situation. The reunion of the Methodist Episcopal Church, South, and the Methodist Episcopal Church in 1939, moreover, had forced white Methodists to discuss the subject of race. Some northern Methodists wanted the reunited denomination to be racially integrated, but the church adopted a compromise measure. In exchange for the appointment of additional black bishops and greater representation at the national level, African Americans were formed into a "Central Jurisdiction," a body separate from (but in theory equal to) the four regional jurisdictions into which the denomination's white conferences were placed. Among Southern Baptists in the early twentieth century, the great number of African Americans who already belonged to their own Baptist churches had been regarded as an insurmountable barrier to the successful operation of a special black missionary program. In the late 1930s, however, even white Baptists began to address the social and legal consequences of racial prejudice, and church conventions in Virginia, North Carolina, and Texas created interracial committees to make contact with middle-class African Americans and explore ways to improve race relations.[4]

Despite such encouraging signs in other denominations, many in the Episcopal Church were still uncertain about the need for a separate racial ministry. In late 1942 George Wieland, director of the church's Home (i.e., domestic missions) Department, contacted forty-one bishops in dioceses that kept statistics on "colored parishes" and requested their opinions on the proposal to create an "Executive Secretary for Negro Work." The responses he received were almost equally divided between positive and negative—a division apparent when the House of Bishops debated the missionary district plan two years before. Although most southern bishops thought a senior black staff person would be a useful addition to the denomination's national program, a few worried that he might unwittingly undercut their own local, white-controlled efforts. Some bishops in northern dioceses feared that the establishment of a national racial program would suggest that the church tacitly approved of segregation; other northerners said they applauded any effort to lift the morale and self-esteem of black church members. Most of the bishops admitted their church needed to provide better leadership in the black community, but they disagreed about whether it was the complacency of white Episcopalians or the native inadequacy of African Americans that caused the problem. Finally, some critics of the plan, most notably Middleton Barnwell of Georgia, insisted that black Episcopalians would be better served if several bishops of their own race, rather than just a single priest, ministered to their needs.[5]

In spite of the bishops' inability to unite and affirm that their church needed a coordinated, national racial ministry, the National Council approved the program and set July 1, 1943, as its starting date. Presiding Bishop Henry St. George Tucker appointed Bravid Harris, archdeacon of the Colored Convocation in the diocese of Southern Virginia, as the new Secretary for Negro Work, and he named twelve people to serve on the Bi-Racial Committee that was created to supervise and assist Harris's activities. Mirroring the ambivalent attitudes held by many Episcopalians on this subject, the announcement about the new program reflected a mixture of optimism and caution regarding what the church hoped to accomplish. Speaking for the National Council, George Wieland indicated that the program's main focus would be an aggressive campaign to evangelize African Americans in rural areas in the South. Because the majority of the denomination's black communicants lived in cities in the North while most African Americans lived in the South, a southern-oriented missionary program was essential, Wieland said, in order to attract "this fundamentally religious group" to the Episcopal Church. Yet he was well aware that southern bishops might be skeptical of the efforts of leaders at the denomination's headquarters in New York to work directly with African Americans in those bishops' dioceses. Countering these expected fears of interference by outsiders from the North, Wieland emphasized that the Secretary for Negro Work would always be under the complete control of local diocesan authorities. Because Harris himself was a respected priest from a southern diocese, he was viewed as an ideal person to undertake the evangelistic tasks the National Council envisioned.[6]

At the same time that Harris began his new job, the National Council adopted a set of "Guiding Principles Designed to Govern the Church's Negro Work," based upon resolutions passed at the 1937 Oxford Conference—an ecumenical gathering that had assembled to discuss the church's role in countering the disintegration of modern society. According to the Oxford Conference, the Christian churches possessed a divine mandate to demonstrate within their own fellowship "the reality of community as God intends it" by gathering all people into their ranks as "a divine society" transcending ordinary national, ethnic, and racial lines. Applying this dictum to the Episcopal Church, the National Council resolved that it would uphold four main criteria in ministering to African Americans:

1. *Fellowship is essential to Christian worship.* Since there are no racial distinctions in the Mind of the Father, but "all are one in Christ Jesus" we dare not break our Christian fellowship by any attitude, act or arrangement in the House of God which marks our Negro brethren as unequal or inferior.

2. *Fellowship is essential in Church Administration.* Only through the privilege of exercising initiative and responsibility in Church affairs, through fair representation and voting power in all Church legislative assemblies, and the enjoyment of Christian hospitality with their white brethren will Negro churchmen be assured that their membership in the Episcopal Church is secure.

3. *High standards must be maintained to secure the best possible training for the Negro Ministry.* . . . Provide the same opportunities as those which are available to other racial groups.

4. *It is both the function and the task of the Church to set the spiritual and moral goals for society, and to bear witness to their validity by achieving them in her own life.* The Church is commanded to break through the encirclement of racial segregation in all matters which pertain to her program . . . and lead the way towards the fulfillment of our Lord's desire that they all may be one.[7]

Harris's tenure with the National Council proved to be relatively brief, for early in 1945 he was elected bishop of the missionary district of Liberia. Because the southern bishops with whom he had been working were pleased with his ministry in their dioceses, they warmly supported his candidacy for the episcopate in Africa. His consecration service in April 1945, however, sparked a controversy that highlighted the ongoing divisions within the church about its approach to race.

Since Harris had been rector of Grace Church, the black parish in Norfolk, Virginia, Christ and St. Luke—the largest Episcopal church in the city—was selected as the site for his consecration. On the morning of the ceremony, that parish was host to a rare event—hundreds of African Americans crowding into a nave where only whites usually worshiped in order to see the first black priest raised to the episcopate since Henry Delany in 1918. In many ways, this service was both a model of racial harmony and a showcase of the National Council's "Guiding Principles." Black and white Episcopalians knelt side by side at the altar rail as they received communion, and following the service they disregarded segregation laws and had lunch together in the parish house. Yet the warm glow of interracial fellowship was quickly dispelled when white Episcopalians from the North complained about where the service had been held. Although southern church leaders believed that Harris's consecration symbolized the start of a new era in the South, northerners dismissed it as simply another example of "Jim-Crowism" and insisted that it should have taken place at the National Cathedral in Washington, D.C., instead. The northern leaders were appalled that the service had not been moved to the prominent site in Washington, where a connection between Episcopal theological ideals and American democratic values might have been unequivocally demonstrated.[8]

The debate surrounding Harris's consecration took place during a period of social change occasioned in part by the country's participation in World War II. Between 1942 and 1945, almost five million men and women from across the United States (including approximately 80 percent of all the African Americans in military service) trained on southern military bases—an eye-opening experience for those who were previously unfamiliar with the South's racial mores. At the same time, Gunnar Myrdal's *American Dilemma* articulated in voluminous detail how white Americans had failed to practice the color-blind tenets of the "American Creed." When the war ended, most Americans looked upon their country as the world's most prosperous, righteous, and successful nation, and leaders in the mainline Protestant denominations reflected this mood. On the one hand, they hoped, in the words of Episcopal bishop Henry Knox Sherrill, that the churches eventually would "move forward to the goal—a Christian America in a Christian world." On the other hand, they wondered how they could fight for democracy abroad when they were depriving racial minorities from enjoying its benefits at home.[9]

As William Scarlett, the bishop of Missouri, observed in his introduction to *Christianity Takes a Stand* (1946), American Christians had been sobered by the fight against the racist nationalism of Nazism, and they now realized "that our world is one, that humanity is one." Scarlett, who had been strongly influenced as a young man by social gospel advocate Washington Gladden, chaired the Joint Commission on Social Reconstruction of the Episcopal Church. Assigned the task of planning the denomination's postwar role in "building a better world for all peoples," his commission articulated three principal objectives for which the Episcopal Church should aim: international peace (recognition of "the basic Christian principle of the unity . . . of all mankind in God"); interracial cooperation (acceptance of "the Jewish-Christian tradition that all mankind is one Family in God"); and economic justice (application of the belief that "the economic order exists to serve God by increasing the welfare of all men").[10] In *Christianity Takes a Stand,* Scarlett and other writers explored specific applications of these general social and theological concerns. Their discussion of race, for example, reflected Myrdal's insights, and Scarlett noted that "segregation . . . contradicts the basic Christian principles of the dignity of every man as a child of God." But despite these strong words, the church commission itself stopped short of endorsing an immediate end of segregation. It focused instead on the need for "equalization of opportunity" in states where segregation laws still existed, and it emphasized that discrimination and inequality, not racial separation as such, were the true evils against which Christians should contend.[11]

Most white Episcopalians in the mid-1940s understood this logic, and they continued to accept legal segregation while hoping that their Negro Work program would at least ameliorate conditions in black parishes in the South. Disturbing reports about the dilapidated buildings and inadequate curriculum at the church's black seminary in Petersburg, Virginia, however, soon caused embarrassment for those who believed in the viability of segregation within the church. When the board of trustees (a body composed almost entirely of southern white clergy) considered moving Bishop Payne Divinity School either to St. Augustine's College in Raleigh or to Virginia Theological Seminary in Alexandria, the Joint Commission on Negro Work of the General Convention advised against it. This biracial commission argued that higher educational standards, not simply a new location, ought to be the trustees' principal concern. The Episcopal Church should either maintain Bishop Payne on a par with other seminaries, or it should close the school entirely.[12]

Recognizing that a crisis point had been reached, the school's trustees published a fund-raising appeal in 1944 and requested a total of $260,000 to help renovate the Petersburg campus. Because most southern bishops still resisted sending black candidates to northern seminaries, the trustees emphasized that Bishop Payne was the "key-stone" of the church's mission to African Americans and needed strong support. In the eyes of a group of black clergy in Pennsylvania, however, the white trustees' appeal for funds to refurbish a segregated seminary was a grave mistake, and they wrote Presiding Bishop Tucker and the National Council in protest. Although the objections of those black Episcopalians were ignored, several white church leaders did receive a hearing when they later protested at a National Council meeting. Aware of the recent condemnation of racial segregation by the Federal Council of Churches, Malcolm Peabody, the bishop of Central New York, inquired whether his denomination's support of a special seminary for African Americans in the South constituted "segregation." Fearing that it did, he requested further study of the situation before the National Council included funding for Bishop Payne in the denominational budget.[13]

The status of the black seminary remained a source of controversy over the next two years. At the December 1946 meeting of the National Council, Cyril Bentley, the white priest who directed the ACIN, asked whether the council intended to allocate funds to his organization. Bentley conceded that racial segregation existed in the schools the ACIN aided, but he thought church leaders also needed to be "realistic and take the Negro where we find him." Northern members of the council attacked Bentley's statement, saying that the church should not support segregation in any way. Shortly thereafter, several black clergy who were rectors of parishes in the North also wrote Bentley to express disagreement with his position. F. Ricksford Meyers, a priest in Detroit, charged that Bentley's words were "loose unchristian statements" and deeply offensive to "Negroes who in an Atomic Age are looking forward and not backward to the bedeviled past." Kenneth Hughes, rector of St. Bartholomew's Church in Cambridge, Massachusetts, thought white Episcopalians were "fatuous to try to rationalize segregation" in any way, for it was an evil that needed to be completely stamped out. Bentley, in contrast, expressed surprise and confusion at the position his correspondents assumed. He insisted that any Episcopalian who supported Bishop Payne was not interested in strengthening segregation as such, but only wanted to give black southerners "larger opportunities, better facilities and the finest education" the church could provide them.[14]

Segregation was "the *result,* not the *cause* of racial tension," Middleton Barnwell of Georgia argued a few months later, when bishops from dioceses in which ACIN schools were located spoke to the National Council on behalf of Bishop Payne Divinity School. There were two races living in close proximity but in different worlds in the South, Barnwell continued, and the church could do little to change that situation. Edwin Penick, the bishop of North Carolina, claimed, moreover, that the debate over the black seminary concerned "an educational problem, not a racial problem." The refusal to continue funding Bishop Payne, he thought, would hamstring the church's ministry among African Americans in the South.[15] The remarks of Barnwell and Penick, like those of Bentley before, were immediately criticized by northern church leaders. John Johnson, a member of the Bi-Racial Committee and a black rector in New York, expressed amazement at the moral blindness of white southerners, who refused to see that segregation laws not only were wrong but also could be overturned if Christian leaders took a conscientious stand against them. An editorial writer for the periodical *The Living Church* agreed with that position and believed Episcopalians should challenge "Nazi-like" segregation laws by opening the denomination's two southern seminaries (Virginia Theological Seminary and the School of Theology at the University of the South) to black students. Bentley, however, came to the bishops' defense. Formal laws aside, he said, "there would always be segregation among minority groups as a means of their attaining self-expression." That was just one of the realities with which those involved in instructing black southerners had to deal.[16]

Despite this disagreement over whether Bishop Payne helped or hindered the work of the Episcopal Church in the black community, the National Council eventually recognized its value "as a temporary expedient" in educating African Americans and made a financial commitment to the seminary.[17] Pleased that the denomination had committed itself to rebuilding their school and improving its curriculum, the trustees of Bishop Payne furthered the spirit of compromise by announcing that applications from white as well as black students would be accepted in the future. But by then it was too late to save Bishop Payne. With segregation now clearly under suspicion, black ministerial candidates and the bishops who supported them sensed how tenuous the seminary's existence had become, and no new students entered the school in either 1947 or 1948. Opponents of Bishop Payne on the National Council took the lack of students as a signal to postpone the funding that had earlier been approved—a decision that further depressed whatever commitment southern Episcopalians had to the school. As a consequence, a committee of the three groups in charge of Bishop Payne (the trustees, the ACIN, and the National Council) voted to close it after the commencement exercises in May 1949 and to transfer the faculty and the one remaining student to other Episcopal seminaries. At the same time, trustees from Bishop Payne and Virginia Seminary met to discuss a possible merger of their schools. Since Virginia had been instrumental in founding Bishop Payne in 1878, the trustees decided it would be appropriate to shift the remaining financial assets of the black school back to Alexandria. After the plan was officially approved in June 1953, the administration of Virginia Seminary sold the property in Petersburg and used the money it received to create a fund designated for the recruitment and education of African Americans on its own campus.[18]

Even before the assets of Bishop Payne were transferred to Alexandria, the color line was broken at Virginia Seminary when John T. Walker enrolled as a B.D. student in the fall of 1951. Walker had grown up in the African Methodist Episcopal Church but joined the Episcopal cathedral in Detroit, Michigan, in the late 1940s. When he approached Richard Emrich, his diocesan bishop, about attending seminary, Walker said he wished to attend the Episcopal Theological School in Cambridge, Massachusetts. But Emrich—a white bishop with a reputation for social liberalism—had other plans. He advised Walker to attend Virginia Seminary, so that he could not only desegregate the school but also experience some of the racial hostility from which he had been generally protected in Detroit. Since his bishop was determined to make him a test case, Walker enrolled at Virginia with reluctance, and though the faculty and most of the students in his own class made him feel welcome, he was given a cold shoulder by some of the seminarians in the classes above him. He later remarked that his three years at the seminary were "okay," but Alexandria in the 1950s was still "a very southern community," and he sometimes felt that he was "sitting in a movie called *Gone With the Wind*."[19]

The most troubling and difficult aspect of desegregation at Virginia Seminary occurred not in public, but in a private exchange of letters between Stanley Brown-Serman, the school's dean, and Jessie Ball duPont, the wealthy philanthropist. DuPont had been raised in tidewater Virginia after the Civil War, and she adamantly retained the racial prejudices of the white South of her youth. Nothing caused her more concern than the movement that had recently begun to challenge the South's racial mores. A devoted supporter of the Episcopal Church and a close friend of Frank Juhan, the bishop of Florida, duPont was a major contributor both to Virginia Seminary and to the University of the South. When she learned that the seminary had admitted a black student in the fall of 1951, she wrote Brown-Serman in protest. The dean insisted that he, too, did not favor full racial integration, but he also argued that, with the closing of Bishop Payne, it had become necessary for white schools to provide theological training for young black men so the church's ministry to African Americans could continue. In duPont's estimation, that was an absurd argument for a white person to make. Since Brown-Serman refused to retreat from his position, she withdrew the aid she gave to Virginia Seminary and declared that it would receive no further contributions from her.[20]

During the same period in which Virginia Seminary was desegregated, the leaders of other Episcopal institutions felt similarly challenged to end racial distinctions and discrimination in the organizations over which they had control. Although many observers considered the Episcopal Church to be the least segregated of all the major Protestant denominations, the refusal of white Episcopalians to form a separate jurisdiction for African Americans had also managed to keep black Episcopalians largely out of the management of national and diocesan affairs. John Hines, the bishop coadjutor (assistant with the right of succession) of Texas, for instance, was one of the first Episcopal leaders in the South to see the need for his diocese to end its quiet acquiescence in the culture of segregation.

In his address to the Texas diocesan convention of 1947, Hines questioned delegates about a long-standing practice that troubled him both as a Christian and as an American. Warning them against that "the threat of militant Communism," he argued that unjust segregation laws were giving subversive elements all the ammunition they needed to attack and undermine American society. The future of American freedom was at stake, he declared, and unless Christians in the United States supported the standards of the New Testament with respect to race, they would forfeit the position of world leadership they had recently attained. It was especially tragic that local ordinances had prevented church members of different races from eating together in the same banquet hall the night before. Segregation laws in Beaumont (the city where the convention was meeting) had forced Clinton Quin, the diocesan bishop, and him to split their time between two racially separate gatherings. Stop this ludicrous and unfair practice, Hines demanded, and either schedule one common meal or have no banquet at all. Although the 1947 diocesan convention pointedly rejected this suggestion, Hines was successful in preventing the scheduling of diocesan banquets over the next few years. By 1952 his reasoning proved fully persuasive, and white and black Episcopalians ate together for the first time at an annual convention.[21]

The success they achieved in desegregating the Texas diocesan banquet soon led Quin and Hines to propose that the 1955 General Convention be held in Houston, the see city of their diocese. The bishops wished to show that, with sound leadership from the church, white and black southerners could live and work harmoniously together. Although racial segregation was still enforced by law in Houston, Quin and Hines guaranteed that black Episcopalians would experience no discrimination there. Quin even pledged that, if the need arose, the diocese not only would construct facilities where people of all races could be housed and eat together but would also create "a volunteer motor corps" to transport convention delegates. Quin made this offer at the General Convention of 1952. Some bishops and deputies thought Chicago would have been a safer choice as the convention city, but the fact that no General Convention had been held in the South for several decades, coupled with a desire to assist in the improvement of race relations there, ultimately led to Houston's selection as the site for the 1955 gathering. Since the 1952 convention had already taken a strong stand in favor of "the clear duty of Christians to lead, in seeking justice and equality of opportunity for all men," many bishops and deputies saw Houston as a chance to test the sincerity of the denomination's official racial views.[22]

Although Hines and Quin made one of the most publicized commitments to the desegregation of the church, several other southern dioceses enacted comparable measures eliminating discriminatory canons that had been enacted in the late nineteenth century. The diocese of Upper South Carolina, for instance, which had been created in 1922 out of the upcountry counties in the state, had continued the practice of the diocese of South Carolina in excluding black representatives from its annual convention. The thirteen parishes and approximately 350 black communicant members in Upper South Carolina were organized into an "annual council of colored churchmen," which functioned separately from the rest of the diocese. The question of black participation was raised several times in the early 1930s, yet resolutions to include African Americans were repeatedly defeated. But in response to pressure from John Gravatt, the diocesan bishop, the convention of 1946 finally changed this racial policy. It removed the words "of the white race" from the diocesan constitution, thereby allowing African American parishes to send two priests and nine lay people to the next convention in 1947.[23]

When the diocese of Southern Virginia separated from the diocese of Virginia in 1890, racial lines were similarly drawn by the passage of a canon forming African Americans into a separate missionary jurisdiction. At the same time, black representation in the annual convention of the new diocese was limited to two clergy and two lay people. Although all black clergy were accorded convention seats in the early twentieth century, black lay people still experienced discrimination. Black parishes were not allowed to send delegates in numbers proportionate to their congregational size (the formula whites used); they were allotted a total of only two delegates, who were seated as the "Colored Convocation." At the diocesan convention of 1946, however, African American priest Odell Harris initiated the process by which this discriminatory canon was repealed. Beginning with the 1949 convention, identical regulations were applied to all self-supporting parishes in the diocese regardless of racial makeup. Five years later the Colored Convocation itself was disbanded. As Richard B. Martin, a black priest from Southern Virginia and a member of the National Council's Bi-Racial Committee, observed, Episcopalians had finally realized that, though church members must necessarily respect local laws, "we . . . feel in the depths of our hearts the magnetism of the laws of the Commonwealth of the Kingdom of God."[24]

Between 1947 and 1949, the dioceses of Georgia, Arkansas, and Virginia also amended their constitutions and granted equality to black parishes and lay people. And in Georgia in 1951 and in Mississippi in 1953, African American clergy were elected for the first time to the executive committees of those dioceses. These actions left the diocese of South Carolina (the coastal portion of the state) as the only Episcopal jurisdiction in which black church members were still excluded from full participation in its decision-making process. Although this process of desegregation often seemed painstakingly slow to African Americans and to liberals in the North, change had at least begun to take place in the Episcopal Church in the South. By then most white leaders in the church recognized that the desegregation of diocesan conventions was just and "Christian." As long as Episcopal parishes remained segregated—as much by custom as by law—southern Episcopalians were generally able to accept the appropriateness of interracial gatherings at the diocesan and national levels. As a result those changes took place without either major or prolonged conflict.[25]

The only notable exception to the pattern of slow but peaceful change occurred at the University of the South—the symbolic heart of the Episcopal Church in the southern states. The idea of a "university of the South" had been conceived by Leonidas Polk, the bishop of Louisiana, during the antebellum controversy over slavery. A leading slaveholder and later a general in the Confederate army, Polk was troubled by the fact that few Episcopal clergy were trained in the deep South and taught to appreciate the "peculiar type of civilization" for which the region stood. Inspired by the thought of using education to strengthen the institution of slavery, Polk wrote to the diocesan bishops in nine other slave states in July 1856 and asked them to assist him in founding a college where the future political and religious leaders of the South could learn the tenets of "Anglo-Saxon Christianity." He emphasized that enslaved African Americans would also benefit from his plan, for it was to their advantage, he said, to have cultivated and well-informed masters aiding their advance from savagery to civilization. According to William Polk, his son and chief biographer, Leonidas Polk thought it was critical that "the ruling race of the South should realize the greatness of the trust which had been providentially committed to them in the care of an ignorant and helpless people." With this purpose firmly in mind, Polk—with the blessing and assistance of other slaveholders and proslavery leaders in the denomination—established his university on a secluded Tennessee mountain plateau just before the outbreak of the Civil War.[26]

Because of the disruption caused by the war and by Polk's own death in battle in 1864, the University of the South was not able to begin operations until three years after the hostilities ended. During the first decades of its existence, it functioned more as a military school than a college; more than half the faculty were former Confederate officers, and until 1892 all students were required to wear Confederate gray uniforms. The ten-thousand-acre "domain" on which the university was located was owned by the twenty-two Episcopal dioceses in the former slave states, and the bishops of those dioceses provided the nucleus of its board of trustees. Despite the opening of the School of Theology in 1880 and the presence of the eminent theologian William Porcher DuBose on the faculty, the university (known affectionately as "Sewanee") retained its unrelenting adherence to the cultural values of "the Lost Cause." A Confederate battle flag hung in the university chapel, and people from all the southern states were encouraged to send flags and other Civil War mementos to the school, where they were reverently displayed and preserved. Well into the twentieth century, in fact, students still imbibed the spirit of the Old South. A few of the School of Theology faculty in the 1940s were involved with the interracial Highlander Folk School in nearby Monteagle, but this involvement was highly unusual. And though race relations on the university campus were harmonious, the interaction between whites and blacks at Sewanee was conducted almost exclusively along master-servant lines.[27]

Given the background and history of the University of the South, conflict at the school was inevitable when the Episcopal Church began to stress the need to desegregate its institutions in the post–World War II era. The stage was set for controversy in June 1950, when the Supreme Court rulings in the *McLaurin* and *Sweatt* cases undermined the concept of "separate but equal" facilities for African Americans in higher education. Although the court left segregation formally in place, it required that black schools had to be equal to white ones if racial separation laws were to remain constitutional. At a synod meeting of the province of Sewanee in October 1951, the bishops, priests, and lay people present debated the issues raised by both the closing of Bishop Payne Divinity School and the release of the Supreme Court decisions. Rather than proposing the organization of another, *better* segregated seminary (an idea favored by a few southern church leaders), the provincial synod declared that existing seminaries in the South should be made open to students of all races—a mandate directed specifically at Sewanee. When the Sewanee trustees discussed that resolution at their own annual meeting in June 1952, they rejected it on practical grounds. The trustees argued that it was unwise for them to encourage black students to apply at the present time, for such an action not only would violate state segregation laws but would also create a contentious atmosphere that was contrary to "the happiness and mutual good will of both races" at the university. Since at least one bishop admitted to being concerned about a catastrophic loss of contributions from such important donors as Jessie Ball duPont, the pressure to postpone desegregation and to maintain the Confederate heritage at Sewanee was intense.[28]

When the theology faculty at Sewanee learned of the trustees' decision, eight of its ten members sent an immediate letter of protest to R. Bland Mitchell, the bishop of Arkansas and chancellor (chairman of the board of trustees) of the university. Those men—F. Craighill Brown (the dean), Robert M. Grant, Claude E. Guthrie, R. Lansing Hicks, Robert M. McNair, J. Allen Reddick, Frederick Q. Shafer, and Richard H. Wilmer Jr.—charged that the trustees' position was "untenable in the light of Christian ethics and of the teaching of the Anglican Communion," for it reduced the critical issue of race relations to "the level of expediency only." In order to emphasize their outrage, the eight faculty members (and a ninth, Howard Johnson, who later added his name to the protest) threatened to resign unless their concerns were heard. The faculty's protest was soon circulated throughout the religious press, where it was widely praised for its concern for American democratic and Christian ethical ideals. At the General Convention that met in Boston in September, moreover, a resolution was introduced that backed the faculty and condemned any Episcopal college or seminary that used race as a criterion for denying admission to students.[29]

Within the Sewanee community, many expressed shock that the theology faculty had chosen to make segregation a major public issue. In his response to the faculty ultimatum, Bishop Mitchell emphasized that he and other trustees were by no means opposed to the recent church statements on desegregation. Their stance was based upon "the practical application of the Christian principles to the particular situation" and "the method or timeliness of applying those principles" to student life at the University of the South. He simply believed that further study of the possible effects of desegregation on life at Sewanee was necessary before that process could proceed.[30] Speaking on behalf of many members of the college faculty, Eugene Kayden, a professor of economics, asked the protesters why they were so eager to destroy "the Sewanee ideal" for the sake of a few hypothetical black applicants. "It is part of Christianity to hold the social fabric together," Kayden said, and faculty members ought to be teaching their students "the arts of social adjustment and the attitudes of mind required for getting along" with one another. He also suggested that the demands made by the theology faculty threatened to transform Sewanee into an ideological battleground in which the true values of the university would be lost. Rather than trying to promote unrealistic goals, he reiterated, their concern should be "the education and nurture of the mind and spirit in right social attitudes"—a mission that had nothing to do with the presence of African Americans in the student body of the university.[31]

The original stage of the crisis at Sewanee took place during the summer months, when most students were absent from the campus. When they returned to school in September 1952, the controversy escalated further. Rumors began to circulate about the moral integrity of several of the faculty. Robert Grant, who was accused of public drunkenness, resigned to avoid dismissal, and J. Allen Reddick and Robert McNair were also charged with similar offenses. In the eyes of most of the seminarians, however, these men were only the victims of falsehoods created by a few of their fellow students whose bishops (notably, Frank Juhan of Florida) wished to see the faculty punished for its outspoken opposition to the trustees. Eventually, all the active faculty of the School of Theology except Bayard Jones (who had refused to sign the earlier letter of protest) made good on their threat to leave the school. Since they did not wish the personal attacks to which they had been subjected to obscure the more substantial theological issues involved in the case, they submitted their resignations, effective at the end of the academic year. Jones, on the other hand, opposed the admission of black students and questioned the grounds on which the other faculty had made their protest. Religious and theological principles were not really at stake, he said. Rather, it was the indefensible "claim of the Negro to social equality—and ultimately . . . to the right of intermarriage" that his colleagues had chosen to advocate.[32]

Jones's opinions, of course, reflected those of many other administrators, faculty, and students at the University of the South in 1952. No one was more determined in his racial views than the newly appointed vice chancellor, Edward McCrady. McCrady belonged to a family that was "proudly Charlestonian," and he had taught biology at Sewanee for fifteen years before his election as vice chancellor (university president).[33] True to the patrician heritage in which he had been raised, McCrady maintained that "the salvation of any Negro soul is as important to God" as the eternal destiny of a white person, but he questioned the intellectual abilities of African Americans and saw no benefit in social interaction between the races. Fearing the consequences of intermarriage, he adhered to his belief in the essential distinctiveness of "the three Great Races (Hauptstrassen) or 'Stocks,'" and he was distressed that it had become "the vogue . . . to talk as if there are no differences among the races except a little pigment of the skin."[34] As a scientist, moreover, McCrady wondered why Christians always needed to oppose "discrimination." After all, he observed, "to promise not to discriminate between men on the ground of race would mean . . . not to be able to distinguish or recognize the differences which do exist." McCrady based his opposition to desegregation on commonplace grounds as well. Arguing that the university was "not equipped to solve . . . all the social and economic problems which beset it and the rest of the world," he emphasized that his administration simply wished to keep "a small school, in a small and isolated community" running efficiently.[35] With this purpose in mind, he recruited and hired five new faculty members to replace the nine protesters who had resigned—an action for which both he and the so-called "scab" professors were roundly denounced in many quarters of the denomination.[36]

McCrady and the trustees, however, still had numerous supporters during the controversy. Even before the trustees officially voted in June 1952, the vestry of Christ Church in Nashville, Tennessee, had expressed their amazement that some people were trying to convince African Americans to enroll at Sewanee—an action they regarded as an affront to the customs of the region. Albion Knight, a lawyer and Sewanee graduate in Florida, saw the admission of black students as "a quick cancer" that would destroy the university. "The University was created for Southern Gentlemen," he said, "and it will be many years before a negro can be classed as a 'Southern Gentleman.'" Albert S. Thomas, the retired bishop of South Carolina, thought it was both "deplorable" and "absurd" to assert, as many in the Episcopal Church were doing, that desegregation was an intrinsically Christian position. If those who professed to be Christians would merely project a loving and tolerant spirit toward the Sewanee trustees, he argued, those men would be able to handle the situation on their own in a responsible fashion. And approximately 80 percent of the undergraduates at the University of the South in early 1953 signed a statement affirming the traditions of their school: they backed the trustees' position on segregation and commended McCrady for behaving throughout the debate on campus in a manner that was "characteristic of a Christian gentleman."[37]

The conflict within the church expanded further in February 1953, when James Pike, the dean of the Cathedral of St. John the Divine in New York, was chosen to receive an honorary degree from Sewanee and preach at the university's baccalaureate service in June. As soon as he learned of that decision, Pike wrote McCrady to decline the honor and released the letter to the *New York Times* and other newspapers for publication. He did not wish to receive "a doctorate in the white divinity which Sewanee apparently is prepared to offer the Church," Pike declared, and he had no desire to become even an honorary alumnus of a school that still maintained an "apartheid policy." Pike also insisted that the university not only had erred in refusing to challenge Tennessee segregation laws, but it had also hurt the cause of Christianity in the United States. How could a church that so easily blends with its cultural surroundings, he asked, hope to attract new members or increase its influence in the nation? "The Church has never regarded the civil law as the final norm for the Christian conscience," he concluded, and a church-sponsored school like Sewanee should be willing to challenge the constitutionality of immoral laws.[38]

Though the tremendous uproar that Pike aroused eventually pushed the university trustees toward desegregation, it worsened the plight of many students already at the School of Theology. Ministerial candidates from southern dioceses were caught in a quandary, for they were forced to decide whether they could in good conscience continue as students at the seminary. The majority of the bishops asked their candidates to leave the university and enroll at another seminary, while a few bishops insisted that their seminarians must stay at Sewanee. Of the fifty-six first- and second-year students at the school in 1952–53, thirty-five of them eventually transferred to other schools. Approximately one-third of that number enrolled at Virginia Seminary, which accepted the transfer students in spite of the overcrowding and housing problems caused by their entrance. For the handful of students committed to the desegregation of Sewanee but under the care of bishops who wished the school to keep its all-white status, the situation was particularly difficult. Bishop Carpenter of Alabama, for example, believed that the time had not yet come to accept African American students at Sewanee, and he made it clear to his seminarians that he would not tolerate any public disagreement with the trustees' decision. "I have told my Alabama boys up there to sit tight, sign no resolutions," he wrote Bland Mitchell. When one candidate from Alabama refused to follow this advice, Carpenter withdrew support and quickly arranged his transfer to the diocese of Western North Carolina, where the bishop (M. George Henry) fully supported desegregation.[39]

The crisis at Sewanee ended finally in June 1953, when the largest gathering of trustees in the university's history met for a special session before their annual board meeting. For several months, Edwin Penick and Edmund Dandridge, the bishops of North Carolina and Tennessee, respectively, had pressed for a meeting to overturn the June 1952 decision, but Bland Mitchell and several lay trustees had successfully delayed that gathering. Thus, when the trustees finally assembled, all the protesting faculty had left Sewanee for other places of employment, and a new faculty, officially neutral on the racial issue, was in position. Although the majority of the trustees believed that applications from black candidates ought to be accepted, a determined minority, consisting primarily of lay men, still argued that desegregation was contrary to the best interests of both African Americans and whites at that time. Augustus Graydon, a South Carolina lawyer who led the lay minority, resisted the attempt by clergy to place "the matter on a theological or ideological plane," and he sought to focus attention instead on what he called "the practical situation" at the school.[40] Graydon said he believed in segregation "unashamedly and unabashedly" because, "more basic . . . than some provisions of the Federal Constitution," it had originated in the unchanging "mores and folkways of our people."[41] Meanwhile, a survey of all Episcopal clergy revealed that nearly 80 percent of the respondents favored the admission of African Americans to Sewanee. Furthermore, eighteen out of the twenty diocesan bishops present at the trustees' meeting supported desegregation, and fourteen of them repeated their pledge to remove their students from Sewanee as long as it remained racially segregated. The decision, therefore, was never really in doubt. Following a day of discussion and debate, the trustees (by a 78–to-6 vote) repudiated the position of a year before and declared that the School of Theology henceforth would be open to African American applicants.[42]

As the student editor of the *Sewanee Purple,* the weekly campus newspaper, noted astutely following the trustees' vote, opening the School of Theology to black students was not necessarily a radical step for white church leaders to take and might ultimately be in their best interests.

After all, if the Episcopal Church hoped to keep a hand in the black community, it could use black priests, raised in the South and trained by white teachers with southern roots, to undertake that ministry. What better place to educate such clergy than at a quintessentially southern school like Sewanee? Augustus Graydon made a similar, albeit disingenuous, point about the subversive nature of white paternalism, when he tried to convince the Sewanee trustees that segregation was what most blacks really desired. The Episcopal Church could best succeed in the black community, he thought, if it maintained a relatively benign policy of segregation and let African Americans run their own affairs without interference from whites. Thus, when slaves gained their freedom after the Civil War, they quickly fled the authority of white Episcopal clergy in order to organize their own independent churches. If the Episcopal Church tries to force integration too fast, Graydon warned, its work among black southerners could be irreparably damaged.[43]

Graydon's argument had a certain merit, for though African Americans were the primary objects of the discussions at Sewanee, their actual voices were never heard. As had happened at the Sewanee conference in 1883, the fate of black people within Episcopal circles was assumed to lie entirely in white hands. Meanwhile, black Episcopalians in the South were left to focus on the maintenance and support of the few church institutions over which they had control. Having struggled throughout the nineteenth and early twentieth centuries to achieve recognition of the usefulness of a separate racial ministry, African Americans in the Episcopal Church found themselves facing an entirely new set of questions and obstacles in the 1950s. What value, for example, would black parishes and ACIN schools now have if African Americans were not automatically excluded from white ones? Would the elimination of racial segregation mean the end of all-black colleges? Indeed, how useful was the Negro Work program that the Bi-Racial Committee and National Council administered, if the Episcopal Church were to become racially integrated? Should "Negro Work" be eliminated as an embarrassing vestige of the Jim Crow era, or should it be continued and strengthened as a symbol of black achievement and uplift?[44]

In the eyes of most African Americans connected with colleges supported by the ACIN, their schools were not just inferior, segregated institutions (as northern liberals charged), but "a secure place" and one of the best "opportunities for self-expression" that educated black southerners possessed.[45] M.M. Millikan, the executive secretary of the ACIN, came to this conclusion from research he conducted following the release of the

*McLaurin* and *Sweatt* decisions. Millikan wrote to the black presidents of ACIN schools in the summer of 1950 and asked them what effect the Supreme Court cases and desegregation might have on their programs. Harold Trigg, the president of St. Augustine's College, expressed his hope that, when some necessary improvements were made, white applicants one day might enroll at his school—at least in numbers equal to the black students who left to study at colleges that were predominantly white. Earl McClenney, the president of St. Paul's Polytechnic Institute in Lawrenceville, Virginia, had similar expectations. Since the court decisions mandated only the equalization of black and white facilities, he anticipated marked improvement in what was offered to African Americans in the South. At the same time, he warned that African American educators should be on guard against "arguments coming from our friends in the North and geographically-border-line-men-of-color" who—in the name of racial integration—might try to close down, rather than improve, black Episcopal colleges.[46]

Despite the cogent argument that Trigg and McClenney advanced, their fears were soon realized as liberal Episcopalians in the North used the *McLaurin* and *Sweatt* cases to scrutinize more closely the "separate but equal" racial ministry the church sustained. The first major criticism of the Negro Work program appeared in a July 1951 editorial in the church's most socially progressive periodical, *The Witness*. Referring to the recent Supreme Court decisions, the editorial, written by William Spofford, a prominent white priest and activist, asked whether the church-sponsored summer conferences held every year at black colleges in the South were still justifiable. Although Spofford was pleased that those gatherings provided some opportunity for white and black Episcopalians to meet, he was also concerned that nothing in their agenda challenged either segregation or the second-class status of black institutions in the South. Instead of attacking racial segregation, those meetings seemed only "to make jim crow function more smoothly." And instead of tearing down "the jim crow ghetto wall which we all abhor," Spofford complained, many black Episcopalians and their white allies in the South seemed far too comfortable functioning within a race-specific context.[47]

These criticisms continued in a series of articles that were published in *The Witness* a few months later. In them Alger Adams, a black rector in Yonkers, New York, and a member of the magazine's editorial board, bitterly condemned what he called "Church Jim Crow." Although South Carolina was the sole diocese that kept its official business segregated, Adams objected strenuously to the fact that many other dioceses still allowed parishes to organize themselves along racial lines. He was especially critical of the Bi-Racial Committee and the Guiding Principles the National Council had adopted in 1943; he thought they exemplified the "lackadaisicalness" with which Episcopal leaders approached the task of integration. Few Episcopalians, either black or white, seemed motivated to question the segregated parish system that remained in existence nationwide, and as a result African American church members usually received a "second-class ministry." The Episcopal Church ought to have been engaged in advancing the spread of the kingdom of God, but "our spiritual blindness, our moral cowardice, and our double-tongued . . . mortal sin in not knowing good from evil" were preventing Episcopalians from following the racially inclusive teachings of Jesus Christ.[48]

Tollie Caution, the black priest who had succeeded Bravid Harris as secretary for Negro work in 1945, had worked quietly and effectively in his position for many years, but he was stung by Adam's criticisms. Those articles and the public rebuke they contained also placed the National Council and the Bi-Racial Committee on the defensive, and they became an important subject of discussion when the two bodies assembled in early 1952. In preparation for those meetings, Caution composed a determinedly upbeat report, entitled "A Decade of Progress in Negro Work," in which he rehearsed the advances African Americans had been able to make in the Episcopal Church since his program started. He began by noting the increased interest among white Episcopalians in recruiting and educating young black men to become church leaders. For example, in 1941 several Episcopal seminaries (in the North as well as in the South) still refused either to admit African Americans or to house them in dormitories with white students. In 1951, in contrast, there were twenty-five black men studying for the priesthood in all but one (i.e., Sewanee) of the church's seminaries. Caution also emphasized the dramatic expansion in funding that had occurred over the previous ten years. The National Council had spent only twenty-three thousand dollars on its black ministry in 1941, but by 1951 it had increased its financial outlay almost tenfold. The Bi-Racial Committee itself had come into existence in 1943, and the ACIN, which had had no African Americans on its eighteen-member board of trustees in 1941, now had two. Finally, Caution said, the summer conferences that Spofford's editorial assailed had proved to be particularly beneficial for young African Americans. Those gatherings not only encouraged participants to become involved in local parishes and diocesan programs, but they also enabled black people in the South to develop an awareness of the ministry of the Episcopal Church at the national level.[49]

Despite Caution's optimistic viewpoint on the program he directed, he could not escape being questioned about the criticisms that the Bi-Racial Committee members all had read. At the committee's January 1952 meeting, he was asked to comment specifically on the accusations in *The Witness*. Caution admitted that Adams and Spofford had made some valid points: all Episcopalians ought to be striving to achieve the ideal of full racial integration. Separation, however, remained the dominant form of race relations throughout the country, and until the Episcopal Church and American society were truly integrated, segregated meetings often were still the most effective means of involving African Americans in the life of their denomination. M.M. Millikan made a similar point a few months later, when he reported to the 1952 General Convention about the activities of the ACIN. He emphasized that the Episcopal Church would continue to maintain "Negro schools . . . not to support segregation but because of segregation." Good schools for black southerners were still in short supply, he said, and in the eyes of those who ran the ACIN colleges, the Episcopal Church was right in offering educational opportunities to African Americans.[50]

Confusion about the purpose of racially based programs also appeared in the official actions of organizations for church women in this period. Starting in 1921, several southern dioceses had formed Woman's Auxiliary chapters for African Americans and allowed those all-black groups to send delegates to the Triennial Meeting, the gathering of church women that met in conjunction with each General Convention. As a result black and white women from those dioceses had been represented in equal numbers at national church gatherings. Opposition to this policy, however, led to the creation of new rules in 1943 stipulating that only a single, integrated Woman's Auxiliary chapter could exist in each diocese. Recognizing that this change effectively eliminated the presence of African Americans at the Triennial Meeting, the church women altered their policy once again. At the 1946 General Convention, they decided that any diocese containing at least three black congregations and 225 black communicants could elect an additional "minority racial" delegate—their leadership emphasizing that this measure was designed not to affirm segregation, but to insure greater interracial cooperation.[51] The Girls' Friendly Society, a social service organization for young women, dealt with virtually the same issue in regard to its regulations. At a meeting in 1949, the society's executive committee decided to revise their statement on race relations and emphasize "justice and equal opportunity for all racial groups" in the church. Consistent with that ideal, the committee declared that whenever "a parish made up of one racial group asks to organize a . . . branch on the basis of segregation, that privilege shall be granted." Although this rule was intended to encourage black women to join the society, charges of racial discrimination were soon raised against it. The offending clause was therefore quietly dropped, and special enticements were no longer offered to African American parishes and women's groups.[52]

In the midst of social changes occurring throughout the country and with the denomination's own distinct African American ministry undergoing increasing scrutiny, all church organizations were necessarily sensitive to the charge that they appeared to practice discrimination. Understanding, therefore, that it was no longer wise even to use racial terminology in reference to Tollie Caution's program, the Bi-Racial Committee suggested, and the National Council approved, a small but significant change in the title of his position. In mid-1952, the term *Negro Work* was removed, and he received the more neutral designation "assistant secretary in the Division of Domestic Missions of the Home Department." Caution's responsibilities were the same, but the distinctly racial aspects of his job were de-emphasized.[53] The CCW, meanwhile, was similarly challenged to examine whether its self-designated role as "a watch-dog group for things concerning Negroes" had become counterproductive in the 1950s. Perhaps an organization concerned about the place of African Americans in the church was—as *The Witness* suggested—no longer an aid but a hindrance to the advance of God's kingdom. Thus, the CCW, which had struggled for more than seventy years to convince white Episcopalians to recognize the presence of African Americans in the denomination—a goal apparently realized in 1943—found itself pushed once again toward the margins of church life as whites began to awaken to the evils of racism. In response to these pressures, the group declared at a meeting in April 1954 that it would alter its focus in the future and concentrate on creating Christian fellowship without regard to racial differences.[54]

A few days after the CCW reached its decision, the last major obstacle in the way of complete desegregation in the Episcopal Church was overturned. The diocese of South Carolina had been debating for several years about opening its annual convention to representatives from black parishes. The subject was first raised in 1945, but segregationists had been able to use parliamentary procedures to block the reform. However, a motion was carried successfully in 1953 that invited parishes in the "Negro Convocation" to apply for membership in the diocesan convention. The test came in 1954. In his convention address that year, Thomas

Carruthers, the diocesan bishop, expressed his wish that the diocese would finally "clear up an irregularity" that had existed since 1875. He praised black Episcopalians for their continuing loyalty to a church that had often rebuffed them, and he asked white Episcopalians to do the right thing and admit black clergy and congregations into their fellowship. When St. Mark's of Charleston (the parish rejected in 1875) and two other African American parishes applied for admission to the convention on May 4, 1954, they were accepted, and—less than two weeks before the release of the historic *Brown* decision—the desegregation of that body was at last achieved.[55]

# Part II

# Integration

Where does the Church stand in the movement toward an integrated society? The Church stands solely upon the Gospel which it celebrates in the preaching and the sacraments. The Church stands as a community integrated in Baptism and Holy Communion. The Church stands upon Jesus who has effectively established the unity of the human family. . . . Through the Freedom Movement our Lord is bringing about a confrontation among men which is often painful and confusing. Yet in the midst of the pain and confusion is a call to prophecy and reconciliation.

—James P. Breeden,
"The Prophecy and Reconciliation,"
1963.

# 3

# *The Impact of the* Brown *Decision*

J Waties Waring, a federal district court judge in South Carolina, seemed
  an unlikely person to become involved in the desegregation of public
  schools in the South in the 1950s. Raised and educated in Charleston,
Waring embodied the aristocratic pretensions and conservative social
values of the Carolina lowcountry. The descendent of slaveholders, he
had been nursed during childhood by a black woman owned by his grand-
parents before the Civil War. Both his parents were committed Episcopalians, and he faithfully attended St. Michael's Church, Charleston, where
(as he later said) he learned to appreciate the interrelationship of religion, ethical values, and "respectability." Following many years of devoted service in South Carolina's all-white Democratic party, he was
appointed a federal judge in 1941, and his supporters fully expected him
to uphold the laws and traditions of white supremacy. But when he came
to the bench in Charleston, Waring's views began to change. Although he
never wholly abandoned the paternalistic racial attitudes of his youth,
his opinions about the political status of African Americans evolved considerably as he awoke to the realities of bigotry and injustice. He read
books such as W.J. Cash's *Mind of the South* (1941) and Myrdal's *American
Dilemma,* and he saw the truth of their analyses about the effects of racism on his society. At the same time, he grew impatient with the moral
timidity of the churches in the region, and he even chided his bishop,
Thomas Carruthers, for not doing enough to overcome racial prejudice.[1]

As Waring's reputation for racial liberalism grew during the late
1940s, both African Americans in South Carolina and lawyers for the
NAACP recognized that they had a friend on the bench in Charleston.
Increasingly sympathetic to the arguments they advanced, Waring handed
down a series of decisions that undermined the legal foundations of dis-

crimination in his state. The final break with his past occurred in 1947. Before that date white legislators in South Carolina had effectively prevented African Americans from casting ballots in Democratic primary elections. After hearing the arguments of NAACP attorney Thurgood Marshall in the *Elmore v. Rice* case, Waring ruled that laws enabling the Democratic party to organize itself as a private club were unconstitutional because they were designed to be racially exclusive. As a result of that decision, thirty thousand black voters went to the polls for the first time on primary day in 1948. When white Democrats protested and sought to stop the expansion of the electorate, Waring exploded angrily and accused them of ignoring both the American political creed and "the creed of true religion" in which southern Christians ostensibly believed. "It is time for South Carolina to rejoin the Union," he declared. This outburst and his general disregard for southern racial mores further alienated him from most white people in the state, and as a consequence he endured not only social ostracism by family members and former friends, but also physical attacks on his home in Charleston.[2]

Thurgood Marshall came to his role as an opponent of segregation by a more predictable route than Waring. Although, like the judge, he had been raised an Episcopalian in the South (his mother had been active at George Freeman Bragg's parish, St. James' in Baltimore), the similarity with Waring's upbringing ended there. As a young black Episcopalian, Marshall had been taught by Bragg to resist, not to advance, the racial status quo. Marshall studied as an undergraduate at Lincoln University and received his legal training at Howard University. After graduating from Howard, he opened a law office in Baltimore in 1933 and prepared his first civil rights suit at the end of that year. By 1938, when he took charge of the legal activities of the NAACP in New York, he had become the most important black lawyer in the United States. Over the course of the next decade, Marshall helped shape the practice of civil rights law, and he functioned effectively as an attorney, an office manager, and a public relations expert for the NAACP. Finally, in his arguments in the *Sweatt* and *McLaurin* cases of 1950, he convinced the Supreme Court to endorse the crucial concept that states were responsible for providing equal educational opportunities for African Americans.[3]

Although segregation was then clearly under siege, the *Sweatt* and *McLaurin* decisions left the constitutionality of the "separate but equal" arrangement intact. This concept was challenged by Judge Waring, however, in his dissent in the *Briggs v. Elliott* case. The *Briggs* case involved black children who were not allowed to ride the buses that carried white students to the public schools in Clarendon County, South Carolina. Since the lack of buses for African Americans denied them equal access to schools in that rural county, Marshall and the NAACP originally intended to argue that officials there were in violation of the "separate but equal" principle established by the *Plessy* decision. But when *Briggs* was referred to Waring's jurisdiction in 1951, he suggested another course for Marshall to follow: amend the complaint and address the inherent inequality of segregation. Marshall gladly followed Waring's advice, and he presented his revised argument before a special federal court over which Waring and two other judges presided. Although his colleagues eventually affirmed that segregated schools were constitutional, Waring was able to deliver a long, stinging dissent from their ruling. In his statement he said he wished to "preach a sermon" that would arouse decent white people in the South to understand the necessity of ending segregation and granting basic rights to African Americans. Segregation was nothing more than a remnant of slavery and a denial of full citizenship guaranteed by the Fourteenth Amendment. "Separate but equal" had become an indefensible charade, he said, for any intelligent person could see that "segregation is per se inequality."[4]

Despite being stymied by the decision in the *Briggs* case, the NAACP legal team gained strength from Waring's vigorous dissent and continued its case against segregation in the courts. Kenneth B. Clark, a young black psychologist who had been a research assistant for Gunnar Myrdal, then became the key figure on whom Marshall and the NAACP relied. Clark taught at the City College of New York. He had written several articles about the damage that segregation and prejudice caused to the self-esteem of African Americans. In order to demonstrate the harmful effects of racism on personality development, Clark and his wife Mamie had developed a "doll test" that they administered to very young children. They showed the children two white dolls and two black dolls, and they asked them to choose the doll they liked the best. Since the majority of African American children preferred the white doll, the Clarks saw this as evidence that racial prejudice had produced feelings of inferiority in them. These findings soon became the basis for the NAACP's argument in its appeal of the *Briggs* decision. Clark and Marshall insisted that as long as racial segregation bore the imprimatur of the Supreme Court, it not only implied the inferiority of every black person in the United States but also threatened the stability and vitality of American society. If prevailing racial attitudes and practices were changed, however, all American children would have the opportunity to grow up in a healthier social environment.[5]

Clark believed that churches could also play a critical role in overcoming prejudice, and he assumed that acceptance of the religious principle of human brotherhood was an important element in inspiring white citizens to treat African Americans with fairness and respect. Clark himself had been an active Episcopalian in Harlem as a youth, and his mother even urged him to study for the priesthood. Although he never intended to fulfill that wish, he did believe in the value of religious institutions in creating and sustaining positive attitudes about race. He was considerably troubled, however, by the fact that the Episcopal Church and other major Protestant denominations, which had begun to pass resolutions about the need to end segregation, were themselves still effectively segregated at all levels. Most of those pronouncements had been vague and sounded tentative, he thought, and they showed that the churches were not yet ready to fight vigorously on behalf of interracial justice. In an effort to gather information that could be used by Marshall and the NAACP, Clark also wrote the leaders of churches and other institutions that were involved in the process of desegregation. Among the people he contacted was Edward McCrady of the University of the South, who—as if to confirm Clark's generally low opinion of his fellow church members—responded evasively to his questions about desegregation at Sewanee.[6]

While the Clarks conducted their sociological research, school segregation cases from Kansas (*Brown v. Board of Education*), Virginia (*Davis v. County School Board*), Delaware (*Gebhart v. Belton*), and the District of Columbia (*Bolling v. Sharpe*) accompanied *Briggs* through the tortuous process of review in the federal judiciary. In order to aid the NAACP legal staff in preparing their arguments in cases involving five different jurisdictions, Marshall purchased several copies of a recently published book, *States' Laws on Race and Color* (1951) by Pauli Murray, a black lawyer he knew. Marshall had first met Murray in 1939, when she sought his help in challenging the University of North Carolina for refusing (solely on racial grounds) to admit her to its graduate school. Although Murray's case was not sufficiently strong to merit the attention of the NAACP, she continued to press for civil rights as a legal expert and writer. She was arrested in 1940 in Virginia for violating the state's bus segregation laws, and in 1942 she served as a delegate to the national conference of A. Philip Randolph's March on Washington movement. As Murray wrote in an article published near the end of World War II, she was determined "by every cultural, spiritual, and psychological resource at my disposal . . . to destroy the institution of segregation." She vowed that she would continually attack segregation laws until the heritage that belonged by

right to all Americans—"the prophecy that all men are created equal"—
was fully realized.[7]

Although Murray and her family were Episcopalians (she had been
baptized at St. James' Church, Baltimore, and one of her aunts was married to a priest in North Carolina), it was not an Episcopal agency but the
Woman's Division of Christian Service of the Methodist Church that commissioned her massive study of American segregation laws. The Woman's
Division, one of the largest organizations of women in the United States
at that time, had been active since the 1920s in the effort to improve race
relations. The idea for Murray's book originated with two white staff
members who became interested in knowing what effect segregation laws
might have on the activities of their organization in the southern and
border states. When they consulted the NAACP in the late 1940s, they
were surprised to learn that no comprehensive source existed to supply
them with information about those statutes. Murray was hired to work
with them in 1948, and her *States' Laws on Race and Color* was ready for
publication three years later. Since many states outside the South had
enacted laws that opposed racial discrimination and protected the civil
rights of African Americans, Murray decided to include in her book all
legislation relating to race. The Woman's Division released the book in
the spring of 1951, and it soon became a key document, used by Thurgood
Marshall and others, in the legal attack on the "separate but equal" doctrine.[8]

The efforts of Marshall, Clark, Murray, and other legal experts and
activists finally bore fruit on Monday, May 17, 1954, when the Supreme
Court handed down a unanimous decision in the *Brown v. Board of Education* case—the name under which the five separate school segregation
cases had been classed. Chief Justice Earl Warren delivered the opinion
of the court, and his argument largely embraced the ideas expressed by
Waring's dissent in the *Briggs* case three years before: separation on the
basis of race was an inherently unequal arrangement that caused great
harm to black children. Warren also cited the psychological testing Clark
had conducted as evidence of the damaging effects of segregation. As
long as children attended schools on a racially segregated basis, he concluded, the *Plessy* decision had no legal bearing, for segregation itself
prevented African Americans from enjoying educational opportunities
equal to those of whites. Marshall and others at NAACP headquarters
were, of course, elated by the Supreme Court decision. Marshall himself
was so confident that a deathblow had been dealt to the Jim Crow system
that he predicted all forms of racial segregation would be eliminated by

1963, when the United States celebrated the centennial of the Emancipation Proclamation.[9]

Reactions to *Brown* from many white southerners stood in marked contrast to Marshall's hopeful words. A vocal group of segregationists, for example, quickly labeled May 17th "Black Monday," and they vowed to fight the decision to the bitter end. Marvin Griffin won the Democratic gubernatorial nomination in Georgia with the pledge that the races would never be mixed in his state, and George Bell Timmerman Jr., the governor of South Carolina, expressed an equally defiant sentiment during a national television broadcast. Senators Richard Russell of Georgia and James Eastland of Mississippi each argued that *Brown* represented an illegitimate action on the part of the federal judiciary, for it wrested decision-making in local affairs out of the hands of state legislatures. In July 1954 a group of civic and business leaders in Mississippi founded the first Citizens' Council, the organization around which the so-called respectable, middle-class resistance to desegregation soon coalesced. Eschewing the outright violence of the Ku Klux Klan, members of the Citizens' Council vowed to maintain segregation by more subtle means, such as threats of economic reprisal against those who defied them.[10]

Every denomination had its share of clergy and lay leaders who expressed segregationist views, but most major church bodies affirmed the validity of the *Brown* decision. The Presbyterian Church in the United States had the distinction of being the first denomination to assemble after the decision was released, and at the General Assembly of 1954 it adopted "A Statement to Southern Christians," a report that articulated the church's official position on desegregation. Since God's love transcended race and united all humankind, southern Presbyterians declared, Christians ought to accept the Supreme Court ruling and begin to dismantle the Jim Crow system. The Southern Baptist Convention, which was the largest religious body in the South, also resolved with surprising unanimity that Christian principles necessarily opposed segregation. The General Board of the National Council of Churches, the Presbyterian Church in the U.S.A., the Council of Bishops in the Methodist Church, the American Baptist Convention, the National Baptist Convention of the U.S.A., Inc., and a number of other denominations expressed similar sentiments in support of the Supreme Court. Although some church leaders were disappointed that these religious organizations had spoken only after the court released its decision, American Protestants as a whole expressed agreement with the principle that both segregation and racial prejudice were wrong.[11]

Unlike other denominations, which backed the *Brown* decision
merely with words, Episcopalians first responded in a practical fashion—
resolving an issue that had troubled them since the fall of 1952. Although
Houston, Texas, had been chosen as the site of the 1955 General Convention, many black Episcopalians and white northerners with liberal views
on race were distressed by the thought of gathering in a city where segregation laws restricted African Americans' use of buses, restaurants, and
hotels. Tollie Caution had always been uneasy about Houston, and after
the release of the Supreme Court decision, he and other members of the
church staff advised Presiding Bishop Henry Sherrill to change the convention site. Sherrill and the National Council had been willing to give
Clinton Quin, John Hines, and other Texas diocesan leaders a chance to
arrange workable alternatives to the segregated facilities and public accommodations in Houston, but the monumental nature of the task soon
became obvious to the national church staff in New York. Sherrill was not
especially progressive in his social views (even *Time* magazine called him
"an unswerving steerer down the middle of the road"), but he had served
on President Truman's Committee on Civil Rights in the late 1940s and
recognized that Texas segregation laws were inconsistent with his denomination's evolving position on race.[12]

Although Quin and Hines had hoped their diocese would be able to
provide hospitality for convention delegates of any race, church members in Texas could neither overturn segregation nor remake Houston on
their own. Faced with a dilemma, Episcopalians engaged in a national
debate about the site of their 1955 convention. The majority of whites
were not particularly troubled by the discrepancy between their professed
belief in "Christian brotherhood" and the harsh realities of racial prejudice in the South. Frank Rhea, the bishop of Idaho, for example, thought
that discrimination based on money and class, not on race, was the most
severe problem the Episcopal Church faced. Since Christians in the past
had not felt the need to change society but had witnessed to their faith
"amid pagan injustices, both civil and political, amid the exploitation of
the unfavored, and amid slavery," there was no reason, Rhea said, why
twentieth-century Episcopalians could not do the same thing. Despite
such indifference on the part of some church leaders, a reversal occurred
when the three black members of the Texas diocesan committee charged
with planning arrangements for the convention made public their belief
that the meeting should not be held in Houston. Black Episcopalians in
Boston, New York, and Washington joined their protest and demanded a
change of location. As Hubert Delany, then a lay delegate to the New York

in convention, remarked, he had grown up under segregation when his father served at St. Augustine's College in North Carolina, but he left the South as an adult because he could no longer accept the conditions under which black people were forced to live. He thought that if Episcopalians removed their convention from Houston, they would send the clearest possible message about their sincerity in seeking to end racial segregation.[13]

Sherrill now had to make an extremely difficult decision—"an ecclesiastical Dunkirk," one editorial writer called it.[14] Although he had the authority as presiding bishop to change the location of the General Convention, he was hesitant to invoke that privilege. Quin and Hines remained adamant about keeping the convention in their diocese, and Sherrill knew that most white Episcopalians in the South—whether they were personally opposed to segregation or not—would be offended if the meeting were removed from their region. Texas was also one of the fastest growing dioceses in the Episcopal Church, and Sherrill was loathe to turn his back on the rapidly expanding population of the Southwest. Opposition to the Houston site, though, came from dioceses in the Northeast, the region from which a major portion of the denomination's financial support derived and where the Episcopal Church remained an inescapable part of "the American establishment." In the immediate aftermath of the *Brown* decision, furthermore, Sherrill did not wish to seem indifferent to the concerns of African Americans about segregation. After weighing these considerations, he made his choice and announced on June 8, 1954, that the General Convention would not be held in Houston. Nine days later he named multiracial Honolulu, Hawaii, as the site of the 1955 meeting. Although he made his choice partly on mainstream political grounds, arguing that Episcopalians needed to disprove Communist propaganda about racial discrimination in the United States, white Episcopalians in southern dioceses were still outraged. Quin was personally devastated. He charged that Sherrill had undermined the church in the South and hinted that malicious "underground work" by Tollie Caution and others at the denomination's headquarters had unfairly demeaned his diocese.[15]

While national leaders resolved this complicated and telling controversy about the General Convention site, other church members—in far less prominent positions than Sherrill and Quin—sat down to formulate an official response to the *Brown* decision. Duncan M. Gray Jr., a white priest in charge of two small parishes in Mississippi, was the somewhat unexpected catalyst for these deliberations. Gray had been a theological student at the University of the South during the crisis in 1952–53, and he was convinced that the Episcopal Church ought to be desegregated at all levels. One of four people who made up the committee in charge of Christian social relations in his diocese, he prepared a statement in June 1954, which the other committee members enthusiastically endorsed, about the Supreme Court pronouncement. Gray's document, entitled "The Church Considers the Supreme Court Decision," invoked a wide variety of authorities in favor of desegregation: biblical teachings about "the Fatherhood of God and the brotherhood of Man"; national belief in "inalienable rights with which every human being is endowed by his Creator"; and official statements from the worldwide Anglican Communion about the need for racial inclusiveness in the church. From the standpoint of both the Christian faith and American democracy, Gray and his colleagues concluded, the *Brown* decision was absolutely "just and right," and Mississippi Episcopalians were morally bound to adhere to the law as interpreted by the Supreme Court. However difficult the present crisis might seem, Christians in the South had been presented with a God-given opportunity to transform both their society and their church.[16]

Gray's statement was powerful enough to gain the attention of several church officials in New York, who invited him to meet with them and present his views. M. Moran Weston and other members of the National Council's Division of Christian Citizenship were already engaged in preparing a report on *Brown*, and Gray was asked to work with that group. At its meeting in December 1954, the National Council adopted a resolution based in part on the Mississippi statement; it too urged all church members to affirm the Supreme Court decision. Christian theology with its emphasis on "the sacredness of human personality in the eyes of God," the council's statement declared, required Episcopalians not only to help desegregate public schools but also to foster interracial fellowship at all levels in their denomination. "The Court's ruling is more than a matter of law and order," the resolution said; "it has to do with the will of God and the welfare and destiny of human beings" as well. Based on "religious faith and democratic principles," Episcopalians recognized that "the Court's decision is just, right and necessary."[17]

The early 1950s were an extraordinarily hopeful period in American life, and political, cultural, intellectual, and religious leaders throughout the country greeted the *Brown* decision with expressions of optimism. Since belief in progress, democracy, and education were deeply held national ideals, the notion of open schools where young Americans could all learn the country's core values had a broad appeal. Episcopal leaders reflected this trend, seeming confident that the application of sound theology and Christian good will would eventually halt racial prejudice in society as a whole.[18] When the 1955 General Convention assembled in Honolulu, for example, the bishops and deputies of the church officially endorsed *Brown* and declared that "unjust social discrimination and segregation are contrary to the mind of Christ and the will of God."[19] The department of Christian social relations in the diocese of Virginia reported in 1955 that "no problem of race relations exists within the Protestant Episcopal Church," because in Jesus Christ all "ancient prejudices, hatreds and contempts" had been overthrown.[20] Girault Jones, the bishop of Louisiana, composed a pastoral letter released in December 1954 that linked desegregation with the celebration of Christ's incarnation. "The rising demand for justice under the law and for equality of opportunity without regard to race," he wrote, is "part of the redemptive work of Almighty God begun, continued, and in His good time to be ended in Him." And Henry Louttit, the bishop of South Florida, thought a few "sincere but deluded folk" still believed in segregation and used scripture to justify their prejudices, but they were swayed more by ignorance than by an informed, modern understanding of what the Bible really taught on race.[21]

Such sanguine statements notwithstanding, Episcopalians were actually far from unanimous in their opinions about desegregation. As a 1952 study suggested, ordinary Episcopalians were generally more conservative on social matters than the official pronouncements of their denomination suggested, and approximately 10 percent of the bishops and priests and 25 percent of the lay people still believed in the validity of racial segregation. As if to prove this point, pockets of resistance to desegregation began to appear in several southern dioceses in mid-1954. One of the strongest voices of dissent came from Edward Guerry, the rector of two small parishes near Charleston, South Carolina. Guerry questioned the psychological evidence on which the *Brown* decision was based, especially the assertion that "Negro children cannot be normal children unless they mingle and mix with White children." While he conceded that forced separation had caused hardship for some black southerners, he did not think all forms of racial separation were necessarily "un-Christian, undemocratic, unconstitutional, or insulting to Negroes." Albert Thomas, the retired bishop of South Carolina who was associated with Guerry's parishes, also raised objections to the *Brown* decision. He argued that segregation was neither contrary to the Bible nor inconsistent with Christian belief in the unity of humankind in Christ's body, the church. Thomas, like Guerry, acknowledged that the system of segregation had its faults, but those, he said, were "due to man's fallen nature, not to segregation itself."[22]

Encouraged by Guerry and Thomas, further organized opposition to the *Brown* decision soon surfaced within the diocese of South Carolina. In January 1956 the vestry of St. Michael's Church, Charleston wrote the National Council to protest its statement on desegregation. The Supreme Court's pronouncement was "not a matter of religious faith," the vestry declared, nor was desegregation "just, right and necessary."[23] Three months later, at the annual convention of the diocese, B. Allston Moore, a lawyer who belonged to St. Michael's, submitted a resolution stating that "there is nothing morally wrong in the voluntary recognition of racial differences and . . . voluntary alignments can be both natural and Christian." Declaring that "the integration problem caused by the Supreme Court decision . . . should not be characterized as Christian or unChristian," the resolution also advised that the mandatory desegregation of Episcopal parishes would be both "unnatural and unwise."[24] John Morris, a white priest in Dillon, South Carolina, led the opposition to Moore's resolution. Morris had long believed that racial prejudice and original sin were interconnected, and most of his clerical colleagues supported that theological view. Guerry and a handful of other clergy, however, said they favored voluntary racial separation on pastoral grounds. As G. Milton Crum, another white priest in South Carolina, remarked a few months later, bigotry was more a form of mental illness (like alcoholism) than a sin, and just as "moral condemnation only worsens the alcoholism of the alcoholic," so "the racialism of the racialist" is also increased when he or she is challenged too harshly. Swayed by that "pastoral" argument, the lay delegates to the convention solidly backed the segregationist position, and the resolution was carried by a two-to-one vote.[25]

For southern white liberals in the Episcopal Church, theological debates about segregation were certainly of symbolic importance, but social and political struggles taking place in their states demanded even greater attention. In May 1955 the Supreme Court had released a second *Brown* decision, which ordered local authorities to proceed with "all deliberate speed" in the desegregation of public schools. This action precipitated the campaign of "massive resistance," as segregationists throughout the South advanced the doctrine of "interposition," reminiscent of the states' rights tradition of the nineteenth century, in order to hinder federal intervention in state and local affairs. Another symbol of the region's defiant stance appeared in March 1956, when more than a hundred senators and congressmen signed a "Southern Manifesto." This document contained each signer's pledge to use all lawful means available to stop the enforcement of the two Supreme Court decisions, and the majority of southern legislatures eventually adopted laws that allowed the closing of public schools if desegregation could not otherwise be stopped. Finally, individual threats of violence, of economic sanctions, and of social ostracism fostered a chilling atmosphere that discouraged opposition to prevailing racial mores in the South.[26]

Despite many pressures, a small group of white southerners sought to oppose the massive resistance campaign and reached out to African Americans. One of the South's most prominent racial moderates was Hodding Carter II, the editor of the *Delta Democrat-Times* in Greenville, Mississippi. A native of Louisiana, Carter had come to Mississippi in 1936 and quickly established himself as an advocate of fair play for ordinary people, both white and black. Thanks to his efforts, the city of Greenville developed a reputation for decency in a state usually caricatured for its political and racial extremism. In addition to writing in his newspaper, Carter published books and articles in national magazines; he was regarded as a perceptive analyst of southern race relations. He did not think of himself as particularly militant on racial matters, however, and prior to the *Brown* decision he had condemned only blatant outrages, not segregation itself. Thus, after the murder of Emmett Till in 1955, he suggested that if justice were not done in the case, Mississippi would deserve whatever criticisms it received from the North. And when white southerners reacted with fury against the Supreme Court's pronouncements, he could not resist saying "I told you so," for he knew that whites had never taken seriously the "separate but equal" arrangement supposedly guaranteed by segregation laws.[27]

Carter was an active Episcopalian as well, and he was very much concerned about the social outreach of his denomination. He served on the vestry of St. James' Church in Greenville and represented his parish at the meetings of the diocesan convention. He feared that churches in the South had done little to transform their region but had allowed themselves to become merely "the mighty fortress of the *status quo*."[28] He also lamented the existence of a "yawning chasm between Sunday and Monday," and he thought that if Jesus Christ were alive in the 1950s, "he would espouse first the cause of the submerged, long-denied minorities who live among us." During the desegregation controversy at the University of the South, Carter had praised the seminary faculty for thinking that "Jesus Christ is more important than Jim Crow," and he applauded the Christian wisdom in the trustees' eventual decision to open the school to black applicants. These views on race not only earned him a large amount of hate mail, but they also led to his ouster from the vestry of St. James'. When Carter and another vestry member admitted that they would not stop African Americans who wished to worship at St. James' from entering the church, the two men were defeated in the next election of parish officers.[29]

Sarah Patton Boyle of Charlottesville, Virginia, was another southern white moderate who felt called to side with African Americans during the desegregation crisis in her state. Raised in a pious Episcopal home, she thought of herself as an insider in southern society. Her forebears had had important roles fighting for the Confederacy in the Civil War, and she was the daughter of Robert Patton, the longtime director of the ACIN, who taught her to regard black southerners with an affectionate, paternalistic eye. After her marriage to Roger Boyle, a professor at the University of Virginia, she settled comfortably into a life of middle-class domesticity in Charlottesville and became active at the white Episcopal parish near the college campus. Still motivated by a deep-seated sense of social superiority and noblesse oblige, Boyle became involved in facilitating the process of desegregation at the university in 1951. She considered segregation to be "distasteful, ridiculous and inexcusably undemocratic," and for a while she assumed that well-meaning white people like herself would be able to end it without much difficulty. Although she was distressed by the rabble-rousing tendencies of political leaders, she believed there was nothing fundamentally wrong with the South, because "love of Negroes is a far deeper tradition" in it than white supremacy.[30]

After the *Brown* decision, however, Boyle's religious thinking began to change dramatically: she became aware of the depths of both white racism and human sinfulness. The Supreme Court's pronouncement initially gave her hope about the inevitable demise of segregation, and in early 1955 she published a widely read article with the provocative title "Southerners Will *Like* Integration." The response to the article was immediate and visceral, and for many months afterward she received a deluge of crank calls and mail laced with obscenities and threats of violence. The campaign of intimidation against Virginia's most outspoken pro-integration white woman reached its height on a night in the summer of 1956, when Boyle and her thirteen–year-old son woke up and saw a six-foot cross burning on their lawn. But rather than frightening her, the cross-burning stiffened her resolve and ultimately helped strengthen her faith. Although she had once depended solely upon humanistic values ("the loftiness of man, the mellow loveliness of Dixie, the steadfastness of friends"), the feelings of rejection Boyle felt during the desegregation crisis in Charlottesville led to a spiritual rebirth.[31] "Man is as lost as the Church has long claimed he is," she wrote a friend in early 1958, and "bitterly I've learned that only God is good."[32] After this experience, Boyle believed she had a religious mission to help better race relations in the South. An indefatigable member of the Virginia Council on Human Relations and of the NAACP, she traveled widely throughout her state—lecturing in every Virginia town over a three-year period in the mid-1950s—in order to drum up support for desegregation.[33]

While Sarah Patton Boyle faced obscenities and social ostracism, Anne and Carl Braden, two white Episcopalians in Louisville, Kentucky, endured an even worse fate because of their commitment to interracial justice. Anne Braden's background was remarkably similar to Boyle's. She grew up in a genteel, middle-class home in Anniston, Alabama, and both her parents were active in the Episcopal Church. She was an extremely religious child and loved the Episcopal communion service, which was "rich with the words of brotherhood: 'O God, the creator and Preserver of all mankind . . . who hast made of one blood all nations of men.'" She was particularly moved by the biblical passage in Matthew 25 in which Jesus described how God would judge human beings based on their treatment of one another—whether they had fed the hungry and clothed the naked. When she attended college in Virginia during World War II, she became acutely aware of the South's racial problems, and she sensed the connection between the racist philosophies of Nazism and the segregated system in which she had grown up. After college she became a newspaper reporter and eventually married Carl Braden, a coworker on the staff of the *Louisville Times*. Although Carl had been raised as a Roman Catholic and had even studied for the priesthood, he thought of himself as an agnostic socialist at the time of his wedding. However, since he found many of the teachings of the Episcopal Church to be consistent with his socialism, he eventually joined the denomination, and when the Bradens' first child was born in the late 1940s, they began attending an Episcopal parish in Louisville. Anne was also appointed to the committee on Christian social relations of the diocese of Kentucky, and as she later observed, she tended to make a nuisance of herself at meetings, when she would always talk about the injustice of segregation.[34]

The release of the *Brown* decision in 1954 deepened the Bradens' commitment to fighting segregation, but it made them an easy target for racist whites as well. A few months before the historic case was decided, Andrew Wade, a black friend of the Bradens, asked them to buy a house for him in a new "white" neighborhood on the outskirts of Louisville. The Bradens readily agreed, and when the real estate deal was completed, they transferred ownership of the house to Wade. He moved into the house on May 15, 1954, just two days before the *Brown* decision was released, and this unintended timing helped trigger a campaign of terror and intimidation against both Wade and the Bradens. The house was eventually damaged by a bomb blast, but rather than indicting the men who attacked the property, a grand jury charged the Bradens and five of their supporters with engaging in a criminal conspiracy. Vulnerable to charges of Communism because of Carl's earlier socialist involvement, the Bradens were arrested under an old state sedition law and accused of masterminding a plot to overthrow the governments of Kentucky and the United States by stirring up racial strife. Caught in the hysteria surrounding McCarthyism, Carl was given a fifteen–year prison sentence and fined five thousand dollars; he spent a year in jail until sufficient bail money could be raised to release him. Although an appellate court exonerated Carl and the other defendants, the Bradens were unable to secure further work as journalists in Louisville. Fortunately, they were hired by James Dombrowski, then director of the Southern Conference Educational Fund (SCEF), who was also under siege for alleged "un-American" activities. Dombrowski employed the Bradens to work for SCEF as field secretaries, traveling throughout the South and encouraging attention to interracial justice.[35]

Throughout this period the Bradens felt isolated from their fellow Episcopalians, and although they received important aid from such left-of-center organizations as the NAACP, the American Civil Liberties Union, and the National Lawyers Guild, few supportive voices were raised within the church. Only William Howard Melish, a priest in Brooklyn, New York, and members of the Episcopal League for Social Action, with which he was closely associated, came to the Bradens' defense. In a sermon Melish preached in February 1955, he called attention to Anne Braden's upbringing as an Episcopalian, her parish membership in Louisville, and her active service on the Christian social relations committee of her diocese. How odd it was, he said, that Christians who accepted "the explicit injunctions of the Master" against social injustice now found themselves accused of sedition in Kentucky. And wasn't it strange that Episcopal communicants who wished to put into practice their denomination's teachings on race relations received no public support from either the National

Council or other church leaders?[36] Melish, however, was no stranger to controversy himself, and thus he was unable to win any general sympathy for the Bradens. In 1949, *Life* magazine had accused him of being one of a group of Communist "dupes and fellow travelers" working in the United States, and his outspoken support for civil rights in the 1950s caused many white Americans simply to dismiss him as a "subversive."[37]

In this toxic political environment—"a climate of fear," as one Episcopal rector in the South characterized it—those who were committed advocates of interracial harmony often had to emphasize how their views on desegregation were "reasonable" and "moderate" rather than "extreme."[38] Pressure to conform was especially heavy on men and women living in small towns, where support networks were weak, and on clergy in Protestant churches, who usually needed the good will of their parishioners to sustain livelihood. Although such "moderates" might wish to speak out and condemn the segregationists' massive resistance campaign, they were keenly aware of the consequences of too much frankness. Within these limitations, a highly effective effort was organized by John Morris in South Carolina. Morris enlisted four other neighboring white clergymen—two Episcopalians (Ralph Cousins and Joseph Horn), a Methodist (Larry Jackson), and a Presbyterian (John Lyles)—and formed them into a group called Concerned South Carolinians. Motivated by both their religious beliefs and their political ideals, the ministers announced that they wished to encourage citizens of their state to consider desegregation "thoughtfully in the light of Christian love and our democratic heritage, believing that we can go forward together even though slowly."[39]

Morris and his colleagues eventually recruited twelve men and women who were respected civic leaders and active church people, and they assigned each the task of writing an essay discussing how white southerners might cooperate with the Supreme Court decision without betraying their regional heritage. James McBride Dabbs, the Presbyterian lay leader and president of the Southern Regional Council, was originally asked to contribute an article, but Morris withdrew the invitation ("with misgiving and a realization that I was compromising with sin," he admitted) because Dabbs had a reputation for being too outspoken on racial matters. Although Dabbs was not among the contributors, the collection of essays, entitled *South Carolinians Speak,* was published in October 1957 and soon gained considerable praise from those who favored desegregation. More than nineteen thousand copies were distributed, and the booklet occasioned a number of newspaper editorials and several hundred generally favorable letters. Two of the people who worked on the project, however, suffered for their actions. John Lyles was forced to resign from his pastorate and find employment in another state, and the home of Claudia Sanders, one of the Episcopal contributors, was severely damaged by a bomb blast.[40]

During this period, the National Council of Churches authorized the creation of a program designed to offer aid to southerners like Lyles and Sanders who were attacked because they publicly supported desegregation. Known as the Southern Project, it became operational in late 1956 with the hiring of Will Campbell, a Southern Baptist minister and chaplain at the University of Mississippi. Campbell placed his office in Nashville, Tennessee, and he began to crisscross the South, making contact with various sympathetic church people. His principal responsibility was to be a "trouble-shooter" offering aid to harassed local activists. When the efforts of John Morris came to his attention, for instance, Campbell offered to circulate information about *South Carolinians Speak* to his mailing list of several thousand southern clergy known to be interested in improving race relations.[41]

The Episcopal Church followed the example of the National Council of Churches, and in December 1956 it hired Cornelius C. ("Neil") Tarplee, a white priest from Lynchburg, Virginia, to work toward what was called "intergroup cooperation" in the South. With the help of a sizable grant from the Fund for the Republic, Tarplee organized the project "Bridge Building in Areas of Racial Tension," which involved visiting twenty-six dioceses during the first four months of his employment. His activities were purposely given little publicity: he was expected to act quietly as a liaison with individuals facing crisis situations involving desegregation in the South. Tarplee reported that it was "clear to all but the most determinedly myopic that racial segregation in the United States is doomed," but he was concerned that the Episcopal Church was failing to keep up with secular organizations such as the armed forces, labor unions, and professional sports in the pace at which it desegregated. Although many white clergy in the South desired desegregation, they often felt stymied by hostile lay men and women beset "with deep-seated and spiritually crippling prejudices," he said. As a result, the denomination had been unable to provide prophetic moral leadership and was forced to watch social changes occur over which it could exert little control.[42]

As Tarplee's argument suggests, some Episcopalians who braved local disfavor to support desegregation assumed that the initiative in the struggle would come from educated white southerners like themselves—an attitude strikingly reminiscent of earlier generations of well-meaning but paternalistic church leaders. This tendency is illustrated by the experience of R. Emmet Gribbin Jr., the Episcopal chaplain of the University of Alabama and a son of the retired bishop of Western North Carolina. Gribbin's mettle was tested in February 1956, when Autherine Lucy attempted to become the first African American student to take classes at the university. An NAACP lawsuit led to Lucy's admission to the school, but on her third day of classes a mob gathered in Tuscaloosa and forced her to leave the campus. During the day of the riot at the university, Gribbin, along with two administrators and several students who were members of the Episcopal chapel, tried to calm the crowd and offered protection to Lucy. Gribbin himself was cursed, hit with an egg, and jostled by the mob. Believing this had proven his goodwill, he later volunteered to work with representatives of the university administration and the NAACP to resolve the situation at Tuscaloosa. But when he asked for help from John Burgess, the Episcopal chaplain at Howard University and a member of the denomination's Bi-Racial Committee, Gribbin received a jolt. Since Burgess knew Thurgood Marshall, Gribbin wanted him to contact Marshall about the negotiations, but Burgess refused. African Americans appreciated Gribbin's bravery during the campus riot, Burgess said, but most black people were still not prepared to trust southern white clergy in the area of race relations. Such a view might be cynical, he acknowledged, but it was a perspective "born of bitter experience."[43]

The controversy surrounding Autherine Lucy at the University of Alabama occurred in the midst of an even more momentous event taking place in Montgomery, the state capital. Black southerners had periodically defied the Jim Crow system before 1956, and they had even won an important victory after a bus boycott in Baton Rouge, Louisiana, in June 1953. The *Brown* decision, however, provided them with fresh incentive to push against the barriers of white racism, and thus when Rosa Parks was arrested in December 1955 for defying a local segregation law, her protest not only helped trigger a mass movement in Montgomery but also proved to be a watershed in the black freedom movement in the South. Although the Baton Rouge action received little outside attention, the lengthy bus boycott in Montgomery and the rise to prominence of Martin Luther King Jr. won considerable sympathy for black protesters among whites in the North. Successfully challenging segregation in the city known as "the cradle of the Confederacy," the Montgomery movement that King led clearly demonstrated to the nation as a whole the effectiveness of nonviolent confrontations with the white power structure of the South.[44]

The victory of King's coalition, however, proved to be the undoing of one white Episcopal priest, whose growing racial liberalism brought him into conflict with members of his parish. Thomas Thrasher, rector of the Church of the Ascension in Montgomery, had been a member of the local chapter of the Alabama Council on Human Relations for a number of years before the bus boycott, and he had engaged in respectful dialogue with clergy and other leaders in the black community. Since the mayor of Montgomery belonged to his parish, Thrasher was also able to function behind the scenes as an intermediary in the negotiations between white politicians and the black movement during the boycott. Inspired by what had been accomplished in his city, he began to preach more frequently about human brotherhood, and he also encouraged white Episcopalians to open their churches to people of all races. This was intolerable to many of his parishioners, who denounced him for betraying Montgomery's Confederate heritage and sought his dismissal from their church. Eventually, Thrasher was forced to leave Alabama and he found employment as a college chaplain in the relatively tolerant climate of the University of North Carolina at Chapel Hill.[45]

Throughout the conflict in Montgomery—first, during the boycott itself, and then in the controversy with his parishioners—Thrasher received virtually no assistance from his bishop, Charles Carpenter. Although Carpenter could have exercised his episcopal authority and come to Thrasher's aid, he essentially agreed with the segregationist position. He thought the Supreme Court had placed all southerners in "a very difficult predicament," for he believed that "time-weathered social modes are not changed overnight by law." In Carpenter's mind, the *Brown* decision had already proved to be a setback to the interracial harmony he believed the South had enjoyed under segregation; the events in Montgomery, he claimed, had further retarded the ability of white and black southerners to communicate effectively with one another. Although he sometimes displayed a willingness to aid individual black Episcopalians in pastoral matters and had even commended Emmet Gribbin privately for his part in helping to restore peace in Tuscaloosa, he condemned discrimination only in general terms and had no wish to promote sweeping social changes. As a consequence, he felt little sympathy for clergy like Thrasher who seemed intent on aiding a direct attack on segregation, thus causing what Carpenter regarded as needless discord within the church in Alabama.[46]

A similar economic boycott by African Americans led to the dismissal of Henry Parker, a black deacon, from his position at St. Paul's Church in Orangeburg, South Carolina. Parker, a New Jersey native, had received his theological education at Harvard Divinity School and had become a ministerial candidate in Cambridge under the tutelage of Kenneth Hughes, one of the more radical priests in the Episcopal Church at that time. Parker arrived in Orangeburg in August 1955, when the city was embroiled in a bitter struggle between its white and black residents over the pace of school desegregation. He was active in the NAACP, and because many of the black clergy in Orangeburg also were members, he joined them in supporting a boycott of white-owned businesses. Parker's situation was complicated, however, by his status within the church. Since St. Paul's was not a self-supporting parish, and since he had not yet been ordained a priest, he was under the direct supervision of Bishop Carruthers and of the rector of the Church of the Redeemer, the white parish in Orangeburg. Vulnerable to criticism from whites, Parker gained a reputation within his diocese for being "over-enthusiastic and very rough on the segregation problem."[47]

Although Carruthers was still regarded as relatively enlightened about racial issues and had been instrumental in bringing St. Paul's, Orangeburg, into the diocesan convention the year before, the *Brown* decision had seriously altered traditional expectations about black-white relations in the South. After scrutinizing Parker's activities over several months, Carruthers accused him of shirking his ministerial duties and told him to leave St. Paul's as soon as he could find employment somewhere else. Parker eventually became the curate (assistant minister) at St. Cyprian's Church in Detroit, but before his departure he discussed the matter at length with his mentor, Hughes. Hughes in turn contacted the church press and accused Carruthers of dismissing Parker solely on the basis of his membership in the NAACP. Parker himself charged that his racial militancy, not his shortcomings as a clergyman, had brought on the conflict with his bishop. "Real preaching is a disturbing factor," Parker said, and if Jesus had taken the course set by the bishop of South Carolina, "it wouldn't have led to the cross." Hughes, meanwhile, compared leading Episcopalians to Pontius Pilate. Although the official statements of the church had called the *Brown* decision "just, right, and necessary," he said, the National Council had chosen to remain aloof from the controversy in South Carolina and thereby allowed a good Christian to suffer a fate he did not deserve.[48]

Although Hughes's charge surely stung members of the National Council, he was essentially correct: the Episcopal Church as a whole had not done anything in Montgomery, in Orangeburg, or in any other place where African Americans were actively challenging segregation laws.

Central to the problem on which Hughes commented was the manner in which Episcopalians had traditionally viewed black southerners—namely, as objects for education, evangelism, and cultural uplift, but not as political beings taking action for themselves. As the senior black employee of the National Council, Tollie Caution had provided effective leadership in the denomination's Negro Work program. Yet the meaning and implications of "Negro work" had changed dramatically since the program's inception in 1943, and an exclusively evangelistic approach to the African American community no longer seemed appropriate—indeed, it seemed equivalent to segregation—in the post-*Brown* era. In Alabama, moreover, where the relationship between white and black Episcopalians had become particularly strained, the black clergy even asked diocesan leaders to bring their traditional, paternalistic ministry to a halt and recommended that they completely rethink their efforts with African Americans.[49]

In the aftermath of the *Brown* decision, the Bi-Racial Committee was placed in a predicament. Its members were forced to revise the rationale for their corporate existence—creating and sustaining distinctly black church institutions. The first stage of this process occurred in early 1955, when the committee decided that the 1943 statement "Guiding Principles Designed to Govern the Church's Negro Work" was no longer adequate. Over the next few months, Moran Weston, Tollie Caution, and other national church staff met and discussed possible revisions. In their initial draft they retained the original idea of the church as "a divine society" commissioned "to set spiritual and moral goals for society," but they proposed several changes reflecting important developments since 1954. Although the first article of the 1943 text decried the treatment of black Episcopalians as "unequal or inferior," the revision criticized any action that "sets brethren of different races apart from one another"—a clear reference to Kenneth Clark's emphasis on the harmful effects of racial separation. The third article (1943) called for "high standards" and "the same opportunities as those which are available to other racial groups" in the training of black clergy; the new document simply declared that high standards were necessary for everyone—African Americans, it assumed, neither lacked full opportunities nor needed remedial assistance. Finally, the proposed revision added wording that emphasized that "desegregation is the ultimate goal" of every aspect of the church's work and stated that desegregation was "more than a matter of law and order"; it was "the will of God."[50]

The subsequent debate on the new "Guiding Principles" reveals much about both the hopes of racial liberals and the realities of the Episcopal Church in the mid-1950s. After Caution introduced the text on which his subcommittee had worked, the full Bi-Racial Committee discussed it at length and adopted the statement with only one notable alteration, insisting that "the integration of all races," not merely "desegregation," should be the ultimate goal of the church's work with African Americans.[51] Since the members of the Bi-Racial Committee acted in an advisory function to the National Council, Caution took their proposal to the council for approval. In that process two significant changes were made in the text. In the "Guiding Principles" eventually adopted at the February 1956 meeting of the National Council, desegregation was no longer called "the will of God." In addition a neutral phrase, "free access to all institutions," was substituted for the term "integration," which was thought to be too inflammatory and suggestive of racial intermarriage. "With full and sympathetic appreciation for the real difficulties faced by the Church and Churchmen in the desegregation of our institutions," the final version of the Guiding Principles declared, "we affirm that the free access to all institutions is our ultimate goal for all our work." While the official thinking of the Episcopal Church had advanced considerably since 1943 and most members of the National Council recognized that "separate but equal" was no longer acceptable as a stated objective for the denomination, full racial integration was a concept from which the majority of church leaders still shrank.[52]

As the National Council accepted (in theory, at least) Episcopalians' responsibility for creating a desegregated society, members of the Bi-Racial Committee necessarily wondered whether any additional differentiation, including the operation of a separate missionary program, should be made between African American and white Episcopalians. The experience of holding the General Convention in Honolulu had raised the further question of what role minority groups other than African Americans should play in the life of the church. Presiding Bishop Sherrill wondered, for example, why "race relations" only meant "Negro-white," when Asian Americans, Hispanic Americans, and Native Americans were also active in the Episcopal Church in various areas of the country. In the fall of 1956, therefore, the Bi-Racial Committee discussed altering both its name and its mission, so that the black-white aspect was subordinated to a wider multiracial focus. Caution expressed concerns about that proposal. The integration of the church's mission was desirable, he admitted, but the great disparity of physical and financial resources that still existed between white and black parishes needed to be rectified before the special African American ministry could be abandoned. By broadening the church's racial ministry, Caution warned, the denominational leadership might fail to give sufficient attention to the particularly tenuous position of African Americans in relation to whites both in society and in the church.[53]

Changing attitudes about race nevertheless caused well-meaning white liberals in the North to ignore Caution's advice and press for modifications of the program he led. In December 1956, for example, Robert Spears, vicar of the Chapel of the Intercession in Harlem and head of the Christian education department of the diocese of New York, wrote the National Council about materials it had mailed to parish Sunday schools. The council had designated "the Church's Mission to Negroes" as one of three projects it wished Episcopal children to support in 1957, but Spears and his committee wondered why African American communicants were singled out in that way. Wasn't the Episcopal Church, he asked, now meant to conduct its mission on a nonracial basis? Caution and the Division of Domestic Missions responded to Spears by arguing that the church contained a multitude of ethnic groups, all of whom were part of the "rich diversity" created by God. Unless nonwhite children learned to recognize and take pride in their racial heritage, they would not be able to love and value the ethnic background of other people within the Christian fellowship. "Our differences are transcended in a new unity of the Spirit," Caution's division concluded, but "they are not obliterated."[54]

Whether right or not, Spears's words carried considerable weight, for those who led the African American ministries of the Episcopal Church were beginning to work against the intellectual temper of the times. By the late 1940s, leading social scientists were abandoning the concept of race as a biological phenomenon and talking in terms of "intergroup relations" instead. Gordon Allport noted in the preface to his influential book, *The Nature of Prejudice* (1954), "Race . . . is in reality an anachronism." He considered "ethnic" to be the most reliable term in discussing American prejudices, for (he wrote) "many 'colored' people are racially as much Caucasian as Negro." Among historians of racism, Kenneth Stampp received considerable attention when he stated in *The Peculiar Institution* (1956), his revisionist study of slavery, that "Negroes *are,* after all, only white men with black skins." And in the world of mainline Protestantism, Liston Pope, the dean of Yale Divinity School, declared in *The Kingdom beyond Caste* (1957) that "where God truly reigns and his kingdom prevails," Christian people recognize no racial differences. Martin Luther King reiterated Pope's views when he complained that "the most segregated hour of Christian America is eleven o'clock on Sunday morning."

Chastened by these various contemporary views, members of the National Council realized they could no longer sustain a program that regarded African Americans as essentially different from other church
members. In February 1957, therefore, the council again changed the
title of Caution's position and placed him at the helm of a new Division of
Racial Minorities. In that position he was responsible not only for African
American church members, but also for Native Americans, Asian Americans, and Hispanic Americans. In addition, the Bi-Racial Committee was
transformed into the Advisory Committee on Racial Minorities, and one
representative of each of the newly recognized ethnic groups was added
to its membership.[55]

The initial meeting of the reconstituted Racial Minorities Committee was held in late September 1957, but as the committee members gathered to attend it, their attention was diverted from church affairs to a
crisis in the real world, where racial differences obviously still mattered.
Although Central High School in Little Rock, Arkansas, had been scheduled for desegregation on September 3, 1957, Orval Faubus, the governor of the state, called out National Guardsmen to prevent African
Americans from entering the school. After a three-week impasse during
which racial tensions rose precipitously, a federal district court judge ordered Faubus to stop interfering with desegregation. When the state troops
were withdrawn and Central High opened on September 23, a mob of
angry whites gathered outside and demanded that the black students leave
the school. Finally, President Dwight Eisenhower intervened and dis-
patched both state and federal soldiers to Little Rock to restore peace.
Against this backdrop, Kenneth Hughes of the Racial Minorities Committee introduced a resolution at their meeting that asked Presiding Bishop
Sherrill to express publicly his denomination's approval of the president's
actions. It was not a matter of race, Hughes cannily argued, but a concern
for "law and order and obedience to constituted authority" that should
motivate Episcopalians to back the intervention of the federal government in Arkansas.[56]

The leadership of the diocese of Arkansas soon offered its support
in helping to defuse the explosive situation in Little Rock. Although Robert Brown, the diocesan bishop, released no immediate statement about
the crisis, he contacted one of the assistant secretaries of state in Washington (a member of the parish he had once led in Richmond) and volunteered to act as a peacemaker. Brown believed that the churches had a
responsibility to strengthen democracy by becoming intermediaries between forces on the political left and the political right that threatened to

destabilize American society. When Eisenhower learned of this suggestion, he thanked Brown and affirmed the idea that church leaders should encourage all their members to join in support of law and order. Brown followed Eisenhower's advice, and in mid-September he presided over an assembly of Little Rock's white clergy, held at Trinity Cathedral, for the purpose of organizing "a Ministry of Reconciliation" in the city.[57] Brown's ecumenical group agreed to hold a day of repentance and prayer in mid-October in which eighty-five churches (including all of Little Rock's Episcopal parishes) took part. As Brown said in a pastoral letter he released to his diocese, he expected Episcopalians "to refrain from every word or deed which is not consistent with the teachings of Jesus Christ concerning the brotherhood of man" and to resist any pressure to engage in mob violence.[58]

Despite his stated desire to bring peace between the races, Brown's overall approach to desegregation failed to take into account the needs and concerns of African Americans in the Little Rock community. As he later mentioned in his reflections on the events of September 1957, he intentionally limited participation in the gathering at his cathedral to white clergy. He believed that only whites could resolve the crisis, and he feared that the presence of black clergy in the discussions would divide the city further. In addition, when the public high schools were closed to prevent desegregation, Trinity Cathedral made its facilities available to white students as "Trinity Academy," thus becoming one of several segregated private schools opened in Little Rock. The deficiencies in Brown's approach—equating the church's "ministry of reconciliation" solely with the restoration of harmony among white citizens—were made obvious a few months later with the release of a sociological study about the Little Rock clergy. In that work Thomas Pettigrew (an Episcopalian) and Ernest Campbell (a Methodist), two southern-born social scientists on the faculty at Harvard University, concluded that white clergy like Brown who believed in the justice of desegregation could have been a significant force working for racial justice. However, because the great majority of white lay people accepted the segregation system, the clergy feared a loss in membership and financial giving if they pushed their parishioners too hard. Another similar study of the attitudes of Episcopalians on race revealed, moreover, that the strongest opposition to desegregation came from *active* members. As Pettigrew and Campbell argued, mainline clergy tended to be cautious in their advocacy of social change, because they knew their lay people would probably not follow them.[59]

The conflict in Little Rock also presented problems to the national leadership of the Episcopal Church, for it coincided with a meeting of the House of Bishops at the University of the South. The location of the bishops' gathering was itself unfortunate and doubtless caused anxiety for many who had been involved in the controversy at Sewanee five years before. Although the bishops discussed the possibility of issuing a pastoral letter affirming the morality of desegregation, they eventually decided to say nothing. Speaking for the group, Henry Sherrill suggested that the timing of the proposed statement was inauspicious, for in the absence of a clear signal about the direction of the crisis—Eisenhower had not yet committed federal troops—the bishops should simply remain silent. Despite the church's prior advocacy of public school desegregation as "just, right, and necessary," Sherrill felt constrained to admit that the issue was actually "a delicate question, and it must be worked out locally." He received a number of letters from Episcopalians in response to his statement after the meeting at Sewanee, among them a cordial note from Edward Guerry of South Carolina. "I am relieved that I do not have to read . . . a Pastoral Letter from the House of Bishops on integration," Guerry told Sherrill. "My people are firmly convinced that the Supreme Court has opened the door to forced integration in our public schools," and they believe that such an approach would not be "the Christian answer to our racial problem."[60]

As Sherrill's statement and Guerry's response suggest, most white church members were still not ready to lend their wholehearted support to racial desegregation. Although lay Episcopalians such as Thurgood Marshall, Kenneth Clark, Pauli Murray, and Waties Waring had done their part to bring about significant legal change, they were not involved in the inner circle of the denomination's leadership. And even Episcopalians who were active in parish and diocesan affairs—Sarah Patton Boyle, Carl and Anne Braden, Thomas Thrasher, and Henry Parker—received little support from their church when they directly challenged racial mores in the South. Shifting the site of the 1955 General Convention had represented a major statement on behalf of desegregation, for that decision unmistakably affected the institutional affairs of the Episcopal Church. But having taken that stand, the denomination seemed to withdraw from the fray, watching distrustfully as African Americans in Alabama, Arkansas, and other southern states made it clear that the full implications of *Brown* had not yet been realized. The increased determination of black southerners, moreover, threatened accustomed patterns of race relations in the church. Though white Episcopalians continued to congratulate themselves for supporting law and order and for shunning the violent excesses of those who burned crosses or threatened black schoolchildren, they remained reluctant about sharing control—whether political or ecclesiastical—with African Americans.

# 4

# Theology, Social Activism, and the Founding of ESCRU

Do white church members in the South owe their primary allegiance to Jesus Christ or to Jim Crow? This question, posed by Episcopal priest Das Kelley Barnett of Texas, became the focus for discussion at an ecumenical gathering of four hundred clerical and lay leaders in Nashville in April 1957—the first major interracial and interdenominational assembly in the South since the release of the *Brown* decision. In his address to the Nashville conference, Barnett spoke about the lack of a sound Christian social ethic in southern church circles, where most churchgoers seemed ignorant of the Bible's teaching on the unity of humankind. Once a Southern Baptist minister, Barnett had recently joined the Episcopal Church because he believed its comparatively strong emphasis on clerical authority would enable him to advance liberal views on race with greater ease than he could in the decentralized, lay-dominated Southern Baptist Convention. But Episcopalians also disappointed him, for while he thought parish clergy in the South ought to have been leading the struggle against segregation, "smugness, complacency, and indifference" kept them from taking action. When he looked at the laity, Barnett was even more discouraged. Was there anything the church could do, he asked, to draw lay people away from "the general cultural trends of our time"— "the excitement of television, the thrill of driving [their] fin-tipped automobile, the drudgery of keeping up with the Joneses"— and convince them to support the movement for racial equality instead?[1]

Like Barnett, Neil Tarplee of the Division of Christian Citizenship deplored what he called the "wide gulf between the pulpit and the pew" in southern churches. Tarplee was one of several church leaders who, in the aftermath of the crisis in Little Rock, were asked by the editors of *Christianity and Crisis* to discuss how their denominations were coping with the problems surrounding desegregation. The central issue for the Episcopal Church, he wrote, was the sharp discontinuity between the theological ethics practiced by most clergy and the rigid adherence of "culturally-conditioned laymen" to the folkways of the South. Although the South's pervasive, but superficial, evangelical piety often fooled white lay people into thinking their culture was a Christian one, their views on race actually revealed how ignorant they were about both theology and the Bible. Despite numerous condemnations of racial discrimination by various ecclesiastical bodies, white laity in the South had been deaf to the church's call for repentance. Lay people had "all but imprisoned the church within the sanctuary," Tarplee charged, and they were threatening to undermine the world-transforming power of the gospel.[2]

This critique of southern folk religion was echoed by several other Episcopalians concerned about race relations. In his reflections on the process of publishing *South Carolinians Speak*, for example, John Morris maintained that too many southerners had become accustomed to practicing "a cultic, pietistic or mental health religion which has shut out the world." What American Christianity really needed, he said, was the "revival of a 'social gospel' . . . grounded in contemporary theology" that would inspire the intelligent engagement of church people in political affairs. Francis Walter, a white priest with parish experience in both Alabama and Georgia, thought young white southerners had trouble relating the beliefs of the church to the social issues of their day. When he asked a group of teenagers to discuss the relationship between Christianity and racial integration, for instance, those who favored segregation hardly mentioned Jesus, but those who believed in integration based their position entirely on Christ's teachings. Walter lampooned the children with segregationist views by observing that they might have made "good Jews and Muslims," but in terms of their religious faith "they were not yet Christians." Helga Sargent, a laywoman in Washington, D.C., objected to the attempt by some church members to limit the involvement of the denomination in secular affairs. Despite the segregationists' desire to "lock our Lord away in the tabernacle at the end of every Mass and leave Him there," the spirit of Christ could not so easily be divorced from real life, she insisted.[3]

Emphasis on the interrelationship of ethics and Christian doctrine was commonplace among Episcopal theologians in the 1950s. Although the period after World War II was a time of tremendous expansion and

statistical growth in all of American Protestantism, clerical and lay leaders often worried that there was too little internal unity within the Episcopal Church and that the average member had little grasp of the doctrines
and ideas for which the denomination stood. Accordingly, the Department of Christian Education commissioned a six-volume series, *The
Church's Teaching*, which was intended to provide adult communicants
with a comprehensive grounding in the Christian faith and in the theological heritage of Anglicanism. As Powel Mills Dawley, a professor at
General Theological Seminary, observed in his volume, *The Episcopal
Church and Its Work* (1955), "for centuries the Church has been the conscience of society," but insufficient Christian education as well as an inadequate commitment to the faith often kept people from seeing "the
relevance of the Gospel . . . in specific problems of contemporary life."
Stephen Bayne, the bishop of Olympia, repeated that theme in *Christian
Living* (1957), the final volume published in the series. "The theology of
political action is clear," he wrote. Since all worldly power is derived ultimately from God, Christians have a religious duty to engage in political
activities in order to ensure that society conforms to God's purposes. Thus,
despite the American tendency to see a separation between the sacred
and the secular—between "the church" and "the world"—no such distinction exists, for every aspect of human life has been created by God
and redeemed through Jesus Christ.[4]

As all the writers in *The Church's Teaching* series knew, the Episcopal Church was heir to a rich tradition of social Christianity that had
influenced Anglicans in Britain and the United States for over a century.
F.D. Maurice, the most significant English theologian of his day, helped
introduce the "Christian socialist" ideal with the publication of *The Kingdom of Christ* in 1838. Writing within the context of an established church
and eschewing the individualistic emphasis of Protestant evangelicalism,
Maurice and his followers stressed both the unity of human society and
God's engagement in the world through the incarnate Christ. All human
life including the civil order, he emphasized, had been created by God
and renewed in Jesus Christ. The themes that Maurice outlined were further refined a generation later by Charles Gore and the scholars who
collaborated with him on *Lux Mundi* (1889), the groundbreaking collection of essays that related the doctrine of the incarnation to late-nine-
teenth-century intellectual and social movements. Gore's ideas provided
a means by which Anglicans could come to terms with modernity without rejecting the theological and liturgical traditions of the past. One of
his disciples, William Temple, emerged as the most respected leader of

English social Christianity after World War I. The church had a duty, Temple believed, to set the moral tone of its nation. Because God entered human affairs in the life of Jesus Christ, and because the church as "the Body of Christ" represented the continuing presence of God in history, no worldly activity could be outside the scope of either God's or the church's concern. As the Lambeth Conference (the worldwide gathering of Anglican bishops) declared in 1920, "the converted life . . . means the acceptance of Christ as King," who "must be King everywhere" and thus "cannot be excluded from politics, or industry, or from our social relationships."[5]

Anglicans in the United States, no less than their counterparts in England, were deeply affected by the idea that the church had responsibilities not simply for its own internal affairs but for society as a whole—a phenomenon on which a number of historians have commented. According to Henry May, Episcopal leaders never lost touch with their English establishmentarian roots—"the medieval dream of society guided and led by the church." And William Hutchison notes that "the issue was hegemony . . . or, to put it precisely, custodianship."[6] Wishing to affirm the church's rightful concern for the spiritual, moral, and cultural values of the nation, Episcopalians organized some of the earliest institutional expressions of the social gospel. The Church Association for the Advancement of the Interests of Labor (CAIL), for instance, was founded in 1887. Dedicated to the principle that "God is the Father of all men and that all men are brothers," CAIL members viewed social problems in the light of Christian belief in the incarnation.[7] William Rainsford, rector of St. George's Church in New York, and other Episcopal clergy were also key figures in the development of the so-called "institutional church" movement. Convinced that their parishes had an obligation to care for the practical needs of people in their neighborhoods, they led the way in transforming urban churches into social service centers. Among Episcopal lay people, Vida Scudder was noteworthy for her insistence on the compatibility of Christianity and socialist political tenets; she argued that the image of the incarnate, crucified Christ signified that no division existed between the social and the spiritual expressions of the church's faith. Scudder was also one of the founders of the Church League for Industrial Democracy (later known as the Episcopal League for Social Action), which helped engage church members in the pressing social issues of the 1930s and early 1940s.[8]

After the end of World War II, these hegemonic impulses were reinvigorated by white middle-class clergy and lay people working in urban

Henry Beard Delany, suffragan bishop of North Carolina, about 1920. Courtesy of The Archives of the Episcopal Church, USA.

Charles C.J. Carpenter, bishop of Alabama, about 1940. Courtesy of The Archives of the Episcopal Church, USA.

*Above*, Tollie L. Caution(seated, far right) with students at Fort Valley College in Georgia, 1951. Courtesy of The Archives of the Episcopal Church, USA. *Left*, Clarence A. Cole, bishop of Upper South Carolina, and Tollie Caution (left to right)at St. Anna's Mission in Columbia, South Carolina, June 1955. Courtesy of The Archives of the Episcopal Church, USA.

Edward McCrady, vice chancellor of the University of the South, about 1952. Courtesy of The Archives of the Episcopal Church, USA.

*Above*, Pauli Murray (second from right)at the publication of her book *Proud Shoes*, 1956. Courtesy of Schlesinger Library, Radcliffe College. *Right*, Hodding Carter II, 1959. Courtesy of Betty Werlein Carter and the Special Collections Department of the Mitchell Memorial Library, Mississippi State University.

Carl and Anne Braden, April 1963. Courtesy of Anne Braden and the State
Historical Society of Wisconsin.[Negative no. WHi(X3)44637]

*Above*, Racial Minorities Committee of the Episcopal Church at Tuskegee Institute in Alabama, September 1957. Courtesy of The Archives of the Episcopal Church, USA. *Below*, Street procession at St. Augustine's Mission on the Lower East Side of New York, about 1955. Courtesy of The Archives of the Episcopal Church, USA.

*Above*, Conference of Church Workers among Colored People at the 1958 General Convention in Miami Beach. Courtesy of The Archives of the Episcopal Church, USA. *Below*, Sarah Patton Boyle (at left) with (from right to left) Henry Mitchell (vicar), Gertrude Mitchell, and Otelia Jackson of Trinity Church, Charlottesville, Virginia, 1963. Courtesy of the Special Collections Department, University of Virginia Library.

areas. The expansion of the automobile industry, the phenomenal growth of the suburbs, and the discrimination that excluded African Americans from sharing in the postwar prosperity all hastened the development of large racial ghettos in northern cities. Since the flight of middle-class parishioners to the suburbs and the subsequent economic decline of downtown areas threatened both the property values and the institutional fabric of many Protestant parishes, church leaders began to emphasize the need to reevangelize the city. They saw "a vast missionary opportunity" awaiting those who were willing to reach out to poor urban neighborhoods, and pioneering ecumenical efforts such as the East Harlem Protestant Parish in New York were initiated by white religious activists wishing to reassert the presence of the mainline denominations in the city.[9] William Stringfellow, a lay Episcopalian who worked as a legal counselor for the East Harlem Parish in the mid-1950s, wrote extensively about his experiences amid what he called the "squalor, depression, poverty, and frustration" of upper Manhattan. Despite the suffering he witnessed in the city, Stringfellow was convinced that neighborhoods like East Harlem represented a primary mission field for the Episcopal Church and other denominations. "The Christian faith is not about some god who is an abstract presence somewhere else," he said, "but about the living presence of God here and now, in this world, in *exactly* this world, as men . . . live and work in it."[10]

The most celebrated Episcopal inner-city ministry of the postwar period was organized and led by Paul Moore, C. Kilmer ("Kim") Myers, and Robert Pegram, priests who worked at Grace Church in the Van Vorst section of Jersey City, New Jersey. Although Grace Church had once been a thriving parish in a prosperous neighborhood, Jersey City had become economically depressed, and the church was virtually deserted and without clerical leadership when the three men began working there in 1949. They had been friends at General Seminary, where many of the faculty and their fellow students were suspicious of their interests and referred to them derisively as the school's "social conscience crowd."[11] In an era when many young white clergy were thought to be priming themselves for jobs in comfortable suburban settings, Moore, Myers, and Pegram were excited instead by the prospects of immersion in "the throbbing life of a city slum."[12] They were inspired, moreover, by the French worker-priest movement and by Abbé Michonneau's influential book, *Revolution in a City Parish* (1949), with its emphasis on the clergy's identification with the poor and downtrodden. When they approached Benjamin Washburn, the bishop of Newark, about working in his diocese, he gave them his enthusiastic support and urged them to help restore Grace Church in Van Vorst. Myers and Pegram were bachelors, and they shared the rectory on the church's grounds with Moore, his wife Jenny, and the Moore children. The priests immediately instituted an "open rectory" policy and were in continual contact with the struggles of the poor people who were their neighbors and parishioners. Paul Moore believed that this demonstrated how the church was incarnate and fully identified with the culture of the city. And as Jenny Moore later observed about her experiences in Jersey City, "the difference between a non-Christian and a Christian is that the former may work to alleviate suffering but that the latter attempts to share in it as well."[13]

Social ministries similar to the one in Jersey City—white Episcopalians making a conscious choice to live and work with minority groups—were started in a number of urban areas in the Northeast in the 1950s. Kim Myers, for example, was recruited in 1952 by Trinity Church, Wall Street—one of the wealthiest parishes in the Episcopal Church—and asked to serve as vicar of St. Augustine's Chapel, a mission it supported on New York's Lower East Side. Thanks to his earlier work at Grace Church, Myers soon established a nationally renowned program with the neighborhood's street gangs and juvenile delinquents, offering them an experience of God's presence in places where, he admitted, "the light of Christ's Gospel shines but dimly."[14] Similar but less publicized work was led by two white priests, Warren McKenna and Robert Muir, at St. John's Church in Roxbury, Boston's largest African American neighborhood. McKenna and Muir had known each other at the Episcopal Theological School in Cambridge, where they were taught by faculty like Joseph Fletcher, who were thoroughly committed to the social implications of the faith. After Muir came to St. John's in 1950, McKenna and he formed the Workers of the Common Life, an organization based on the model of Dorothy Day's radical Catholic Worker movement. Although charges of Communism soon forced both men to leave St. John's, their work was continued by John Harmon, who became rector of the parish in 1952. Harmon, strongly influenced by the postwar liturgical movement, stressed the historic relationship between Anglo-Catholic ritualism and social ministry in urban neighborhoods. He believed in Christ's mystical identification with the world's suffering, and he asked Episcopalians to acknowledge and recognize "the marks of grace already present" in everyday life.[15]

Although these postwar urban ministries were inspired largely by traditional Anglican social teachings, new emphases in American theology also influenced the rise of an activist mentality among mainline church leaders during that period. No thinker was more critical in the development of these ideas about the engagement of Christians in secular affairs than Dietrich Bonhoeffer. Bonhoeffer, whose final writings were published in English in the early 1950s, built upon the theological foundation laid by Karl Barth, but whereas the neoorthodox Barth saw a deep gulf separating God and creation, Bonhoeffer emphasized (and personified through his martyrdom in 1945) God's relationship with the world. Bonhoeffer's insistence that what is distinctly Christian is found in the secular realm further challenged believers to think of God not on the boundaries, but at the center, of human existence. This theological focus had significant implications for the mission of the church as well. "The church is the church only when it exists for others," Bonhoeffer wrote shortly before his death. A number of other thinkers certainly strengthened the popularity of the "religionless Christianity" and "worldly holiness" that Bonhoeffer advocated—Paul Tillich's talk of religion as "ultimate concern," Rudolph Bultmann's "demythologizing" of scriptural language, Reinhold Niebuhr's pragmatic approach to Christian social action, and Harvey Cox's celebration of "the secular city." But it was Bonhoeffer's statement that "Jesus claims for himself and the Kingdom of God the whole of human life" that helped foster an activist mentality among a critical number of Protestant clergy trained after 1945.[16]

In contrast to this vigorous image of ministry popularized by theologians such as Tillich, Niebuhr, and Bonhoeffer, actual expressions of American religion in the 1950s often seemed wan and domesticated. Although church membership levels had reached new heights (nearly half of the population said they attended church each week, and more than six out of ten Americans belonged to one of the Christian denominations in 1958), the postwar "religious revival" was usually dismissed as just "culture religion" and a bland "faith in faith."[17] Episcopal priest Gibson Winter (who coined the phrase "the suburban captivity of the churches" that epitomized the activists' disdain for contemporary American religiosity) claimed that the "anti-Christian forces" dominating suburban parishes were insulating churchgoers from the world for which Jesus died. It was especially tragic, he thought, that at a time "when America's position of world leadership requires a prophetic church," white middle-class Protestants were rejecting their responsibilities in the public sphere and concentrating only on satisfying their inner, personal needs.[18] Paul Moore, who had been severely wounded in combat during World War II, was even more blunt in his analysis of the problem. He contrasted the virile character of the urban ministry in which he engaged with the feminine, family-oriented milieu of Protestantism in the suburbs. Since God called Christians "to redeem society and to love and heal as the body of Christ," the true "battle line of the Church is the inner-city," Moore insisted, not "the matriarchal child-centered suburban parish" with which the majority of Episcopalians were affiliated.[19]

Arthur Walmsley, a priest who left a parish in St. Louis to become director of the Division of Christian Citizenship in New York in 1958, agreed substantially with this analysis of the contemporary American religious scene. He conceded that a revival of sorts had taken place in many Episcopal parishes, but the therapeutic emphasis in churches at that time— the "preoccupation with small-group, face-to-face relationships, family life, [and] the parish family"—was undermining the traditional Anglican understanding that the Christian's "warfare is in the world." The average Episcopalian, Walmsley argued, seemed to have forgotten that Christ came "not to redeem the Church but the world," and few church members were willing to look beyond their local parishes to wider social, political, and economic affairs. This tendency was especially troubling in relation to the church's recent progress in addressing desegregation. Although the national leadership of the Episcopal Church had affirmed the value of the *Brown* decision, their various social directives had only a minimal impact on everyday church life. Although the denomination's "Guiding Principles" on race relations asserted that the church had a God-given responsibility "to set spiritual and moral goals for society," most white Episcopalians were content to let the emerging civil rights movement take shape without rousing themselves to aid it in any way.[20]

To counteract what they regarded as a disturbing trend, Walmsley and his associate Neil Tarplee circulated a report among Episcopalians known to be sympathetic to their views on race. The two priests outlined some of the major events that had taken place in the field of race relations since 1945, and they discussed possible strategies their denomination might adopt in order to break out of its "suburban captivity" and accelerate the desegregation process. Tarplee and Walmsley knew their suggestions would meet strong resistance in some circles in the South. Was the church prepared to pay the price of courageous and prophetic leadership, they asked, even if it meant a decline in importance or a loss in membership? Were clergy willing to condemn the "flouting of Biblical and theological doctrine" and the "repudiation of the duly constituted government" of the denomination by prominent lay people? Though it was tempting simply to stand back and watch events take their course, such passivity posed a grave threat to the church: failure to practice what they preached made Episcopal clergy look like hypocrites. "The Church must reassert and demonstrate its unity with complete disregard of race and nationality in the segregated South," Walmsley and Tarplee concluded; otherwise it was in danger of slipping into a state of "functional irrelevance" in American society.[21]

In order to inspire the next General Convention to address the interrelationship of race, theology, and social action, Tarplee helped convene a gathering of like-minded people in mid-September 1958 in Eaton Center, New Hampshire. The invitation list was small, and only about a dozen people eventually traveled to the meeting: Episcopalians from the South (such as John Morris and Sarah Patton Boyle) to whom Tarplee had offered assistance during his travels, and church staff from New York (Tollie Caution and Walmsley, as well as Will Campbell of the National Council of Churches) who were committed to supporting the civil rights movement. The gathering had no expressed agenda; it was intended mainly to encourage prointegration Episcopalians to stand against the tide of "massive resistance" in their home communities. Nevertheless, with the beginning of the General Convention close at hand, the group decided to compose a statement for the bishops and deputies to read. Because the church had a dual responsibility, to proclaim its belief in the unity of humankind and to offer prayerful support to the leadership of its nation, the statement said, Episcopal leaders ought to urge church members to condemn racial prejudice and join black Americans' struggle for civil rights.[22]

When the convention assembled a few weeks later, race was one of the central questions the church addressed. As a result of the controversy over Houston three years before, Miami Beach, a southern city where participants were expected to be minimally troubled by segregation, had been chosen as the site for the meeting. The governor of Florida, LeRoy Collins, who was both a popular southern moderate and an active Episcopalian, was invited to address the opening session of the convention. Affirming that the American people were capable of finding "a constructive way out of the darkness" of racial conflict, Collins challenged the leaders of his denomination to help defuse tensions and formulate "a plan for progress in the field of human right . . . which can be supported with honor by people of every race, creed and color."[23] In addition, the House of Bishops released the pastoral letter on race on which it had been working for over a year. The bishops declared that the Lambeth Conference from which they had recently returned had been crucial in helping them decide what to say to their church. They noted how the ethnic diversity they had experienced at that meeting reinforced their sense of "the oneness of mankind in Christ," and they referred to conversations with fellow Anglican bishops representing "the colored races," who told them that the United States was losing friends abroad because of its continuing hypocrisy about race. Unless their nation proved itself superior to Soviet Communism in the attention it gave to social justice, the American bishops said, the prominence of the United States in world affairs might quickly come to an end. Finally, the bishops expressed admiration for the intimate relationship that existed between church and state in England. Emphasizing that "government is a structure appointed by God for the common good," the House of Bishops condemned segregationists who broke the law or engaged in mob violence in resisting the mandates of the Supreme Court.[24]

Despite the hopeful tone of both the bishops' pastoral letter and Collins's address, other realities regarding race undermined the effect those official statements were intended to create. One problem concerned the diminishing number of black communicants in the Episcopal Church. This issue surfaced when the Conference of Church Workers held its own triennial meeting at St. Agnes' Church, a prominent black parish in Miami. The theme of the meeting was "The Responsibility of Minority Groups in an Integrated Church and State," but a number of participants questioned whether African Americans were actually making the progress that the title suggested.[25] Though members of the CCW were generally appreciative of the willingness of some white clergy to challenge segregation in the South, they were also concerned about the impact that integration might have on the position of African Americans within the Episcopal Church itself. Tollie Caution reported, for example, that there were ten thousand fewer black communicants in 1958 than ten years before—a decline due in part to the closing of black parishes and the transfer of their members to predominantly white congregations. Since racial integration was not empowering black Episcopalians but merely absorbing their congregations into white ones, African Americans asked what place, if any, they still had in their Episcopal Church. Although the achievements of white clergy involved in inner-city churches had received considerable attention in recent years, the important ministry of black clergy and congregations in urban areas (e.g., St. Philip's and St. Martin's in New York; St. Cyprian's in Boston and St. Bartholomew's in Cambridge; St. Thomas' in Philadelphia; St. James' in Baltimore; and All Saints' in St. Louis) was either ignored entirely or dismissed as just "slum work." In addition, the CCW was troubled by the fact that racial customs in Miami

Beach were far less enlightened than white leaders claimed. Economic considerations impelled Miami merchants to serve black visitors who wore official General Convention badges, but African Americans without badges were still treated as second-class citizens by most whites in the city.[26]

The statement from the Eaton Center meeting also proved to be a source of serious discord at the convention. As soon as the statement was introduced for debate in the House of Deputies, B. Allston Moore of South Carolina (the Charleston lawyer with whom John Morris had clashed at the convention of their diocese in 1956) presented a substitute motion that affirmed the continuing validity of racial segregation. Both resolutions were referred to a committee for further study, and when the subject of race was raised again a few days later, Edward Guerry (one of the four clerical deputies from South Carolina), Moore, and a contingent of white lay deputies loudly opposed all attempts to endorse desegregation. Eventually, the deputies adopted a compromise measure. Although the final resolution affirmed "the natural dignity and value of every man, of whatever color or race, as created in the image of God" and asked church members "to work together, in charity and forbearance, towards the establishment . . . of full opportunities in fields such as education, housing, employment and public accommodations," it cautioned that there were "no easy answers" to problems created when theological convictions were applied "to special and local situations." The deputies also stated—with almost droll equivocation—that statements about race adopted by church bodies "may or may not be the will of God," and that "honest differences of opinion" about courses of action would always exist among committed Christians.[27]

Disappointed by the continuing failure of Episcopalians to speak as a single voice about desegregation, Morris and Tarplee remained in close touch and discussed strategies for fostering the course of action they had been unable to convince General Convention to undertake. They were heartened when Arthur Lichtenberger, the bishop of Missouri, was elected as the new presiding bishop at the convention. In the sermon he preached at his installation in January 1959, Lichtenberger clearly identified the church's mission both with transforming the society in which it lived and with restoring unity across boundaries that traditionally separated ethnic groups. Morris and Tarplee realized, however, that even under Lichtenberger's leadership the denomination would still be slow to endorse the concept of racial integration. They therefore discussed the idea of creating an independent organization, committed to the church's official theological positions, but free of the entanglements that usually restrained the activities of National Council staff such as Tarplee himself. Tarplee thought that activists were needed who could bring together a knowledge of the social sciences and theology and apply that expertise to the mission of the church. They played around with possible names of the organization until Morris suggested a title they both liked: Church Society for Racial Unity—a name based on the first verse of Psalm 133 ("Behold, how good and joyful a thing it is, for brethren to dwell together in unity!") from *The Book of Common Prayer* (1928). Morris was in an ideal position to help organize the society they envisioned, for he had just left his parish in South Carolina and moved to Atlanta. He originally had expected to pursue graduate studies at Emory University, but the challenge of the desegregation crisis convinced him that he should work on his own responding to events in the South.[28]

As it turned out, the times were right for the plans that Tarplee and Morris were making; other organizations were also forming to address the religious and social concerns they raised. In February 1957, for example, approximately a hundred delegates assembled in New Orleans and founded what eventually became known as the Southern Christian Leadership Conference (SCLC). The SCLC was firmly rooted in the black church in the South. Virtually all of its formal leadership positions were held by clergy, and its purposes—spiritual as well as political—were reflected in the motto the ministers adopted: "To Redeem the Soul of America."[29] White Roman Catholics in the North organized the National Catholic Conference for Interracial Justice in early 1958. Delegates to the inaugural meeting of that body resolved to act both "as Catholics and Americans" in implementing "the principles of Christian Social Justice and American Democracy in regard to race relations." Because of the popularity of neoscholastic thought, Roman Catholic theologians had been stressing the importance of social unity within the Body of Christ since the 1930s. This philosophical emphasis gave the organizers of the conference a critical tool, for it enabled them not only to condemn segregation as morally sinful but also to identify racial integration as an expression of Catholic orthodoxy.[30]

Against this background of a growing religious critique of segregation, Morris and Tarplee composed a proposal that they sent to approximately eight hundred Episcopalians considered to be sympathetic to a policy of racial inclusiveness in the church. Inviting suggestions about the society's name and purpose, they asked for assistance in planning a conference they hoped would meet in the South sometime in the fall of 1959. The real trouble, as Morris and Tarplee saw it, was not the lack of clearly stated principles about race—the Episcopal Church had made many formal statements—but the reluctance of Episcopal leaders to challenge segregationists and put those official principles into practice. How could the Episcopal Church possibly provide a wholesome example to American society or advise the government about race relations unless it fully committed itself to integration? One of the most glaring problems in Morris's estimation was the continued existence of racially distinct Episcopal parishes—the maintaining of small, usually struggling black parishes in close proximity to white churches. Though he acknowledged that many African Americans might resist the elimination of their parishes, Morris also believed that separate black congregations in the Episcopal Church were truly "a sign of our sin."[31]

Over 60 percent of the people to whom the proposal was mailed responded, and most of those were positive. Sarah Patton Boyle remarked that she knew many people working for civil rights who were eager to take a stand as Christians, for unlike secular organization such as the NAACP, the church provided not only "a means but . . . a motivation for social justice." Because of the large number of responses, Morris was extraordinarily busy during the summer of 1959, writing to supporters and critics alike. He kept track of the dioceses where his respondents lived—a list that clearly reveals where the strength of the proposed organization was situated. Although most of the key backers expected that the focus of the society would be in the segregated South, over a quarter of the positive responses came from church members in three major urban dioceses in the Northeast: New York, Massachusetts (metropolitan Boston), and Pennsylvania (metropolitan Philadelphia). In addition, a large number of positive responses were received from the dioceses of Chicago, Washington (D.C.), and Michigan (metropolitan Detroit). Among the southern dioceses, though, only those in the upper South were well represented, and the responses received from deep South states such as South Carolina, Georgia, Alabama, and Mississippi were just half as many as those from New York City alone.[32]

Because Morris and Tarplee contacted only those known to be generally friendly to their ideas, few respondents expressed outright segregationist views. Nevertheless, a number of letters contained criticisms of what the men were attempting to do. The most common complaint from white correspondents concerned the term "racial unity," which—expressed in euphemisms such as "intermarriage," "amalgamation," and "race mixing"—raised the specter of interracial sex. Deeply troubled by this idea, these Episcopalians suggested alternatives that raised fewer hackles than "racial *unity*." Several people also questioned the wisdom of creating an organization outside the official structures of the Episcopal Church. If the responsibility to confront racism were the mission of only a special society, those critics argued, its existence alone might salve the conscience of denominational leaders and thus allow the vast majority of church members to ignore the need to work for full integration. Other critics contended that, because three officers of the National Council (Tollie Caution, Arthur Walmsley, and Tarplee himself) already exercised responsibility in the area of race relations, the formation of a new society would undermine the effectiveness of their work. Tarplee explicitly rejected that argument, reiterating his belief that the denomination would never seriously discuss racial matters unless a significant number of church members vigorously pressed for action.[33]

Since Morris and Tarplee were white male clergy, a few respondents asked whether they intended to give lay people, women, and African Americans an effective voice in the proposed society. There would be strategic as well as philosophical advantages to expanding the leadership base of the organization, they said. One laywoman observed that with the widening gap between clergy and laity in the South, the inclusion of lay leaders might help heal that potentially destructive division over race relations. A clerical correspondent echoed these words and warned Morris that, if the society were dominated by clergy, its existence would only aggravate the mistrust that already existed between white laity and their generally more liberal bishops and priests. McRae Werth, a white priest who had worked in Virginia, was particularly candid about the apparent absence of African Americans in the new organization: "For Pete's sake, quit making like white southern liberals and include a Negro clergyman and a Negro layman immediately," he said. "Southern churchmen are forever forming outfits like this, and bringing in Negroes later." Several prominent black clergy, in contrast, expressed approval that white Episcopalians were beginning to recognize the need to do their part in pushing the church forward on civil rights issues. Jesse Anderson, rector of St. Thomas' Church in Philadelphia, thought "such a society has long been needed in our Church especially since so many of us have felt frustrated by the paucity of leadership." In New York, Walter Dennis, a priest on the staff of the Cathedral of St. John the Divine, hoped the society would maintain constant pressure on the House of Bishops in order to encourage that body to condemn racial injustice. The new society, Dennis said, was called to speak "not so much *for* the Church as *to* the Church," pointing out wrongs that average churchgoers seldom even noticed.[34]

As the several hundred responses to their proposal indicated, interest was strong enough for Morris and Tarplee to arrange a meeting to organize the new society. They chose St. Augustine's College as the site for the meeting, because it was one of the few church-related institutions in the South where a large interracial group could assemble without arousing undue attention from white opponents. Approximately one hundred people were able to come to Raleigh in late December 1959. Before the meeting, Morris created a banner that he hung in the auditorium where the group was to gather. This sign bore the words of the first verse of Psalm 133, which Tarplee and he had discussed a few months before as a possible motto for their proposed society. Morris thought that the unity of all people in Christ represented the religious principle that should inspire participants at the conference, and most of the people there agreed with Morris's idea. They named the organization "The Episcopal Society for Cultural and Racial Unity" (later known by the acronym ESCRU) and proclaimed that the concepts of race, ethnicity, and social class had no place in the church. A statement of purpose was also adopted that enumerated some of the objectives for which the society stood: the elimination of single-race parishes; an end to racial criteria in the admission of people to schools, camps, hospitals, and other institutions affiliated with the Episcopal Church; support for Episcopalians working for integration; appreciation of the church's "prophetic role" in overturning racial barriers in society as a whole; and the fostering of "that condition of harmony among peoples which is the benefit of a mutual recognition of the Lordship of Jesus Christ, so that brothers may dwell together in unity."[35]

The name and purpose of the new organization notwithstanding, crucial disagreements about its mission quickly began to divide the membership even at the outset of its existence. First, Kim Myers caused a stir at the Raleigh meeting by publicly lambasting the Episcopal Church as a "racist, caste-ridden" institution. Next, as the meeting was ending, Das Kelley Barnett told the church press that he would not accept his election to the board of directors because he believed that ESCRU was to become merely "a protest sect," not an effective policymaking organization. Finally, several key white supporters in the South withdrew from membership in the society. For example, when Duncan Gray, then rector of St. Peter's Church in Oxford, Mississippi, learned that he was the only clerical member of ESCRU in his state, he decided he could not take "the risk of alienating his people and impairing what little effectiveness" he had in working for desegregation under highly volatile conditions. Moultrie Guerry, a North Carolina priest who was one of the founders of the Fellowship of Southern Churchmen in 1934, had also been expected to be active in the society. Unlike his outspoken brother Edward in South Carolina, Moultrie had been generally supportive of desegregation. He disagreed, however, with one of the central premises on which ESCRU was founded. Since "the Church . . . holds *diversity* in the Unity of the Spirit" as a fundamental tenet, Guerry told Morris, he could not join a church-related organization that defined the faith in such a narrow way as ESCRU did.[36]

After these initial disagreements arose and ran their course, the ESCRU leadership focused on strengthening itself internally. Participants at the Raleigh meeting elected a board of directors of twenty-four people, who then hired John Morris to be the executive director of the society. He immediately set up the national office of the organization in Atlanta, and by mid-1960 over a thousand Episcopalians had joined ESCRU. Morris also reproduced two striking images that were to serve as symbols of the society's mission. One depicted Jesus, robed as a high priest, offering his benediction to two figures, one black and one white, who knelt facing each other in front of him. The other, borrowed from the Anglican Church of South Africa, showed the crucified body of Christ bisected by a barbed wire fence emblazoned with the word "Apartheid" that separated a kneeling white man from a kneeling black man. Since "Apartheid" was still a relatively unfamiliar term in the United States, Morris decided to replace it with the words "Segregation-Separation" to symbolize for Americans the stark effects of racism on Christ's body, the church.[37]

The genesis of ESCRU coincided almost exactly with the beginning of an important new stage in the civil rights movement, as sit-in protests started to take place in southern cities. Although African Americans had always been encouraged to shop in commercial establishments such as Woolworth and Kresge, segregation laws had kept them from eating with whites at the lunch counters in those stores. In February 1960 African American students at North Carolina Agricultural and Technical College challenged those laws by sitting down and asking for service at the Woolworth lunch counter in downtown Greensboro. This sit-in sparked a series of similar protests, which the board of directors of ESCRU quickly endorsed. A few weeks later, Arthur Walmsley, Neil Tarplee, and Tollie Caution—all now prominently identified with ESCRU—along with other staff of both the Division of Christian Citizenship and the Division of Racial Minorities, published a long, carefully worded report affirming the sit-ins that were spreading throughout the South. The report invoked William Temple's dictum that "it can be known whether Democracy is true to its own root principle . . . by the careful regard which it pays to the rights of minorities." In addition it noted that Anglican social teaching recognized the right of Christians to disobey unjust and immoral laws such as the ones the students were violating.[38]

These public statements by denominational staff, ostensibly on behalf of the National Council, immediately came under attack from conservative white Episcopalians in the South. B. Powell Harrison, a lawyer in Virginia, for example, accused church leaders in New York of committing the same mistakes that northerners had made "during the horrors of the Reconstruction Era." Although Anglicans in the South during the revolutionary era of the eighteenth century had led the struggle "to gain for the individual the right to protect his property against the trespassing of unwanted people," Harrison claimed, the twentieth-century church now seemed bent on destroying those property rights by endorsing the black students' illegal sit-ins. Edward Guerry also condemned "this endorsement of public demonstrations which threaten the peace and security of Southern people." Resist the temptation to meddle in southern affairs, he implored the National Council staff: "We do not need your resolutions; we need your love and prayers." No one was more vocal, though, than Charles Carpenter of Alabama, who accused national church leaders of utter recklessness in allowing a few of their employees to speak for the whole denomination. Since in the wake of the recent Little Rock crisis the House of Bishops had urged *obedience* to the law, it was entirely inappropriate for the church to reverse this course. "'Civil disobedience' . . . is just another name for lawlessness," Carpenter warned, and the church was courting danger by paying more attention to social protests than to the gospel of Christ.[39]

This outburst from Carpenter and other church people in the South inspired a counterblast from Morris and the ESCRU leadership. Morris lambasted Carpenter for advising Episcopalians to ignore the National Council statement and the support it offered to the black students' just and peaceful witness against segregation. Morris predicted that the burgeoning civil rights movement would prove to be "a plumb-line in the South," dividing bishops and clergy ready to implement the church's teaching on race from those who wished merely to be "chaplains to the dying order of the Confederacy." The latter remark was particularly timely, for James Silver, a historian teaching at the University of Mississippi, had recently published a book documenting the critical role Episcopal bishops and other southern clergy played in defending slavery and leading their states into secession prior to the Civil War. Morris saw evidence that a similar conspiracy was emerging a hundred years later among white southern Christians like Carpenter. Since his protest against the integration movement occurred in the context of the centennial celebration of the Civil War, when the theme of reconciliation—racial as well as sectional—was receiving a good deal of national attention, Morris suggested that Carpenter's views were not only outdated but also vaguely disloyal to American democratic ideals.[40]

Other Episcopalians associated with ESCRU joined the attack on white southerners who seemed content to maintain the racial status quo. Despite Carpenter's argument that he was really a "moderate," holding the middle ground between the extremism of diehard segregationists and militant integrationists, critics called his position a preposterous one. Thomas Pettigrew, who was then a member of the ESCRU board of directors, charged that every so-called moderate was really "a paternalistic segregationist of 19th century vintage." Such a person was not offering a reasonable alternative to the two extremes but was just standing on the sidelines, meekly "wringing his hands in despair" and clinging to archaic ideas about race relations. Arthur Walmsley also questioned the motives of church members who thought it was difficult to put abstract ideals such as integration into practice in real-life situations. The issue, Walmsley thought, was whether people respected the official teachings of their church on the universality of salvation. "To avoid involvement in the tensions brought about by social change is to deny God's world," Walmsley argued, for the present racial crisis was summoning Episcopalians to witness to the fatherhood of God and their unity in Jesus Christ.[41]

Because of the strategic advantages of identifying ESCRU with religious values in the mainstream of American life the original leaders of the organization took pains to distinguish their goals not only from the segregationist positions of men like Charles Carpenter and Edward Guerry, but also from people with left-wing affiliations who wished to join forces in the antiracist cause. Carl and Anne Braden, for example, were extremely enthusiastic when they learned about the founding of ESCRU, and they wrote Morris about helping form an ESCRU chapter in Louisville. But since Carl Braden had been imprisoned for refusing to answer questions before the House Un-American Activities Committee, Morris was wary of tainting ESCRU with Braden's alleged Communist sympathies. Rebuffing the Bradens' offer to assist ESCRU, Morris compared their single-minded commitment to interracial justice with the "Churchmanship" issues that had divided Anglicans since the nineteenth century. Just as a "person of decidedly Anglo-Catholic tendencies would not be the best representative of the Society" in a low-church diocese, Morris argued, so the Bradens' social activism likewise would raise unnecessary suspicion about ESCRU's mission in most southern dioceses. Though Morris's cold war mentality was hardly unique among liberals at that time—red-baiting remained a persistent theme in American politics throughout the 1960s—it reveals the essentially centrist political leanings of the ESCRU leadership.[42]

In spite of Morris's best efforts, some of the most outspoken members of ESCRU soon caused embarrassment for the organization. The issued concerned the perennially inflammatory question of interracial marriage and—more specifically—the fears and fantasies of whites about sex between black men and white women. At the first annual meeting of the society in January 1961, members adopted a series of resolutions on the civil rights movement that were certainly progressive for their day but not inconsistent with the official theological and social positions of the Episcopal Church. One of the resolutions offered the society's approval of the so-called kneel-ins that had started to take place in many white segregated churches in the South. Like the sit-ins, the kneel-ins represented the attempt by African Americans to enter places where white southerners were not accustomed to welcoming them. The ESCRU membership affirmed the value of the kneel-ins as "practical dramatizations of the Christian teaching that the church is not color conscious." To strengthen the ideals of racial inclusiveness, ESCRU also urged diocesan bishops to uphold the rights granted to parish clergy by the denomination's canon law: particularly, complete authority in questions concerning the liturgy, control of parish property, and the admission of worshipers to services. If disagreements arose between a white rector who wanted to admit African Americans to his church and a lay vestry that wished to exclude them, ESCRU stressed the supremacy of Episcopal clergy in all matters relating to public worship.[43]

Although Morris hoped to keep the annual meeting focused on what he believed were attainable goals, McRae Werth, then serving on the meeting's program committee, pressed the gathering to affirm the propriety of interracial marriage. Werth himself was a controversial figure in southern church circles, for he had recently lost a parish position in the diocese of Southwestern Virginia because of his undeviating advocacy of racial integration. That diocese had been engaged in a bitter and prolonged struggle over the desegregation of youth events at Hemlock Haven, the conference center it had purchased in the late 1950s. Although William Marmion (the diocesan bishop) and most of the clergy in the diocese favored the scheduling of racially integrated events at Hemlock

Haven, the "massive resistance" policy of Virginia's political leaders encouraged a group of lay Episcopalians to fight that plan. Werth, the most
outspoken of the clergy, charged that it was scandalous to exclude African American youths in order to satisfy members of the Citizens' Council
and a few other whites "who worship a biological doctrine of the master
race." An early supporter of ESCRU, Werth's stubbornness about racial
issues had forced him to leave Virginia and move to a parish in Delaware
in 1959.[44]

Since the dread of possible sexual contact between black and white
teenagers had been a major factor stirring emotions in the Hemlock Haven controversy, Werth decided to address that topic directly at the ESCRU
annual meeting. He introduced a resolution stating that the Episcopal
Church recognized "neither theological nor biological barriers to marriage between persons of different color" and considered state laws for-
bidding such marriages to be "contrary to Christian teaching, natural
law, and the Constitution of this country." While few Episcopal clergy at
that time would have publicly disagreed with Werth's statements—indeed, interracial marriage was not forbidden by the church—most also
recognized that the subject itself was, in the words of George Cadigan,
the bishop of Missouri, a "bete noir for the people of the south." Although Werth's resolution passed after an extended debate, the issue later
returned to haunt John Morris, when scores of Episcopalians wrote him
objecting to the position the society had taken. Moderately liberal southern bishops such as Henry Louttit of South Florida and Albert Stuart of
Georgia canceled their membership in ESCRU because, they claimed, the
statement on intermarriage was too inflammatory for the conservative
dioceses in which they ministered. Angus Dun, the bishop of Washington, criticized the society for making "a serious strategic mistake," and
Anson Phelps Stokes, the bishop of Massachusetts, reported that most of
the southern bishops he knew thought ESCRU had unwittingly "created
an atmosphere in which they were not helped." Ordinary clergy and lay
people also protested. John Turnbull, a priest in Texas, thought the resolution was "impolitic"; Samuel Wylie, a rector in Boston, called it "love-
less, snide . . . and ingenuous"; and Barbara Kalif, an otherwise sympathetic
laywoman in Virginia, believed it had been "unnecessary and undesirably
dramatic."[45]

Wilburn Campbell, the bishop of West Virginia, next entered the
fray and raised the stakes even higher by contacting the press and charging that the top leadership of ESCRU contained at least one "card carrying Communist."[46] Committed to the tradition of white paternalism in

his dealing with black people, Campbell lashed out in anger against the resolution on intermarriage, which threatened his assumptions about the proper relationship of the races. The situation was complicated by the fact that Campbell had received his information about the ESCRU meeting from reports that Carl Braden released. Distressed by the implications of Campbell's charge, Morris traveled to West Virginia to meet personally with the bishop. In their discussion Morris repudiated Braden and convinced Campbell to retract his allegations, noting that the society's elected leadership (to which Braden did not belong) were all "committed Churchmen and loyal citizens" who were "inherently opposed to Communism." Meanwhile, Morris wrote Braden and demanded that he refrain from any future involvement in ESCRU's affairs.[47]

Having been raised in coastal Georgia, Morris understood quite well the conservatism of the South. As he wrote a friend soon after his meeting with Campbell, he wished he could tell everyone who had known him as a young man "how I have such compassion for the agony of the region."[48] In his responses both to Campbell and to Braden, therefore, he took pains as a white southerner to clarify the distinction between "the perfect" and "the possible"—between "a militancy that is responsible and grounded in basic Christian attitudes" and the "kind of exploitative and self-aggrandizing action" of which he thought men like Braden and Werth were guilty.[49] Because McCarthyism remained a potent force in southern culture and threatened to cripple the effectiveness of his young organization, Morris was determined to keep it free of any taint of disloyalty to mainstream American values. He was cognizant of the tragic nature of the situation and the spiritual dangers of trying to steer a middle course that might offend some well-meaning supporters. Because of the ambiguity in which church people in the South had to work, Morris believed that the objectives he sought justified the tactics that sometimes had to be employed. The task of reconciliation for which Christ died—uniting an "assortment of persons at the foot of the Cross, the multitude of races and tongues at Pentecost"—was the noble goal for which ESCRU was striving, and if his organization could just keep focused on that religious vision, it had the potential to end all forms of segregation and foster true interracial harmony within the Episcopal Church.[50]

# 5

# The Church's Response to the Civil Rights Crisis

I n the spring of 1961, James Farmer, the director of the Congress of Racial Equality (CORE), announced that his organization would send an integrated team of "freedom riders" on buses from Washington, D.C., to New Orleans. This action coincided with the seventh anniversary of the *Brown* decision and was intended to test the South's compliance with court-mandated desegregation in interstate transportation terminals. CORE had sponsored a similar action fourteen years before when the Supreme Court banned segregated seating on interstate buses, and its leaders hoped the new effort would again prod the federal government to protect the rights of African Americans. Seven black men and six white men boarded two buses in Washington on May 4, 1961, and they traveled safely through Virginia, North Carolina, South Carolina, and Georgia. On the road from Atlanta to Birmingham, Alabama, however, the freedom riders were attacked by mobs of racist whites. One of the buses was destroyed by a fire bomb near Anniston, Alabama, and occupants of the second vehicle were beaten savagely when they arrived in Birmingham. The country as a whole reacted with shock at this violence, and Attorney General Robert Kennedy was eventually compelled to send federal marshals to ensure the safety of the freedom riders. Although local police arrested the interracial group when they entered the segregated waiting rooms at the bus terminal in Jackson, Mississippi, the first freedom ride had achieved its objectives by drawing attention both to the continued resistance to federal laws and to the grave dangers faced by activists who challenged segregation in the deep South.[1]

Over the next few months, while hundreds of other Americans participated in freedom rides and kept up pressure on southern officials, the Episcopal Church maintained what Kenneth Clark and Arthur Walmsley called a "deafening silence" on civil rights. Walmsley and Clark were working together on civil rights issues at national church headquarters, and they expressed frustration that leaders in their denomination seemed paralyzed as events of tremendous long-term significance took place all around them. Even if the denomination could not corporately endorse the actions of CORE and other civil rights organizations, they argued, individuals should still be encouraged to join the protesters.[2] One of the first Episcopalians to respond in this way was Grant Muse, the vicar of an urban mission in Berkeley, California, who joined a group of CORE members from the San Francisco area who were traveling to Mississippi. Following his arrest at the Jackson bus station in mid-June, Muse said that his decision to fight injustice in the South was motivated by his belief in the social teachings of his church, especially the prayer for social justice in the Prayer Book: "Almighty God, who hast created man in thine own image; Grant us grace fearlessly to contend against evil, and to make no peace with oppression. . . ." Muse saw himself "as a priest exercising his prophetic role" with the freedom riders, and with the sympathetic assistance of Edward Harrison, rector of St. Andrew's Church in Jackson, he was able to celebrate the eucharist in his cell on Sunday morning.[3]

John Morris, meanwhile, was engaged in making plans for his organization to undertake its own freedom ride. ESCRU, he said, would sponsor a "Prayer Pilgrimage," in which a multiracial group of priests would ride together on a bus between New Orleans and Detroit—a demonstration of interracial harmony coinciding with the General Convention scheduled to assemble in Detroit in mid-September that year. During the three months prior to the convention, Morris and Walmsley contacted clergy who were sympathetic to the freedom rides and asked them to volunteer for the ESCRU prayer pilgrimage. Although Morris had hoped to have clerical representatives from a variety of minority groups, he was disappointed by the response he received: only five out of the twenty-eight prayer pilgrims were African Americans, and no Native American, Asian American, or Hispanic American priest asked to join it. Other minor problems also plagued the preparations. Despite agreeing originally to serve as chaplain of the group, Kim Myers withdrew at the last minute because he felt uncomfortable that comparatively few black and southern white clergy were taking part. Morris agreed with Myers's concern and expressed annoyance at the apparent failure of African Americans to answer his appeal—the symptom of what he called a general "uncle tomism" among black Episcopalians in the South. In addition, the group was not as geographically balanced as Morris wished, for most of the participants lived in either the Northeast or the Midwest.[4]

On the evening of September 11, 1961, the twenty-seven priests who agreed to join Morris on the prayer pilgrimage all gathered in New Orleans, and the next morning they boarded a chartered bus to take them northward. Though thoroughly committed to the cause, many of the white priests had little firsthand knowledge of the South, and some were quite naive about the everyday experiences of African Americans. In spite of the clerical collars they wore, they also had reason to fear violence, given what had happened earlier to the freedom riders in Anniston and Birmingham. Whatever their doubts or second thoughts, the men in the group were united in their intention to make a strong statement to the Episcopal Church about the sinfulness of segregation. Malcolm Boyd, one of the prayer pilgrims, said at the time that his colleagues and he wanted to teach the church about the relationship of piety and ordinary life. They were ready to face arrest, physical abuse, and possibly even death because they believed Christians had a duty to enter the world and witness to the universal lordship of Jesus Christ. Quoting a portion of the prayer of self-dedication in the Episcopal communion service, the clergy declared to their fellow church members: "It is in His Name that we go forth, and to Him we *offer our selves, our souls and bodies* for what we pray may be used for the spread of His Kingdom."[5]

The prayer pilgrims planned to stop at various segregated church institutions located between New Orleans and their destination in Detroit. In preparation, Morris wrote clergy in Mississippi and Alabama, the two states he thought needed the most attention, and asked for their support as his group traveled through their dioceses. Charles Carpenter and George Murray, the bishop and bishop coadjutor of Alabama, promptly responded and told him that the prayer pilgrims would receive absolutely no sympathy or assistance from them, especially if they decided to break state or local segregation laws. The bishops suggested that, rather than causing "irritation and disharmony" in southern dioceses, the ESCRU clergy should encourage better race relations through lawful means such as negotiation and mediation. Morris also contacted John Allin, then the head of All Saints' College in Vicksburg, an all-white school operated by the diocese of Mississippi, to inquire if his group could visit and discuss why All Saints' had not yet complied with the official policies of the denomination on race. Allin begged Morris not to come. He admitted his school had not yet desegregated—indeed, it received important funding from Jessie Ball duPont because of its continuing commitment to segregation—but he argued that Episcopal clergy in Mississippi should be given more time to ameliorate the situation before outsiders started to interfere with its operations. Despite Allin's plea, Morris and the prayer pilgrims made All Saints' College the first major stop on their trip. They were received politely, but the meeting was not a very satisfying one for either side. Allin continued to regard the prayer pilgrimage as "poor strategy and ill-timed," and he insisted that only Mississippi residents could handle racial tensions in the church in their state.[6]

Although Allin was far too sophisticated to allow the prayer pilgrims to embarrass him, the ESCRU contingent did not have to wait long to force the type of confrontation they were seeking in Mississippi. On the second day of the trip, fifteen of the men were arrested when they entered the bus terminal in Jackson as an interracial group. The police waited respectfully while the priests, all in clerical attire, offered prayers for the people of Mississippi, but then they led them away to jail. Since Robert Pierson, one of the clergymen arrested, was the son-in-law of Governor Nelson Rockefeller of New York, the national press gave considerable coverage to the ESCRU effort. After spending a brief period in jail, the men were convicted of disturbing the peace, fined two hundred dollars, and sentenced to a four-month jail term. When he handed down this sentence, the judge (a fellow Episcopalian) lectured the clergy about the "Articles of Religion" in the Prayer Book, which mandated the need for "respectful obedience to the Civil Authority." Thirteen of the men quickly appealed the conviction and were released on bond. While they headed for the General Convention in Detroit, the other two prayer pilgrims who had been arrested agreed to stay in jail so that their case would remain in the news.[7]

At the same time, the other half of the prayer pilgrimage contingent left Jackson and headed toward Sewanee, Tennessee, where they hoped to instigate a confrontation with the administration of the University of the South. Despite the acrimonious national controversy over the desegregation of the School of Theology during the 1952–53 academic year, segregation remained the de facto policy at the undergraduate level at Sewanee until June 1961, when the trustees finally agreed to consider applications from African Americans. During the spring of 1961, another furor had arisen over the university's decision to confer an honorary degree on Thomas Waring, a noted segregationist from South Carolina. Waring, a nephew (and outspoken critic) of Judge J. Waties Waring, was an Episcopalian, valedictorian of Sewanee's class of 1926, and editor of the *Charleston News and Courier.* His professional accomplishments certainly qualified him for recognition, but he was also a leader of the prosegregation forces in his state and a strong supporter of the Citizens' Council. Waring and his newspaper consistently attacked the NAACP, the Supreme Court, and even Thomas Carruthers for threatening white supremacy, and in 1952 he had argued vociferously against allowing the theological school at Sewanee to desegregate. Despite protests from many faculty members and from Episcopalians throughout the country, vice chancellor Edward McCrady and the trustees of the university chose to grant Waring the honorary degree—a decision that especially offended the ESCRU leadership and made Sewanee an obvious target for the prayer pilgrims.[8]

Although the Waring uproar quickly abated after the commencement exercises, a second and more protracted controversy arose over the racial policies in effect at the Sewanee Inn and Claramont Restaurant, a facility operating on land owned by the university. Troubles began there in the summer of 1961 when a group of white trustees, white faculty members, and black graduate students attempted to have a meal at the restaurant. When the men asked to be seated, the restaurant owner, Clara Shoemate, told them politely but firmly that she did not serve African Americans. Despite the outcry arising over this incident, the university administration insisted that it was not responsible for the racial attitudes of local people like Shoemate to whom it happened to rent property. The disingenuous nature of this argument was exposed by the fact that Shoemate's strongest defenders were the same three men who had been Waring's most insistent supporters a few weeks before: the university chancellor, Charles Carpenter; the vice chancellor, McCrady; and the director of development, Frank Juhan, retired bishop of Florida and close friend of Jessie Ball duPont. Because of the stance taken by these Sewanee officials, the restaurant and the inn were designated as the focus for the prayer pilgrims' protest when they arrived at the campus in September. Although the university administration knew the clergy were coming and hoped to mollify them enough to avoid further trouble, Shoemate stubbornly refused to back down and allow the black prayer pilgrims to enter her restaurant. Having made their point, the ESCRU clergy did not stay long at Sewanee but headed for Detroit to rejoin their comrades coming from Jackson. They were extremely pleased that they had succeeded in embarrassing both the university and its supporters within the church.[9]

When the two separate groups of prayer pilgrims were reunited after an intense and exciting week on the road, they were met with a warm welcome at the convention, and as they talked with their fellow church members, they sought to explain their goals in theological terms. Echoing ideas made popular by Dietrich Bonhoeffer and Gibson Winter, Malcolm Boyd announced that he and the other clergy were "acting out a sermon" on behalf of mainline American Christianity.[10] Although the church in the United States seemed content to be merely "a country club . . . , a dispenser of spiritual tranquilizers . . . , a kind of pseudo-holy dollhouse with starched lace-curtains," the prayer pilgrimage had demonstrated religion's relevance within the real world.[11] Another prayer pilgrim, Merrill Orne Young, emphasized that what the group had done was "less for the sake of the Negro directly, or of the nation or the world, than for the sake of the church." The church was so divided by race, he said, that most people could not see within its everyday life the unity that the Holy Spirit had created on the day of Pentecost. By witnessing to racial integration, therefore, Young believed that he had engaged in an evangelistic exercise that contributed to the renewal of the church.[12] For Robert Chapman, his participation represented a natural extension of his priestly ministry, for the prayer pilgrims were helping to transform society and thus bringing God's kingdom closer to reality.[13]

The presence of the prayer pilgrims in Detroit helped make the 1961 General Convention an especially lively affair—an event mirroring the expansive, idealistic tenor of the country in the early 1960s. As if evoking President John Kennedy's promise to lead the United States toward a bold "New Frontier," Arthur Lichtenberger's opening sermon summoned Episcopalians to mission work at home and abroad. "Repent, believe, go— these are our orders," he declared. "The ends of the earth for us today are the frontiers in this city, in New Orleans, in San Juan, Manila and Monrovia. . . . We dare not temporize, for the time is short." The church should not be viewed as "a place of refuge from the disturbing and threatening events" of the twentieth century, he emphasized; rather, it had been set by God squarely in the midst of the world. In an address at the Triennial Meeting of Episcopal churchwomen, Paul Moore struck a similar note: the churches in the United States had reached "a new Kairos," a time for extending the reach of human freedom, and at such a moment they needed to be ready to undertake their vocation, bearing "in action and in power" the liberating truth of Jesus Christ. Stephen Bayne, then serving as the executive officer of the Anglican Communion, highlighted the same themes in his convention address. He lamented the tendency to regard the Episcopal Church as an effete institution that embodied "the captive Christianity of Gothic arches and Tudor prose." Episcopalians, he reminded the gathering, should focus on the vigorous demands of the gospel, for everything American Christians held dear "came not from pleasant people who wanted to get along," but from those who chose "to follow Christ into an altogether new kind of country."[14]

Encouraged by the progressive tone of the convention, Morris decided that ESCRU should advance once more against the still intransigent administration of the University of the South. Some progress appeared to have been made at Sewanee after the embarrassment of the summer protests, when pressure from the university's regents and faculty forced Clara Shoemate to open her establishment to all registered students and authorized guests of the school regardless of race. (In previous academic years, visiting dignitaries such as Bishop Bravid Harris of Liberia and the entertainer Louis Armstrong had been forced to find food and lodging at private homes on the campus.) However, when James Woodruff, Robert Hunter, and Warren Scott, black clergy from nearby cities, asked for service at the restaurant based on the fact that they were Episcopal priests, they were rebuffed by Shoemate. She welcomed any white tourist seeking a meal at the Claramont Restaurant, but Shoemate was adamant about her right to exclude African Americans, clergy or not, who had no official status at the university. When Edward McCrady refused to overrule her decision, Morris announced that ESCRU would undertake a series of sit-ins at Shoemate's establishment in order to shame the university into action. "Sewanee still wrestles with the specter of Bishop Polk," Morris observed, and the school needed to cut "the umbilical cord" binding it to the bygone culture of the antebellum South and bind itself instead to the eternal gospel of Jesus Christ.[15]

When an interracial team of ESCRU clergy came seeking a confrontation at the campus in April, they entered the Sewanee Inn but discovered that Shoemate had decided not to open her restaurant in the building that day. The men remained at the restaurant for several hours, during which time a few students came and talked politely with them about their views on racial integration. At one point during the standoff, Frank Juhan also spoke to the ESCRU group and told the black priests that they were interlopers who were not welcome at Sewanee. Meanwhile, a rowdy crowd of young men from the college gathered outside the restaurant. They heckled the white priests, called the African Americans "niggers," threatened to beat up anyone who tried to leave the building, and in the evening set fire to a cross outside the restaurant. Although the ESCRU demonstrators left the campus after midnight, they returned the next morning and again found that the restaurant had been shut down. The protest continued for another day before the clergy decided that they had made their point and left Sewanee for good.[16]

The impasse continued for several more months, as moderate and liberal elements within the university sought to effect change without appearing to bow completely to the demands made by ESCRU. John Allin, a graduate both of the college and of the theological school, admitted that ESCRU had embarrassed the university and hoped a compromise could be reached. The university at least ought to be willing to welcome the black clergy of the Episcopal Church at all its facilities, he thought. John Gessell, a faculty member at the School of Theology, was in full sympathy with ESCRU's goals, but—repeating John Morris's sentiments from a year before—he urged its leadership to distinguish more carefully between "the actual and the possible" with Sewanee. "Responsible action can be taken best by those who live in a given situation," he reasoned, and it was dangerous for those seeking justice for African Americans "to assume that the segregationist is neither neighbor nor redeemable." Christian social action, furthermore, should be understood "within the context of sin and grace"—a religious framework in which the whole church, North and South, integrationist and segregationist, fell together under God's judgment.[17] Although the ESCRU leadership did not find his arguments convincing, Gessell, FitzSimons Allison, and other members of the theological faculty at Sewanee sought to establish a common ground on which white Episcopalians like themselves could take a stand that was not only principled but also effective within the community in which they lived. Eventually, their approach was successful, for with a virtually united front against her, Shoemate finally capitulated in the spring of 1963. Nearly two years after ESCRU exposed the problem at the school, she removed her business from the official "domain" of the university and opened a private, racially segregated club on the outskirts of Sewanee instead.[18]

In the midst of this controversy, administrators at the school received strong support from a number of concerned white southerners who urged them to stand their ground and resist desegregation at all costs. Saying how much they appreciated the history and Confederate heritage of the university, these men and women realized that issues far more critical than just the status of a campus restaurant were at stake. Although John Morris and members of ESCRU believed that an Episcopal university should be faithful to the teachings of its denomination, especially on the hotly contested subject of race, segregationists such as Edward Guerry stressed the importance of loyalty to the tradition of white supremacy. Proud of their association with the Citizens' Council, the prosegregation

Episcopalians were quick to criticize even the most halting steps toward racial justice by church leaders in the South, and they were dismayed when McCrady and others at Sewanee at last backed away from their commitment to Shoemate.[19]

As historian David Chappell has observed, few articulate segregationists remained in the mainline denominations by the early 1960s, but a handful of Episcopalians were among the most visible and outspoken at that time. These men had published an important and revealing collection, *Essays on Segregation* (1960), in which they presented reasons why church people should reject both the *Brown* decision and the desegregation of southern institutions. T. Robert Ingram, the book's editor and rector of St. Thomas' Church in Houston, Texas, insisted that, despite their strong emphasis on biblical texts, those who favored integration did not really understand either the Bible or the lessons of early Christian history. When the apostolic council of Jerusalem, for example, decided that Gentiles did not need to become Jews before joining the church (Acts 15), it recognized the reality of a bifurcated society. In Christ, Gentiles could remain Gentiles, Ingram argued, and Jews were still free to be Jews. Although some twentieth-century Christians thought a biracial church was contrary to God's will, the opposite in fact was true: Christ promised "not that the nations shall be demolished, . . . but that all nations, remaining nations, shall come unto him." Other authors in the collection echoed this theme of the importance of racial diversity. G. MacLaren Brydon, the former Archdeacon for Negro Work in the diocese of Virginia, wrote that pride in one's race is not inherently sinful. Because God created distinct races and nations, he said, the church was called to gather each separately into the fellowship of Christ's body. Essays by Edward Guerry and Albert Thomas of South Carolina espoused similar views: though human beings belong to different races, all have separate but equal access to Christ through faith.[20]

In contrast to the conservative, decidedly paternalistic tone adopted by Ingram, Brydon, Guerry, and Thomas, two other authors in the collection unleashed venomous attacks against African Americans and whites who advocated desegregation. Henry Egger, rector of St. Peter's Church, Charlotte, North Carolina, had been censured in 1957 by the other Episcopal clergy of his city for his outspoken opposition to the *Brown* decision. Egger emphasized the indelible character of racial differences, equating blackness with ignorance and criminality and warning that "the breakdown of racial integrity" would lead inevitably to social degeneration. He also revived the classic racist stereotype of the "tragic mulatto" and claimed that "pure-blooded Negroes" resisted integration whereas only "Negroes of mixed blood" (with directions from "the council-rooms of Moscow") sought it.[21] James Dees, rector of Trinity Church, Statesville, North Carolina, was even more aggressive than Egger in his fight against integration, which he equated with the desire to create an "amalgamation of the races" that was "abhorrent to God." Dees was a leading member of the Citizens' Council as well as one of the founders of the North Carolina Defenders of States' Rights. In the fall of 1959, he had defied Bishop Jones of Louisiana, who sought to bar him from speaking at a Citizens' Council meeting in New Orleans. Dees's extremist views placed him so at odds with the rest of the denomination that he ultimately renounced the Episcopal priesthood. Charging that the Episcopal Church had fostered the growth of a variety of social and theological heresies, Dees organized the Anglican Orthodox Church in 1963 and appealed to disaffected, prosegregation church members to join his denomination.[22]

Other leading white Episcopalians in the South attempted to make their peace with the new racial environment that was emerging in the early 1960s. One of them was Ralph McGill, the editor of the *Atlanta Constitution* and one of the founders of the Southern Regional Council. He still considered himself a segregationist when the *Brown* decision was released and had not been above launching red-baiting attacks on individuals and groups suspected of having ties to radical organizations. Over the course of his long and distinguished journalistic career, however, McGill moved steadily leftward, and though proud of his regional heritage, he understood the evils of the racism it often harbored. Raised a Presbyterian, he found his religious faith waning in the 1930s, but in the fall of 1953 he officially joined the Episcopal Church and became affiliated with St. Philip's Cathedral in Atlanta, where he later served on the vestry. As McGill's racial attitudes evolved, he became increasingly impatient with his denomination and accused its leadership of providing little positive guidance to the civil rights movement. Too many parishes had allowed themselves to become merely "gymnasiums where we exercise with the reading of the Book of Common Prayer, neither sweating nor breathing hard in the stuffy air of sanctity." The inability of organized Christianity to respond creatively to the challenges of modern society, he lamented, was "the single most melancholy aspect of what has been called the moral decline of our time."[23]

McGill was especially concerned about the lack of support from diocesan leaders in states in the deep South where civil rights workers were consistently harassed and assaulted. The problem had become particularly acute for Episcopal activists in Alabama, for the ecclesiastical as well as the political authorities there were adamantly opposed to the civil rights movement. Robert DuBose, a black priest in Montgomery, discovered that fact when he ran afoul of Bishop Carpenter in March 1960. DuBose, who served as vicar of the Church of the Good Shepherd and as chaplain of Alabama State College, had been participating quietly in the Montgomery Improvement Association since the bus boycott four years before. However, when nine students were expelled from Alabama State because of their involvement in sit-in demonstrations in the city, SCLC leader Ralph Abernathy and he marched at the head of several hundred black protesters who gathered in front of the state capitol. Since the two clergymen had planned to offer prayers on the steps of the capitol, each man was dressed in the appropriate liturgical garments of his denomination—Abernathy, the Baptist preacher, in a dark suit and tie and DuBose, the high-church Episcopalian, in a cassock, surplice, stole, and biretta. This striking image of clerical activism appeared on the front page of the *New York Times* the next day, and since it clearly dramatized the religious impulse behind the civil rights movement in Montgomery, it outraged DuBose's bishop. Although he had always treated the black priest in a kindly, paternal manner before the incident, his attitude changed overnight when it became clear that DuBose was no longer going to behave in a manner befitting what Carpenter called a "good Negro." Unwilling to accept any insubordination from the black clergy in his diocese, Carpenter removed DuBose from both his church positions and forced him to find employment in a northern diocese instead.[24]

Carpenter was equally unforgiving in his treatment of white clergy who challenged the racial status quo in Alabama. Robert Man, a priest in Bessemer, noted in a letter to Arthur Walmsley that his personal relationship with the bishop was cordial, but he also knew Carpenter's weight and influence lay entirely on the side of the segregationists. If an open clash over race were to occur in any parish in his diocese, Man predicted, Carpenter would do little to support prointegration clergy. Francis Walter, rector of St. James' Church in Eufaula, learned this to his chagrin when his active support of ESCRU became a cause of conflict in his parish. Carpenter tolerated young white priests like Walter as long as they were circumspect about their liberal views, but when he heard that Walter had become active in ESCRU and would not repudiate that involvement, Carpenter asked for his resignation from St. James' and ushered him out of the diocese. A few months later at St. Peter's Church in Talladega, another young rector, Kenneth Franklin, learned that students from the

nearby black college intended to worship at the town's white churches on
Easter Sunday in 1962. He advised his parishioners to welcome them
when they came, and though the atmosphere was tense at St. Peter's that
morning, it was the only white church in Talladega that permitted African Americans to enter and participate in the service. Although Carpenter expressed his approval in private—it had been customary for African
Americans to worship with their white masters even in the days of slavery, he admitted—Franklin felt isolated and uneasy after the crisis. Fearing possible reprisals by the Ku Klux Klan and concerned about Carpenter's
equivocal posture on race, Franklin decided to resign from St. Peter's and
enrolled for graduate study at General Seminary in New York.[25]

The situation in Mississippi was only marginally better than in Alabama. Thanks principally to the efforts of Duncan Gray Jr. and the committee on Christian social relations on which he served, Mississippi
Episcopalians at the diocesan level had responded quickly and positively
to the idea of desegregation. Nearly a decade after the *Brown* decision,
however, the mood at All Saints' College in Vicksburg had become typical
of the diocese—a gnawing sense that segregation was wrong but an inability to develop a strategy by which desegregation could be implemented.
Edward Harrison of St. Andrew's, Jackson, moreover, was forced to leave
his parish in 1962 when a rift occurred as a result of his restrained but
clear support of the civil rights movement. Harrison had been under fire
for several years because of his desire to modernize services and the Sunday school curriculum at the church. Criticism of his leadership broadened and intensified during the freedom rides in 1961, when he was
attacked not only for offering aid to Grant Muse and other civil rights
workers jailed in Jackson but also for attending interracial meetings that
discussed race relations. Despite his relatively moderate political views,
approximately one hundred members left the parish in protest during
that period. The final break occurred in May 1962, when Harrison's name
was forged on a telegram urging T. Robert Ingram not to come to Jackson
and speak at a Citizens' Council gathering there. Although diocesan and
parish leaders officially supported him during that crisis, Harrison decided he could no longer minister effectively in such a highly charged
atmosphere. He resigned and accepted a position at a parish in Florida
instead.[26]

Jane Schutt was one of the few white Episcopalians in Jackson to
come publicly to Harrison's defense during the period he was under fire.
Like Anne Braden of Kentucky, Schutt had been an Episcopalian since
childhood, and she never wavered from the lessons she learned in Sun-

day school about the unity of all people and races in Christ. Well known because of her involvement in the United Church Women, a national ecumenical organization that had pledged to bridge the gap between the races, she was appointed to the state advisory committee of the U.S. Commission on Civil Rights when it was organized in Mississippi in 1961. (The national commission had been created as part of the 1957 Civil Rights Act, and it was authorized to form advisory committees that investigated charges of discrimination against African Americans on the state level.) Schutt served on the committee for three years, and under her chairmanship it issued a stinging report on conditions faced by African Americans in Mississippi. This challenge to racial orthodoxy made Schutt the target of acts of terrorism by local Klan members. A cross was burned on her lawn and on another occasion her house was damaged by a dynamite blast, but she remained staunchly committed to interracial justice. Despite personal attacks by segregationists who accused her of Communist sympathies, Schutt insisted that her civil rights activities were motivated primarily by her religious beliefs.[27]

Although Edward Harrison and Jane Schutt were virtually unknown outside of Mississippi, Duncan Gray of St. Peter's Church in Oxford became a celebrated figure nationally because of his presence and bravery at the center of one of the most shameful episodes in the history of the state: the riot at "Ole Miss." After trying for over a year and a half to break the color line at the University of Mississippi, James Meredith finally registered as a student in September 1962, but on the night he took up residence in a dorm room, a mob composed of thousands of angry whites descended upon the school. Gray had first walked to the campus in the early evening in response to a telephone call from a distraught parishioner, who asked him to locate her daughter and take her to the safety of his rectory a short distance from the school. Later, as a battle between the mob and the federal marshals protecting Meredith broke out, Gray returned to the campus with Wofford Smith, the Episcopal chaplain at the university, and two faculty members who were St. Peter's parishioners. All four men plunged into the crowd and attempted to talk with students and do whatever they could to restore order. Gray soon encountered Edwin Walker, one of the ringleaders of the mob. Since Walker was a retired general and an Episcopalian, Gray hoped that he might be willing to help him, but Walker adamantly refused. When Gray next saw Walker exhorting a bunch of men at the Confederate monument near the campus entrance, he climbed up on the monument and begged them all to disperse. This did little good, for he was immediately grabbed by several members of the crowd and dragged away. Although state and federal soldiers eventually brought rioting at the school to a halt, scores of people were injured in the melee, and two men were killed by random gunfire that night.[28]

In the aftermath of the riot, Gray continued his courageous efforts to work for peace throughout the state. Some members of St. Peter's, Oxford left the parish in protest against what their rector had done, but leading Episcopalians such as Arthur Lichtenberger and John Allin publicly commended Gray, and his personal bravery was praised by the National Council and by editorial writers in several church publications that fall. This reaction to Gray's courage and the attention he received was itself rather noteworthy. Like the fictional character Atticus Finch in Harper Lee's prize-winning bestseller *To Kill a Mockingbird* (1960), Gray seemed to symbolize middle-class decency standing against the vicious and destructive racism of lower-class whites. During a period of rapid and confusing social change, his example provided reassurance to white Episcopalians, for he represented not only Christian rectitude and quiet moral strength, but also an embodiment of the church leaders' hopes that *they* still could control the racial crisis in the South. And in spite of his strong personal belief in the incompatibility of segregation and the gospel, the message Gray preached during the campus riot—respect for law and order—did not directly threaten the position of the still-segregated Episcopal Church in Mississippi. Winsome and sincere, his stance was consistent with the highest ideals of a paternalistic racial tradition that extended back to the early-twentieth-century episcopate of Theodore DuBose Bratton.[29]

Their well-publicized support of Gray notwithstanding, Lichtenberger and the National Council were—at virtually the same moment—engaged in suppressing a report that was highly critical of the church's overall approach to race relations. This report was the product of two years' worth of deliberations by the Committee on Intergroup Relations, an ad hoc body organized by Neil Tarplee and Arthur Walmsley in mid-1960. Composed of six Episcopalians who were widely regarded as experts in the area of race (Sarah Patton Boyle of Charlottesville, Virginia; Will Campbell of the National Council of Churches; Kenneth Clark of the Department of Psychology, City College of New York; Thurgood Marshall of the NAACP; Thomas Pettigrew of the Department of Social Relations, Harvard University; and Frederick Routh of the Michigan Fair Employment Practices Commission), the committee was intended to advise the Department of Christian Social Relations about how to bridge the gap between the church's lofty social principles and its actual racial practices on the local and national levels.[30]

From the outset, the committee had run into a number of problems that defied easy solution. The most difficult concerned their relationship with Tollie Caution and the Division of Racial Minorities of the Home Department. Although Caution attended meetings of the intergroup relations committee, its members reported not to him but to the two white staff members (Tarplee and Walmsley) of the Division of Christian Citizenship in the Department of Christian Social Relations. The committee viewed the evangelistic, community-building concerns of Caution and the Racial Minorities Committee as anachronistic, and Clark and Pettigrew in particular questioned the educational value of the black colleges that were supported through the American Church Institute (the words, "for Negroes," had recently been dropped—quietly—from its name). Many white activists in the church agreed with that judgment. John Morris, for example, despaired that black Episcopalians in the South might actually prefer the old "separate but equal" parish system out of which the Division of Racial Minorities first emerged. All church members should now be willing to worship in integrated parishes, he insisted. Other whites also challenged the assumption that minority groups needed special recognition within the organizational structures of the church. Thus, when *The Episcopalian* (the principal mouthpiece of the denomination) published several articles honoring "the Negro Episcopalian" in its April 1962 issue, an editorial writer in *The Witness* immediately attacked the series. Although *The Witness* had a well-deserved reputation as a progressive journal, it had long been critical of Caution's Negro Work program, reasoning that race was irrelevant to the church's mission. In an editorial mockingly entitled, "Let's Have a White Episcopalian Issue," the *Witness* staff questioned why in 1962 their denomination continued to treat "Negro Episcopalians" as an entity distinct from other churchgoers.[31]

Frustrated by what they regarded as continuing segregation at the highest levels of the Episcopal Church, the Committee on Intergroup Relations still pressed national church leaders to support desegregation in society at large. Arthur Lichtenberger at first seemed receptive to this appeal, and in anticipation of a meeting of the House of Bishops in October 1962, he asked them to provide him with some concrete recommendations he could share with that body. Pleased with Lichtenberger's initial openness, committee members began to draft a report for the bishops but then were crushed when the invitation was abruptly withdrawn. Lichtenberger claimed that the bishops had chosen to consider more pressing theological issues instead—their meeting coincided, in fact, with the opening of the Second Vatican Council—but the committee entirely rejected that explanation. Since the gathering was held in Columbia, South Carolina, where segregation laws were still rigidly enforced—Bishops Bravid Harris and Dillard Brown of Liberia, the only two African Americans at the meeting, were forced to eat and sleep apart from their colleagues—the committee assumed that most of the bishops simply wanted to pretend that the civil rights movement was not happening. Charging that "the institutions of Caesar . . . have moved ahead of the institution of God" in supporting racial inclusiveness, Boyle, Pettigrew and the others accused the Episcopal Church of "failing its mission and its Master."[32]

In the end, four members of the committee were allowed to submit individual statements to the National Council. The reports they eventually presented are revealing documents, for they reflect not only the committee's quarrel with the leadership of the church but also the disagreements members had had with one another during the course of their deliberations.

Will Campbell's report, "Theological Imperatives within the Church," examined American race relations from the perspective of neoorthodox theology and concluded that redemption and grace were at the heart of the race issue. Since all people—integrationists and segregationists, black people and white people—were sinners for whom Jesus had died, the presumption that race or social class made one person superior to another was fundamentally sinful. For Christians, "the only reference is God," Campbell said, and the church needed to remember that its unity was created solely by Christ. This argument reflected Campbell's frustration as much with the leadership of his employer, the National Council of Churches, as with Episcopalians. Despite his strong commitment to interracial justice and his genuine concern for poor people of all races, Campbell was ambivalent about the direction the civil rights movement was starting to take, and he feared that many liberal whites lacked a solid theological foundation on which to support their involvement in social action.[33]

Sarah Patton Boyle gave the most personal report of the four: "The Witness of a Lone Layman." She referred to her overwhelming sense of isolation as a white person advocating racial equality during the bitter period of massive resistance in Virginia, when neither black people nor white people seemed to trust her. Nevertheless, she continued to affirm her belief in "the brotherhood of man," and she accused the Episcopal Church of being lax in its obligation to help fashion a humane society. White Episcopalians in the South, she said, ought to learn to identify more with the Christian gospel than with the secular racial customs with which they had been raised. Boyle also thought Episcopal bishops tended "to be more executives than spiritual leaders," but unlike other members of her committee, who had all but given up on the institution and its clergy, she believed that the church might still play a prophetic role in race relations.[34]

Kenneth B. Clark, the sole African American to submit a report, titled his presentation "Policy and Implementation: Problems of Race Relations in the Protestant Episcopal Church." He struck the most bitter note, distinguishing between the denomination's stated positions on racial discrimination and its inability to transform its beliefs into action. He criticized Arthur Lichtenberger for his personal failure to support the freedom rides and other civil rights initiatives, and he condemned the church for maintaining segregated schools through the auspices of the American Church Institute. Although the concept of race had become outmoded in academic circles, he acidly remarked, the Episcopal Church seemed blissfully unaware of that development. Because of its refusal to take risks on behalf of justice for all Americans, the church had managed to maintain itself as a social institution while forfeiting all claims to moral leadership. "This is practical impotence," Clark concluded, "and mockery of the spirit of Christ."[35]

Thomas F. Pettigrew, in his report, "Why We Have Failed," outlined four reasons for the glaring discrepancies between the church's official position on race and day-to-day practices on the local level. First, the church had emphasized the need for raising money and membership levels at the expense of theological ideals. Second, Episcopalians had allowed respect for individual freedom to devolve into an utter lack of responsibility for society as a whole. Third, the church had fallen prey to "the ideology of so-called 'moderation'" and had simply maintained traditional patterns of racial paternalism in its outlook on African Americans. Finally, church leaders had tried to alter attitudes about race rather than practices, naively assuming that practices would change once minds had been educated. Quoting fellow Episcopal sociologist Gordon Allport, Pettigrew warned that "the day of reckoning has come for the Christian Church," which must either keep up with a rapidly changing world or cease to have an impact on the lives of ordinary Americans.[36]

National Council members were given an opportunity to read and reflect on the four-part report, but they eventually decided that the document was too inflammatory to be released to ordinary churchgoers. Instead of circulating the report throughout the church, council members simply told the committee what they thought of its recommendations.

One of the most vehement and negative responses came from Donald Wattley, a priest in New Orleans. Given "the long years during which both Church and State have condoned the status quo, the 'separate but equal' theory of race relations," he began, it was impractical to think that changes were going to occur overnight. Furthermore, since the Episcopal Church was "historically, theologically, culturally and structurally a distinctly 'moderate'" organization, it tended to attract people who were well-to-do and content with their lot in life. Although he agreed that racial integration was a noble goal, Wattley emphasized that church leaders had no right to allow the denomination to be torn apart by pressing too hard on controversial issues, for despite the committee's implication that white Episcopalians ought to support desegregation at any cost, the church also needed to preserve its own institutional fabric. Many leading lay people in the South were at best lukewarm about desegregation, and bishops and priests were wise not to press them, especially when "millions of dollars in property and investment . . . would go down the drain" in that effort. Quoting the reaction of Edwin Penick, the former bishop of North Carolina, to the *Brown* decision eight years before, Wattley concluded, "A human problem so vast in its dimensions, involving the welfare of millions of people . . . cannot, by its very nature, yield to a quick solution. To attempt a speedy answer, or even to expect it, seems to me unrealistic, for it ignores the experience of history, including an era of tragic fratricidal strife. . . . This is a mountain of fact and circumstance that only faith in Christ can remove. And with all my heart I believe that this realistic mountain will be moved and cast into the sea. But the process, inevitably, must be slow."[37]

Wattley's remarks about the lessons of "an era of tragic fratricidal strife" had an unintentionally ironic tone, for many in the United States were about to celebrate, not lament, the legacy of the Civil War and Reconstruction by commemorating the centennial of the Emancipation Proclamation. Precisely because denominations like the Episcopal Church were so slow in confronting the problems of racial discrimination, activists within various religious bodies had been pressing for an ecumenical gathering that would finally prod Christian and Jewish leaders into action. At the resulting National Conference on Religion and Race, more than 650 representatives from various Roman Catholic, Greek Orthodox, Jewish, and Protestant organizations and denominations (including 38 Episcopalians, most of whom were associated with ESCRU) assembled in Chicago in January 1963. Timed to coincide with the date when American slavery had been abolished, the conference featured speeches by prominent figures such as Martin Luther King, Benjamin Mays, and Will Campbell, and in their concluding "Appeal to the Conscience of the American People," participants called racism the nation's "most serious domestic evil" and summoned their fellow citizens "to work, to pray and to act courageously in the cause of human equality and dignity." As King remarked in his address, most American church people had been content to "remain silent behind the anesthetizing security of stained-glass windows." The time had now come for them to wake up and see the involvement of God in the civil rights struggle.[38]

Although the Conference on Religion and Race proved to be a turning point for the Episcopal Church and other predominantly white denominations, several participants later complained that the white leaders who had presided at the meeting had little understanding of the problems faced by most African Americans. As William Stringfellow bluntly remarked, the gathering had simply been "too little, too late, and too lily white"—a judgment, he knew, that was applicable as much to his denomination as to the conference itself. Arthur Walmsley also was critical of white Episcopalians' hesitation about taking action, and he was especially concerned that black militants and the federal government had been far more involved than church members in encouraging positive changes in race relations. Despite Stringfellow's and Walmsley's pessimistic outlook, however, the South experienced a series of crises in the spring and summer of 1963 from which few but the most apathetic white Americans could turn away.[39]

This change in attitude began to occur on the same day that the Conference on Religion and Race assembled in Chicago—January 14, 1963. On that day George Wallace, the newly elected governor of Alabama, stood before a cheering crowd in Montgomery and announced his unwavering commitment to the tradition of white supremacy. Proclaiming "segregation now . . . segregation tomorrow . . . segregation forever," he promised to take a firm, public stance against all attempts to desegregate institutions in his state.[40] Judged even by the standards of deep South governors in that period, Wallace's inaugural address was angry and melodramatic, and it made a profound impression on the Episcopal bishops of Alabama. Troubled particularly by the governor's promise to block the desegregation of the state university, George Murray and Charles Carpenter helped organize and publish a response by eleven major white religious leaders. Objecting not only to Wallace's threat to break the law but also to the demagogic tone he adopted, the clergy sought to articulate a middle position between the governor's blatant appeal to white racism and the full acceptance of black demands for equality. Condemning all who were "advocating defiance, anarchy and subversion," they called upon "people of goodwill to join us in seeking divine guidance as we make our appeal for law and order and common sense" throughout Alabama.[41]

In an attempt to put those words into action, Murray had made the diocesan offices in Birmingham available as a place where clergy and other representatives of the black community could meet with whites and discuss the bettering of race relations in the city. Although Birmingham had often been called the most segregated city in America, its government was in the process of being transformed, as white moderates sought to wrest political control from hard-line segregationist Eugene "Bull" Connor. Worried that further protests from black groups might lead to outbreaks of violence that would hinder the moderates' efforts to ameliorate the Jim Crow system, white political and religious leaders tried to convince Martin Luther King to stop demonstrations that had been planned for April. When King refused to take their advice, Carpenter, Murray, and five other white clergymen released a public letter criticizing him for heightening racial tensions in the city. The implication that the civil rights activity of African Americans, not the racism of whites, was the cause of the continuing unrest in Birmingham infuriated King, and in the now legendary "Letter from Birmingham Jail," he blasted the white clergy. King lectured them on the Christian's responsibility to distinguish between just and unjust laws, and he charged that they were far more concerned with maintaining a stable social and economic environment than with upholding the spiritual values of the Judeo-Christian heritage. African Americans would win freedom, he declared, because their demands were consistent with both the religious and political traditions of their nation.[42]

Even two weeks later, after Connor and the police had unleashed attack dogs and used high-pressure fire hoses against black protesters in Birmingham, Murray still attempted locate a moderating position where he and other white clergy who wished "to minister to the . . . segregationists" could stand in good conscience. As he insisted in a letter to a church periodical, the "long and deeply ingrained traditions and prejudices" held by whites in Alabama could not be quickly and easily removed. He admitted that "some police tempers were frayed" and that Connor's use of such extreme measures as fire hoses and dogs was unwise, yet he defended those methods as "more merciful than the use of guns" on young African American protesters. Despite impressions created by the media, he said, "Birmingham is not just a city of mean, nasty, violent white people, and good, gentle, mistreated Negroes." All kinds of people lived there, and they all needed support, not condemnation, from outsiders. "Honest and prayerful negotiations" between whites and local blacks, Murray believed, not irresponsible protests by outside groups such as SCLC, offered the best solution to his city's long-standing racial troubles.[43]

By the end of May, when Murray's remarks were published, however, the full brutality of white authorities in Birmingham had been exposed via television, and those events demanded a response from the leadership of the Episcopal Church in New York. In preparation for Whitsunday (Pentecost) on June 2, 1963, therefore, Arthur Walmsley helped the presiding bishop prepare a pastoral letter discussing the racial turmoil in Birmingham. In Lichtenberger's "Whitsuntide Message" circulated extensively in the secular press as well as in the church, he spoke of "the necessity of the Church to act" in the face of "the possible imminence of catastrophe" facing the entire nation. As Christians hailed the ascension of the universal lord and celebrated the unifying power of the Holy Spirit at Pentecost, he said, they should also "take every step possible to join with each other across lines of racial separation, in a common struggle for justice." The freedom "to vote, to eat a hamburger where you want, to have a decent job, to live in a house fit for habitation" were rights that should not be denied to anyone in the United States. Although the church had been silent before, it could no longer afford to take that stance, Lichtenberger concluded, during "this, our greatest domestic moral crisis."[44]

In the wake of the mayhem in Birmingham and the apparent unraveling of the country's social fabric—African Americans lying senseless and bloodied on the street while white police faced counterattacks from young men throwing bottles and stones—national leaders, both ecclesiastical and secular, at last began to acknowledge the seriousness and legitimacy of the civil rights movement. President Kennedy asked his aides to draft a civil rights bill, which he introduced to a national television audience in mid-June; at the same time he contacted officials in the Episcopal Church and other major religious bodies, inviting them to meet with him to discuss the American racial crisis. Meanwhile the General Board of the National Council of Churches created a new organization, the Commission on Religion and Race, which was designed to respond as rapidly as possible to developments in the civil rights struggle. Because of the attention his recent Whitsuntide message had received, Lichtenberger agreed to chair the commission, and Robert Spike, a white United Church of Christ minister, was selected as the executive director of the organization. Arthur Walmsley was also released from some of his duties at Episcopal headquarters to work directly with the commission as a staff member.[45]

Over the next three months, numerous Episcopalians participated in various public events that were intended to demonstrate their denomination's newfound commitment to the civil rights movement. For example, when NAACP field secretary Medgar Evers was murdered outside his home in Jackson, Mississippi, John Morris quickly organized a contingent of priests to attend his funeral as honorary pallbearers. Because Morris had been in contact with Evers about holding possible kneel-ins at Episcopal parishes in Jackson, the ESCRU group also met with local church leaders to discuss the progress of desegregation in the diocese of Mississippi. Although a few laity such as Jane Schutt were sympathetic to the ESCRU clergy, most of the other Episcopalians expressed concern that such a highly visible contingent of outsiders might arouse further violence from segregationists. Since Byron De La Beckwith, the killer of Evers, was a notorious and troublesome member of the Church of the Nativity in Greenwood, where he had regularly argued about racial issues with the former rector, Duncan Gray, and with his son Duncan Jr., diocesan officials felt understandably apprehensive about the situation in their state. The ESCRU representatives, however, remained committed to the goals of their mission in Jackson. As one of them later wrote, "knowledge of the unity of the Church overriding the disunity of man" had been constantly on his mind there, but he confessed that he also felt "like a piece of blotting paper absorbing more and more pain and torment and sadness" during the brief time he was in Mississippi.[46]

Further demonstrations, in which priests in clerical collars were prominent among the protesters at segregated public facilities, followed throughout the summer of 1963. A particularly well-publicized event occurred on July 4 at Gwyn Oaks amusement park outside of Baltimore. On that day 275 people (including Eugene Carson Blake, the highest-ranking executive in the United Presbyterian Church, and a small interdenominational group of clergy) were arrested as they attempted to enter Gwyn Oaks. Episcopal bishop Daniel Corrigan, the director of the Home Department, also proudly accompanied Blake into a Baltimore police wagon that day. After he was released on bail, Corrigan noted that he had been on legitimate church business during that protest, for it was the responsibility of Christian leaders "to be where there is action" in the world. Michael Allen, rector of St. Mark's-in-the-Bowery, New York, was arrested, too. Allen claimed that a priest always had a duty to obey "a higher law" than that of the state and to "go wherever his people go" in the struggle for social justice. Since a large number of people from the poor neighborhood in which his parish was located were committing themselves to the fight against racial prejudice in the South, Allen went along to symbolize that the church was ready to work with them in that cause.[47]

The climax of the evolution to which Corrigan and Allen referred—the institutional church finally placing itself "where there is action"—occurred in late August 1963 during the momentous March on Washington for Jobs and Freedom. Prior to the event, Episcopalians took careful steps to prepare for the small but significant role they were to play in it. At a special meeting held in mid-August, the House of Bishops officially endorsed Kennedy's civil rights legislation and recognized the right of church members to join the march as an expression of their Christian beliefs. The Department of Christian Social Relations of the National Council also encouraged dioceses and parishes to charter buses and send groups en masse to Washington. Although black activists had originally planned the demonstration, the participation of these middle-class white people significantly altered its focus, transforming it from a protest against years of injustice and abuse into a supportive statement in favor of Kennedy's civil rights legislation. Thus, the National Council stressed that the march was an expression of mainstream American values, coordinated in cooperation with federal agencies. As J. Stuart Wetmore (the suffragan bishop of New York) remarked, "What began as a segregated movement by self-conscious groups has become thoroughly integrated." Neil Tarplee similarly argued that a noticeable white presence was essential to success: those men and women not only would demonstrate their belief in the justice of the civil rights movement to millions of other Americans at home, but they would also lend respectability to the march. William Stringfellow was less enthusiastic than Wetmore and Tarplee about the meaning of the interracial partnership they touted. Many white leaders who had once been uncertain about the civil rights movement, he quipped, now seemed eager—on the verge of a victory won by African Americans—to become generals of the winning side.[48]

Although the idea of having all Episcopalians walk together by dioceses was soon abandoned as impractical, more than 1,000 people gathered for a service at St. John's Church at Lafayette Square on the day of the march. Thanks to the efforts of Arthur Walmsley, an advertisement announcing the Episcopal Church's full support of jobs and voting rights for African Americans had appeared in the *Washington Post* that morning. Bolstered by this statement and by hymns and prayers, a procession of

Episcopalians emerged from St. John's and—with a cross and an ESCRU banner carried by members of St. Stephen and the Incarnation (an interracial parish in the city) leading the way—joined the massive body of demonstrators on the way to the Lincoln Memorial. Between 200,000 and 300,000 people streamed into Washington to take part in the march and to rally on behalf of the civil rights movement. The ecumenical religious contingent represented only a handful of the total number of participants, but Russell Baker of the *New York Times* remarked that the whole event had "the spirit of a church outing." More than 40,000 laity and clergy from all the major American denominations (including 10 bishops and approximately 300 priests of the Episcopal Church) helped swell the ranks of that imposing contingent of concerned Americans. As Martin Luther King declared in his climactic "I Have a Dream" speech later in the afternoon, it was "the greatest demonstration for freedom" in the history of the United States.[49]

Afterward, conservative elements within the church in the South loudly condemned both the march and the identification of their denomination with its goals. Bishop Jones of Louisiana, for example, had supported the *Brown* decision in 1954, but he questioned the wisdom of endorsing mass civil rights demonstrations. These not only were illegal in many localities, he argued, but they also confused people about the true, supernatural mission of the church. Even Jesus himself had been familiar with many evils in his day (e.g., "slavery, a ruthlessly cruel imperialism, a demoralizing paganism"), but rather than trying to change the societies that spawned them, he sought to convert *individuals* through his "winsomely personal ministry." Charles Arny, a lay member of the diocese of Louisiana, agreed with his bishop and remarked (with some justification) that, since he had never been aware of "any noteworthy militancy on the part of the national body of the Episcopal Church concerning major moral questions" before, he saw no reason why the church needed to change its course now. Other objections came from the diocese of Alabama, where John Mandeville, a lawyer from Mobile, accused the Department of Christian Social Relations of being "more interested in the furtherance of 'total integration of the races' than . . . in fostering peace, togetherness, and solidarity" among white Episcopalians. Evans Dunn, the diocesan chancellor, threatened to withhold funds that Alabama owed to the national church, and Charles Carpenter blasted the denominational staff for offering assistance to the March on Washington. Instead of giving funds away in support of protest demonstrations that offered no benefit to the Episcopal Church, Carpenter asked, why wasn't more money spent on worthwhile activities that aided the schools and parishes of law-abiding black church members in the South?[50]

Despite such attempts to undercut their endorsement of the civil rights movement, the national leadership of the Episcopal Church felt encouraged and empowered by the involvement of so many people in the March on Washington. In the fall of 1963, approximately three hundred Episcopalians returned to Washington to press Congress to adopt the civil rights bill. Along with the National Council of Churches and other religious bodies, these Episcopalians insisted that the legislation involved an issue of public morality about which all churches were rightly concerned, and they exhorted their congressional representatives to see that it was passed. In his description of this lobbying effort, Robert Spike of the Commission on Religion and Race recounted an unidentified bishop's meeting with John McCormack, the Speaker of the House of Representatives. The bishop, "looking every inch an Anglican divine, broad-brimmed hat and umbrella as part of the equipment, . . . pointed his umbrella at the Speaker and said, 'I have been coming to Congress for many years, asking for one reform after another. It was presumed that I represented at least some church people. Now, Mr. Speaker, I *know* I speak for thousands.'"[51] With public opinion strongly favoring the bill, the House of Representatives approved the legislation in February 1964, and the Senate followed suit four months later. When he signed the 1964 Civil Rights Act in July, President Johnson observed that white and black Americans would be equal not only in the eyes of God but in polling booths and other public places as well. Speaking for his denomination, Arthur Lichtenberger gave thanks for what Congress and the president had accomplished. He admitted that legislation alone could not change racial customs, but he urged Episcopalians to do all they could to uphold the law and support the constitutional rights of all Americans.[52]

Whatever Lichtenberger's good intentions as he sought to provide moral guidance at a critical juncture in American history, his church still remained sadly divided over the meaning of the civil rights movement. Certainly black protests in Birmingham had caught the nation's eye and forced prominent white Episcopalians to engage themselves in action, but overall there was still little consensus beyond recognizing the need to maintain law, order, and a semblance of civility in the midst of the racial crisis. Indeed, the most telling event for the church in the early 1960s was not the bus pilgrimage of priests exposing the continued existence of segregation and prejudice in the South, nor the individual bravery of Duncan Gray in Mississippi, nor even the presence of neatly dressed clergy

and lay people at civil rights rallies in the nation's capital, but the suppression—little noticed in comparison to those other, highly publicized
activities—of the report from the National Council's own intergroup relations committee. As committee member Sarah Patton Boyle warned at
the time, the Christianity that most white Episcopalians practiced had
done virtually nothing to help African Americans, and in the future few
black people would listen to them. Whites, she said, needed to change
their attitude and demonstrate "a new spirit, the true Spirit of Christ,"
humbling themselves enough to accept the leadership of African Americans in the civil rights struggle. Boyle's advice went unheeded, however,
for whether they were conservative bishops in Alabama or umbrella-point-
ing, liberal establishment figures in Washington, white Episcopalians
seemed unready to step out of the limelight and aid African Americans in
authentic but less obtrusive ways.[53]

# 6

# *Christian Witness and Racial Integration in the Deep South*

At the end of 1961, Martin Luther King and the SCLC leadership took command of a crucial civil rights campaign in Albany, Georgia. Believing that only mass demonstrations and pressure from outside groups would win concessions from the white power structure in that town, King enlisted support from various allies throughout the country. John Morris was one of many white clergymen who responded to King's appeal, and he in turn engaged the ESCRU membership in the Albany protests. After participating in one of those demonstrations in August 1962, Morris happened to sit next to Coretta Scott King on an airplane flying back to Atlanta. Conversation quickly turned to the subject of their children, who were roughly the same age. At that time Morris's oldest daughter attended Lovett School, an all-white private institution affiliated with the Episcopal Church in Atlanta, and he recommended it to Mrs. King. Critical of black Episcopalians in his diocese for refusing to press the school's officials about their racial policies, Morris hoped that the well-known Baptist minister and his wife might be the first African Americans to break the color line at Lovett. The Kings took his advice, but when they submitted an application for their son Martin III, the trustees of the school curtly refused to accept it.[1]

The rejection of the famed civil rights leader's son began a protracted and acrimonious dispute between Morris and Randolph Claiborne, the bishop of Atlanta, over the desegregation of Lovett School. Although the school had an unmistakably Episcopal character—its charter stipulated that at least two-thirds of the board of trustees had to be Episcopalians committed to furthering "the cause of education and religion with reference to the teaching of the Episcopal faith"—Claiborne insisted that the internal affairs of Lovett were beyond his jurisdiction because it had no formal connection to the diocese. Even after the applications of two black Episcopalians were similarly rejected, Claiborne maintained his position, pronouncing the school "an independent autonomous corporation, subject to no ecclesiastical control." Though he was by no means a diehard segregationist and was one of many Atlanta clergymen who had signed a statement advocating acceptance of the *Brown* decision in the public schools nine years before, Claiborne was determined that no one other than he would decide the racial policies of the Episcopal Church in his diocese. When Morris demanded that the bishop obey national directives about the desegregation of church institutions, Claiborne reacted with anger. Exasperated by the ESCRU director's refusal to accept that nothing further was going to be done about Lovett, Claiborne took a drastic measure and revoked Morris's license to officiate as a priest.[2]

In the fall of 1963, as both the *New York Times* and *Time* published reports about the growing conflict among Episcopalians in Atlanta, Morris announced that interracial groups of clergy and laity from other states would picket in front of Lovett until the school admitted African Americans. On approximately half the school days in October and November, delegations of ESCRU members from several northern dioceses joined local protesters on the picket line at the entrance to the school. On the first days of the picketing, parents and children arriving at the school looked aghast as they saw priests in dark suits and clerical collars walking beside lay women and men with placards condemning segregation. As if this were not embarrassing enough, journalist Ralph McGill, then the most prominent lay Episcopalian in the city, publicly charged that diocesan officials were dishonest and hypocritical in pretending that a church-related school—operated by Episcopalians, using the *Book of Common Prayer,* and located on land owned by St. Philip's Cathedral— was not actually an "Episcopal" institution. He called it outrageous that the Lovett administration chose to retain the full liturgical trappings of the church but rejected its most important social teachings. As soon as Bishop Claiborne's assistant learned that McGill's criticisms were about to appear in the diocesan newspaper, he canceled the issue and confiscated copies that had already been printed. Infuriated that his own denomination had resorted to censorship, McGill withdrew from St. Philip's Cathedral (to which many Lovett trustees belonged) and transferred his membership to another parish in downtown Atlanta.[3]

As the picketing of Lovett School continued in early 1964, the con-

flict between Morris and Claiborne became increasingly personal and vituperative. Morris was left in an extremely awkward position as an unli-
censed priest who, because he had offended Claiborne's sense of deference,
lacked authority to conduct worship services in the diocese where he
lived. It was tragic and absurd, he said, that Episcopal clergy who were
avowed segregationists were able to officiate at services in their parishes
every week, while someone like himself who fully respected national directives on race was no longer allowed to function as a priest in Atlanta.
Refusing to bow to outside pressure but seeking a compromise, Claiborne
eventually concluded that the solution lay in ushering the school completely out of the Episcopal Church. In the end, therefore, the school's
trustees thoroughly revised their charter and removed all references to
"the Episcopal faith"; Lovett thus became a school with religious, but not
specifically Episcopal, ties. Although this decision was hardly satisfac-
tory to critics such as Morris and McGill, Claiborne could again claim
that his diocese was in full compliance with national church policies, for
no Episcopal institutions in Atlanta were segregated.[4]

The protracted battle over Lovett School proved to be the first of
several racial clashes that unsettled Episcopalians in southern dioceses in
1964. A short-lived but even more dramatic confrontation occurred in St.
Augustine, Florida, in early April. St. Augustine presented an inviting
target to civil rights groups, for though its tourist-based economy was
heavily dependent upon vacationers from the North, most of its white-
owned motels and restaurants refused to welcome African American cus-
tomers. The opening assault against segregation in St. Augustine was
planned by the Massachusetts chapter of SCLC, in which James Breeden,
a priest who served as the bishop's vicar on civil rights at the Episcopal
cathedral in Boston, was a key member. Breeden had been one of the
ESCRU prayer pilgrims, and with the assistance of his wife Jeanne, he
recruited several prominent church women to be part of the SCLC delegation heading to Florida that spring: Esther Burgess, wife of John Burgess, the newly consecrated suffragan bishop of Massachusetts; Mary
Peabody, wife of Malcolm Peabody, the retired bishop of Central New
York; and Hester Campbell, wife of Donald Campbell, a former suffragan
bishop of Los Angeles. Breeden had originally hoped that the bishops
would also accompany the SCLC demonstrators, but while all the men
were strong supporters of the civil rights movement, they were concerned
that their presence in St. Augustine might cause embarrassment for their
colleague, E. Hamilton West, the bishop of Florida. Since the three women
were not constrained by the same sense of ecclesiastical protocol as their

husbands, they gladly volunteered their services. Christian ideals compelled them to present a witness for racial integration in St. Augustine, they declared.[5]

The day after they arrived in the city, the women attempted to eat breakfast together at a segregated restaurant, but when the manager realized that the light-skinned Esther Burgess was a "Negro," she was asked to leave the building. Although all three women left the restaurant together, Mrs. Burgess was arrested later in the day for "trespassing and being an undesirable guest" at the bar of the Ponce de Léon Motor Lodge. The next morning, Mary Peabody and Hester Campbell accompanied a delegation of African Americans to worship at Trinity Church, the largest Episcopal parish in the city. They were unable to enter the church, however, because the vestry of the parish had pressured the rector, Charles Seymour, to cancel the regularly scheduled service that day. Stymied at the church, but seeing the value of their being arrested as civil rights demonstrators, the two women then returned to the Ponce de Léon bar with an interracial group and were quickly taken into custody by the police. Photographs taken of the three well-dressed ladies, looking both determined and bemused behind bars in a Florida jail cell, immediately appeared in the national press and demonstrated the absurdity of the city's segregation laws. Seventy-two–year-old "Grandmother Peabody"— "the indomitable *grande dame* of an old New England dynasty" as she was dubbed in the *Saturday Evening Post*—received special attention because she was the mother of Endicott Peabody, the governor of Massachusetts, who had encouraged her action. After the three women were released on bail, they returned to Boston, where they were greeted with warm expressions of admiration and support from church officials and various SCLC leaders.[6]

Although this initial foray by SCLC was aimed primarily at segregated commercial establishments in St. Augustine, John Morris was so encouraged by the publicity surrounding the arrest of the three Episcopalians that he decided to place further pressure on the rector and vestry at Trinity Church. Bishop West released a statement claiming that fears of violence had forced the temporary closing of Trinity Church when Peabody and Campbell came for worship, but Morris believed otherwise. West had a poor reputation among ESCRU members; even before the incident in St. Augustine, he was alleged to have kept clergy who belonged to ESCRU from receiving church positions in his diocese. As a result, Morris sought to test West's commitment to desegregation by sending interracial groups to attend services at Trinity Church throughout the spring and summer. John Snow, a white priest, and Edward Chase, a black vestry member, from Christ Church in Cambridge, Massachusetts, were among the first to attempt to worship together at the parish. Along with three African Americans who were not Episcopalians, they were seated and took part in a Sunday morning service. Despite being physically threatened by some white youths when they left the church, Snow actually was impressed by the polite reception his group received inside, and he later admitted that Bishop West's statement may have been correct: there had not been a formal policy of segregation at the church, but local racial customs alone had been sufficient to keep the races apart. Snow and Chase had tried to convince their fellow Episcopalians at St. Cyprian's Church, the African American parish in the city, to join them at Trinity, but the black Episcopalians refused to participate. Snow concluded that the people at St. Cyprian's were so "intimidated" by whites that they simply found it easier and more congenial to maintain their own parish—a position he thought was understandable.[7]

In late May, when SCLC resumed its campaign in St. Augustine, several ESCRU members offered their support. During the course of the protests, violence broke out when civil rights marchers were attacked by Klan members at the city's former slave market. A series of "wade-ins" at segregated city beaches also required a large contingent of police to stand in the water and protect demonstrators from mobs of angry whites. Sarah Patton Boyle was among the protesters taken into custody during those clashes. Arrested for the first time in her life, Boyle spent a week in jail in St. Augustine but took pride in the fact that she had been able to demonstrate the depth of her commitment both to the Christian faith and to the civil rights cause. Robert Hampshire, another former prayer pilgrim, was beaten up when he attempted to offer prayers for racial harmony at one of the wade-in demonstrations. Meanwhile, Henri Stines, a black priest who had recently joined the ESCRU staff, sought to worship at Trinity Church on a Sunday morning in June, but on that occasion he and the contingent of African American Episcopalians he led were barred by the ushers. When Stines pointed to the familiar church sign that said, "The Episcopal Church Welcomes You," one of the ushers remarked that the message did not apply to local black people, who could just as easily worship at St. Cyprian's. At that point Charles Seymour appeared, asserted his prerogative as rector to admit whomever he chose, and personally escorted Stines and his group into the church.[8]

This willingness to admit African Americans to worship soon cost Seymour his job. His vestry had already voted to withhold funds from their diocese because of support the national leadership of the Episcopal Church had given the civil rights demonstrations in St. Augustine. After Seymour made it clear that he did not intend to lead a racially segregated parish, the vestry demanded that he resign. When Hamilton West learned of the situation, he took the rector's side and upheld his authority; although the excitement caused by protests in St. Augustine might have upset parishioners, he said, they had no warrant to defy their rector on a matter concerning worship and would face excommunication if they continued to do so. Seymour, however, was not prepared to stay at Trinity and fight. Despite the encouragement he received from numerous Episcopal clergy during the crisis, he eventually accepted an offer to serve under less stressful conditions, and in the fall he left for a parish in New Orleans.[9]

In the midst of this controversy over civil rights in St. Augustine, an even more serious and violent conflict was under way in the state of Mississippi. Thanks to the leadership of Bob Moses and the Student Nonviolent Coordinating Committee (SNCC), black activists had been hard at work since 1961 pressing African Americans in Mississippi to register as voters. Despite repeated threats and random acts of violence against civil rights workers, youths connected with SNCC continued to flock to Mississippi in the hopes of transforming the most openly racist of all the southern states. In late 1963, SNCC also started to recruit white students from northern universities as temporary workers whose presence in the state was intended to focus national attention on black efforts to win political rights. In connection with that strategy, the Commission on Religion and Race of the National Council of Churches established ties with SNCC, and as a result more than fifty Protestant clergymen came to Hattiesburg in January 1964 to assist (as well as quietly protect) African Americans who were attempting to recruit new voters. Because the later departure of those ministers made the black community vulnerable again to attacks by local whites, both the Commission on Religion and Race and ESCRU discussed the creation of a continuing "ministry of presence" in Hattiesburg and in other key Mississippi towns.[10]

Thanks to the success of those efforts, SNCC leaders designated the summer of 1964 as the time for an even stronger drive to register black voters throughout the state. Although some SNCC workers thought African Americans should organize and run the program by themselves, the fact that whites were also involved had certain strategic advantages given the abysmal history of race relations in Mississippi. During the first half of 1964, therefore, SNCC and other civil rights organizations helped build support in the North for what was called the Mississippi Summer Project. Optimistic about what they hoped to accomplish, the corps of SNCC volunteers experienced a rude shock at the very outset of the project. On June 21, three civil rights workers (James Chaney, Michael Schwerner, and Andrew Goodman) disappeared in the vicinity of Philadelphia, Mississippi, and a few weeks later their bodies were found buried in an earth-filled dam outside the town. Despite the very real dangers they faced during the "Freedom Summer," hundreds of white Americans eventually put their lives and ideals on the line by serving alongside African Americans in Mississippi.[11]

What started as a project principally for white college students soon expanded as an influx of older "minister-counselors" joined the other volunteers coming down to Mississippi. As organizers of the 1964 summer project reasoned, the presence of clergy from outside the state not only reduced the risk of further violence against civil rights workers but also provided mature role models for the students—an important consideration due to the increased media attention that was expected. In April the Commission on Religion and Race had issued a call for clergy and laity to volunteer to serve during the summer months, and it hired Warren McKenna, then rector of a small parish in Holbrook, Massachusetts, to work in Jackson as the director of orientation for those recruits. An activist throughout his ministry, McKenna had been arrested during a civil rights protest in North Carolina the previous November, and he was thought to be an excellent choice to introduce volunteers from the North to the civil rights struggle. Arthur Walmsley, who had recently been placed in charge of civil rights matters for the Episcopal Church, also began to recruit Episcopalians for the program, and eventually almost three hundred clergy and lay people, including approximately fifty Episcopalians, spent time in Mississippi, most of them coming for two-week stints as part of their summer vacations.[12]

The experience in Mississippi proved to be eye-opening and deeply troubling to many of the Freedom Summer volunteers. Believing they would be able to affirm democratic values while achieving reconciliation between white and black southerners, they had come to Mississippi with high hopes. The situation, however, seemed unbelievable and almost demonic to many of them, and several participants reported that the culture of the state was alien and thoroughly unAmerican. A number of Episcopalians believed that their church affiliation also made them especially suspect in the eyes of local whites. One Episcopal priest who had driven his car from Texas decided to scrape the seal of the Episcopal Church off his bumper when he reached the Mississippi state line; he worried that the church seal might call too much attention to his car and thus place him in special danger. And when another car filled with white clergy drove across the state, the men intentionally decided to remove their clerical collars so they could not instantly be identified as civil rights workers. Whether or not to wear distinctive clothing, in fact, was a critical question each priest had to answer for himself. Some refrained from wearing clerical shirts and collars in order to appear less conspicuous, while others deliberately dressed as priests in the hope (often mistaken) that their appearance might deflect the resentment of hostile whites.[13]

Despite the fears and anxiety they felt, the volunteers tended to say that their faith had been deepened and profoundly changed by participating in the movement. Harry Bowie, a black priest from New Jersey, for example, viewed the breakthroughs that occurred in the voter registration drive in McComb as visible proof of God's intervention in history. Others said that the suffering they witnessed had given them an appreciation of what the true mission of the church should be. According to Malcolm Boyd, then on assignment as a special representative of ESCRU, "the only way to understand this twilight world . . . is to meditate on Christ hanging upon the cross in intense human pain but affirming, through the torture and death, that he was the Son of God." Boyd also said that the lively camaraderie among the activists he met reminded him of the spirit that had infused the early church. Indeed, Christ was more truly present in the homes of poor black people in Mississippi, he thought, than in the stained-glass windows and fine church buildings of pious white Christians who barred their doors to African Americans.[14]

Paul Moore was another clerical participant who shared Boyd's understanding of the theological significance of the ecumenical summer project. Although Moore had been elected suffragan bishop of the diocese of Washington in late 1963, he had no intention of allowing himself to become merely a church bureaucrat. Because of his prominent position in the church, he was free to spend significant amounts of time in Mississippi, principally in Hattiesburg and McComb, and he was given the sobriquet "the Big Fisherman" in order to confuse the Citizens' Council and the Klan concerning his whereabouts. Moore conferred with SNCC leaders, with church officials such as John Allin, and with ordinary citizens such as Red and Malva Heffner of McComb. The Heffners were Episcopalians who had told their priest, Colton Smith, that they were interested in talking with some of the civil rights workers in their town, and with his help they conferred with several activists at the church rectory. As news of that meeting began to circulate, the Heffners were harassed so viciously by their neighbors and other whites in McComb that they were eventually forced to flee Mississippi entirely.[15]

Despite the hardships suffered by so many people that summer, Moore regarded the freedom struggle in Mississippi as a movement in which the Holy Spirit was active, summoning church members to become engaged, in a highly unconventional setting. Colton Smith, for instance, wished to support the efforts of Harry Bowie, who had been his classmate in seminary just three years before. Although he knew his vestry would not tolerate the regular presence of a black priest at the parish, Smith gave Bowie a set of communion silver and an ironing board to use as an altar on which to celebrate the eucharist at the "freedom house" in McComb. Moore, too, used Smith's unusual liturgical equipment when he led an ecumenical contingent in worship there one Sunday morning. "The altar was an ironing board," he wrote, and "the reredos was the blasted out side of the Freedom Headquarters; the gospel began, 'And when [Christ] was come near, he beheld the city and wept over it.' We were there to weep with him. More deeply though, we were there to celebrate with him the glory of his kingdom as it appeared around us in courage, in patience, in love, in fire, in faith. We were there just to be there, just to say this is the Church, these purposes are of God. Through these young people, whether they know it or not, the Holy Spirit is working." When Moore reflected on this experience a few years later, he emphasized how it had taught him about "the presence of God in the flesh, the blood, the sweat, and the love" of the ordinary women and men, many with no formal religious affiliations, whom he met during the summer of 1964.[16]

In the aftermath of the excitement of their engagement in the civil rights struggle with hundreds of other idealistic Americans during the Freedom Summer, leaders such as Moore and Boyd traveled to St. Louis in mid-October for their denomination's General Convention. Far from affirming the progress that was being made on the civil rights front in secular circles, however, the church gathering revealed many of the divisions over race that still troubled the denomination at various levels in its institutional life. The convention opened in Kiel auditorium with a worship service at which Arthur Lichtenberger preached. Since the onset of Parkinson's disease had forced him to retire prematurely, the sermon was the last one Lichtenberger was to preach as presiding bishop—a fact that perhaps encouraged him to speak frankly about the state of his church. He said he wanted to register "a protest against the angry men . . . who, in their criticism of the Church, the establishment, if you will, never speak a word of hope or joy." In the past year he had received letters from hundreds of church members that reflected a "mood of dark despair" in many parishes and dioceses throughout the country. "Instead of . . . sticking to religion and having our bishops dress up and conduct confirmation services, like the heads of our religion," one letter said, "you want them to get mixed up with minority groups [and] with issues that have nothing to do with religion." In Lichtenberger's view, such words represented an outright denial of the Christian faith: the belief that "God so loved the world—*the world*—that He gave His only begotten son, Jesus Christ." "Religion in general," he feared, had taken the place of "solid Christian convictions" in the hearts and minds of many Episcopalians. Instead of retreating into houses of worship and closing their doors, church people needed to step out into the world and involve themselves in politics and in the fight against injustice.[17]

Lichtenberger's warning notwithstanding, the convention had barely begun when a political matter made an unwelcome intrusion into the ecclesiastical affairs over which bishops and deputies were deliberating. The convention coincided with the final month of the presidential campaign pitting Lyndon Johnson against Republican challenger Barry Goldwater. Goldwater, himself an Episcopalian, was known for his archconservative views; because of the strong backing he received from numerous right-wing ideologues and segregationists, liberals feared that his election might bring the gains of the civil rights movement to a halt. William Stringfellow, one of Goldwater's most vocal critics in the Episcopal Church, decided that the convention gathering was an ideal time for liberal Episcopalians to speak against their fellow church member and denounce his ideas. With the support of John Morris, who wanted to keep goading the church into taking a stronger position on race, Stringfellow released "a Statement of Conscience on Racism in the Presidential Campaign," which condemned Goldwater's "transparent exploitation of racism among white citizens," accused him of seeking "the votes of white racists," and invited unbiased Episcopalians to join together in expressing their displeasure with the Republican candidate's views. Approximately eight hundred clergy and laity eventually signed Stringfellow's document.[18]

Stringfellow never said he was speaking for the Episcopal Church as a whole, but reports in the national press indicated that his statement was an official pronouncement of the General Convention. That suggestion outraged conservatives in the church, and the House of Deputies immediately formed a special committee to investigate the matter. Although Joseph Harte, the bishop of Arizona; National Council member Stephen Shadegg; and the vestry of Goldwater's parish, Trinity Cathedral in Phoenix, had already endorsed the candidacy of the Republican senator, the convention committee returned with a resolution deploring what Stringfellow had done and affirming the denomination's official neutrality on the election. Despite this censure and the criticism he received, Stringfellow expressed satisfaction with his mission; he had succeeded not only in calling attention to the implications of racism in the Goldwater campaign but also in exposing some of the hypocrisy about politics among Episcopal leaders. Morris agreed with his assessment, and a few weeks later ESCRU helped raise funds to reimburse Stringfellow for the expenses he had incurred at the convention.[19]

The church's divisions over the civil rights movement continued throughout the convention. Episcopalians officially honored Martin Luther King by inviting him to address a session of the House of Deputies on the eve of his winning the Nobel Peace Prize. Although a few white deputies refused either to stand for King or applaud his speech, he was generally well received as he called upon Episcopalians to assist in the struggle of African Americans for human rights in the South. He also spoke to a banquet sponsored by ESCRU, commending Morris and others in that organization for doing "so much to make the Gospel of Our Lord and Saviour Jesus Christ relevant and meaningful in this period of social transition" and warning Episcopalians about the consequences of ignoring the great revolution that was stirring the nation.[20] However, when the House of Deputies debated a resolution supporting one of the central principles for which King stood—the right of citizens to disobey unjust laws—the measure was defeated. Although a majority of the clerical deputies approved the resolution, it failed to obtain the necessary concurrent majority from the lay deputies. This decision so angered first-time deputy Thurgood Marshall (then serving as a judge on the federal appeals court in New York) that he stormed out of the meeting hall and left the convention. For Marshall, his fellow lay deputies' rejection of the civil disobedience resolution was extremely irksome, since based on his previous experience with the church, he had expected that the white clergy, not the laity, would block the motion. Further confusing the matter, the American Church Union, an otherwise conservative Anglo-Catholic organization, backed the resolution strictly on theological grounds. Since the church and its clergy were ultimately subject to an authority higher than the state, the Anglo-Catholics argued, they had a divinely ordained right to take principled positions that were contrary to mere human laws. Meanwhile, the House of Bishops reversed the position it had taken at the 1958 General Convention (when it condemned the "civil disobedience" of white citizens heading the massive resistance campaigns in southern states) and passed its own resolution favoring what it called "Christian obedience." Agreeing with the American Church Union, the bishops contended that human laws were at best reflections of "immutable divine law which man did not devise." Christians therefore were not expected to respect all secular laws equally: when one was clearly unjust, they had a moral obligation to violate it.[21]

In spite of this disagreement over the propriety of church members' involvement in protest activities, the convention passed two other critical resolutions on race that directly affected the institutional church. The first resolution added a new statute to the denomination's canon law: "Canon 16, Sec. 4. Every communicant or baptized member of this Church shall be entitled to equal rights and status in any Parish or Mission thereof. He shall not be excluded from the worship or Sacraments of the Church, nor from parochial membership, because of race, color, or ethnic origin." The second resolution affirmed "the supernatural unity of mankind in the common waters of Baptism" through belief in the universal lordship of Christ. Based on this theological reasoning, the bishops and deputies together agreed that "racial discrimination, segregation, and the exclusion of any person in the human family, because of race, from the rites and activities of the Church" were wrong. On the one hand, the two resolutions did no more than continue the denomination's long-standing policy of recognizing no racial barriers in worship. All people were welcome to receive communion or present their children for baptism or confirmation in the Episcopal Church. On the other hand, as both the most vocal advocates and the most adamant opponents of the resolutions insisted, the convention was also implicitly recognizing the legitimacy of interracial marriages. As a result of those pronouncements, the church had placed itself at odds with the antimiscegenation laws that still existed in seventeen states.[22]

The 1964 General Convention made one further important decision, when the House of Bishops elected John Hines of Texas to replace Arthur Lichtenberger as the presiding bishop. Some black Episcopalians were at first uneasy about Hines because he had grown up in South Carolina and had served only in southern dioceses. They also remembered the problem of segregation in Houston that had caused the removal of the 1955 General Convention from that city. Hines's record on racial issues was commendable, however, and after succeeding Clinton Quin as diocesan bishop in Texas, he spent the early years of his episcopate battling—often against stout resistance from T. Robert Ingram and others—for an end to racial prejudice and for the desegregation of all church-related institutions in Texas. Unlike Randolph Claiborne of Atlanta, Hines thought these theological convictions ought to be put into practice, and—as Lyndon Johnson did—he pressed his fellow white southerners to come to terms with the nation's changing racial mores. In his initial statements after his election in St. Louis, moreover, Hines named racial equality as the primary issue facing the church in the 1960s, and he said his denomination needed "to speak out, loud and clear—and pay up personally" through firsthand involvement in the social ferment of the times.[23]

It did not receive the headlines surrounding either the election of John Hines or the debates over civil disobedience, but one further troubling question lurked behind the scenes at the 1964 General Convention—an issue whose full importance would not become clear to white Episcopalians until later in the decade. This concerned the status of the five black colleges supported by the church through the American Church Institute. When the ACI trustees, most of whom were white, submitted their triennial report to the 1964 convention, they mentioned the need to reconsider the future of those schools and to decide whether "the so-called Negro colleges would continue to serve an important function in American society, regardless of the integration movement."[24] At approximately the same time, one of the ACI schools had become the target of an investigation conducted under the auspices of ESCRU. In that investigation Naomi Long, a white Australian employed as a consultant by the Girls' Friendly Society in Michigan, and Malcolm Boyd examined a controversy surrounding the firing of three faculty members at St. Paul's College in Lawrenceville, Virginia. Long and Boyd maintained that the faculty members had been dismissed because of their civil rights activities and that the school itself had become no more than "a breeding place for 'Uncle Tomism'" in the South—a stinging accusation that the African American president of St. Paul's, Earl McClenney, vigorously denied.[25]

These charges sparked a heated exchange between the ESCRU leadership and officials of the Home Department, the denominational agency responsible for the operations of the ACI. Daniel Corrigan, the director of the Home Department, complained that Boyd and Long had failed to speak with people on both sides of the controversy and thus had not presented an impartial account. Tollie Caution and other officers of the ACI thought the ESCRU investigation, which had been conducted by two white people with little prior experience with or knowledge of black colleges in the South, failed to appreciate the importance of such institutions for African Americans. Far from encouraging "Uncle Tomism," colleges like St. Paul's were in fact "the birthplace of the Negro student non-violent movement," Caution said.[26] John Morris refused to retreat from the position his organization had assumed, and he continued to stress the importance of integration for all members of the church. Another ESCRU report that spring, in fact, had raised a similar question: since African Americans were often as reluctant as white southerners to change their habits, was it wise to allow black Episcopalians to maintain their own separate camps and conference centers? Because of the importance of fostering the "inclusive nature" of the church, that report concluded, "Negro Churchmen must venture away from the security of old patterns" and attempt to integrate all-white facilities.[27] For the sake of the unity of the church and in witness to the unity of humankind, then, the "subsidized separatism" of black Episcopalians would have to end.[28]

Alleged black self-segregation was an important concern of John Morris and ESCRU—and thus remained a touchy subject for Tollie Caution and the denomination's domestic missionary staff over the next few years. Most Episcopalians involved with the civil rights movement, however, still regarded it as secondary to the larger struggle for racial equality. Although the issue returned with a vengeance in the late 1960s, no definitive solution to the quandary was either required or possible in 1964, and thus discussion of the matter quietly subsided. Instead, as soon as the convention adjourned, the church's African American and white activists refocused their energy and attention on the highly explosive situation in Mississippi.

In the aftermath of the Freedom Summer project, the leadership of the Commission on Religion and Race had developed an organization, the Delta Ministry, through which mainline Protestants could make a long-term commitment to community development in Mississippi. The organization opened a permanent office in September 1964 in the relatively liberal city of Greenville (Hodding Carter's home and the chief town in the fertile but impoverished Delta region that stretched along the Mississippi river from Memphis, Tennessee to Vicksburg). An ecumenical agency under the direction of the National Council of Churches, the Delta project was conceived as "a ministry of reconciliation" that would work for the alleviation of poverty and an end to paternalistic patterns of race relations. Paul Moore was chosen to chair the executive board that supervised the overall operations of the program, and Arthur Thomas, a white

Methodist minister, and Warren McKenna became the director and the assistant director of the Delta Ministry at its Greenville headquarters. The organization also opened satellite offices in McComb, headed by Harry Bowie, and in Hattiesburg, headed by Robert Beech, a white Presbyterian minister.[29]

From the outset, however, the predominantly white, northern establishment leadership of the National Council of Churches in New York was viewed with skepticism by people within the state—black activists as well as white conservatives—who questioned both the tactics and the strategic goals of the Delta Ministry. John ("Jack") Pratt, for example, the lay Episcopalian who served as legal counsel of the Commission on Religion and Race, had no civil rights experience before being hired by the National Council of Churches in 1963, and though he learned a good deal in a year, his relationship with Bob Moses and the SNCC staff in Mississippi was consistently shaky. At one of the planning sessions for the summer project, Pratt opposed the participation of the National Lawyers' Guild, a left-of-center organization that had been invited by SNCC and CORE to provide legal assistance to the student volunteers. Jack Greenberg of the NAACP, Robert Spike of the Commission on Religion and Race, and Pratt threatened to pull their organizations out of the summer project if the National Lawyers' Guild joined it. Pratt also prevented the Southern Conference Educational Fund (SCEF) representatives Anne and Carl Braden from joining the Mississippi movement. The cold war mentality of the early 1960s continued to exert a powerful hold over the white liberals in the National Council of Churches leadership, and just as John Morris and ESCRU had kept the Bradens at arm's length in 1961, so they were excluded from working as allies of the mainline denominations in Mississippi three years later. Finally, at the Democratic national convention in August, Pratt was a member of the middle-of-the-road coalition that backed Lyndon Johnson's decision not to recognize the delegates of the Mississippi Freedom Democratic Party—a bitter blow to the left-wing activists registering black voters in the state.[30]

The Delta Ministry faced even stronger opposition from white church members in Mississippi, most notably John Allin, the bishop coadjutor of the Episcopal diocese. Allin was by no means a rigid segregationist, but he was at home in the paternalistic culture of the church in Mississippi. He had often worked with conservative black leaders in an effort to better race relations in the state, and he was a leading figure in the Committee of Concern, an interfaith and interracial organization that aided African American congregations by restoring over fifty churches destroyed by white arsonists in 1964 and 1965. When other white Protestant churches in Mississippi closed their doors to black worshipers, he declared forthrightly that his denomination intended to welcome all of God's people. Allin believed, however, that responsibility for the state's racial situation belonged to local leaders, so he deeply resented the flood of northerners who came to Mississippi during the summer. He especially disapproved of Episcopal clergy from the Northeast who assisted civil rights organizations but failed to coordinate their efforts with his. As he said to John Morris, he disliked "free and somewhat detached agencies deciding to override the judgment of other duly constituted agents" in southern dioceses. As a result the two Episcopal priests most actively involved in the Delta Ministry—Warren McKenna and Harry Bowie—came under intense scrutiny from him in the fall of 1964.[31]

Allin's opposition started even before the National Council of Churches officially launched the Delta Ministry, for he questioned why a church organization with headquarters in New York wished to form an agency that essentially bypassed the white clergy in Mississippi. Since the social outreach programs of the National Council of Churches were already viewed with suspicion by many conservative lay Episcopalians, his challenge received ample support. After the Delta Ministry began its operations, Allin also accused it of ignoring spiritual concerns altogether and bringing conflict, not reconciliation, between the races. He was joined in that attack by Hodding Carter III, then a member of the Delta Ministry executive board and his father's associate at the *Delta Democrat-Times* in Greenville. From the perspective of the Delta Ministry staff in Mississippi, however, Allin's and Carter's views were outdated, paternalistic, and—at their worst—racist. And though white church leaders in New York such as Robert Spike and Arthur Walmsley at first sought to gain the cooperation of Carter and Allin, they were realistic about the overall situation and knew that one of the Delta Ministry's underlying goals was the subversion of traditional patterns of race relations in the South.[32]

Although Allin's initial objections to the Delta Ministry did not affect his denomination directly, the issues he raised later surfaced in the course of discussions about finances at the meetings of the National Council of the Episcopal Church. After the release of Arthur Lichtenberger's Whitsuntide message in 1963, several thousand dollars had been contributed by church members in support of the denomination's work in race relations. As a result the National Council not only created a "Church and Race" fund in which it placed that money, but it also appealed for an additional $150,000 to aid the civil rights movement in 1964. At the council meeting in December 1963, however, two critical restrictions were placed on the use of that fund: first, National Council employees would not be allowed to engage in civil rights activities without obtaining the approval of the diocesan bishop in whatever southern state was affected; and second, the "Church and Race" money had to be employed primarily to aid programs sponsored by groups affiliated with the Episcopal Church. Arguing that the diocese was the basic organizational unit of the church, conservatives wished to curtail the ability of national officers such as Arthur Walmsley and Neil Tarplee to initiate civil rights actions without local white support. A number of people protested, arguing that such provisions would also curtail the constitutional right of denominational officers to participate as private citizens in demonstrations in southern dioceses, but the National Council expressed its hope that "Christian courtesy" would ultimately prevail whenever conflicts arose between diocesan bishops and national church employees.[33]

In the aftermath of civil rights activities in which Episcopalians had been prominent participants in the spring and summer of 1964, conservatives on the Executive Council (the National Council had changed its name in the fall of that year) were determined to limit future actions by clergy and denominational employees. At its final meeting in 1964, therefore, the council passed a "compromise" similar to the one developed a year before; it authorized an appeal for another one hundred thousand dollars for the Church and Race fund but stipulated that no Episcopal priest could work for an agency receiving money from the fund without the approval of the local bishop—a provision designed specifically to give John Allin veto power over the ministries of the Episcopalians on the Delta Ministry staff. After the ESCRU leadership and other liberals loudly complained about that policy, John Hines sought to reopen the issue in early 1965 and invited Paul Moore, Harry Bowie, Robert Spike, and Allin to explain their positions at an Executive Council session. No one questioned that a diocesan bishop was ultimately responsible for church affairs in his diocese, but how far did that authority extend? Did the bishop coadjutor of Mississippi have a right to curtail the secular activities of two priests (McKenna and Bowie) who were not "canonically resident" in his diocese but who were fully supported by their own diocesan bishops (Anson Stokes of Massachusetts and Alfred Banyard of New Jersey), by the ecumenical church agency that employed them, and by the local black people with whom they worked in Greenville and McComb? After an extended debate that raised important questions about church governance as well as about civil rights issues, the Executive Council divided roughly along regional lines. Most members from the South—the minority—backed Allin's position, but the council as a whole voted to rescind the earlier resolution, thus removing the restrictions on the use of the Church and Race fund by Delta Ministry personnel. A few weeks later, an advertisement appeared in several church magazines, depicting a racially mixed group of Episcopalians walking together behind a cross and an ESCRU banner at the March on Washington. "Men are on the move in our land today," the ad triumphantly declared; "every Church person, of every race," had a responsibility to assist the civil rights movement by making a financial contribution to the Church and Race fund.[34]

Nonetheless, national church leaders again found themselves arguing about the value of the Delta Ministry a few months later. The new controversy was started unwittingly by Daisuke Kitagawa, the head of the Division of Domestic Mission, who thought that if the church wished to address race relations in a responsible fashion, it needed to concentrate on the "cure of souls" and minister pastorally to segregationist and integrationist alike. He well understood the impact of racial prejudice—as a Japanese American, he had experienced the tangible effects of racism in an internment camp during World War II—but he was still committed to an approach that offered Christian forgiveness, not simply condemnation, to bigots. Since this strategy also appealed to clergy like Duncan Gray and Will Campbell, who had attempted to minister in a similar way to whites in Mississippi, Kitagawa traveled to that state in May 1965 in the hopes of fostering further racial reconciliation. When he returned to New York, he circulated a report that was critical of the Delta Ministry and accused it of failing to attend to its ostensibly religious mission. Not only had the Delta Ministry heightened racial tensions in Mississippi, he claimed, but it had also subtly undermined the involvement of middle-class African Americans with "the Negro masses," who now looked to the New York-based National Council of Churches for support. Although most white Episcopalians in Mississippi were comforted by these findings and applauded Kitagawa's efforts, Paul Moore immediately blasted the report, charging that Kitagawa had consulted only whites and had not been shown the true situation in the Delta. In addition Moore accused him of violating Executive Council procedures, for Arthur Walmsley of the Department of Christian Social Relations, not Kitagawa of the Home Department, was the proper liaison between national church headquarters and the Delta Ministry.[35]

This dispute over Kitagawa's trip to Mississippi and his subsequent report reveals a number of unresolved questions concerning the denomination's handling of race relations in that period. At the most fundamental level, it shows the disagreement over the proper way for a religious body to approach civil rights issues. Which model should the church use to confront racism: a pastoral-theological (condemn the sin, not the sinner) or a social-action (attack the evil and the system that sustains it) approach? As Moore complained, a gap had developed in the Episcopal Church "between those who feel the Church must be involved in shaping society . . . and those who would be content to remain on the sidelines in peace." Second, on a personal level there was considerable irony in the fact that Moore, a white establishment figure from an extremely privileged background, accused Kitagawa, a member of a minority group who had suffered personally because of his race, of misunderstanding the marginal position of African Americans in Mississippi. While Moore and his family had always been "involved in shaping society," Kitagawa had been a victim of white, Anglo-Saxon hegemony. Kitagawa's empathy for the black middle class, on the other hand, contrasted sharply with Moore's belief that the poorest blacks should have been the primary subjects of the church's concern. Finally, from a bureaucratic perspective, Moore's complaint that Kitagawa had acted outside his assigned jurisdiction paralleled Allin's criticism of Moore and the Episcopalians on the Delta Ministry staff for allegedly failing to coordinate their work with him. Since Moore doubtless was aware of this dynamic, he was determined to turn denomination protocol to his advantage on that occasion.[36]

The Executive Council was never required to respond to this controversy, because while Moore and Kitagawa argued behind the scenes, two well-known prosegregation parishes, St. John's Church in Savannah, Georgia, and St. Paul's Church in Selma, Alabama, seized the national spotlight instead. St. John's was the largest and wealthiest parish in the diocese of Georgia, but its rector, Ernest Risley, had continued to maintain the policy of racial segregation that had been in place when he began his ministry there in 1936. Although the church had been the target of periodic kneel-in attempts by interracial groups in the early 1960s, ushers had successfully barred the doors every time African Americans attempted to enter. Albert Stuart, the diocesan bishop, was displeased with that situation, but he did not think he should use his authority to override it. With the passage of canon 16:4 at the 1964 General Convention, however, he had told Risley that the Episcopal Church now unquestionably required the removal of racial barriers in parish life. Risley remained adamant about resisting change, and when Henri Stines and John Morris attempted to lead a contingent of ESCRU members into St. John's on

Easter Sunday in 1965, the rector refused to let them enter. Soon after
that confrontation, St. John's decided to follow a logical course and disas-
sociate itself from the Episcopal Church. Risley also renounced his priestly
orders, and in his parting words he accused the denomination of having
slipped into heresy by substituting ideas about racial equality and social
relevance for the classic theological beliefs of Christianity.[37]

A conflict similar to the one in Savannah arose at St. Paul's Church
in Selma, which became the focus of protests during the larger civil rights
struggle in Alabama in 1965. SNCC workers had been pressing for voting
rights for African Americans in Selma since 1963, but the critical moment occurred in March 1965 when city police and state troopers assaulted a force of activists who were attempting to march to Montgomery
to present a petition to Governor Wallace. Reports about this attack at
the Edmund Pettus Bridge, in which scores of defenseless marchers were
bloodied and beaten, were broadcast over national television on the
evening of March 7. John Morris had been in Selma at the time, and he
stood with Andrew Young of SCLC observing the attack a short distance
away. After aiding the injured marchers, Young and Morris were among
the people who telephoned Martin Luther King to discuss how the movement should respond. They convinced King to send telegrams to several
hundred prominent religious leaders, inviting them to take part in another march in Selma, and in the next few days thousands of people from
across the United States came to Alabama to express their solidarity. Eventually, more than five hundred Episcopalians—including Presiding Bishop
Hines and approximately ten percent of all Episcopal clergy in the country—joined the civil rights entourage in Selma. Bishop Carpenter called
the Selma protest "a foolish business and sad waste of time," and he urged
his fellow church members to go home. Black Episcopalians in Carpenter's
diocese, however, took a far different view of the events in their state.
According to Vernon Jones, the rector of the African American parish at
Tuskegee Institute, Carpenter and the white leadership of the diocese
seemed "to miss the point entirely" when it came to race relations and
simply refused to understand the religious basis that was inspiring so
many Episcopalians to come to Selma on behalf of civil rights.[38]

Since most of the Episcopalians who had come to Selma were also
ESCRU members, Morris encouraged them to turn their attention to St.
Paul's Church. The leadership of St. Paul's had always had a poor reputation even among white Alabamans for their complete indifference to African Americans in Selma. Both T. Frank Mathews, the rector, and his
vestry still maintained that tradition in 1965, and when "a motley, as-

sorted, racially mixed group" of civil rights marchers arrived in the city, they made it clear that none of them were welcome to worship at St. Paul's.[39] Outraged by this response to their presence, representatives of ESCRU made two attempts to enter St. Paul's en masse. The first occurred on Sunday morning March 14, when John Morris and Malcolm ("Mike") Peabody, president of the ESCRU board of directors and one of Mary Peabody's sons, led an interracial group to the church. They were met by a phalanx of ushers—men intent on "guarding the church from the Church," Morris quipped—who informed them that only clergy and white lay people would be allowed to come in. Refusing to accept those conditions, the entire group knelt at the front door, spent a few minutes in corporate prayer, and then somberly left the premises.[40]

The second, more dramatic attempt took place on the day before the climactic march from Selma to Montgomery began. Kim Myers, then the suffragan bishop of Michigan, had been trying for several days to gain access to St. Paul's, arguing that—as a bishop—he had a moral right to celebrate the eucharist at the altar of any Episcopal parish he visited. When he asked Carpenter to make the rector and vestry of St. Paul's respect that episcopal prerogative, Carpenter refused and angrily rebuked him for his arrogance. On Saturday March 20, therefore, Myers led a group of two hundred people from Brown Chapel, the African Methodist Episcopal church where the civil rights marchers were gathering, to St. Paul's, where a line of police kept them away from the building. With television and motion-picture cameras rolling, the ESCRU contingent recited the penitential office from the Prayer Book and then walked solemnly back to Brown Chapel. There Myers celebrated communion on an altar set up on the sidewalk—a gesture intended to symbolize both the presence of Christ in worldly affairs and the church's inherent concern with society. It was a glorious moment for all who gathered around the altar in the black community that afternoon. Many of the people participating in the outdoor eucharist believed that the great day of unity and integration for which they were striving had at last arrived. Transcending not only racial but also denominational divisions, they shared the sacramental bread and wine and experienced for the first time "the oneness of the Body of Christ and the equality of all men."[41]

The next day the "Great March" started at the Pettus Bridge, and it ended on the grounds of the Alabama state capitol four days later. F. Goldthwaite Sherrill, a priest from Massachusetts and son of the former presiding bishop, Henry Knox Sherrill, was designated to represent ESCRU among the three hundred people who walked the entire fifty-four-mile

route from Selma to Montgomery. He envisioned the march as the culmi-
nation of a protracted effort to affirm racial integration throughout the
United States. To Sherrill and many other Americans, victory in the civil
rights struggle seemed imminent, for Lyndon Johnson had just thrown
the weight of the presidency behind their cause by sending to Congress a
bill designed to guarantee voting rights for all citizens. Buoyed by this
support, more than twenty-five thousand people gathered in Montgomery to hear Martin Luther King and others proclaim that the long years
of oppression and segregation in Alabama were about to end. King
praised those who had joined black southerners on the march to Montgomery. There had been a veritable "pilgrimage of clergymen and laymen of every race and faith pouring into Selma to face danger at the
side of its embattled Negroes," he said, and thanks to their help, African
Americans would finally be able to cast off "the centuries-old blight" of
racial prejudice.[42]

After the cheering in Montgomery had subsided and most of the
participants returned home, the church members who had been present
when King spoke offered their own unique religious interpretations of
the event. John Morris, for example, thought that church members in the
United States had reached a time of unprecedented opportunity, when
God was calling them to be "a light set on a hill" and giving them power
to "revive the American Dream and clothe it with meaning for multiracial America." William Workman, a canon at the National Cathedral in
Washington, was similarly hopeful; he described the gathering in Alabama as "another Jerusalem, . . . another Bethlehem," a point when God's
purposes for humankind had again been revealed to believers. Roberta
Walmsley, a laywoman and wife of Arthur Walmsley, found the experience at Selma to be tremendously uplifting, for she believed it symbolized the church itself moving toward a transcendent goal. And William
Stringfellow said that the Selma-Montgomery march was one of the greatest
ecumenical religious assemblies that had ever taken place, drawing a diversity of people together as at Pentecost and restoring spiritual vitality
to their churches.[43]

ESCRU even achieved a measure of success at St. Paul's Church a
few days after the march concluded. Bishops Carpenter and Murray and
Mathews the rector were sufficiently embarrassed by the national attention the parish had received that, after further negotiations with the St.
Paul's vestry, they persuaded the ushers to obey the denomination's canon
16:4 and admit African Americans to services. As a result Judith Upham
and Jonathan Daniels, two white seminarians from the Episcopal Theo-

logical School, quietly brought an interracial group into the church on the last Sunday in March. Carpenter was still miffed, however, that several national church officers had not given him sufficient warning before entering his diocese to take part in the Selma demonstrations. Wishing to exact some revenge, he came personally with his complaint to the May 1965 meeting of the Executive Council. Arguing that he expected the staff of his denomination to work for the advance of God's kingdom not for the civil rights movement, he demanded that all the church's guidelines be obeyed in his diocese. Staff members could take part in demonstrations as private citizens, he conceded, but those who were priests had no authority either to wear clerical clothing in civil rights marches or to imply that they represented the Episcopal Church at those events. Murray and other conservatives on the council strongly supported Carpenter, and a lengthy debate about the church's appropriate social role ensued. When a vote was taken, the Executive Council divided evenly on the issue, and only John Hines's tie-breaking vote ended the deadlock and overruled Carpenter's protest.[44]

Concerned about the conditions under which African Americans in Alabama lived, Morris Samuel (a former prayer pilgrim), Judith Upham, and Jonathan Daniels remained in Selma for several weeks after the march as special representatives of ESCRU. Upham and Daniels met repeatedly with Frank Mathews and other members of St. Paul's to explain their theological reasons for supporting racial integration, and they continued to bring interracial groups to worship at the church on Sunday mornings. Although Mathews was cordial and patient with the seminarians throughout this period, the ushers of his parish were not cooperative but insisted that black worshipers had to sit at the back of the church and take communion only after all whites in the congregation had received it. Distressed that St. Paul's was fulfilling the letter, but not the spirit, of the denominational canons, Upham and Daniels went to Birmingham to discuss the matter with Carpenter. When Carpenter remarked that sitting at the back of the church might give African Americans a beneficial lesson in "humility," the seminarians responded that there was a profound "difference between humility and humiliation"—humility being a quality that all church people, white as well as black, needed to practice. When the conversations with Carpenter proved unproductive, Upham, Daniels, and other ESCRU members picketed outside the diocesan headquarters with signs proclaiming that white Episcopalians in Selma had resurrected the "slave gallery" custom of antebellum times.[45]

Upham left Alabama to spend the summer working at a camp for inner-city children in St. Louis, but Daniels chose to remain in Selma and assist SNCC with voter registration in the rural areas outside the city. He saw his civil rights involvement as intimately connected with his religious faith, and believing that the Holy Spirit had led him to Selma, he wanted to be engaged in what Dietrich Bonhoeffer had called "worldly holiness" by witnessing to the unity in which God had created humankind. Daniels was eventually arrested during a civil rights demonstration in Lowndes County. Released from the jail in Hayneville, Alabama, on August 20, he went with Roman Catholic priest Richard Morrisroe and two black teenagers, Ruby Sales and Joyce Bailey, to buy soft drinks at a small store in the town. As they started to enter the building, Tom Coleman, a white man armed with a shotgun, accosted them and abruptly opened fire. Sales was closest to Coleman, but Daniels pushed her to the ground and received the shotgun blast in his chest at point-blank range. He was killed instantly, and as Morrisroe and Bailey turned to run, Coleman also fired at them, severely wounding Morrisroe in the back. Coleman was charged with manslaughter, yet though there was no question he had killed Daniels, the jury acquitted him when the case came to trial in the fall—a verdict that John Hines and other church leaders assailed as a fundamental "travesty of justice."[46]

As soon as John Morris learned of Daniels's death, he made arrangements for the body to be flown back to Daniels's home in Keene, New Hampshire, for burial. In place of a formal eulogy at the funeral service, excerpts from Daniels's theological writings were read aloud to the mourners gathered at St. James' Church. In one of those selections, he wrote that he had stopped being afraid of death in Alabama, for he realized that "I had truly been baptized into the Lord's death and Resurrection, that in the only sense that really matters I am already dead, and my life is hid with Christ in God." Stokely Carmichael, the SNCC organizer with whom Daniels had worked most closely in Alabama, was deeply upset by the murder and remarked that Daniels had "lived like Christ." In tears at the interment following the funeral, Carmichael joined hands with other mourners, who softly sang "We Shall Overcome" beside the grave. At the same time, memorial services were held in many other churches throughout the country, and the slain seminarian received numerous tributes. Frank Mathews expressed shock at what had happened and offered prayers at St. Paul's. William Stringfellow, who had been one of Daniels's mentors, called him "an authentic Christian" who had died simply for doing what the gospel demanded; Judith Upham believed his witness demonstrated that "God requires not extraordinary people, but ordinary people with an extraordinary commitment as channels for His grace-full action in the world."[47]

Charles Carpenter and George Murray also condemned Daniels's murder, but they saw it as the logical consequence of increasing lawlessness, for which civil rights activists were at least as responsible as racist whites. On a visit to the Episcopal Theological School in the fall of 1965, Murray spoke with faculty and students there about factors that had led to the seminarian's death. Emphasizing the importance of the House of Bishops' condemnation of civil disobedience at the General Convention of 1958, he argued that prointegration Episcopalians had committed a serious error by reversing their position and endorsing the concept in 1964. Civil disobedience was always "a two-edged sword," he insisted, because it could be used by men like Coleman, who did not understand the "technical niceties" of church resolutions, to commit acts of mayhem. Carpenter introduced a similar theme when he addressed his annual diocesan convention in January 1966. The prior year had been an extremely difficult one for the Episcopal Church in Alabama, he said, but he prayed that all "unwanted interlopers" from the North would now return home and work to improve race relations in the places where they lived. Like those who came to make a witness on behalf of racial integration at Selma, therefore, Carpenter was concerned about fostering social and ecclesiastical harmony. Unlike those who favored integration, however, he was not interested in creating a new world in which equality was the source from which peace and concord flowed. Rather, he hoped that by preserving the old order, based on the strict subordination of one race to another, all people would learn to accept their proper place within a benevolent but stratified society.[48]

Despite the seemingly implacable views of the bishops of Alabama, and despite even the sadness surrounding Jonathan Daniels's murder—one of several that occurred within the context of the civil rights struggle in Selma—church leaders who emphasized integration as the goal of their work could feel well satisfied by mid-1965. The climactic eucharistic celebration in front of Brown Chapel seemed to embody perfectly the vision they were seeking, and for a few minutes at least, a small gathering of Episcopalians experienced the full measure of unity—racial, cultural, national, and religious—that had first inspired the formation of ESCRU. At the eucharist in Selma, black and white, male and female, southerner and northerner, Protestant and Catholic worshiped together and prepared themselves spiritually to march together to Montgomery as part of a great, diverse assortment of Americans. Not only was the dream of integration finally being realized that day, but the church (or at least a portion of it) was present at the event, witnessing to its theological ideals in the heart of the deep South. John Morris and his colleagues were right to describe the occasion in millenarian terms, for it was an extraordinary—and ephemeral—moment.

# Part III

# Fragmentation

American attitudes towards the Church and church life are changing rapidly. It is not civil rights or social action militancy which has created the gap (though to some extent it has exacerbated bad feelings in some places), but the difference in attitude towards the place and function of the Church in society. . . . We were all traumatized by the political year of 1969. . . . The impact of the last couple of years has been fragmentation; it seems desperately important to begin to rebuild a coalition.
—Arthur E. Walmsley, 1969

# 7

# Black Power
# and the Urban Crisis
# in the North

Although the passage of legislation in both 1964 and 1965 had represented a tremendous advance for black people nationwide, most African Americans still had a long way to go before they experienced appreciable change in their day-to-day lives. Despite receiving the guarantee of a few basic political rights, black people did not yet enjoy economic and social equality with whites; better schools, housing, and jobs were also going to be needed, critics pointed out, before the promise of the civil rights movement would be fulfilled. According to Kenneth Clark, power was central to the ongoing "American Dilemma," for blacks were tired of having their fate determined simply according to the charity of paternalistic whites. They were no longer interested, he said, in hearing liberal whites tell them how "*they* contribute to civil rights causes, *they* marched to Washington and journeyed to Selma and Montgomery to demonstrate their commitment to racial justice."[1] A change of attitude on the part of African Americans was necessary as well, and that would mean a willingness to confront the white power structure and, in so doing, risk disapproval. Though Clark himself did not reject the belief in racial integration that had inspired the civil rights movement in the South, that ideal had little relevance to most city dwellers he knew in the North. "The black cat in Harlem wasn't worried about no damn bus—he'd been riding the bus for fifty years," one New Yorker quipped. "What he didn't have was the fare."[2]

In his highly influential book, *The Other America* (1963), Michael Harrington had warned about the racially-tinged "culture of poverty" hidden beneath the veneer of post–World War II abundance and affluence enjoyed by most white Americans. Harrington's critique inspired liberal politicians and government leaders to develop a legislative strategy aimed at redirecting economic capital into what Lyndon Johnson called a "an unconditional war on poverty." But despite Johnson's hopes for the emergence of a "Great Society," his ambitious program proved incapable of bringing most African Americans into the nation's mainstream—a fact starkly demonstrated by the explosion of rioting in the Watts section of Los Angeles in August 1965. As the focus of black leaders shifted from questions of status (the original objective of middle-class African Americans in the South) and the reform of a basically sound political system to far less tractable economic issues, and as disappointment with Johnson's Great Society program increased, some activists were left wondering whether whites really wanted to help black people after all. Arthur Walmsley, for example, was pleased that outrage over attacks on civil rights workers had inspired unprecedented numbers of church people to commit themselves for short periods to the freedom struggle in Mississippi and Alabama. When the regional outlook and the goals of the civil rights movement changed a bit, however, most white northerners could "muster little but apathy" toward the continuing pockets of black poverty close their own homes.[3]

Daniel Patrick Moynihan, a Labor Department official as well as a professor at Harvard University, was concerned about convincing the federal government to strike with greater intensity at the "culture of poverty" Harrington described. In his now notorious report, *The Negro Family* (1965), Moynihan argued that three centuries of social and cultural degradation—the legacy of slavery and segregation—had produced a "tangle of pathology" in the black community and had taken a devastating toll upon the African American family structure.[4] Yet, though he did not mean to downplay the role of white racism in creating dysfunctional conditions in the black community, he appeared to suggest that poverty in northern urban ghettos was largely attributable to the neighborhood residents themselves. Moynihan intended to say that whatever was wrong with black families could be improved by a significant infusion of money from the federal government, but most people who read his report focused only on the problems he outlined. Activists, black and white alike, were infuriated by the Moynihan report, and they condemned his ideas as part of the ideology of white supremacy. One critic even coined the phrase "blaming the victim" to describe what he perceived to have been Moynihan's purpose in releasing his report to the general public.[5]

Despite the heated controversy that Moynihan unintentionally aroused, neither his thesis nor the sociological evidence he presented was particularly new. Stanley Elkins's *Slavery* (1959)—a work cited by Moynihan—had drawn parallels between the plantation system in the antebellum South and Nazi concentration camps. Elkins reasoned that slavery had encouraged the development of a "Sambo" personality among enslaved African Americans that continued to handicap the black community well into the twentieth century.[6] Moynihan also relied heavily upon the research published in Kenneth Clark's *Dark Ghetto* (1965). Clark's book, based upon his work in Harlem, emphasized the "chronic, self-perpetuating pathology" of ghetto life and argued that most poor African Americans had been stripped of their self-respect. The impact had been particularly acute upon black males, Clark wrote, for they tended to fall into patterns of "sexual impulsiveness, irresponsibility, verbal bombast, posturing, and compensatory achievement in entertainment and athletics," thus achieving status only in ways that were "antisocial, escapist, socially irresponsible."[7] Although Clark once thought that simply eliminating segregation laws might solve many of the problems in the ghetto, he now admitted his naïveté. Thus, when a storm of protest engulfed Moynihan, Clark staunchly came to his defense. "Is a doctor responsible for the disease simply because he diagnoses it?" Clark asked.[8]

Whatever Moynihan's intentions or the true source of his ideas, the controversy surrounding his report revealed the clear fissures that had developed in the interracial coalition that once supported the civil rights movement. The condemnation Moynihan endured from outraged African Americans helped set the stage for an even more dramatic split between white liberals and black activists a few months later. SNCC organizers such as Stokely Carmichael had already questioned the value of coalition politics during the voter registration campaign in Alabama during the summer of 1965, and a separatist faction within SNCC soon began to resist the involvement of both white workers and prointegration blacks in the organization. With these racial tensions rising, James Meredith announced that he would undertake a 220–mile pilgrimage on foot from Memphis, Tennessee, to Jackson, Mississippi, in order to inspire African Americans in his state to register to vote. On June 5, 1966, however—just two days after his journey began—Meredith was shot by a member of the Ku Klux Klan. As he lay recuperating in a Memphis hospital, Stokely Carmichael of SNCC, Martin Luther King of SCLC, and Floyd McKissick of CORE made plans to bring their organizations into what became known as the "James Meredith March against Fear." Although leaders from many different civil rights groups convened in Mississippi for that event, the unity that had marked the Selma-Montgomery march had all but vanished. After being arrested during the course of the Meredith march, Carmichael spoke to a rally of African Americans about his rejection of integration with whites and his new desire to seek and demand "black power." The concept of black power gained immediate popularity among African Americans associated with SNCC: it called black people to unite, "to reclaim their history, their culture . . . their own sense of community" and to repudiate assimilation into mainstream American society."[9]

Carmichael had thrown down the gauntlet in the face of liberal whites, and initial reactions to his slogan were as mixed among church people as they were in the nation as a whole. The earliest positive statement from a religious group was presented by an assortment of black church leaders convened by Benjamin Payton, a National Baptist minister who had recently succeeded Robert Spike as director of the Commission on Religion and Race. Calling themselves the National Committee of Negro Churchmen (later changed to the National Commission of Black Churchmen [NCBC]), Payton's group purchased advertising space in the *New York Times* in July 1966. Signed by forty-eight people, mainly northern black clergy, this statement endorsed the black power concept and affirmed the need for solidarity in the strengthening of African American institutions. As church leaders, the NCBC condemned the "distorted . . . view of *an other worldly* conception of God's power" and expressed the belief "that Jesus Christ reigns in the 'here' and 'now.'" Emphasizing that integration was not useful unless it allowed black people to share power fully with whites, they also noted that the church organizations African Americans controlled represented one of the few areas in which black people in the United States already exercised power. In fact, "the Negro Church" had come into existence, they said, because African Americans refused "to submit to the indignities of a false kind of 'integration' in which all power was in the hands of white people." According to Quinland Gordon, one of the Episcopal priests who signed the NCBC statement, black power meant that African Americans were seeking a chance to gain control over their own lives, and he hoped white Episcopalians would join with black church members in supporting such reasonable and attainable goals.[10]

The concepts of self-determination and self-respect to which Gordon and the NCBC referred were particularly critical to black Episcopal clergy, many of whom believed their position in the church was eroding even as the civil rights movement opened up ostensibly wider opportunities for them. Black Episcopalians made up only a handful of the denominational membership—about 2 percent in the early 1960s—and they were confined to approximately three hundred congregations, almost exclusively in the South and in northeastern dioceses around New York and Philadelphia. For a brief period, in fact, John Burgess, Kenneth Hughes, and other leading African American clergy had hoped that true integration might be achieved in the church, and they joined with white liberals in urging an end to the practice of identifying "colored" parishes and "Negro" deacons and priests. By the mid-1960s, however, African American clergy began to see that the continuation of such racial classifications actually provided them with a *place* in a denomination whose national and diocesan leadership was still dominated by whites.[11]

Under the old segregated parish system (de jure in most southern dioceses and de facto in cities in the North), African American priests had at least been assured of employment; very few were given the opportunity to serve in white parishes, yet there were enough black parishes to provide them with support. This situation began to change dramatically in the 1950s and early 1960s. The destruction of black neighborhoods and churches in the wake of urban renewal (called "Negro removal" by some); the well-meaning desire of young white clergy and their families to improve race relations—"breaking down barriers," as Jenny Moore called it—by taking charge of failing inner-city parishes; and the belief that black church members ought to be integrated with whites in nearby white-controlled parishes—all of these trends caused a number of African American priests in northern dioceses either to lose or to be denied jobs. In addition, since Episcopal bishops in the North did not wish to be accused of favoring "segregation" by supporting separate racial churches, it was always easier to close a black parish that was financially marginal than to continue providing assistance from diocesan funds. Ironically, clergy and lay people in black parishes in the South may have fared better than those in the North during this period, since most southern bishops were still willing to admit that black religious institutions existed and had a useful, if circumscribed, role. By contrast, the white liberal approach to "integration" (i.e., absorbing black parishes into white ones) proved to be an essentially one-way proposition that further undermined the black presence in the Episcopal Church. Seen in this light, the "integration" of parishes in the North even appeared to mimic antebellum times, when masters made their slaves worship (in a subordinate position, of course) in the same churches with them.[12]

A classic example of good intentions gone awry had occurred in

May 1964 when ESCRU announced plans for a "Whitsunday Witness."
Concerned about making integration more equitable for all Episcopalians, the ESCRU leadership summoned church people to observe the
tenth anniversary of the *Brown* decision (May 17, 1964) by transferring
their membership to a parish racially unlike their own: black Episcopalians moving to white parishes, and vice versa. Since May 17th also corre-
sponded with the feast of Pentecost that year, this massive, corporate
shift was meant to be symbolic of the biblical day of Pentecost, when the
Holy Spirit "overcame all barriers of tongue and race" among God's people
and brought the universal church into existence. Although few Episcopalians actually responded to the appeal, the ESCRU plan heightened
fears among African American clergy that liberal whites did not comprehend the tenuous nature of their position within the church. What was
the purpose of a program, black priests wondered, that encouraged African Americans to leave rather than strengthen their own parishes? Since
the employment of most black clergy depended realistically upon the pres-
ervation of racially distinct parishes, the suggestion that those churches
should be closed down posed little threat to white priests but placed the
jobs of black rectors and vicars in serious jeopardy.[13]

Feeling under siege as a result of these various developments, a
contingent of black clergy—Kenneth Hughes, Jesse Anderson, James
Breeden, Quinland Gordon, Robert Hood, and Henri Stines—asked per-
mission to air their concerns at a special gathering of the House of Bishops in September 1965. The bishops had assembled in Glacier Park,
Montana, mainly to discuss whether their colleague James Pike of California should be tried for heresy. Since Pike had offended many southern
bishops by refusing to accept a degree in "white divinity" from the University of the South little more than a decade before, the black priests'
presence and their misgivings about the church's commitment to full integration added a decidedly ironic twist to the meeting. Hughes and others asked why African Americans were rarely considered for employment
in white parishes and still treated "as aliens and strangers" in the Episcopal Church. The bishops' reaction at first was positive, and they passed a
resolution expressing their commitment to recruit African Americans to
serve in a number of capacities throughout the denomination—as rectors
and parish assistants, as chaplains and teachers at all church-related
schools, as staff members at cathedrals and diocesan offices, and as officers employed by the Executive Council. In response to that resolution,
Tollie Caution later circulated a letter to black clergy asking for information that would facilitate the hiring of "duly qualified persons whose handi-

cap is chiefly their racial heritage" at all levels in the church. Yet despite these official actions, white leaders (including many of the bishops who openly supported the black clergy at the Glacier Park meeting) essentially disregarded the House of Bishops' resolution on employment practices in the Episcopal Church.[14]

Approximately half the black Episcopal clergy, led by Quintin Primo, rector of St. Matthew's Church in Wilmington, Delaware, signed a statement that was released to the press early in 1967. Entitled "A Declaration by Priests who are Negroes" and addressed to the white leadership of the Episcopal Church, it denounced the continued second-class treatment of African American clergy. Primo and the many other signatories demanded to know why their denomination was actually lagging behind secular institutions in the inclusion of black people in key positions in its corporate life. They noted, for example, that Moran Weston and Tollie Caution were the only African Americans who had ever been hired to fill the numerous executive positions available at the national church level, and Caution had even been demoted when the Division of Racial Minorities was eliminated in the early 1960s. In fact, so inattentive was the church to its black members that no African American was involved in the management of either the Church and Race fund or the Joint Urban Program, the body then in charge of the denomination's inner-city work. As John Burgess ruefully observed in a discussion about the "Declaration" with John Hines, the Episcopal Church was quick to give recognition to inexperienced white priests for their supposed expertise on black issues, but it inevitably downplayed the contributions and ideas of skilled black rectors in ghetto parishes. As a result, African Americans had usually been made to feel both unwelcome and "invisible" within their own denomination.[15]

The racial character and outlook of the staff of the Joint Urban Program was especially nettlesome to black Episcopal clergy. That program represented a continuation of the new urban focus that had developed in the churches in the aftermath of World War II, when mainline Protestants came to see decaying areas in northern cities as an appropriate place for them to exercise public responsibility. Inspired by the accomplishments of white clerical pioneers such as Paul Moore, Kim Myers, and Robert Castle in the New York metropolitan area, and John Harmon, Warren McKenna, and Cornelius Hastie in metropolitan Boston, the Episcopal Church gradually brought these piecemeal local efforts together under the broader care of the National Council. The process began at the 1961 General Convention, when the denomination officially decided to revise its work among racial minorities by de-emphasizing traditional evangelistic and social-service ministries and by stressing the church's role in the transformation of society instead. The National Council then formed a task force under the direction of James Morton, a white priest who had earlier worked with Paul Moore at Grace Church in Jersey City. Composed of staff from both the Department of Christian Social Relations and the Home Department, Morton's group was authorized to study and formulate strategies by which the church could buck the trend of suburbanization and maintain a foothold in major American cities. At the 1964 General Convention, the status of the program was formalized and its responsibilities were further expanded. When Morton left to become head of the ecumenical Urban Training Center in Chicago, G.H. (Jack) Woodard, a white priest from the diocese of Texas, was placed in charge of the operations of the Joint Urban program. Trained in the fields of engineering and business management prior to entering seminary, Woodard was picked for the position because Episcopal leaders believed that their denomination "was almost totally unrelated to the world of industry and city" and that his skills would enable him to bridge that gap.[16]

Absent from this otherwise carefully constructed plan was any substantial role for black Episcopalians who already lived and ministered in inner-city areas. Instead of looking for leadership within the major black Episcopal parishes or providing financial support for their ongoing work, the overwhelmingly white National Council and its staff had turned to a cadre of talented and capable upper-middle-class white Episcopalians like themselves—men not unlike "the best and the brightest" who served in the Kennedy and Johnson administrations in Washington. The original staff of the Joint Urban Program were, in James Morton's words, "a very in-group," and a number of them had come from privileged social and educational backgrounds. In addition to those leaders at the national church level, the people chosen to head local diocesan projects were also uniformly white. Although all were fully committed to the goals of the civil rights movement, they tended to view African Americans more as beneficiaries of the denomination's largesse than as actors in their own right. Thus, instead of empowering indigenous black ministries, the rhetoric used by the leadership of the Joint Urban Program seemed to imply that nothing effective could take place until whites ventured forth from their suburban enclaves and aided people who had no resources to help themselves. From the perspective of black Episcopalians, therefore, their church's national urban program was the epitome of white racial pater-

Episcopal Society for Cultural and Racial Unity symbol, about 1960. Courtesy of The Archives of the Episcopal Church, USA.

*Above*, ESCRU Prayer Pilgrims at the 1961 General Convention in Detroit. Courtesy of The Archives of the Episcopal Church, USA. *Below*, Episcopal clergy and lay people meeting with Senator Philip Hart in Washington, D.C., October 1963. Courtesy of The Archives of the Episcopal Church, USA.

*Above*, Henri A. Stines and Malcolm Boyd (left to right) picketing Lovett School in Atlanta, fall 1963. Courtesy of John B. Morris, Atlanta. *Below*, Thomas W.S. Logan, Robert C. Chapman, and Jesse Anderson Sr. (from left to right) picketing Lovett School in Atlanta, fall 1963. Courtesy of John B. Morris, Atlanta.

*Above*, Kenneth B. Clark, Thomas F. Pettigrew, William Stringfellow, and James Forman (from left to right), about 1963. Courtesy of the Division of Rare and Manuscript Collections, Carl A. Kroch Library, Cornell University. *Left*, Arrest of Mary Peabody in St. Augustine, Florida, March 1964. Courtesy of The Archives of the Episcopal Church, USA.

*Above*, Presiding Bishop John E. Hines (at right) with Greek Orthodox Archbishop Demetrios Iakovos in Selma, Alabama, March 1965. Courtesy of Arthur E. Walmsley, Deering, N.H. *Below*, Judith E. Upham (at left) with civil rights workers in Selma, Alabama, April 1965. Courtesy of The Archives of the Episcopal Church, USA.

Stokely Carmichael (second from left-facing camera) with mourners at the funeral of Jonathan Daniels in Keene, New Hampshire, August 1965. Courtesy of The Archives of the Episcopal Church, USA.

ESCRU members Virginia Shields and Robert F.B. Hunter picketing St. Philip's Cathedral, Atlanta, May 1965. Courtesy of John B. Morris, Atlanta.

*Above*, ESCRU members Robert F.B. Hunter (priest at left) and Albert R. Dreisbach Jr. (priest at right) with Martin Luther King Jr. (center) at St. Philip's Cathedral, Atlanta, June 1966. Courtesy of The Archives of the Episcopal Church, USA. *Below*, Muhammed Kenyatta and James Woodruff (left to right) of the Union of Black Clergy and Laity at the 1969 Special Convention in South Bend. Courtesy of The Archives of the Episcopal Church, USA.

nalism; church leaders had observed the problems of inner-city ghettos but had failed to identify fully with the residents of those neighborhoods.[17]

Although subtle forms of racism undoubtedly played a role in the inability of white liberals to recognize the presence of black Episcopalians in their midst, new theological and social fashions also contributed significantly to this trend. According to Gibson Winter, an early proponent of urban ministry, "*history* rather than the *religious institution*" was the proper context of the Christian life. The typical congregation with its emphasis on worship, education, and pastoral care was becoming gradually less important, he argued; in the secular Christianity of the future, ministry would be defined by its ability to discern the gospel and locate the church in society and in the public realm.[18] As James Morton also stressed, the church should not be described statically as an institution but should be viewed as "the revolution of God in the world, God's avant-garde, his spearhead."[19] Even Kim Myers, who had served in parish-based ministries in Jersey City and New York, fell prey to this tendency to downplay the importance of formal organizations in inner-city neighborhoods. Because of these theological and intellectual biases, white clergy involved with the formation and administration of the Joint Urban Program were not attuned to the importance of urban parishes, run by black clergy, and the pastoral ministries they offered their communities. Though those white leaders did not consciously intend to discount the work of black priests, their theology simply envisioned no place for African Americans within the institutional church they were seeking to reform.[20]

Social class was another factor contributing to the devaluation of black parishes and clergy in the mid-1960s. It had long been a truism that middle-class African Americans gravitated toward the ordered ceremonies and rituals of denominations such as the Episcopal Church, and black Episcopalians were generally perceived to be the upper crust of the African American community. Educated and comparatively well-to-do African Americans, whether Episcopalians or not, also strongly resented the homogenizing effects of racism. As W.E.B. Du Bois remarked at the turn of the century, "nothing more exasperates the better class of Negroes than this tendency [of white people] to ignore utterly their existence" and to lump them with the most downtrodden members of their race. The "Great Migration" of African Americans from the rural South to the urban North compounded this class division. Migrants were often viewed as uncouth by African Americans whose families had lived in northern cities for many years, while white racism contributed to the decline in status of the old "black aristocracy" as the black community expanded in the North. The final and most ironic blow was dealt by the civil rights movement itself, as the social revolution of the 1960s overturned traditional ideas about class and culture throughout every segment of the American population. Black militants—many of them raised in middle-class homes—began to ridicule African Americans at the top of the social structure as self-serving elitists, out of touch with ordinary people of their own race. White activists followed suit and suggested that only those who were most alienated from mainstream American society could truly lay claim to being "black." As a result of these broad cultural changes, the bourgeois mentality that black Episcopalians had once cultivated as a defense against racial bigotry became a source of further scorn from whites at the height of the civil rights movement.[21]

While black clergy demanded recognition of their place within the Episcopal Church, significant changes were also taking place in the leadership of ESCRU as it came to terms with the rejection of racial integration by African Americans. Despite their commitment to the black freedom struggle, the membership of ESCRU had always been predominantly white and middle-class. When John Morris joked in the summer of 1965, for example, that ongoing civil rights protests in the South had helped keep "everybody's Selma sun tan in shape," he inadvertently revealed a significant fact about the complexion of most of his organization.[22] Even Tollie Caution and John Burgess, black clergy who faithfully supported ESCRU, confessed that they were uneasy when whites like Morris either assumed they spoke for African Americans or carelessly disparaged black church institutions. And as the black power movement gained strength in 1966, divisions between white and black members became increasingly more pronounced. Even though Morris admitted that black power was the logical outcome of the suppression of African American voices by white racists, he called it "tragic historically, practically untenable, morally and theologically unacceptable." Since Morris and other white leaders in ESCRU continued to believe in the validity of integration and viewed appeals to racial self-consciousness as misguided, black Episcopalians openly wondered whether the society really had their best interests at heart.[23]

The seriousness of these issues became apparent at the meeting of the ESCRU board of directors in November 1966. Forced like many interracial groups in this period to reassess both its mission and the location of authority within its organization, the board excluded Morris from an executive session in which it candidly discussed the future direction of ESCRU. A number of issues were debated, the two most heated being whether ESCRU should redirect its regional focus by moving its head-quarters to a northeastern city such as Philadelphia or New York and whether it should emphasize work within the secular community rather than in the church. Morris was adamant that the church in the South should continue to remain the society's principal concern, but in the face of growing opposition to his views, he offered to resign from his position as executive director. Although dissuaded from taking that step, Morris clearly was under attack, and he felt frustrated by the impending shift away from the course he had championed since ESCRU's inception. He thought the society should concentrate on what it could do well—encouraging the Episcopal Church to become more racially inclusive—not on a task for which it was unequipped—being a conventional civil rights organization. Indeed, Morris emphasized that "when I do anything worthwhile in ESCRU, it is for Christ's sake—and not for the cause of civil rights or . . . to 'help the Negro.'" Morris was not the only person to be upset by the implications of the ESCRU board meeting. Judith Upham admitted that it was "profoundly disturbing—a six hour fight," and she wondered whether ESCRU really had much future as an organization at that point. After a period of soul-searching, Morris decided to take a six-month leave of absence beginning in April 1967. Some board members argued that an African American should take his place, but this option was never seriously pursued. Instead, assistant director Albert R. ("Kim") Dreisbach, a white priest, took charge while Morris was away. As Dreisbach commented at the time, "the child which John nurtured from a pup" had grown up and was about to set off on its own.[24]

In the summer of 1967, midway through Morris's leave, a series of riots broke out in northern cities, the worst occurring in July in black neighborhoods in Detroit and Newark. Fires and looting caused millions of dollars of property damage in the two cities, and a total of sixty-six people died during those outbreaks of violence. Newsweek labeled the disastrous situation in Detroit "Battlefield, U.S.A.," and it opined that "the message of this longest, hottest summer was plain: America could no longer run away from the endemic sickness of her cities." Time followed suit by stating that the riots were "the most sensational expression of an ugly mood of nihilism and anarchy" that had gripped the African American population in the North. The nation was traumatized by the social upheaval it was witnessing, and middle-class white Americans seemed shocked not only by the widespread disorder that confronted them but also by their inability to intervene and keep it under control.[25]

Against this seemingly cataclysmic backdrop, ESCRU too appeared to descend into chaos as Morris engaged in an acrimonious public debate with Mike Peabody of the society's board of directors. Peabody, a Bostonian, was deeply troubled by the unrest and destruction in Newark and Detroit; he urged ESCRU to concentrate on those urban areas, not merely on the now relatively peaceful South. He was also distressed that Morris was determined to focus on the South at a time when northern cities seemed to demand the most attention. "Why do we stand aside paralyzed," he asked, "while the United States disintegrates?" Peabody also resented Morris's tendency to speak unilaterally on behalf of the organization, and he wanted the board of directors that he headed to exert greater authority and control. Morris, on his part, feared that Peabody was unwilling to challenge the "separatism and hate" of black power advocates, who seemed bent on nullifying the successes achieved by Martin Luther King and the civil rights movement in the South. ESCRU would function best, Morris believed, if it helped transform the Episcopal Church into a model of harmonious racial integration on which the nation as a whole could pattern itself. If the church could first heal its own ills and divisions, it truly might become a beacon pointing the United States toward racial healing.[26]

This internal division (as well as a growing financial crisis) occupied the attention of the ESCRU leadership throughout the remainder of 1967. At the annual meeting in September, the membership called for a complete revision of the society's statement of purpose, abandoning the former emphasis on integration and affirming instead black self-determination and the importance of racial and cultural *diversity*. Since most of the people who attended the meeting also favored Peabody's strategy of intervention in the urban North, Morris immediately resigned as executive director and Dreisbach replaced him in the capacity of acting director. Peabody's term expired at the same time, and he too stepped down; he was succeeded as president by Jesse Anderson, who, as rector of St. Thomas' Church in Philadelphia, was one of the most prominent black priests in the United States. Because the focus of ESCRU had shifted dramatically from the time of its initial formation in the late 1950s, Morris departed with a sense of despondency and regret. He remained troubled both by the implications of black power and by the support it received from northerners like Peabody, whom he regarded as "compulsively guilty, sick white liberals." Although racial tensions in the South were easing, and Bishop Claiborne had finally licensed him again as a priest, Morris did not return to regular parish work after leaving ESCRU but eventually joined the staff of the Southern Regional Council in Atlanta.[27]

While the new emphasis on black power was causing considerable turmoil in the ranks of ESCRU, the Executive Council also struggled to find a suitable course of action for the Episcopal Church as a whole to take in response to the troubling racial unrest in the North. The status of the Church and Race fund clearly reveals the difficulties the council was facing in this period. Despite the excitement that initially surrounded the creation of the fund, it had not lived up to expectations and had actually raised only half the amount that had initially been projected as its financial goal. With the apparent success achieved by the civil rights movement in 1965, moreover, interest in the program had decidedly waned. The indifference of most ordinary Episcopalians to the continuing existence of the fund and the fact that it was based solely on voluntary contributions just added to its difficulties. Although some members of the council thought the fund should be augmented with money from the general budget of the denomination, the majority no longer wished to commit the church to race-related projects but preferred to let the 1967 General Convention make the definitive statement on the future, if any, of the fund.[28]

These ominous signs of fading interest notwithstanding, John Hines was determined that the Episcopal Church would continue to have a positive impact on American society by helping ease racial tensions. The presiding bishop had, after all, started his ministry in Missouri under the influence of William Scarlett, arguably the most outspoken advocate of the social gospel in the Episcopal Church in the 1930s and 1940s. Inspired by Scarlett's hopeful, action-oriented approach, Hines was very aware of the position of his denomination within the American "establishment," and he believed that it should be fully engaged in the task of solving social ills, not barricaded into what he called "a kind of 'Maginot-mind-set.'" Christian institutions had to place themselves at risk just as Jesus himself did and, if necessary, die in order to accomplish their world-transforming mission. The Episcopal Church should never worry about its institutional survival but should seek renewal through sacrificial service on behalf of the larger community. "Christianity is turned towards the future, not towards the past," Hines argued, "towards creation, a new heaven and a new earth, not towards a safe and static world."[29]

In order to prove his point, Hines made a dramatic change in his own plans in anticipation of the upcoming 1967 General Convention. In mid-August, he left a meeting of the World Council of Churches in Crete and returned home early when members of his staff warned him that "things might soon blow sky high" in the United States.[30] He also decided to look beyond the world that was familiar to him and observe firsthand an alien one—a culture far removed from the white establishment circles in which he had served throughout most of his ministry. He asked Leon Modeste, an African American layman working in the Division of Community Services of the Executive Council, to show him "real life" on the streets of New York. Although Modeste initially resisted the idea of having Hines and a group of white people walking around a black ghetto "as if they were sightseeing or visiting a zoo," he agreed to take Hines as long as he came by himself and did not wear a clerical collar.[31] On a hot August day, therefore, Hines substituted a shirt and necktie for his usual clerical attire and walked with Modeste around the Bedford-Stuyvesant section of Brooklyn—an experience that he later described as a "searing," "depressing," yet "exhilarating" moment. Hines talked casually with numerous people that day, and he thought what they told him was extraordinarily meaningful: the poor, he concluded, had a far better sense of God than those, like himself, who had been raised in privilege. Feeling energized and wishing to put what he had learned into action, Hines left for Washington, D.C., where he attended a gathering of major political, business, and religious figures who had assembled to discuss the urban crisis. There he called for a massive reordering of government priorities, including allowing the poor to have direct control over their own economic destinies.[32]

Based on what he had experienced in Bedford-Stuyvesant, Hines directed his staff to arrange a series of planning sessions with African American activists and others familiar with the situation in the northern cities in preparation for the General Convention. The goal of those meetings was the development of a program that would offer a significant portion of the financial resources of the Episcopal Church to groups working with the poor in ghetto areas. As a number of social analysts were suggesting at the time, churches had a potentially useful role to play as allies with the government in the war on poverty. According to Sterling Tucker, a black lay Episcopalian who served as executive director of the Urban League in Washington, the white leadership of the major American denominations needed to do more than merely wring their hands and decry the existence of poverty; they also needed "to take a stand in the streets" with the poor and place the management of the ghetto in the hands of those who lived there. One of the ad hoc committees Hines assembled expressed this theme in the report it submitted: whatever funds the Episcopal Church committed to alleviating poverty should be given away entirely "without strings" to representatives of the poor people themselves. Although this process might be an extremely painful one for white church members, who would have to relinquish control over their money, it would help purge whites of racism and simultaneously empower African Americans.[33]

Preparing his plan for presentation required a great deal of work, but Hines had the proposal ready for approval by the Executive Council when it met two days before the start of the convention. Caught somewhat off guard but distressed by the urban crisis in which the nation was immersed, the council listened intently as the presiding bishop described what he thought was needed. Approximately $2 million per year should be allocated to urban work, although most of that money, he explained, would be gained through cutbacks in other departments and through the elimination of the Joint Urban Program, with many of its responsibilities being adopted by the new program. In addition, the leadership of the General Division of Women's Work would be asked to contribute $1 million per year from its own United Thank Offering. (At every General Convention, the Episcopal Church Women presented a "United Thank Offering" for use in various missionary projects of the denomination; almost $4.8 million had been given to the church at the 1964 General Convention.) If this plan were carried out, Hines insisted, the Episcopal Church would not only enable black organizations to gain and exercise economic and political power, but it would also demonstrate forcefully its own willingness to "stand with the dispossessed and the alienated, sharing their pain and their agony" in the ghetto. A few conservative council members objected that Hines's proposal seemed last-minute and panicky, and they worried about the possibility that it would undermine some of the denomination's more traditional ministries. Was it advisable, they asked, to turn large sums of money over to the poor without some assurance that it would be used responsibly and in accordance with Christian moral principles? The majority on the Executive Council, however, believed the presiding bishop had outlined an appropriate new mission for their denomination and a way to shore up a rapidly crumbling society, and they gave him authorization to proceed with the plan.[34]

Hines introduced his vision to the church as a whole in his sermon at the opening service of the convention. Episcopalians did not have to stand by helpless while the United States disintegrated into chaos, he proclaimed. Instead, they could set aside $9 million over the next three years—a figure roughly equivalent to one-quarter of the church's operating budget—for the empowerment of the country's poorest citizens. One scholar has called Hines's sermon "a primary document of the era."[35] That is an accurate assessment, for the themes on which the presiding bishop touched reflected both the self-confidence and the sense of national responsibility that still prevailed in mainline Protestantism in 1967: (1) concern for the stability of society: he called for an end to "the appallingly destructive bloody rioting which has destroyed much inner city fabric, damaged communications between black and white, waved the flag of 'black power' menacingly, and wasted precious human lives, setting at naught respect for law and order"; (2) patriotic pride: the denomination must recognize that people in the streets of Watts, Newark, and Detroit are fighting "for the right of self-determination, for the rights of dignity of every human being, for freedom under law, for deliverance from discrimination, and for a dream which for nearly two centuries has been a brilliant torch to which the shackled and oppressed everywhere could look up in hope"; (3) liberal political zeal: Hines said "the quest of a people for self-determination, the exercise of freedom, and the right to participate in the decisions that affect their destiny" should be nurtured and "the use of political and economic power to support justice . . . for all men" should be encouraged, so that "their power for self-determination may be increased and their dignity restored"; (4) apprehension about the continuing relevance of the church: he wanted to convince "these unfortunate people [who] have written off the churches as possible allies in their quest for justice . . . that church people are concerned about their plight or will take the necessary risk to help redeem it"; thus "the credibility and integrity of 'mission' for this Church could be preserved for generations to come"; and (5) theological hopefulness: the Episcopal Church should place itself "humbly and boldly alongside of, and in support of, the dispossessed and oppressed peoples of this country for the healing of our national life," embrace this "'moment of passing grace' given to us by God, that may never again re-occur—and in which we are given together the opportunity to act," and discover that "only through our sharing in the pain and the agonized frustration of the dispossessed . . . our own renewal can come to be!"[36]

Hines's energetic and moving appeal had the effect he intended: following a surprisingly quiet discussion and debate, both the House of Bishops and the House of Deputies approved the substance of his plan. As he had hoped, the women's Triennial Meeting also enthusiastically supported what he proposed. The leadership of the General Division of Women's Work pledged a portion of its own funds, as well as whatever additional money was needed from the United Thank Offering, in order to add $1 million each year to the budget of the new urban program. So strong was the support Hines received that only a single dissent was heard at the convention. J.L. Caldwell McFaddin, a white attorney from Beaumont, had opposed Hines on a number of occasions during his tenure as bishop in the diocese of Texas. Now a General Convention deputy, McFaddin questioned the wisdom of the denomination's placing its whole missionary program at risk for the sake of pursuing what he regarded as essentially secular goals. "Our offerings, made on our altars to God," he insisted, "should not be diverted to achieve economic and political power for any group, White or Black." McFaddin also feared that awarding funds to nonchurch groups unconditionally, without safeguards, could backfire: Episcopalians might withhold contributions if they thought their financial offerings were not being used for the proper religious purposes. Despite these objections, Hines gained the approval he needed, and when the convention had ended, he set out to find a staff to administer what soon was dubbed the General Convention Special Program (GCSP).[37]

In the midst of that process, however, a voice more formidable than McFaddin's was also raised against Hines's strategy. Nathan Wright, a black priest who directed the urban work program of the diocese of Newark, begged white leaders not to repeat the serious mistakes they had made with the Joint Urban Program. Give knowledgeable African American clergy—the church's main link with the black community—positions of authority within the new empowerment program, he urged. Wright, the organizer of the National Conference on Black Power that had recently met in Newark, saw the concept of black power as a necessary step toward a just society. While the civil rights movement had placed emphasis on what white Americans owed to their fellow citizens who were black, black power focused on what African Americans could do for themselves. Wright certainly understood the value of white-owned businesses and other establishment groups like the Episcopal Church assisting black people in achieving economic self-development. But he was extremely wary of paternalistic whites who professed goodwill but did not allow African Americans freedom to work and plan on their own. Those men, he charged, were part of "a suburban, white elite of power whose 'culture, history, beliefs, and race' differ from those in our inner cities." They regarded all African Americans, even middle-class professionals, with a "colonial mind-set" that encouraged both dependency on whites and the separation of "successful Negro men and women from the black poor who should look to them for leadership."[38] Thus, to ignore the resources of African American clergy and their parishes would merely perpetuate "the insolence and paternalism" with which white Episcopalians from the South—Wright was acutely aware of Hines's southern roots—had always regarded their black colleagues.[39]

Although Wright made a concerted effort to change the presiding bishop's mind, Hines ignored his suggestions and appointed Leon Modeste—a lay Episcopalian, not a parish priest—to direct GCSP. Hines thought Modeste would be able to communicate effectively with both white church members and African Americans in the ghetto. Because he knew Modeste well and trusted him, Hines gave him a free hand in hiring his assistants. As a result few of the people who were chosen to work in the new program were active churchgoers, let alone Episcopalians, and they were generally suspicious of all clergy, black as well as white. Modeste wanted to find staff members who were single-minded about aiding the empowerment of the poor, and he saw no value in asking them to placate middle-class church people as well. In fact, he was convinced that polarization along class as well as racial lines was necessary because racist attitudes would be changed only through the radical destabilization of society. And since the purpose of GCSP was to transfer power from the powerful to the powerless, the feelings of the powerful were essentially irrelevant. The bottom line, Modeste asserted, was not the "orderly disciplined process" prized by most church leaders, but simply "getting the job done" for the sake of the poor.[40]

Without intending it, Hines, the Executive Council, and the General Convention had created a situation in which four constituencies within their church were about to be placed at odds against one another: African American rectors and their parishioners, liberal white clergy, middle-class white lay Episcopalians, and the staff at the denomination's headquarters in New York. In fact, even as GCSP was still in the process of being organized, Hines and Modeste came under galling fire from black parish clergy—the one constituency on whom (as Nathan Wright had tried to explain) they should have most relied.

Most African Americans hoped that, with the advent of GCSP and with the growing national attention to black power, their moment for recognition and respect might finally have come, though their position within the Episcopal Church had always been marginal. Furthermore, many had assumed that Tollie Caution, who had served at national headquarters for over twenty years, was the logical person to direct GCSP. Part of the traditional black leadership class in the South, Caution had learned to use the old politics of accommodation to his advantage throughout a long and distinguished ministry. But by the mid-1960s, his style and his approach to social issues were viewed as out of date, and he had been dubbed an "Uncle Tom" and treated in patronizing manner by young white liberals working in the Department of Christian Social Relations and in the Joint Urban Program. Hines, too, had reason to resent Caution, for he had been instrumental in convincing Presiding Bishop Sherrill to move the 1955 General Convention out of racially segregated Houston—a bitter blow to Clinton Quin and most white Episcopalians in the diocese of Texas. As a result Hines deliberately passed over Caution when he chose a director for GCSP. In addition, since Caution's experience in the church undoubtedly posed a threat to the authority Modeste exercised, and since the black Episcopalians whom Caution represented were regarded as "an aggravation" by the people Modeste initially hired, he was summarily dismissed from his position at the same time GCSP began its operations. Caution had just turned sixty-five, and Daniel Corrigan, the Home Department director under whom he worked, declared that it was time for him to retire. So complete was Corrigan's contempt for the senior African American priest in the Episcopal Church that he composed the letter of resignation he expected Caution to sign![41]

Making matters even worse and further insulting black Episcopalians, the Executive Council voted to dissolve the American Church Institute, thus ending what white liberals in the North had long regarded as an embarrassing anomaly. Although the formation of the ACI was inextricably bound up with the paternalistic racial attitudes of Robert Patton and the other white southern men who founded it in 1906, it had also served as an important link connecting denominational headquarters in New York, aspiring middle-class African Americans in the South, and the general black population whom the church leadership said it wished to evangelize. Yet other modern cultural trends undermined it, and as one National Council member observed in 1961, the ACI schools had become "essentially segregated schools and a dwindling type of educational institution." Mindful of this charge, liberals at national church headquarters saw little justification for continuing to fund either the ACI or the denomination's three remaining southern black colleges, St. Augustine's in North Carolina, St. Paul's in Virginia, and Voorhees in South Carolina. Rejecting Tollie Caution's advice against abandoning the education (and consequent betterment) of black southerners, Daniel Corrigan and the white staff of the Home Department pressed for the dissolution of the ACI. In December 1967 the Executive Council officially terminated the organization and placed the colleges it supported under Corrigan's decidedly unsympathetic direction.[42]

By demonstrating so vividly the vulnerable position of African Americans in the church, Caution's forced retirement and the end of the ACI galvanized black Episcopalians and forced their simmering conflict with the Executive Council into the open. Letters of protest poured into the offices of Corrigan and Hines. As those letters emphasized, liberal white Episcopalians seemed bent on reforming society before they looked critically at some of the racist assumptions under which they themselves operated. Why, for instance, had well-to-do white men, who had never shown much interest in assisting faithful, law-abiding black church members, suddenly become so concerned about African Americans outside the church who destroyed property and threatened the status quo? Corrigan especially came under fire. Kenneth Hughes told him that he could not understand how "a place has always been found for your *white* employees, but this one *black* employee must be kicked out after giving 22 years—the best of his life—to his church."[43] John Burgess also stated that he was tired of seeing the national church pass over African American clergy who had toiled for years in poor ghetto parishes, while raising up "less qualified white clergy" and "inexperienced white Johnny-Come-Latelies," who instantly were given recognition as authorities on urban problems and black affairs.[44] "Who should be more knowledgeable of the situation and predicaments of people in the ghettos," African Americans asked Corrigan and Hines, "than those whose lot it is to live . . . and work in them almost all their lives?"[45] In the opinion of Walter Dennis of New York, the answer to that question was obvious: "The Church still thinks white when it goes about its business."[46]

Troubled by the continuing unwillingness of white leaders either to hear or respond adequately to their concerns, a group of black clergy under the leadership of Quintin Primo took matters into their own hands. In early February of 1968, seventeen priests assembled at St. Philip's in Harlem, Moran Weston's church and the strongest black parish in the denomination at that time, to organize the Union of Black Clergy and Laymen (UBCL). The founders of the UBCL protested their continued second-class treatment, and they said they were determined to remove "racism . . . by any means necessary to achieve full participation on the basis of equality in policy making, decision making, program and staffing" throughout the denomination. They believed they were upholding a venerable legacy extending back to the ministries of Alexander Crummell and George Freeman Bragg, and so strong was their resolve to achieve self-determination that some even considered reviving George Alexander McGuire's African Orthodox Church as an ecclesiastical alternative for

Afro-Anglicans in the United States. As Austin R. Cooper, rector of St. Philip's Church in Jacksonville, Florida, emphasized, black priests had suffered many indignities in the past, especially from southern bishops who resented any aggressiveness on their part. In the future, the leadership of the UBCL vowed, whites would always take the interests of black Episcopalians into account before making decisions that affected them, or, like McGuire and his followers, they would leave the Episcopal Church rather than allowing themselves to be treated as inferiors in it.[47]

Since a number of the clergy involved in the creation of the UBCL had also been active in ESCRU, they tried to convince its white members to understand and support their need for an all-black organization. John Morris had remained true to the society's original prointegration ideals throughout his tenure as executive director. After his departure, however, the new leaders of ESCRU were quick to express their sympathy for the goals of black self-determination, and they decided that a reworking of its statement of purpose was in order in 1968. ESCRU's original statement of purpose, formulated mainly by white clergy, emphasized the congruence of traditional Christian beliefs, racial integration, and involvement in the civil rights movement; the revised mission statement, developed principally by African Americans, highlighted the extent to which traditional Christianity had failed to inspire white church people to confront their own racism and respect racial differences. Black members of the board of directors emphasized, for example, that the original focus on racial unity had been "premature and unrealistic," for acceptance of diversity was crucial for African Americans seeking power and acceptance within both society and the church.[48] While affirming belief in the essential spiritual unity of humankind, effected by participation in the sacraments of baptism and communion, the new ESCRU statement also stressed that "talk of Unity between men in the absence of Equality has been in vain, and that talk of Love between them where there is not Justice is meaningless." This assertion led the editors of The Living Church, a church journal that had supported ESCRU consistently since its inception in 1959, to ask why it now refused to condemn all forms of racism, black as well as white. Arguing that black power was essentially a racist concept and that African American militants were as inherently racist as Klan members, the editors insisted that the only legitimate goal for a Christian of any color was the integration and reconciliation of all races.[49]

At the same time Episcopalians were debating about the formation of the UBCL and the change of direction in ESCRU, the National Advisory Commission on Civil Disorders ("the Kerner Commission") released its report on the current state of race relations in the United States. The commission argued that anger over years of discrimination and neglect had sparked the outbreaks of rioting in American cities, and it called for the expansion of government programs to alleviate the effects of the racism that permeated virtually every area of American life. Extensive research was contained in the Kerner report, but the document's most memorable lines appeared in the summary that introduced the commission's findings. Although the civil rights movement had won many gains for African Americans, the opening summary stated, a "deepening racial division" had become apparent across the nation, and "the continuing polarization of the American community" threatened to destroy the basic democratic values on which the country was founded. Members of the predominantly white commission said they were still hopeful about achieving full racial integration one day, yet they acknowledged the fact that, at present, the country was rapidly "moving toward two societies, one black, one white—separate and unequal."[50]

As if demonstrating the validity of what the Kerner report had recently stated, the ESCRU chapter in Philadelphia made the decision to begin dividing into separate caucuses, one black and one white, during all its meetings. Thanks to the leadership of black clergy such as Jesse Anderson and Paul Washington and of black laywoman Barbara Harris, the Philadelphia chapter of ESCRU had emerged as one of the most influential local branches in the organization. Although Anderson had at first assumed that ESCRU would maintain its prointegration stance when he was elected president of the society in 1967, he eventually came to see the usefulness of separate racial caucuses and urged adoption of the practice on the national level. There were times, he advised, when white and black church people needed to be divided in order to build "a more honest, stronger, and truly unified ESCRU." Joseph Pelham, a black priest and an ESCRU board member, agreed with Anderson about the advantages of such a division—whites working against racism in the suburbs and blacks strengthening their own institutions and neighborhoods in the inner city. Since white racism remained the major stumbling block to interracial harmony, Pelham and Anderson argued, whites had to learn how to root it out where they lived before coming into African American communities and presenting themselves as leaders there. What was most important for ESCRU members to support, therefore, was not "'mouthed' integration with practical segregation," but the determination of black church people to express themselves and maintain the religious autonomy for which they had always struggled. As a consequence of those arguments, the ESCRU membership officially divided itself along racial lines at the society's annual meeting in November 1968.[51]

Kim Dreisbach, who had recently been appointed the permanent director of ESCRU, tried to view this shift of direction in a positive light and urged his fellow white members to remain in the organization. He noted that Americans were living in "an age of revolution . . . in which all previous value systems" were under scrutiny, and if some church people felt troubled by the current black militancy, they ought to remember the rabbi Gamaliel's sage advice in the book of Acts and take a wait-and-see attitude.[52] He also emphasized that, while the ESCRU leadership had divided on racial lines to discuss the business of the organization, blacks and whites still observed the sacramental unity of the church by celebrating and sharing the eucharist together at meetings. Dreisbach's words were not sufficient to stem the tide of white members abandoning the society. Although open communion between black and white Episcopalians in the South had once been viewed as a radical act—indeed, it was one of the standards for which ESCRU initially stood—it was no longer enough to satisfy most prointegration white Episcopalians. Troubled by the new assertiveness of African Americans and mindful of the time when "black and white together" had been their rallying cry, angry whites wrote Dreisbach to indicate that the creation of separate racial caucuses was their chief reason for resigning from ESCRU. As one lay member remarked, the church's mission was to proclaim the unity of humankind, and despite the pressure to support black power, he could see no justification for ceasing to believe in integration.[53] Although Dreisbach gamely sought to keep his organization together by mediating between African Americans who now viewed integration as detrimental to their interests and whites who had little appreciation of the new black perspective, he realized he was fighting a losing battle. As he sadly commented in the fall of 1969, keeping ESCRU afloat had become a "lonely and frustrating" job.[54]

ESCRU had come a long way since the Selma-Montgomery march of 1965, and having labored to bring African Americans from the margins to the center of the church's concern, the society had achieved a considerable measure of success. While the ESCRU leadership did not have a direct hand in the creation of GCSP, they had also fostered a climate conducive to the development of that program. But white liberals in ESCRU and at denominational headquarters had overlooked one critical factor: once African Americans were identified as a key focus for the church's ministry, black Episcopalians necessarily had a vital role to play as actors and leaders in deciding how outreach in their community would proceed. Although the mission to African Americans now encompassed social action, not evangelism, the traditional pattern of race relations in the Episcopal Church had remained strong through the mid-1960s. That was an extraordinarily painful time for whites, especially for those who had done the most to assist the civil rights struggle in the South. Yet they were forced to see that white paternalism was pernicious whether it was practiced by conservative southern bishops or by liberal church bureaucrats. Racial unity came at a risk, therefore, even for people who had courageously advocated that ideal when it was not popular. Having once championed equality and integration, liberal white Episcopalians were now distressed to learn that the two qualities apparently were not going to be achieved together.

# 8

# *Backlash and the End of the Civil Rights Era*

In a speech before the National Catholic Conference for Interracial Justice in August 1969, Lucius Walker, a black minister and the director of the Interreligious Foundation for Community Organization (IFCO), lambasted all major religious bodies in the United States for failing to support the revolution taking place outside the doors of their sanctuaries. Recently, "some churches and synagogues have been in the forefront of the retreat from justice," he complained, and religious bureaucrats at all levels "have been more responsive to their racist uptight constituencies than to [pleas] for mercy and justice." Walker's address reflected the frustrations he felt as the director of IFCO, an organization founded in 1967 as a conduit for funds donated by various Christian and Jewish groups to programs aiding the poor in northern cities. Although the Episcopal Church was one of the original members of IFCO and had given more than three hundred thousand dollars to the project, many other denominations and church boards had contributed virtually nothing during the two years of its existence. Walker knew his organization was part of an increasingly shaky interracial coalition and had been walking a tightrope between two competing, if not wholly incompatible, concerns: the desire of white church people to resolve the social crisis in the ghettos and the need of African Americans to gain real economic and political power for their communities.[1]

In addition to his general distress, Walker was annoyed that church and synagogue leaders had refused to respond sympathetically to the provisions of the "Black Manifesto," a document endorsed by IFCO representatives at the National Black Economic Development Conference that was held in Detroit in April. The manifesto had delivered a blistering attack on the racism of white-run religious institutions in the United States. "We know that we were not Christians when we were brought to this country," the document declared, but "Christianity was used to help enslave us." Because the crimes of white Christians and Jews had been so severe, extreme measures were necessary in order to redeem the situation. The manifesto demanded, therefore, that mainline religious bodies surrender a total of $500 million as "reparations" for the cumulative impact of the oppression and discrimination whites had practiced against African Americans for over three centuries. At the end of the Detroit gathering, a permanent Black Economic Development Conference (BEDC) was created as the repository for all funds that the manifesto raised, and James Forman, a former SNCC leader and one of the principal organizers of the Mississippi Summer Project, was appointed its director. BEDC had no funds of its own and few staff members, but Forman called upon African Americans to bring their claim for reparations—just "fifteen dollars per nigger," he emphasized—to the attention of the Protestant denominations by disrupting Sunday morning church services.[2]

Although Forman's most dramatic appearance occurred when he interrupted Sunday worship at the Riverside Church in New York on May 4, his initial confrontation with the white religious establishment had actually taken place three days earlier. On that day he led a delegation of African Americans to the national headquarters of the Episcopal Church, where he hoped to deliver the Black Manifesto in person to John Hines. Impressed by the General Convention Special Program and by Episcopalians' comparatively strong witness in the area of human rights, Forman thought that Hines would at least listen respectfully to what he had to say. Since the presiding bishop was not in New York, Forman instead read the manifesto to the two bishops in charge of church affairs during Hines's absence: Stephen Bayne, then first vice president of the Executive Council, and J. Brooke Mosley, the deputy for overseas relations. The Episcopal Church was such a powerful economic institution, Forman told them, that the time had come for its many wealthy members to liquidate their financial holdings and give those assets to poor people. Specifically, he directed Episcopalians to contribute at least $60 million (as well as 60 percent of the denomination's yearly "profits") to BEDC. They were uneasy about Forman's appearance at church headquarters and flabbergasted by his monetary demands, but Bayne and Mosley received him politely. They even agreed with much of what he said about white racism—in fact, the money that had been committed to black empowerment through GCSP symbolized the church's acceptance of the main goals of the manifesto, they said. Nonetheless, they thought it was unrealistic to expect that their denomination would meet the manifesto's clearly exorbitant provisions. The average Episcopalian was only minimally committed to the mission the church's leadership had articulated, and conservative whites could always choose to withhold contributions to the denominational budget if they disagreed with how their money was being used. In Bayne's estimation, the Episcopal Church was hardly the influential national power that Forman and BEDC imagined it to be, but simply a "tiny, powerless agency" dependent upon an often quixotic membership.[3]

Bayne's response to Forman was certainly well founded, for the overwhelming majority of Americans soon let it be known that they had no intention of taking the Black Manifesto seriously. According to a Gallup poll taken after Forman's appearance at the Riverside Church, 92 percent of all American churchgoers opposed the payment of reparations to African Americans. White Episcopalians were in strong agreement with that position. Peter Doyle, for example, had been such a committed supporter of desegregation that he had been forced to resign from his position as vicar of a parish in Southwestern Virginia during the controversy over the diocesan conference center in 1958. Serving in Kentucky in 1969, Doyle said that he objected to the black power movement for the same reasons he had condemned segregation a decade before: "the deliberate promotion of secular theories of racial 'dignity'" had no place in an institution that believed in the unity of all human beings in Christ. While Doyle's objections were theological, the reactions of numerous lay Episcopalians were simply visceral and blunt. Perry Laukhuff, a layman from Norwalk, Connecticut, wrote Bayne: "To see grown men groveling is nauseating. . . . This is the kind of behavior which long ago took away from me any respect for the national leadership of the Church." And Cornelia McCarthy, a laywoman from Bronxville, New York, stated that she would "never contribute another dime to any Church" that accepted "Forman's vicious demand." Those attitudes had become so widespread, in fact, that the Executive Council was forced to make serious cutbacks in the denominational budget for 1969, and Bayne feared that the Black Manifesto was going to exacerbate the financial crisis in the Episcopal Church even further.[4]

Three weeks after Forman delivered the manifesto at national church headquarters, the Executive Council gathered to decide on an official response. With the backing of a handful of supporters—William Stringfellow and the ESCRU board of directors had endorsed the idea of reparations—John Hines tried to be hopeful and upbeat. Though he rejected the concept of reparations on theological grounds (Christ had already made reparation for the sins of humankind), Hines thought the Episcopal Church could and should do more to aid the powerless and the poor for whom Forman spoke. Despite the conservatives' charge that the manifesto was a "revolutionary, Marxist" document, Hines saw that some of its concerns were also solidly capitalistic, e.g., seeking money for investment in black-owned businesses and institutions. Viewed in this light, the Black Manifesto was merely reemphasizing a goal to which the Episcopal Church had given its approval in 1967 through GCSP and through participation in IFCO. "There is no doubt in my mind that this Church is moving in the right direction," Hines declared. "Our mandate is for full speed ahead—united . . . in the name of Jesus Christ!"[5]

Hines's optimism, unfortunately, was not contagious, and the Executive Council meeting proved to be a difficult and contentious affair. Although a few members did speak in favor of the manifesto—Robert DeWitt, the bishop of Pennsylvania, suggested placing a $1 million mortgage on church properties in order to meet some of the manifesto's financial demands—the council as a whole rejected Forman's statement. Eventually, the council agreed on a compromise measure and formed a committee to explore "new and sacrificial ways" (other than reparations) by which the Episcopal Church could attack poverty and injustice in American society. The committee was placed under the direction of John Coburn, the president of the House of Deputies and former dean of the Episcopal Theological School. Coburn, an advocate of the church's involvement in social outreach, had recently worked as a teacher in Harlem, and he seemed a logical choice for the task of discussing and investigating Forman's demands.[6]

GCSP grants also proved to be a source of sharp disagreement among Executive Council members, with a grant application from the Jackson Human Rights Project in Mississippi receiving the most attention. Opponents of the grant argued that, rather than fostering racial reconciliation, the Jackson Human Rights Project was actually a black separatist organization advocating the use of violence against whites; thus it was at odds with a GCSP regulation that forbade the awarding of a grant to any group engaged in violent activities. At issue in the debate was a poem published in the organization's newsletter, warning the white American to "run, run, run, run!" because "the nigger . . . is gonna kill you man, when he catches your white ass." In addition, Muhammed Kenyatta, one of the project's most vocal staff members, was accused of having demonstrated how to construct a "Molotov cocktail" in another issue of the newsletter. The conservatives who opposed the Jackson project resurrected the "states' rights" theory of ecclesiastical polity that had earlier been used by church officials in Mississippi and Alabama at the height of the civil rights movement. It was wrong, they said, for the Executive Council to send denominational funds into a diocese where the bishop (in this case, John Allin) opposed the grant. Despite strenuous objections from representatives from southern dioceses, however, the council approved the grant by a one-vote majority.[7]

Because a large amount of unfinished business still remained from the 1967 General Convention, and because the times had become so chaotic, a special session of the General Convention had been scheduled to meet in August 1969. With this meeting fast approaching, the new "Coburn committee" was asked not only to deal with the contentiousness surrounding the Black Manifesto, but also to complete and submit a report to the Executive Council before the special convention. Coburn was aware of the larger ecumenical context in which his denomination operated, and his first step was to hold a meeting with three white National Council of Churches officials at the Princeton Club in New York. A few days later he took James Forman himself to dinner (in more egalitarian surroundings—a Chinese restaurant near Columbia University) to ask for suggestions about what he thought the Episcopal Church could realistically do. Since both the men had known and respected Jonathan Daniels, they had a profitable conversation about the recent efforts of white Episcopalians to address racism. Coburn's next hurdle was convincing UBCL members to join his task force. Although the black Episcopalians were initially suspicious of the white-dominated committee and accused the Executive Council of trying to address the manifesto "by rhetoric and pronouncement" rather than by action, they eventually sent four representatives to take part in the deliberations.[8]

The key figure on the Coburn committee proved to be Charles Willie, a sociology professor at Syracuse University and one of the few African American members of the Executive Council. Willie had been a classmate of Martin Luther King at Morehouse College, and he fully supported the social-action focus the church had adopted at the 1967 General Convention. However, he had also gone on record in opposition to black power, arguing that, since the church was "in the business of reconciliation," it should not endorse any concept that divided one group of people from another. Based on his training as a sociologist, Willie believed further that the debate over black power was potentially harmful to the African American community because it deflected attention away from the tangible benefits the civil rights movement had been able to gain for them. He recognized that racial chauvinism might have psychological appeal "for a few persons who are not wise in the ways of social change," but he feared that it was in fact "a backward movement," akin to Booker T. Washington's disastrous acquiescence to segregation at the end of the nineteenth century.[9] Although some African Americans labeled Willie an "Oreo cookie" for continuing to insist on the value of racial integration, he sought to steer a middle course between revolutionary black militancy and reactionary white conservatism.[10] As a consequence he stressed that the Black Manifesto was correct in some regards (e.g., its emphasis on the devastating impact of white racism) but incorrect in its "implication that black people in America can be bought for money." The manifesto was "an awkward cry" by African Americans for recognition, he emphasized, but the church should not mistakenly "pay off blacks to stay where they are, which is outside the mainstream in American life."[11]

The Coburn committee held its meetings during the summer of 1969, and with Willie's mediating presence it was able to submit recommendations to the Executive Council at the beginning of the Special General Convention. While recognizing that the church could not resolve all the diverse problems of American life, the committee's report affirmed that responsible stewardship of denominational resources required a response to Forman and the Black Manifesto. The committee proposed a number of resolutions that the council soon adopted: (1) diversifying the membership of the Executive Council by adding six additional representatives—two for the youth of the church, and four for African Americans and other ethnic minorities; (2) reaffirming the importance of the church's own program, GCSP; (3) supporting the principles of black economic development and self-determination, but repudiating the specific political ideology articulated by the Black Manifesto; (4) calling for an ecumenical conference to study how religious bodies might better support racial and economic justice in the United States; (5) strengthening the church's three black colleges in the South (St. Augustine's, St. Paul's, and Voorhees); (6) forming a permanent Executive Council committee to review and coordinate the church's ministry among ethnic and racial minorities; (7) creating and distributing educational materials about the church's views on race; and (8) encouraging dioceses and large parishes to follow the example of the national church and provide funds for investment in the black community. "Penitence must issue in action," the report concluded, and "the Church must speak . . . out of the courage of its beliefs, which accepts the divisions and brokenness as it seeks to over-come them."[12]

Despite the confident note expressed in this report, the Episcopal Church was about to experience firsthand the very "divisions and bro-kenness" to which the Coburn committee referred. The 1969 Special General Convention, which met (as a cost-cutting measure) on the cam-pus of the University of Notre Dame in South Bend, Indiana, soon be-came a battleground as factions within the church warred over the social outlook their denomination ought to assume. Although John Hines could not have foreseen all that was to happen during the gathering, the bibli-cal text on which he based his opening sermon ("We are troubled on every side, yet not distressed; . . . persecuted, but not forsaken" [2 Cor. 4:8–9]) certainly epitomized his eventual perspective on the events of the week at South Bend. In his address Hines affirmed the recommenda-tions of the Coburn committee's report and urged the church to stick to the course it had been taking since 1967. He distinguished his own views on the church's mission from others that were beginning to polarize por-tions of the church: conservatives, who stressed only "the vertical dimen-sion of our faith," and radicals, who wished to tear down institutional Christianity. Hines asked those factions not to waste time and energy bickering with one another but simply to unite and "heal our broken world," just as the ecumenical movement was beginning to heal historic church divisions. Finally, he begged Americans everywhere, *"Don't give up on the Church*—even in its apparent defeats."[13]

As if to mock the advice of its presiding bishop, the Episcopal Church did not unite but seemed to come apart at the seams in the days that followed. On the first evening of the convention, when a joint assembly of the House of Deputies and the House of Bishops gathered to discuss future trends in the deployment of clergy, the UBCL orchestrated a take-over of the podium that instantly disrupted the deliberations. UBCL lead-ers chose Muhammed Kenyatta, a BEDC-sponsored community organizer in the Philadelphia area and the man whose work in Mississippi had drawn fire at the Executive Council meeting in May, to demand that Episcopa-lians drop their other business and address the Black Manifesto. At the appointed time, Kenyatta strode to the rostrum and wrestled the micro-phone away from John Hines, who, when order was restored, allowed him to speak to the convention. Paul Washington, who had worked with Kenyatta in Philadelphia, took the microphone next. Declaring that white people had no right to set the agenda for the church by themselves, he led a walkout of African Americans from the convention hall. Although some left with reluctance—this was the first General Convention to include significant numbers of African American representatives—the demonstration had its intended effect and helped change the focus of the meeting. Yet when bishops and deputies reassembled the next day to discuss the manifesto, a group of white antiwar activists stood at the back of the convention hall and made their concerns known by reading aloud the names of American soldiers killed in Vietnam. Later in the convention, two military deserters appeared without warning and asked to be granted sanctuary by the church; when the deputies refused to consider this request, separate groups—one white, one black—rose and turned their backs on the gathering. Sallie Eckert, a white observer from Michigan, also interrupted a meeting of the bishops in order to castigate them for refusing to trust black people on the question of the manifesto, while Mary Eunice Oliver, one of the four duly elected lay deputies from the diocese of Los Angeles, was publicly barred from taking her seat at the convention because women were not yet allowed to serve as deputies. And, adding to the many other distractions, it was announced that James Pike, the alleged heretic and erstwhile bishop of California, was missing and presumed dead in the wilderness in Israel. According to John Krumm, the rector of a parish in New York, the "miracle convention of 1969" had revealed the true identity of the Episcopal Church: "It is not the comfortable upper middle-class version of respectable Christianity [but] the most diverse, motley, widely varied group of human beings that could be imagined."[14]

Against this backdrop, the main debate over reparations continued throughout the week. UBCL leaders insisted that the church should give two hundred thousand dollars directly to BEDC, and they were adamant that neither they nor GCSP should be used as a buffer for dealing with BEDC—an action that John Burgess thought would be akin to "using pimps to push drugs in the ghetto." When the convention as a whole voted that representatives from BEDC should apply for money from GCSP just like any other organization, several African American clergy angrily denounced the decision. Since the Executive Council had the final say on any GCSP grant, the convention's action insured that white leaders would continue to decide which black organizations were worthy to receive the church's funds. Although he was a strong supporter of GCSP, Junius Carter, rector of the Church of the Holy Cross in Pittsburgh and one of a handful of black deputies at the convention, stood up to protest what had happened. He declared that the convention had just participated in the "crucifixion" of its black members. "You don't trust me, you don't trust black priests and you don't trust black people," he shouted into the micro-

phone. Then, angry and upset, he left the convention hall. Carter's stinging words had their effect, for the convention reversed its earlier decision
and adopted a new measure, authorizing a two-hundred-thousand-dollar
grant to the National Commission of Black Churchmen. Since NCBC was
at least an ecumenical coalition of *black* church leaders (Tollie Caution
was a representative of the Episcopal Church), the UBCL accepted this
decision: it not only insured that BEDC would receive funding, but it also
gave African Americans ultimate control over the money set aside for
economic development in their communities. Black Episcopalians took
satisfaction from the fact that they had kept the convention from dealing
only with internal affairs and had forced the church to discuss racism in
American society as well.[15]

African Americans had achieved gains at the Special General Convention, but many middle-class white Americans now began to wonder
whether the Episcopal Church had lost its corporate mind. As a result
Hines, Coburn, and other leaders found themselves caught between two
opposing camps: those who wanted the church to become further engaged in the social revolution of the day and those who wanted it to turn
back to strictly "spiritual" concerns. When the front page of the *New York
Times* reported that Episcopalians had voted to give two hundred thousand dollars in "reparations" to BEDC—a decision the *Times* then denounced on its editorial page—Coburn and Hines immediately sent a
response, insisting that the convention had not actually endorsed the
principle of reparations. Though that rebuttal was technically correct,
the *Times* report had already done its damage. Either way Hines turned
he received criticism, for the support his denomination had given to black
empowerment appeared tepid to some observers but outrageous to others. J. Metz Rollins, the Presbyterian minister who directed NCBC, for
instance, was offended that African American church people had been
made to act as intermediaries with BEDC. Why couldn't the Episcopal
Church, he asked, just give the money directly to the black group? In
contrast, vestry members at several white parishes in the South asked
Hines why they should contribute money in order to enable their church
to support black militants. James Stoney, a white priest in Alabama, called
the convention's decision "cowardly, dishonest, hypocritical, immoral,
and against the laws of God." However, he said he did not blame Hines
personally—the presiding bishop had just been living and working in
New York for too long. If the presiding bishop could get back to his regional roots, he would see "a great difference in the way people think in
your Diocese of Texas, and in your home town of Seneca, S.C."[16]

Stoney was correct in many ways. As Hines well knew, the most vituperative opposition he faced came from the Foundation for Christian Theology, based in Victoria, Texas. Organized in 1966 by Paul Kratzig, the rector of Trinity Church, Victoria, the foundation wished "to define and counteract the influence of Humanism as a substitute for Christian beliefs"—a familiar refrain among prosegregation church groups—and said it was dedicated to presenting "a Christian challenge to those who presume to . . . involve the Church in the social, political, and economic activities of our times."[17] Kratzig claimed that many traditional missionary programs had been eliminated under Hines's leadership and that the Executive Council was intent on supporting black power groups instead. He also accused the national church leadership of undermining religious freedoms by attempting to take American Protestants "back to medieval times when the hearts and minds of the people were controlled" by a distant ecclesiastical bureaucracy.[18] The foundation described itself as part of what Richard Nixon later dubbed the "great silent majority"—Episcopalians who were forced to battle against overwhelming odds in order to restore the church to its true mission. The group was particularly strong in the Southwest, where Joseph Harte, the bishop of Arizona, and Senator Barry Goldwater were its most notable supporters. Hines had little use for Kratzig; he spoke of the Foundation for Christian Theology with contempt, calling it "fundamentalistic, pro-segregation, . . . and not willing to face the 20th century and its demands"—a characterization with which even some conservatives on the Executive Council agreed.[19]

Kratzig's organization was clearly far outside the mainstream of the Episcopal Church and thus easily dismissed, but the "loyal opposition" that Hines faced at Executive Council meetings demanded and received a more serious hearing. One of Hines's most articulate opponents was George Murray, who succeeded Charles Carpenter as bishop of Alabama in 1969. A vocal and persistent critic of most forms of social activism in his denomination since the mid-1960s, Murray had grown "weary and embarrassed over dogmatic and simplistic pronouncements by some Church leaders on widely-varied and complicated subjects in which they have no special competence whatever."[20] A few weeks before the South Bend convention, he had published an article in The Episcopalian arguing that the desire for social change was seriously interfering with the tasks of evangelism. Though he believed that the church had some responsibility to help combat poverty, he also feared that the Episcopal Church was in danger of abandoning the gospel's command to "seek . . . first His Kingdom and His righteousness" by substituting ephemeral secular positions in place of evangelism. Contrary to Hines's oft-stated view that God called Christians into full engagement with the world, Murray was adamant that "the kingdom to which the Church calls men is not ultimately a kingdom of this world."[21]

Although Murray based his criticisms on theological grounds, even Episcopalians who claimed to be supportive of the church's social ministry began to question the value of decisions made at the 1969 convention. Several of them (including Murray and a coalition of self-styled moderates from the Midwest and the Northeast) banded together and formed a group known as Episcopalians and Others for Responsible Social Action. Rather than handing money over to radicals who threatened "violence and intimidation as a means of obtaining their objectives," the leaders of the new organization proposed to fund only established, relatively conservative black organizations such as the NAACP and the Urban League. They asked for financial support from Episcopalians that would enable them to assist African Americans without furthering a social revolution.[22] According to Roy Wilkins, the head of the NAACP, the Episcopal Church and other mainline white denominations had recently gone astray by contributing church funds to radical black groups. Echoing one of the charges made by Nathan Wright in 1967, Wilkins thought that by giving away money to African American hucksters—men "without credentials or competence"—some liberal whites actually demonstrated their contempt for legitimate black leaders working patiently through the nation's legal and political system. Whatever the merits of its goals, Episcopalians and Others for Responsible Social Action fell woefully short of the three-hundred-thousand-dollar figure its leadership originally projected. After raising approximately forty-one thousand dollars in its first year of operation, the organization quietly disbanded in the fall of 1970.[23]

The most persistent and widespread complaint against GCSP focused on the threat that it posed to the polity upon which many Episcopalians believed their church was organized—namely, the "episcopal principle." Conservatives argued that their denomination was a federation of independent dioceses, not a national organization as such. Based on the organizational model they supported, leadership was meant to "flow up" from the dioceses to the central administration in New York, not vice versa. But according to the procedures under which GCSP operated, decisions made at the national level could be imposed upon dioceses without their consent. Although a bishop was supposed to be consulted whenever the GCSP staff received an application for a grant within the boundaries of that leader's diocese, his disapproval was a sig-nificant but not absolute factor in how the grant request was handled. Hence, white Episcopalians (in southern dioceses especially) questioned the constitutionality of GCSP. As earlier controversies over the involve-ment of national church employees in Mississippi and Alabama had illus-trated, nothing infuriated bishops and local church leaders more than the idea that outsiders could be involved in decisions on matters in the geo-graphical areas in which they lived, ministered, and exercised ecclesiasti-cal jurisdiction.[24]

Among the many requests for funding that the presiding bishop, GCSP staff, and Executive Council considered between 1968 and 1970, four in particular reveal the complex nature of Episcopalians' response to racial issues during this turbulent period. One of these cases involved the Selma Inter-Religious Project, a program directed by Francis Walter in Tuscaloosa, Alabama. Walter had been forced to leave the diocese of Ala-bama in 1961 after his conflict with Charles Carpenter over ESCRU and racial integration. Following brief stints as vicar of a small parish in Sa-vannah and as priest-in-charge of Grace Church, Van Vorst, the "mother church" of white urban ministry in the North, Walter had returned to Alabama in 1965. Answering John Morris's call for a continuing "minis-try of presence" in the aftermath of the "Great March," Walter was instru-mental in the founding of the Selma Inter-Religious Project, an organization dedicated to improving race relations in the state's Black Belt. Bishops Carpenter and Murray both strenuously opposed him, ar-guing that his work was "a direct insult to the ministry of all those who are working . . . under proper authorization from their churches" in the field of race, and they did all they could to keep him from returning to his native state. Since Walter remained canonically resident in the diocese of Newark, Carpenter and Murray could have no direct control over his secular activities, but their disapproval prevented him from receiving a grant from the Church and Race fund in 1966. Despite those difficulties, Walter was eventually able to obtain funding from the Commission on Religion and Race of the National Council of Churches—another mark against him in the bishops' eyes—and he achieved success in working with the black community in Dallas, Lowndes, and Wilcox counties.[25]

After GCSP began its operations in 1968, Walter assumed that the goals of his organization were consistent with those of the Episcopal pro-gram and that, as a priest serving among African Americans, he would have little trouble receiving a grant. The application process proved far more difficult than he had expected, however. Led by an interracial staff committed to empowering black people in the rural South, Walter's project failed to elicit strong support either from white Episcopalians in Alabama or from the radical GCSP staff in New York. When asked for his reaction to Walter's request for a small grant from GCSP, George Murray responded that the Selma Inter-Religious Project did not meet the criteria set for the church program: it was not organized by African Americans in Alabama themselves, but by a white priest from the diocese of Newark, whose primary financial support came from the National Council of Churches, an agency based in another state. John O'Neal, a black consultant who worked for GCSP, confirmed Murray's decidedly disingenuous critique of Walter's program: the Selma Inter-Religious Project should not receive a GCSP grant because its staff and board of directors, dominated by middle-class whites, could not be truly representative of the rural blacks for whom they said they spoke. Until the racial character of the program leadership underwent a fundamental change—whites giving up their positions to poor blacks—O'Neal concluded that Walter's organization could not expect to receive assistance from the Episcopal Church.[26]

Although the fate of the Selma Inter-Religious Project was decided in relative obscurity, the forty-five thousand dollars given in two major grants to Malcolm X Liberation University in Durham, North Carolina, received headline attention. The school had been opened in the spring of 1969 by African Americans dissatisfied with Duke University's failure to develop an adequate black studies curriculum, and Thomas Fraser, the bishop of North Carolina, at first endorsed the decision by the Executive Council to give it a GCSP grant. Regarding himself as "a transplanted northerner," Fraser had worked hard to remove many traditional racial barriers in his diocese since arriving in North Carolina in 1960. Because of his earlier commitment to racial integration, however, Fraser had immediately gone on record against black power, equating the concept with the racist philosophy of the Ku Klux Klan and threatening to excommunicate any Episcopalian who advocated either white or black supremacy. He also disliked the name of the new black educational institution in the heart of his diocese, and as the impact of the Special General Convention began to be felt in the church in his state, he became more and more uneasy about Malcolm X University.[27]

Fraser wrote Leon Modeste in the fall of 1969 and asked for better warning before any additional grants were made in his diocese. Modeste not only refused to honor Fraser's request, but he also dismissed the idea that the GCSP staff owed anything to local church people. "Risk and controversy were the birthrights of the GCSP," Modeste argued, and he did not think it was wise "to destroy the little confidence in the Church still remaining among the powerless" poor by allowing dioceses and their bishops to stand in the way of the denomination's national mission. This response angered Fraser, and at his next diocesan convention, he condemned Malcolm X University as "an unrealistic experiment in education" and as a direct threat to the essential interracial character of the Christian church. White conservatives in North Carolina were even more outraged than their bishop, and they dramatically curtailed their financial contributions to the diocese in 1970. The unwillingness of Modeste and his staff to listen to local officials about GCSP grants, Fraser charged, caused a shortfall of nearly $165,000 in his diocesan budget, and as a result the diocese of North Carolina was forced to reduce its donation to the national church by nearly 40 percent that year.[28]

The third example—a twenty-five-thousand-dollar grant to the Black Awareness Coordinating Committee of Denmark, South Carolina—illuminates not only prejudiced white attitudes toward black empowerment, but also the ambiguous place of white-supported black educational institutions within the Episcopal Church. Denmark was the home of Voorhees College, founded as an industrial training school for African Americans at the end of the nineteenth century. With the support of William Alexander Guerry, the bishop of South Carolina, the school became affiliated with the Episcopal Church through the American Church Institute for Negroes in 1924. An Episcopal chapel was established on the campus of the school, and during the 1950s it became a significant focus for Tollie Caution's work with racial minorities in the denomination. With the rise of black militancy in the late 1960s, however, life at Voorhees began to change dramatically. The Black Awareness Coordinating Committee was founded in 1967, and it was involved in a series of protests at Voorhees and at nearby South Carolina State College in Orangeburg. In April 1969, after Voorhees officials failed to respond adequately to demands for a black-oriented curriculum and greater black representation on the faculty and board of trustees, a group of students seized the administration building. The state police and the National Guard intervened, and thirty-five protesters were arrested. Pressure from the Black Awareness group kept tensions high; when four black faculty members were suspended from teaching on campus in February 1970, protests again forced the closing of the school and the summoning of the National Guard. While white Episcopalians in South Carolina decried the student militancy at Voorhees, African Americans involved with the protest movement condemned the arrogance and paternalism of white church people, who supported the school with wealth gained from slave labor and assumed they would always be able to control black southerners.[29]

The troubles at Voorhees had come to the attention of the national church when four students from the school interrupted the May 1969 meeting of the Executive Council to ask for help in their struggle with the school administration. Although the council itself took no formal action, John Hines (as a South Carolina native) was authorized to pay the bail bond premiums for three students unable to arrange for their own release. This decision earned a quick rebuke from J. Kenneth Morris, the white priest who was chairman of the Voorhees board of trustees, and set the stage for another round of controversy within the church. At its October 1970 meeting, the Executive Council followed the advice of the GCSP staff and approved (by a 21–to-16 vote) a grant to the Black Awareness Coordinating Committee for its community development work in Denmark. During a particularly heated debate, both Gray Temple, the bishop of South Carolina, and John Pinckney, the bishop of Upper South Carolina, spoke in opposition to the grant and cited the black organization's record of violence during the two campus uprisings. Frederick Williams of the UBCL and Charles Willie argued that racism and the intransigence of college officials were the real cause of the disturbances at Voorhees. And Leon Modeste, who later accused Temple of opposing another GCSP grant in his diocese because it threatened his own financial interests, simply brushed his protests aside and labeled the bishop a racist. The resentment of local white Episcopalians, however, eventually forced the Executive Council to send three of its members (all white) to South Carolina to investigate how the Black Awareness Coordinating Committee was using the grant money. Following the investigating committee's report that there was little evidence that the organization still existed, the grant was suspended. This decision led African Americans on the council to observe that, since blacks and whites in the South "live in different worlds," it was unrealistic to expect African Americans in Denmark to talk honestly with white investigators about the work they were doing. John O'Neal of the GCSP staff declared that persistent intimidation and pressure from "the plantation overlords" who controlled the church in South Carolina were the factors principally responsible for the demise of the radical black organization.[30]

The fourth controversial GCSP grant and the most hotly debated of all the Executive Council actions in this period concerned a Mexican American, not an African American, organization: the Alianza Federal de Mercedes. Since GCSP was created theoretically to assist and empower poor people of all races and ethnic groups, the Alianza, committed to regaining lands in the Southwest taken by the United States after the Mexican War, was eligible and deemed worthy to receive a forty-thousand-dollar grant. Although the group had apparently violated the church's guidelines on nonviolence by supporting an armed assault on a courthouse, Modeste and Hines did not think that should automatically disqualify them; the violence, they argued, was a form of self-defense that had arisen out of frustration at the conditions under which Mexican Americans lived. Based on this reasoning, the Executive Council approved the grant request by a narrow margin of 23 to 21, with three abstentions and four members absent, at its December 1969 meeting. C.J. Kinsolving, the bishop of New Mexico and Southwest Texas, had adamantly opposed the grant, and when the council refused to follow his advice, his diocese immediately withheld the entire sum it owed to the national church (approximately eighty-two thousand dollars) in 1970.[31]

Such reactions point to the clear split that had grown between Episcopalians in the South and Southwest and the leadership of the denomination in New York. Edwin Thayer, the bishop of Colorado, for example, wrote Hines to complain that the "Ivory Tower of the Executive Council . . : is violating a fundamental tenet of the Anglican Communion" by attempting to circumvent the authority of a bishop over his diocese. Thayer also accused the council of acting more like "a medieval curia" than a representative of the ostensibly democratic Anglican polity. The bishop of Southeast Florida, James Duncan, wrote in a similar vein to castigate Modeste for his treatment of Thomas Fraser. Despite the tendency of the GCSP staff to "pontificate from your throne in New York," Duncan asserted, "salvation . . . will come only as the people of God both [sic] black, brown and white, poor and rich, on the local level" learn to work together as Christians. John Ellison, the rector of the Church of St. Clement in El Paso, Texas, remarked that the national church staff was not only acting like a "sacred cow" but also "killing the goose . . . that lays the golden egg." "Something is seriously wrong" in the Episcopal Church, Ellison wrote early in 1970, and it was "time to clean house—now" in preparation for the General Convention that was to meet later in the year.[32]

With dissatisfaction and anger against GCSP growing everyday among white Episcopalians, Hines was forced to appoint a fact-finding committee to evaluate the program. Chaired by William Booth, an African American judge from New York with whom Hines had consulted in the development of GCSP in 1967, the committee presented a largely favorable report to the Executive Council in May 1970. Although the committee had considered the possibility of giving a bishop veto power over grants in his diocese—a safeguard that conservatives increasingly were demanding—it decided not to recommend such a procedural change. "Those who participate in the oppression of people are not capable of designing strategy for the relief of that oppression," the committee reasoned, for few white church people could adequately identify with the poor. The only concession that the Booth committee made was a promise to sponsor hearings in advance in dioceses affected by potentially controversial grants. William Ikard, a committee member representing the diocese of New Mexico and Southwest Texas, strenuously disagreed with the majority's position. As he had insisted a few months before when he opposed the Alianza grant, consultation and trust were central concerns for most of the middle-class Episcopalians on whose donations GCSP depended, and those men and women were not likely to be mollified simply by being allowed to talk at hearings. In addition to Ikard's complaint, twenty-five diocesan conventions across the country adopted resolutions requesting that bishops be allowed to block potential grants within their dioceses. Finally, fifteen members of the Executive Council itself (including George Murray, William Ikard, and nine other white southerners) signed their own report calling for diocesan bishops to have at least limited veto power over grants.[33]

Not surprisingly, GCSP was the main topic on the agenda when bishops and deputies of the denomination assembled in Houston in October 1970. The 1970 General Convention was a homecoming of sorts for Hines; Houston was the headquarters of his former diocese, and he believed that the Episcopal Church had owed a convention to the city ever since Henry Sherrill moved the 1955 meeting from Houston to Honolulu. The timing for a church gathering in the South, however, was still not auspicious. Although segregation no longer existed by law in Texas, racial prejudice was running high, and white Episcopalians in the South and the Southwest were strongly opposed to GCSP. Furthermore, the credibility of the Episcopal leadership seemed to be at an all-time low, represented by a $1 million shortfall in anticipated income for the denominational budget that year. Security was also extremely tight in the convention hall, for police had learned of threats—allegedly from a disgruntled black priest—against Hines's life. Contradicting the optimism in Hines's opening sermon, in which he valiantly defended the church's commitment to the political and economic empowerment of African Americans through GCSP, the 1970 General Convention effectively reversed whatever progress the church had made in that regard at the two previous conventions. As Bishop Duncan of Southeast Florida aptly re-marked, the real issue at stake in Houston was not GCSP or any other program the denominational leadership was going to discuss, but control over the church itself. And at the 1970 convention, white Episcopalians succeeded in regaining control of "their" church.[34]

The convention did not entirely repudiate GCSP—approximately $1 million was still budgeted for the program in 1971—but white church people made sure that African Americans could not make decisions about church money without their approval. By giving veto power to diocesan bishops, for example, white conservatives gained the key provision for which they had been lobbying: a bishop was given thirty days in which to object to any proposed GCSP grant in his diocese; if he objected, only a majority of the full membership of the Executive Council could override his veto. When this decision won the support of even outspoken opponents of GCSP such as C.J. Kinsolving, it was clear that Hines's original commitment to funding "without strings" had been overcome by those who wished to keep tighter reins on the denomination's finances. Although some white Episcopalians had feared that their church was about to fall apart, the results of the Houston convention left them feeling relieved and content. Black Episcopalians had a decidedly different reaction to what had taken place. Speaking on behalf of the UBCL, Lloyd Casson of St. Matthew's Church in Wilmington, Delaware, declared that the forces of negativity and racism had won the day at Houston. Yet despite these strong words, UBCL leaders admitted in private that they had probably gained as much as they could at the convention. Since African American clergy knew that Hines had never envisioned black church members as an integral part of GCSP, most of them viewed the program as symbolic of their ambiguous status within the Episcopal Church.[35]

The 1970 General Convention also marked the official demise of ESCRU. Since the UBCL and NCBC had clearly become the groups most in need of contributions from black Episcopalians, African Americans had little enthusiasm for keeping ESCRU alive. ESCRU's endorsement of the Black Manifesto, furthermore, had cost the organization the last remnants of its support among prointegration whites. Even the remaining whites in the organization who were not intellectually opposed to black power knew they could no longer be leaders in the struggle against racism, and with the rise of antiwar sentiment throughout the country, prominent racial liberals such as Paul Moore and Malcolm Boyd found themselves increasingly drawn to the movement against American involvement in Vietnam. In part because of John Morris's earlier strategic efforts to keep his society focused on race rather than on the emerging peace movement, most antiwar whites had stopped being actively involved in ESCRU and had shifted their energies to the Episcopal Peace Fellowship instead. Although conservative groups still saw ESCRU as a threat to their interests, the society in fact could do little more than limp to the convention in Houston, where Kim Dreisbach hoped its membership might battle the forces of racism one last time before closing down the organization.[36]

The end of ESCRU, when it finally came, was almost anticlimactic. Since it had only a few members and virtually no funds, continuing to operate seemed futile. In a statement hardly noticed in the midst of the larger battle over GCSP, ESCRU vice president Barbara Harris announced that the society would suspend operations by the end of the year. A black laywoman who had been active for several years in the Philadelphia chapter, Harris believed that ESCRU had served its purpose and that the UBCL and GCSP had assumed most of its functions. She counseled African Americans, therefore, to join the UBCL, and she asked white Episcopalians to work against racism within the communities where they lived. A few of the white Episcopalians who were left in the organization objected to Harris's advice. Mary Eunice Oliver, the lay deputy barred from the Special General Convention in 1969, thought whites like herself should have a group to which they could belong, and she resented the fact that her race disqualified her from membership in the UBCL. Kim Dreisbach also lamented the loss of the ideal of racial unity that had inspired the founders of ESCRU. He doubted that GCSP, bound even more closely into the official church structures by decisions made at the Houston convention, had the freedom to attack racism in the way that an independent organization like ESCRU could. Disappointed, he said he still longed to work for the millennial day when "brothers and sisters, of all hues and clans" would bring into reality the ESCRU motto: "Behold, how good and joyful a thing it is, for brethren to dwell together in unity."[37]

With ESCRU disbanded and the autonomy of GCSP seriously curtailed, racial issues seemed less and less to occupy the attention of Episcopalians—and white Americans in general—after 1970. The tone for the nation's social policy was set by Daniel Moynihan, who as Richard Nixon's chief domestic adviser called for "a period of benign neglect" with regard to African Americans. According to a *Newsweek* report, the 1970s paralleled the Reconstruction period of the 1870s, when northern whites backed away from active concern for the freed black minority in the South. The mainline Protestant denominations, too, were engaged in a retrograde movement, and conservatives such as Presbyterian business-man J. Howard Pew loudly opined that it was time simply to "let the Church be the Church." According to Pew, churches had no warrant to trouble themselves with civil rights or any other fundamentally political matter. "The mission of the Church is to redeem souls," he maintained, "and only as she redeems individuals will society be redeemed." The redoubtable Edward Guerry expressed a similar sentiment for conservative Episcopalians. He accused the church of forsaking Jesus' commandment "to make disciples of all nations" (Matt. 28:19, RSV) by making the gift of "large sums of money to secular groups" the primary focus of its mission. Cancel GCSP and return to "the real work" of Christianity, he advised. Helen Smith Shoemaker of the Anglican Fellowship of Prayer also questioned the wisdom of Hines's decision "to help poor people gain social, political, economic power in order to get into the main stream of American life." Spiritual power was what the poor needed the most, she insisted, and despite her own comfortable social position, she wondered if Jesus would "want anyone to be in the main stream of American life today."[38]

At the same time, leaders in the mainline denominations became aware of another, even more disturbing trend, as church membership figures began to decline for the first time in the nation's history—a particularly noticeable reversal after the tremendous growth that had occurred between 1945 and 1965. Dean Kelley, an official of the National Council of Churches, popularized a thesis that linked the decrease in church membership with the tendency of clergy and denominational executives to involve their religious institutions in social change. In his widely read study, Why Conservative Churches Are Growing (1972), Kelley asserted that Protestant church leaders, in their eagerness to become quasi-political statesmen, had unwittingly undermined the one contribution they could make to modern society: providing and maintaining spiritual meaning. And as the Episcopal Church and other resolutely modern mainline denominations continued to decline in membership and influence, Kelley argued, conservative groups adhering to traditional beliefs about sin, forgiveness, and eternal salvation would flourish in their place. Sociologist Jeffrey Hadden insisted, moreover, that an identity crisis had encouraged many "marching ministers" to use their involvement in civil rights activities as a substitute for solid religious faith. This analysis appealed to men such as Will Campbell, Duncan Gray, and William Stringfellow, who all retained a conservative theological outlook and resisted the often uncritical celebration of the social revolution of the 1960s.

Remembering the March on Washington in 1963, Stringfellow thought that, no matter how good the intentions of the clergy and other church people who had participated in it, "something terrible" had taken place that day. By thinking they could operate on the world's terms, American Christians had betrayed their spiritual ideals and made the march "a Palm Sunday, not an Easter, and hence a triumph for Caesar and not for Christ."[39]

Gender was also a subtle factor reinforcing this emergent critique of clerical (i.e., male) activism in the Episcopal Church. Although Episcopal women were still excluded from serving as General Convention deputies when GCSP was created in 1967, they had been asked to donate a large sum of money from their own United Thank Offering toward the new outreach program. In agreeing to do what men such as John Hines and Stephen Bayne requested, the women's Triennial Meeting placed itself at the forefront of the denomination's response to the racial crisis, for the bishops and male deputies of the convention did not officially adopt the program until they received word of the generous pledge the women had made. Conservative church women soon began to question what had happened at the convention. They charged that, by giving away valuable financial resources to a program that was administered mainly by black men, white women (the largest active—but woefully underrepresented—group of Episcopalians) had actually weakened their position within the church. As Ilse Helmus of Uniondale, New York, remarked, "it is all very well to be flexible, but . . . how can the 'powers that be' leave high and dry so much of the work that has enlisted the interest and support of the women of the Church?" Dorothy Faber, one of the leaders of the Foundation for Christian Theology, was even more blunt. Asserting that the male leadership of the Episcopal Church had given the women's money away to black groups that supported "bloody revolution" rather than genuine mission, she organized the "Christian Thank Offering" to which "faithful Christian women" were invited to contribute and over which only they would have control.[40]

In the spring of 1968, furthermore, during the process of restructuring that accompanied the creation of GCSP, the Executive Council had reduced the denominational bureaucracy by eliminating the General Division of Women's Work. Believing that women could now be fully integrated into the organizational structure of the denomination, male leaders took over most of the decision-making roles formerly belonging to women. Just as Tollie Caution's "separate but equal" program of black ministries had been deemed superfluous in 1967, women too were shut out of leadership positions in what liberal white males regarded as an updated, modern denomination. Theodora Sorg, one of the few women on the Executive Council, protested this trend and insisted that "since women are part of the whole Church, then the whole Church has got to take . . . seriously" the work that women themselves could do. Cynthia Wedel, an active Episcopalian as well as the first female president of the National Council of Churches, also wondered why her church had "fallen into the trap of false alternatives" in the late 1960s, appearing to place social action above everything else. Not specifically rejecting the commitment to black empowerment, she did list it as a prime example of "pressure . . . imposed from above" by "a new breed of clergymen . . . insensitive to the average man and woman in the pew." In contrast, Wedel held up the quiet contributions of "women in the rank-and-file church membership" who had carried on a number of ministries with little recognition from their "marching ministers." A change of approach was needed, and though male activists would tend to dismiss what she was saying as "condoning the status quo or 'giving in' to the forces of reaction," the church would be a more nurturing, spiritual place, she thought, if the pace of social action were slowed for a while.[41]

Opinions about the purpose and effectiveness of the social policies of the Episcopal Church in the 1960s were related, therefore, not only to politics, but also to the nature of the church and its membership. For John Hines, personal faith and public religion were inseparable, and he wanted GCSP to change the shape of mission by allowing the Episcopal Church to give itself away for the sake of the poor and dispossessed. Yet he did not fully comprehend how his call for institutional transformation could have been applied equally to black priests, pious lay women and men, and church bureaucrats like himself, ensconced in an imposing office building in New York. There was, in fact, a fundamental paradox in Hines's outlook on the social crisis of his day. Throughout his tenure as presiding bishop, he resisted all efforts to dilute the church's importance as a national institution by decentralizing its program or shifting funds back to parish or diocesan ministries. Yet since the Second Vatican Council had recently downplayed the hierarchical nature of the Roman Catholic Church and stressed that ecclesiastical authority ought to be shared among all the people of God, ordinary Episcopalians began to wonder why their church staff still assumed they had the right to speak for the diverse membership of the denomination. As L. William Countryman, a parish priest in Ohio, sarcastically remarked, "probably the present world scene is more intelligible from the penthouse" in New York than from the small town where he lived. "We now have a church leadership whose only gospel is a kind of social-activist legalism . . . dubbed 'prophecy,'" he complained, while people in parishes throughout the country were crying out "for some guidance in spiritual life, in understanding the Bible and the church's teachings, in prayer and personal renewal." This led Countryman and other critics of the national church to conclude that the presiding bishop and his staff were committed to a rootless form of social justice, "divorced from the real world of the church . . . and incompetent to meet" the religious and spiritual challenges of the coming decade. [42]

Convinced that their national leaders were out of touch with average church people, a few Episcopalians even suggested that Hines's own theological and social ideas were not actually as revolutionary as he thought. Although Hines remained attached to the social gospel concepts that were popular when he began his ministry in the mid-1930s, post–World War II theological trends—Dietrich Bonhoeffer's discussion of "religionless Christianity," Harvey Cox's idea of the "secular city," and a growing emphasis on "the underground church"—had all seriously undermined the presiding bishop's approach to the church's mission in the world. As historian James Findlay has observed, the engagement of the mainline denominations in the civil rights movement actually represented "a last hurrah of sorts" of the social gospel, for by the late 1960s the traditional Protestant "establishment" on which the social gospel depended—relatively affluent white males with interventionist views on public affairs—had lost its exclusive hold on the American religious scene.[43] Moreover, according to theologian Paul van Buren, whose *Secular Meaning of the Gospel* (1963) was a key text in that period, the church per se did not have a role to play in the pluralistic culture of modern times.[44] Warren Shaw, a priest in Chester, Pennsylvania, echoed van Buren's ideas, noting that there had once been a time when people expected the church to "march in formation with our colors flying high" to mobilize communities into action. But in light of contemporary theology, that outlook seemed hopelessly outdated. In other words, what was the rationale for a denominational bureaucracy trumpeting the notion that "the church" was in the forefront of social change when, in a "secular world . . . come of age," the focus should have been solely on the involvement of individuals?[45]

On hearing these various criticisms muttered throughout the denomination in the early 1970s, members of the Executive Council expressed dismay over the apparent crisis in the leadership of the Episcopal Church. When some council members suggested that Hines should address that issue directly by sending a special message to the church, John

Allin of Mississippi asserted that the Executive Council should speak to the church "by doing its job" rather than by delivering another message from on high. Allin understood that, in a sense, the church at large had already sent an unmistakable message to its leaders: so many wealthy parishes in the South and Southwest had withheld funds in protest against GCSP that the Executive Council had been forced to cut its staff nearly in half (from approximately two hundred to slightly more than one hundred employees) in 1971. The extent of this intense dislike of GCSP was further revealed in an Executive Council report entitled "What We Learned from What You Said." An attempt by the church's national leadership to talk with its grassroots membership about why discontent was so widespread, the report revealed that, instead of enabling and empowering "various segments of our society" (i.e., nonwhite non-Episcopalians), most church members wanted to emphasize "personal and corporate spiritual renewal, for knowledge and growth in 'the faith'" and the "empowerment of the individual to be a Christian." As for GCSP, the advice from the people who were interviewed was simple: just terminate it.[46]

At the same time that white Episcopalians were making their doubts about social ministry loud and clear, leading black Episcopalians were working quietly to regain the place at national church headquarters that had been lost with Tollie Caution's dismissal in 1967. The leadership of the Union of Black Episcopalians (UBE)—the UBCL had changed its name in 1971—remained outwardly supportive of the principles of black empowerment for which John Hines stood, but GCSP had never been "their" program, and it was regarded, in the words of UBE president Frederick Williams, as "the most sophisticated bit of paternalism" to come from whites in many decades. Although many in the church hierarchy assumed that African Americans on the GCSP staff fulfilled the functions for which Caution had been responsible, older black clergy such as John Burgess, the bishop of Massachusetts, continued to argue that it was "a fatal mistake" to confuse social action with evangelism in the African American community. In addition, the UBE insisted that, since their membership comprised the largest ethnic minority group in the church, the restoration of a permanent "Black Desk" focused exclusively on the concerns of African American Episcopalians was imperative. That position would give black Episcopalians direct input again into the power structure at church headquarters, and the staff member who held it would be able to direct an effective, centralized evangelistic effort similar to what Bravid Harris and Tollie Caution had accomplished between 1943 and 1967.[47]

The 1973 General Convention, which met in Louisville in the early fall, represented the final chapter in the history of GCSP and the ostensible beginning of a new era for black Episcopalians. As a coalition of white liberals sadly remarked at the time, most of the bishops and deputies who came to Louisville lacked a sense of adventure and wanted only to withdraw from "the painful agenda" of the last three conventions.[48] In place of social outreach, the 1973 convention gave its greatest attention to internal affairs, especially rising interest in the ordination of women. Nevertheless, the lack of discussion about GCSP was unexpected and almost unsettling. The convention approved a plan that not only brought all the church's ethnic minorities (African, Hispanic, Asian, and Native American) together into one large budget item but also effectively terminated GCSP. This decision led the editors of the The Living Church to give thanks that "a give-away program that smacked more of Lady Bountifulism than of apostolic Christianity" had at last been ended.[49] Leon Modeste, on the other hand, delivered a stinging rebuke to the church for which he had worked since the mid-1960s. He blamed the racism of most white Episcopalians for the cavalier fashion in which their program of black empowerment had been closed down.[50]

John Hines, too, chose to cut short his term as presiding bishop and retire in the spring of 1974. Although some speculated that his opponents had succeeded in hounding him from office, it is more likely that Hines was simply exhausted from serving almost thirty years as bishop during a turbulent period of social change. Though he retired prematurely in the midst of severe criticism, he continued to maintain his commitment to GCSP and insisted that it had been the right response to the racial crisis of 1967. He conceded that the staff of the program had made mistakes, but he also trusted them and recognized that they had been forced to work under extremely trying circumstances. It was especially hard for people like Leon Modeste, he said, who "had to stand with one foot in the . . . comfortable, don't rock the boat Episcopal organizational tradition, and . . . the other foot among the fractured elements of society who don't give a damn about the Episcopal Church."[51] Hines's opening address at the 1973 convention had served as a fitting valedictory on both GCSP and his own ministry. In 1967, he said, "the light of burning cities and the cries of the poor and powerless for justice" had made church members recognize that "we were more part of the problem than we were a part of the answer." Since God wanted religious bodies to be involved in the world, GCSP had been created for the sake of "the integrity of the church's life and the credibility of our witness to Christ as Lord of all."

Despite the upheaval it had caused, the program had enabled Episcopalians to develop an understanding of Christian mission, Hines asserted, that did not simply strengthen the church as an institution—the goal of traditional evangelism—but had affirmed "the revolutionary, convicting and renewing nature of the Gospel."[52]

With the announcement that Hines would retire a few months after the convention, the House of Bishops chose John Allin to be his successor. As the bishop of Mississippi who had resisted the civil rights involvement of national church officials in his state, as a persistent critic of GCSP, and as the new chancellor of the University of the South, Allin's candidacy appeared to be a total repudiation of the racial liberalism that Hines had championed. Since the election of a presiding bishop required the consent of the House of Deputies, Allin was forced to wait for several hours while the deputies debated whether or not to approve the House of Bishops' choice. Allin was eventually confirmed, but approximately 20 percent of the diocesan delegations refused to concur with the bishops' decision—a negative vote of unprecedented size. Although one of Allin's supporters maintained that "to pin the racist label on him . . . is about as reasonable as to assume that the Bishop of Milwaukee must be president of a brewing company," his candidacy was strongly resisted by the church's white liberal wing. The leadership of the UBE was concerned about Allin as well, but after an extraordinarily frank discussion with him, they were surprised by his willingness to accept their main requests: the restoration of the Black Desk at national church headquarters, the development of an affirmative action program for the hiring of denominational staff, and a commitment to financial support of the three black colleges in the South. Having worked for most of his ministry in an environment that was thoroughly attuned to the realities of race, Allin accepted the idea that African Americans had a valid *racial* role to play within the Episcopal Church, and he eventually appointed Franklin Turner, an African American priest who had worked with GCSP, to fill the reinstated Black Desk position.[53]

In his remarks following the election, Allin paid tribute to the good intentions of his predecessor in attempting to place his denomination at the forefront of American society in the late 1960s. Both men were white southerners—raised, educated, and trained as clergy in the South—but they had little else in common. Allin not only sensed that the "can-do" leadership style and "Great Society" rhetoric of Hines's episcopate were no longer going to stir most Episcopalians, but he was also attentive to racial differences and had no wish to become the voice of African Americans. Remembering Hines's enthusiasm when he launched GCSP in 1967,

Allin noted that the presiding bishop had imagined he saw his church marching "from coast to coast in serried ranks assembled and prepared for Zion's war." But in point of fact, the people who had gathered for that convention were only "a rag-tag, disorganized, poorly educated group of middle-class Americans." They were men and women of the "great silent majority," he implied, who lacked the spiritual and theological discipline necessary to involve themselves in a radical process of institutional transformation.[54]

Whatever Allin's motives, his observations about the church were essentially accurate. Hines's image of Episcopalians joined in a common cause, laboring to unite a racially fractured society, had brought mainly strife and division to the denomination. Allin, in contrast, hoped to reunify the Episcopal Church by accepting the diversity of its membership. While Hines had presented an inspiring religious vision for a powerful, crusading denomination, Allin displayed a canny understanding of the true nature of the fragmented, culture-bound institution he had been elected to lead.

# *Epilogue*

In November 1990 a slim majority of voters in the state of Arizona defeated a referendum that would have created a holiday honoring Martin Luther King Jr. Although white citizens in Arizona insisted that their vote was not intended as a repudiation of either King or the movement he led, the symbolic rejection of the great civil rights leader was troubling to many Americans. As a result a number of groups stepped forward to condemn the vote; none of those censures was more notable than the announcement by officials of the National Football League that the 1993 Super Bowl, scheduled to take place in Tempe, would be moved to another city. According to Paul Tagliabue, the NFL commissioner, "Americans, of all races and backgrounds, perceive the Arizona opposition as a slap at Dr. King and his message." Since more than 60 percent of the players in the NFL were African American, Tagliabue was determined to have the league's premier event transferred to another, more hospitable site.[1]

The Episcopal Church faced a dilemma similar to the NFL's, and for the second time in the history of the denomination, its leaders were forced to consider changing the location of the General Convention because of a controversy over race. Scheduled to hold their convention in Phoenix in July 1991, Episcopalians hotly debated whether they should do so. Diocesan conventions in New York and Washington asked Edmond Browning, the presiding bishop, to follow Henry Sherrill's example and use his authority to switch the meeting site, and the diocese of Atlanta offered itself as a host, volunteering to hold the event in the city where King had lived. Since Browning had declared "There shall be no outcasts" when he was elected to succeed John Allin in 1985 (a pledge directed implicitly to gay and lesbian church members), black Episcopalians hoped his statement also applied to their position in the denomination. Members of the UBE were particularly vocal in the advice they gave to Browning and other white leaders. Diane Pollard, a laywoman, argued that

keeping the General Convention in Phoenix would send "an inappropriate message" to Americans about the church's stance on racism; Joel
Gibson, a priest, claimed that the refusal of white Episcopalians to resolve the issue in favor of African Americans would cast "a pall over our
moral leadership."[2] In addition, an editorial in *The Witness* maintained
that Browning and the church, not Tagliabue and a professional sports
organization, should have led the way in boycotting a state that rejected
King and his legacy. Paraphrasing a familiar biblical verse, the editors of
the magazine quipped: "Except your righteousness exceed that of the
NFL and the Super Bowl, you will never get into the kingdom of heaven."[3]

Despite these protests and the embarrassment they caused, Browning announced that the General Convention would meet in Phoenix in
1991. A native of Corpus Christi, Texas, Browning could empathize with
the position of whites in Arizona. He had been a first-year divinity student at the University of the South during the turmoil of the 1952–53
academic year, and he had remained at Sewanee even though the conflict
over desegregation compelled the majority of his fellow seminarians to
leave for other schools. A year later, when Sherrill moved the General
Convention from Houston to Honolulu, Browning was entering his senior year as a student sponsored by the diocese of West Texas. Refusing
to allow a racial controversy to disrupt the church's plans and emphasizing the responsibility to minister to all the citizens of Arizona, Browning
insisted that Episcopalians could make their strongest testimony against
"the blatant sin of racism" by going to Arizona and "working with people
of good faith" there. "My gut, my heart, my reason, my prayer, my whole
being says go to Phoenix," he declared. In his eyes and in the eyes of
many other white Episcopalians—including Edward McCrady's son—
voters in the state of Arizona had done nothing to merit categorical rejection, and whatever mistake they might have made, an understanding,
"Christian" approach was preferable to a self-righteous, judgmental one.
As Rustin Kimsey, a bishop who supported Browning's decision, observed,
"I don't want Arizona to think that their sin is worse than my sin."[4]

Black Episcopalians, however, saw the Arizona situation in a far
different light than Browning, and they believed that bishops, clergy, and
powerful lay leaders who were white had once again downplayed the
importance of race and the effects of racial prejudice and indifference on
African Americans. How could blacks make an effective witness against
racism, they asked, when the system in which they were expected to operate was itself oppressive and prevented them from exercising any appreciable authority? Whites, after all, had always called the shots and

simply expected blacks to follow their lead, even in matters that affected blacks more than whites. Thus, as soon as the General Convention was called to order in July, African American church members rose to voice their official disapproval of the proceedings. Antoinette Daniels of the diocese of New Jersey was one of the first people to speak in the House of Deputies. She declared that black Episcopalians were protesting not only the decision to go ahead with the convention, but also the manner in which it had been handled. "Episcopalians of color were ignored and not consulted seriously when the response to the events in Arizona were being formulated," she observed—a fact "more typical than extraordinary of their experiences in the church."[5]

This protest notwithstanding, white Episcopalians at the convention did make an effort to address some of the objections raised by African Americans. They conducted a "racism audit," designed to uncover and analyze racial attitudes throughout the denomination. The gathering also passed a series of resolutions condemning racial discrimination, and the House of Bishops made plans to formulate its own pastoral letter on racism for release at a later time. Finally, thanks to the efforts of John Morris and other former ESCRU members, Jonathan Daniels was added to the denomination's calendar of "Lesser Feasts and Fasts" and commemorated as a martyr in the cause of racial justice. After the close of the convention, many white Episcopalians viewed the meeting as an occasion when their church had honestly examined its racial sins and made an attempt to celebrate "the diversity of races and cultures God has given to us."[6]

Despite this sanguine view, the discussions at Phoenix were actually conducted with little appreciation or understanding of the history behind the church's position on race—a history that the 1991 General Convention simply repeated. Although many of those present at the convention no doubt thought they were making a clean break with the past, the quarrel over the Phoenix site was simply another example of white Episcopalians' long-standing ambivalence about their relationship with African Americans. Between the Emancipation Proclamation of 1863 and the vote on the King holiday in 1990, there had certainly been many worthwhile changes within the Episcopal Church, and bigoted attitudes that were commonplace among white Americans as late as 1960 were no longer acceptable. The civil rights movement truly had transformed the church in numerous and important ways. But even considering those advances, unity with whites was still an ambiguous principle for the black membership of the Episcopal Church. Like many of his forebears raised

in the South, Edmond Browning believed that the church would be most
true to the Christian gospel if it maintained its unity and kept everyone,
both African Americans and white voters in Arizona, together. His
nonjudgmental, ostensibly inclusive approach made sense from a perspective on which slavery, racism, and the black struggle for survival and
self-respect had made little impact. Black Episcopalians, in contrast, knew
that the theological and social model Browning articulated did not come
close to addressing their concerns. In fact, if white church members had
seen the controversy over Phoenix as a matter of race and equality rather
than of reconciliation and unity, they too might have understood the symbolic value in turning their backs on Phoenix and moving the convention
to another site.

# *Notes*

## Abbreviations

ACIN    American Church Institute for Negroes Records, Archives of the
Episcopal Church, Austin, Tex., record group 61

AEC    Archives of the Episcopal Church, Austin, Tex.

AEWP    Arthur E. Walmsley Papers, Archives of the Diocese of Connecticut,
Hartford

BPDS    Bishop Payne Divinity School Collection, Archives, Bishop Payne
Library, Virginia Theological Seminary, Alexandria

BRC    Minutes of the Meeting of the Bi-Racial Sub-Committee, Tollie L.
Caution Papers, St. Mark's Library, General Theological Seminary,
New York

C    *The Churchman*

CaC    *Christianity and Crisis*

CaR    *Church and Race*

CCe    *Christian Century*

CCh    *The Christian Challenge*

CCJC    Charles C.J. Carpenter Office Records, Department of Archives and
Manuscripts, Birmingham Public Library, Birmingham, Ala., collection
241

*CIM*    *Church in Metropolis*

CMCP    Charles M. Crump Papers, Archives of the Episcopal Church, Austin,
Tex., record group 227

CSR-31    Department of Christian Social Relations of the Episcopal Church
Records, Archives of the Episcopal Church, Austin, Tex., record group
31

CSR-85    Department of Christian Social Relations of the Episcopal Church
Records, Archives of the Episcopal Church, Austin, Tex., record group
85

DAR    Diocese of Alabama Records, Department of Archives and Manuscripts,
Birmingham Public Library, Birmingham, Ala.

DAT    Department of Archives, Zenobia Coleman Library, Tougaloo College,
Tougaloo, Miss.

DAW    David A. Works Collection of North Conway Institute, Archives, Bishop

|       |                                                                                     |
|-------|-------------------------------------------------------------------------------------|
|       | Payne Library, Virginia Theological Seminary, Alexandria, accession no. 1992.0013 |
| DCC   | Division of Christian Citizenship, Records of the Executive Director, Arthur Walmsley, Archives of the Episcopal Church, Austin, Tex., accession record 93.34 |
| DMR   | Delta Ministry Records, King Library and Archives, Martin Luther King, Jr., Center, Atlanta |
| E     | *The Episcopalian* |
| EB    | Minutes of the Meeting of the Board of Directors of the Episcopal Society for Cultural and Racial Unity, Episcopal Society for Cultural and Racial Unity Records, folders 7:1–13, Archives of the Episcopal Church, Austin, Tex. |
| EC    | *Episcopal Churchnews* |
| ECBM  | Episcopal Commission for Black Ministries and Coordinator for Black Ministries Records, Archives of the Episcopal Church, Austin, Tex., record group 159 |
| ECEC  | Minutes of the Meeting of the Executive Council of the Episcopal Church, Archives of the Episcopal Church, Austin, Tex., record group 40 |
| EN    | "The Episcopal Society for Cultural and Racial Unity: Newsletter," Episcopal Society for Cultural and Racial Unity Records, folders 36:1–10, Archives of the Episcopal Church, Austin, Tex. |
| ESCRU | Episcopal Society for Cultural and Racial Unity Records, Archives of the Episcopal Church, Austin, Tex., accession record 98.122 |
| GCD   | *General Convention Daily* |
| GCSP  | General Convention Special Program Records, Archives of the Episcopal Church, Austin, Tex., record group 87 |
| HMPEC | *Historical Magazine of the Protestant Episcopal Church* |
| IBS   | "Integration of Blacks at Sewanee" file, Records of the School of Theology, Univ. of the South, Department of Archives, Jessie Ball duPont Library, Univ. of the South, Sewanee, Tenn., record group 24, ser. 12/5 |
| JBCP  | John B. Coburn Papers, Library and Archives, Diocese of Massachusetts, Boston |
| JGC   | Protestant Episcopal Church, *Journal of the General Convention* |
| JHEP  | John H. Esquirol Papers, Archives of the Diocese of Connecticut, Hartford |
| LC    | *The Living Church* |
| MBP   | Malcolm Boyd Papers, Department of Special Collections, Mugar Memorial Library, Boston Univ., Boston |
| MM    | Manuscript in the possession of John B. Morris, Atlanta |
| MSU   | Special Collections Department, Mitchell Memorial Library, Mississippi State Univ., Starkville |
| NCEC  | Minutes of the Meeting of the National Council of the Episcopal Church, Archives of the Episcopal Church, Austin, Tex., record group 40 |
| NCPC  | National Church Publications Collection, Archives of the Episcopal Church, Austin, Tex. |
| NYT   | *New York Times* |
| PB-22 | Records of the Presiding Bishop of the Episcopal Church, Archives of the Episcopal Church, Austin, Tex., record group 22 |

PB-113     Records of the Presiding Bishop of the Episcopal Church, Archives of
               the Episcopal Church, Austin, Tex., record group 113
PP            "ESCRU: The Prayer Pilgrimage of 1961," scrapbook in the possession
               of John B. Morris, Atlanta
RMC        Minutes of the Meeting of the Racial Minorities Committee, Tollie L.
               Caution Papers, St. Mark's Library, General Theological Seminary,
               New York
RVC        Records of the Vice-Chancellor, Edward McCrady, Department of
               Archives, Jessie Ball duPont Library, Univ. of the South, Sewanee,
               Tenn., record group 4:14
SFBP        Stephen F. Bayne Papers, St. Mark's Library, General Theological
               Seminary, New York
SIP           Selma Inter-Religious Project, Department of Archives and Manuscripts,
               Birmingham Public Library, Birmingham, Ala., collection 1044
SPBP        Sarah Patton Boyle Papers, Special Collections Department, Univ. of
               Virginia Library, Charlottesville, accession no. 8003–a–b
TLCP        Tollie L. Caution Papers, St. Mark's Library, General Theological
               Seminary, New York
VTS         Virginia Theological Seminary, Alexandria
VTSA       Archives, Bishop Payne Library, Virginia Theological Seminary, Alexandria
W            *The Witness*
WSP         William Stringfellow Papers, Division of Rare and Manuscript Collec-
               tions, Carl A. Kroch Library, Cornell Univ., Ithaca, N.Y.

## Introduction

1. Ulrich B. Phillips, "The Central Theme of Southern History," *American His-
torical Review* 34 (1928–29): 31 (emphasis added in quotation); and Stanley M. Elkins,
*Slavery: A Problem in American Institutional and Intellectual Life* (Chicago: Univ. of
Chicago Press, 1959), 9–17.

2. Clarence Cason, *90° in the Shade* (Chapel Hill: Univ. of North Carolina Press,
1935), 120–27; Paul Harvey, *Redeeming the South: Religious Cultures and Racial Iden-
tities among Southern Baptists, 1865–1925* (Chapel Hill: Univ. of North Carolina Press,
1997), 230–31; and Grace Elizabeth Hale, *Making Whiteness: The Culture of Segregation in the South, 1890–1940* (New York: Pantheon, 1998), 51–74, 86–87.

3. Regarding the issue of whether "race" actually exists, see, for example, Barbara Jeanne Fields, "Slavery, Race and Ideology in the United States," *New Left Review*
181 (May–June 1990): 95–118. For scholarly studies of the African American presence within the Episcopal Church, see esp. Harold T. Lewis, *Yet with a Steady Beat:
The African American Struggle for Recognition in the Episcopal Church* (Valley Forge,
Pa.: Trinity Press International, 1996), and the works of J. Carleton Hayden cited
throughout this book.

4. For a discussion of the historical importance of the "national church" idea,
see Ian T. Douglas, *Fling Out the Banner! The National Church Ideal and the Foreign
Mission of the Episcopal Church* (New York: Church Hymnal, 1996). On Myrdal, see
especially David W. Southern, *Gunnar Myrdal and Black-White Relations: The Use and
Abuse of* An American Dilemma, *1944–1969* (Baton Rouge: Louisiana State Univ. Press,
1987).

## 1. Racial Paternalism and Christian Mission
## after the Civil War

1. W.E.B. Du Bois, *Black Reconstruction in America* (New York: Harcourt, Brace, 1935), 124; Eric Foner, *Reconstruction: America's Unfinished Revolution, 1863–1877* (New York: Harper, 1988), 1–10; and William E. Montgomery, *Under Their Own Vine and Fig Tree: The African-American Church in the South, 1865–1900* (Baton Rouge: Louisiana State Univ. Press, 1993), 38–40.

2. Albert Sidney Thomas, *A Historical Account of the Protestant Episcopal Church in South Carolina, 1820–1957* (Columbia, S.C.: R.L. Bryan, 1957), 381–85, 446; Charles Joyner, *Down by the Riverside: A South Carolina Slave Community* (Urbana: Univ. of Illinois Press, 1984), 22–23, 154–64, 229–30; Stiles Bailey Lines, "Slaves and Church-men: The Work of the Episcopal Church among Southern Negroes, 1830–1860," Ph.D. diss., Columbia Univ., 1960, 239–43, 260; J. Carleton Hayden, "Conversion and Control: Dilemma of Episcopalians in Providing for the Religious Instructions of Slaves, Charleston, South Carolina, 1845–1860," *HMPEC* 40 (1971): 143–44, 166; and Robert E. Hood, "From a Headstart to a Deadstart: The Historical Basis for Black Indifference toward the Episcopal Church, 1800–1860," *HMPEC* 51 (1982): 273–77.

3. *JGC* (1868): 297–98, 339–40; Hodding Carter and Betty Werlein Carter, *So Great a Good: A History of the Episcopal Church in Louisiana and of Christ Church Cathedral, 1805–1955* (Sewanee, Tenn.: Univ. Press, 1955), 154; George F. Bragg Jr., *The Episcopal Church and the Black Man* (Baltimore: St. James' Episcopal Church, 1918), 12; Donald G. Mathews, *Religion in the Old South* (Chicago: Univ. of Chicago Press, 1977), 136–46; J. Carleton Hayden, "Reading, Religion, and Racism: The Mission of the Episcopal Church to Blacks in Virginia, 1865–1877," Ph.D. diss., Howard Univ., 1972, 87, 90, 96; J. Carleton Hayden, "After the War: The Mission and Growth of the Episcopal Church among Blacks in the South, 1865–1877," *HMPEC* 42 (1973): 410–13; Daniel W. Stowell, *Rebuilding Zion: The Religious Reconstruction of the South, 1863–1877* (New York: Oxford Univ. Press, 1998), 65–99; Lewis, *Yet with a Steady Beat*, 27–35; and Montgomery, *Under Their Own Vine and Fig Tree*, 104–8, 126–27.

4. *JGC* (1865): 168; S.D. McConnell, *History of the American Episcopal Church, 1600–1915* (Milwaukee: Morehouse, 1916), 360–79; Lawrence Foushee London and Sarah McCulloh Lemmon, eds., *The Episcopal Church in North Carolina, 1701–1959* (Raleigh: Episcopal Diocese of North Carolina, 1987), 252–53; Toombs Hodges Kay Jr., "The Role of Selected Protestant Churches in Emancipation and Integration," Ph.D. diss., New York Univ., 1962, 200; and David L. Holmes, *A Brief History of the Episcopal Church* (Valley Forge, Pa.: Trinity Press International, 1993), 80–82. The General Convention is a bicameral body divided into a House of Bishops (all bishops of the denomination) and a House of Deputies (four lay and four clerical representatives from each diocese in the church).

5. *JGC* (1865): 175, 188–89; (1868): 330; H. Peers Brewer, "The Protestant Episcopal Freedman's Commission, 1865–1878," *HMPEC* 26 (1957): 361–67; Hayden, "After the War," 413–20; and Foner, *Reconstruction*, 68–70. Wharton quotation in *Spirit of Missions* 31 (1866): 43–44.

6. *Spirit of Missions* 34 (1869): 122–23; *JGC* (1868): 175–76, 277, 369–72; Walter C. Whitaker, *Richard Hooker Wilmer, Second Bishop of Alabama* (Philadelphia: George W. Jacobs, 1907), 232; Brewer, "Protestant Episcopal Freedman's Commission," 370; and Hayden, "Reading, Religion, and Racism," 132.

7. *JGC* (1871): 513–15; (1877): 491–94; *Spirit of Missions* 42 (1877): 419–21,

479; 43 (1878): 47–48, 124, 185; Commission of Home Missions to Colored People, *Annual Report* 9 (1873–74): 7, 15–16, 19–20 (quotation on 19); Hayden, "After the War," 421–25; and Brewer, "Protestant Episcopal Freedman's Commission," 376–81. For the similar experiences of other Christian denominations in the South, see Harvey, *Redeeming the South,* 31–43; and David W. Southern, *John LaFarge and the Limits of Catholic Interracialism, 1911–1963* (Baton Rouge: Louisiana State Univ. Press, 1996), 66–69.

8. Commission of Home Missions to Colored People, *Annual Report* 9 (1873–74): 5–8 (quotation on 7); 11 (1875–76): 9–11; G. MacLaren Brydon, *The Episcopal Church Among the Negroes of Virginia* (Richmond: Virginia Diocesan Library, 1937), 8–12, 25–26; "The Bishop Payne Divinity School" [1937], 1–5, in BPDS, folder 9:1; John H. Edwards, "Recollections and Reflections on My Clerical Life," [1956], 9–10, in Special Collections, VTSA; Odell Greenleaf Harris, *The Bishop Payne Divinity School: A History of the Seminary to Prepare Black Men for the Ministry of the Protestant Episcopal Church* (Alexandria, Va.: Protestant Episcopal Theological Seminary, 1980), 1–10; and John Booty, *Mission and Ministry: A History of the Virginia Theological Seminary* (Harrisburg, Pa.: Morehouse, 1995), 130–33.

9. H. Shelton Smith, *In His Image, But . . . : Racism in Southern Religion, 1780–1910* (Durham, N.C.: Duke Univ. Press, 1972), 246–47; Thomas, *Historical Account,* 84–92, 297, 448–49; Allen C. Guelzo, *For the Union of Evangelical Christendom: The Irony of the Reformed Episcopalians* (University Park: Pennsylvania State Univ. Press, 1994), 219–24; and Herbert Geer McCarriar Jr., "A History of the Missionary Jurisdiction of the South of the Reformed Episcopal Church, 1874–1970," *HMPEC* 41 (1972): 197–220.

10. Owen Meredith Waller, *The Episcopal Church and the Colored People: A Statement of Facts* (Washington, D.C.: Emmett C. Jones, 1898), 9–10; Lewis, *Yet with a Steady Beat,* 65–71; Montgomery, *Under Their Own Vine and Fig Tree,* 117–27; and Reginald F. Hildebrand, *The Times Were Strange and Stirring: Methodist Preachers and the Crisis of Emancipation* (Durham, N.C.: Duke Univ. Press, 1995), 10–23.

11. *An Account of the Conference on the Relation of the Church to the Colored People of the South, Held at Sewanee, Tennessee, July 25 to 28, 1883* (Sewanee, Tenn.: Wm. H. Harlow, [1883]), 3–14 (quotations on 7); *JGC* (1874): 255, 261; (1883): 69–70, 181, 595–600; and Robert W. Prichard, *A History of the Episcopal Church* (Harrisburg, Pa.: Morehouse, 1991), 179.

12. George R. Fairbanks, *History of the University of the South* (Jacksonville, Fla.: H. and W.B. Dew, 1905), 228–31; *Account of the Conference . . . at Sewanee,* 12–13; C. Vann Woodward, *The Strange Career of Jim Crow,* 3d rev. ed. (New York: Oxford Univ. Press, 1974), 44–59, 69–72; Joel Williamson, *A Rage for Order: Black/White Relations in the American South Since Emancipation* (New York: Oxford Univ. Press, 1986), 70–72, 158–59; Hale, *Making Whiteness,* 51–74; and Lewis, *Yet with a Steady Beat,* 67–72. White Presbyterians also had difficulty competing with black Methodist and Baptist churches for the allegiance of African American members, and the Presbyterian Church in the United States eventually approved an arrangement similar to the one proposed by the Sewanee conference. Through the creation of segregated presbyteries for black clergy and congregations, white leaders maintained control over African Americans while withholding full equality in church affairs. Joel L. Alvis Jr., *Religion and Race: Southern Presbyterians, 1946–1983* (Tuscaloosa: Univ. of Alabama Press, 1994), 13–15; and Montgomery, *Under Their Own Vine and Fig Tree,* 74–78, 125.

13. George F. Bragg Jr., *History of the Afro-American Group of the Episcopal Church* (1922; reprint, New York: Johnson Reprint, 1968), 151–53, 305–7 (quotation on 306).

14. *JGC* (1883): 181, 600; Whitaker, *Richard Hooker Wilmer,* 234–40 (quotation on 235); and David M. Reimers, *White Protestantism and the Negro* (New York: Oxford Univ. Press, 1965), 34–35.

15. *JGC* (1883): 69–70, 181, 191–92, 210, 217–18, 251–52, 280 (quotation on 251).

16. Alexander Crummell, *Civilization and Black Progress: Selected Writings of Alexander Crummell on the South,* ed. J.R. Oldfield (Charlottesville: Univ. Press of Virginia, 1995), 17, 78; Isaac DuBose Seabrook, *Before and After; or, The Relations of the Races at the South,* ed. John Hammond Moore (Baton Rouge: Louisiana State Univ. Press, 1967), 12–14; Brydon, *Episcopal Church Among the Negroes,* 13–18; Thomas, *Historical Account,* 92–99, 448–51; and Smith, *In His Image, But . . . ,* 247–48. Phrase, "a race Church," in Seabrook, *Before and After,* 14.

17. Thomas U. Dudley, "How Shall We Help the Negro?" *Century* 30 (1885): 273–80 (quotations on 274–75); Charles E. Wynes, ed., *Forgotten Voices: Dissenting Southerners in an Age of Conformity* (Baton Rouge: Louisiana State Univ. Press, 1967), 37–38; L. Moody Simms Jr., "Thomas Underwood Dudley: A Forgotten Voice of Dissent," *Mississippi Quarterly* 20 (1967): 217–23; and Ralph E. Luker, *The Social Gospel in Black and White: American Racial Reform, 1885–1912* (Chapel Hill: Univ. of North Carolina Press, 1991), 23–24.

18. Alexander Crummell, "The Best Methods of Church Work among the Colored People," in Crummell, *Civilization and Black Progress,* 155–62; Alexander Crummell, "The Destined Superiority of the Negro," in Alexander Crummell, *Destiny and Race: Selected Writings, 1840–1898,* ed. Wilson Jeremiah Moses (Amherst: Univ. of Massachusetts Press, 1992), 194–205; W.E.B. Du Bois, *The Souls of Black Folk* (Chicago: A.C. McClurg, 1903), 215–27; George F. Bragg Jr., *Afro-American Church Work and Workers* (Baltimore: Church Advocate, 1904), 5–8, 40; Bragg, *History of the Afro-American Group,* 151–53; and Wilson Jeremiah Moses, *Alexander Crummell: A Study of Civilization and Discontent* (1989; reprint, Amherst: Univ. of Massachusetts Press, 1992), 24–43, 196–221.

19. Anna Julia Cooper, *A Voice from the South* (1892; reprint, New York: Oxford Univ. Press, 1988), 33–47 (quotations on 34, 39, 41); Cooper, *The Voice of Anna Julia Cooper,* ed. Charles Lemert and Esme Bhan (Lanham, Md.: Rowan and Littlefield, 1998), 1–14, 306, 331; George F. Bragg Jr., *A Bond Slave of Christ* (n.p., [1912]), 1–4; Kevin K. Gaines, *Uplifting the Race: Black Leadership, Politics, and Culture in the Twentieth Century* (Chapel Hill: Univ. of North Carolina Press, 1996), 128–51; and David Levering Lewis, *W.E.B. Du Bois: Biography of a Race, 1868–1919* (New York: Holt, 1993), 249.

20. *JGC* (1889): 57–59, 265–66, 282, 328–29, 380–81; Bragg, *History of the Afro-American Group,* 152–53; and Bragg, *Afro-American Church Work,* 8–10.

21. Booker T. Washington, "The Colored Ministry: Its Defects and Needs," *Christian Union,* Aug. 14, 1890, in Louis R. Harlan et al., eds., *The Booker T. Washington Papers* (Urbana: Univ. of Illinois Press, 1972–89), 3:71–75; Booker T. Washington, *Up from Slavery: An Autobiography* (Garden City, N.Y.: Doubleday, 1901), 217–25; Williamson, *Rage for Order,* 61–65; Louis R. Harlan, *Booker T. Washington: The Making of a Black Leader, 1856–1901* (New York: Oxford Univ. Press, 1972), 204–21; and Luker, *Social Gospel in Black and White,* 132–36.

22. Edgar Gardner Murphy, *The Larger Life: Sermons and an Essay* (New York: Longmans, Green, 1897), 153–61; Edgar Gardner Murphy, "The Task of the Leader," *Sewanee Review* 15 (1907): 6–30. Hugh C. Bailey, *Edgar Gardner Murphy: Gentle Progressive* (Coral Gables, Fla.: Univ. of Miami Press, 1968), 27–30, 37, 55–56, 134;

Harlan, *Booker T. Washington*, 292–96; Williamson, *Rage for Order*, 153–62, 208–10; and Smith, *In His Image, But . . .*, 285–89.

23. Southern Society for the Promotion of the Study of Race Conditions and Problems in the South, *Race Problems of the South: Report of the Proceedings of the First Annual Conference* (1900; reprint, New York: Negro Universities Press, 1969), 7–9, 114–15, 124–34 (quotations on 130–31, 134); and Ronald C. White Jr., *Liberty and Justice for All: Racial Reform and the Social Gospel (1877–1925)* (San Francisco: Harper, 1990), 152–54.

24. Edgar Gardner Murphy, *Problems of the Present South: A Discussion of Certain of the Educational, Industrial and Political Issues in the Southern States* (New York: Macmillan, 1904), 7–9, 34–35, 41, 160–66, 270–74; Edgar Gardner Murphy, *The Basis of Ascendancy: A Discussion of Certain Principles of Public Policy Involved in the Development of the Southern States* (New York: Longmans, Green, 1909), xii–xvii, 3–12, 55–58, 112–15, 121–24, 242–44 (quotations on xv, 115); White, *Liberty and Justice for All*, 154–58; and Luker, *Social Gospel in Black and White*, 148–52, 282–89.

25. Theodore DuBose Bratton, "The Christian South and Negro Education," *Sewanee Review* 16 (1908): 290–97 (quotations on 291–92); George M. Fredrickson, *The Black Image in the White Mind: The Debate on Afro-American Character and Destiny, 1817–1914* (1971; reprint, Hanover, N.H.: Wesleyan Univ. Press, 1987), 269–71; I.A. Newby, *Jim Crow's Defense: Anti-Negro Thought in America, 1900–1930* (Baton Rouge: Louisiana State Univ. Press, 1965), 88–89; and Paul M. Gaston, *The New South Creed: A Study in Southern Mythmaking* (New York: Knopf, 1970), 167–86.

26. Robert W. Patton, "Notable Recognition Accorded Negro Schools: General Education Board Makes Conditional Gifts to Fort Valley and St. Paul's," *Spirit of Missions* 92 (1927): 11–15 (quotations on 12–13); Robert W. Patton, *An Inspiring Record in Negro Education: Historical Summary of the Work of the American Church Institute for Negroes* (New York: National Council, [1940]), 4–7; American Church Institute for Negroes, *Our Church Schools for Negroes* (New York: Church Missions House, [1921]), 5; Isabel Y. Douglas, *The Story of the Program, 1923–1925* (New York: National Council, 1923), 191–93, 202–6; [Elizabeth H.B.] Roberts, *Hand-Book: Colored Work in Dioceses of the South* (Philadelphia: Geo. W. Jacobs, [1916]), 86–88; and Lewis, *Yet with a Steady Beat*, 125–31.

27. W.E.B. Du Bois, ed., *The Negro Church* (Atlanta: Atlanta Univ. Press, 1903), 139; Samuel H. Bishop to W.E.B. Du Bois, Apr. 16, 1907, and Du Bois to Bishop, May 1, 1907, in *The Correspondence of W.E.B. Du Bois*, ed. Herbert Aptheker ([Amherst]: Univ. of Massachusetts Press, 1973–78), 1:130–31; A.C. Tebeau to Du Bois, Feb. 10, 1940, and Du Bois to Tebeau, Feb. 20, 1940, in *Correspondence of W.E.B. Du Bois*, 2:211–12; Moses, *Alexander Crummell*, 30; and Lewis, *W.E.B. Du Bois*, 16–18.

28. Bragg, *Afro-American Church Work*, 16–30; Bragg, *History of the Afro-American Group*, 152–53; J. Carleton Hayden, "'For Zion's Sake I Will Not Hold My Peace': George Freeman Bragg, Jr., Priest, Pastor, and Prophet," *Linkage* 6 (Oct. 1986): 10–11, 23; Luker, *Social Gospel in Black and White*, 254–56; August Meier, *Negro Thought in America, 1880–1915: Racial Ideologies in the Age of Booker T. Washington* (Ann Arbor: Univ. of Michigan Press, 1963), 180–81, 222–23; David M. Reimers, "Negro Bishops and Diocesan Segregation in the Protestant Episcopal Church: 1870–1954," *HMPEC* 31 (1962): 234; and Lewis, *Yet with a Steady Beat*, 72–73.

29. *JGC* (1904): 49, 57, 98, 100, 286, 318 (quotations on 49, 98). As the above reference to "languages" suggests, Episcopalians were interested not only in the church's mission to African Americans but also in its relationship with non–English-

speaking immigrants from northern Europe, e.g., Germans, Swedes, and Poles. *JGC* (1898): 409–10; (1907): 80; and Bragg, *Afro-American Church Work,* 26.

30. William Montgomery Brown, *The Crucial Race Question; or, Where and How Shall the Color Line Be Drawn,* 2d ed. (Little Rock: Arkansas Churchman's Publishing, 1907), xi–xxx, 150–58, 162–65, 188–92, 245–49, 253–58, 266–70; William Montgomery Brown, *My Heresy: The Autobiography of an Idea* (New York: John Day, 1926), 42–46; Newby, *Jim Crow's Defense,* 87–88, 170–71; Fredrickson, *Black Image in the White Mind,* 228–55, 256–69; Lewis, *Yet with a Steady Beat,* 75–76, 102; and Prichard, *History,* 210–11. Brown's extreme theological and social views—he later became a Communist and declared that the Christian faith was outmoded—led the House of Bishops to depose him in 1924.

31. Gavin White, "Patriarch McGuire and the Episcopal Church," *HMPEC* 38 (1969): 109–41; Randall K. Burkett, *Garveyism as a Religious Movement: The Institutionalization of a Black Civil Religion* (Metuchen, N.J.: Scarecrow, 1978), 71–75, 90–91; Michael Beary, "Wake-up Call, 1907: Bishop Brown vs. Archdeacon McGuire," *Historiographer* 28 (spring 1996): 4–5, 17; and Lewis, *Yet with a Steady Beat,* 100–106.

32. *JGC* (1907): 80–81, 117, 296–99.

33. *JGC* (1907): 518–22.

34. *JGC* (1907): 117, 522–23; and Gaines M. Foster, "Bishop Cheshire and Black Participation in the Episcopal Church: The Limitations of Religious Paternalism," *North Carolina Historical Review* 54 (1977): 50–59.

35. Reimers, "Negro Bishops," 234–35; and M. Moran Weston, *Social Policy of the Episcopal Church in the Twentieth Century* (New York: Seabury, 1964), 143–44; and Lewis, *Yet with a Steady Beat,* 76–78.

36. *JGC* (1907): 83, 118–19, 144–45, 157–58, 160–61, 370–71; (1910): 29, 77–78, 119, 175–76, 185, 191, 230–32, 306, 356, 384, 409; *Constitution of the Protestant Episcopal Church* (1910), 2:4; *JGC* (1913): 29–31, 125–26, 133–35, 158, 323, 342–43, 349, 482–87; (1916): 75–76, 96, 484–95; George Frazier Miller, "The Missionary Episcopate as a Method of Evangelism," in John M. Burgess, [ed.], *Black Gospel/ White Church* (New York: Seabury, 1982), 32–35; Thomas, *Historical Account,* 130–32; Bragg, *History of the Afro-American Group,* 154–55; Reimers, "Negro Bishops," 235–37; Weston, *Social Policy,* 144–46; and Foster, "Bishop Cheshire," 59.

37. James S. Russell, *Adventure in Faith: An Autobiographic Story of St. Paul Normal and Industrial School, Lawrenceville, Virginia* (New York: Morehouse, 1936), 73–81; Bragg, *History of the Afro-American Group,* 293–94; Sarah L. Delany and A. Elizabeth Delany, *Having Our Say: The Delany Sisters' First 100 Years* (New York: Dell, 1993), 165–66, 201–2 (DuBois quotation on 202); J. Carleton Hayden, "James Solomon Russell (1857–1935), Missionary and Founder of St. Paul's College," *Linkage* 7 (Mar. 1987): 10–11; London and Lemmon, *Episcopal Church in North Carolina,* 324–28; Lewis, *Yet with a Steady Beat,* 78–81; Reimers, "Negro Bishops," 237–39; ; and Foster, "Bishop Cheshire," 59–63.

38. *JGC* (1919): 217, 228–29, 300, 507; Gunnar Myrdal, *An American Dilemma: The Negro Problem and Modern Democracy* (1944; reprint, New York: Harper, 1962), 182–97; St. Clair Drake and Horace R. Cayton, *Black Metropolis: A Study of Negro Life in a Northern City* (New York: Harcourt, Brace, 1945), 58–61, 73–75; Gilbert Osofsky, *Harlem: The Making of a Ghetto,* 2d ed. (New York: Harper, 1971), 17–19, 180–81; Milton C. Sernett, *Bound for the Promised Land: African American Religion and the Great Migration* (Durham, N.C.: Duke Univ. Press, 1997), 9–86; Robert E. Hood,

*Social Teachings in the Episcopal Church* (Harrisburg, Pa.: Morehouse, 1990), 111–12; and Weston, *Social Policy,* 163–65.

39. Mrs. Frank Bonynge, "School Rambles in the Black Belt, Aug. 1936," 18–20, in Records of the Woman's Auxiliary to the National Council, Pennsylvania Branch, folder 1:15, AEC; *JGC* (1931): 101, 379–80; (1934): 348, 473–78 (quotation on 476); and Reimers, "Negro Bishops," 237–39.

40. John M. Glen, *Highlander: No Ordinary School, 1932–1962,* 2d ed. (Knoxville: Univ. of Tennessee Press, 1996), 11–21, 50; Charles Donald Donahue, "The Yearning for a Prophetic Southern Culture: A History of the Fellowship of Southern Churchmen, 1934–1963," Ph.D. diss., Union Theological Seminary, 1995, 10–20; Robert F. Martin, "Critique of Southern Society and Vision of a New Order: The Fellowship of Southern Churchmen, 1934–1957," *Church History* 52 (1983): 66–80; and Dewey W. Grantham, *The South in Modern America: A Region at Odds* (New York: HarperCollins, 1994), 126, 162–64.

41. "Report of Provincial Commission on Negro Work to the 1939 Synod of the Fourth Province," [1939], 3–4, in IBS, box 1; [Report of the Synod of the Fourth Province meeting in Tampa, Fla. (Nov. 14, 1939)], 1–5 (quotation on 1), in CCJC, folder 241.2.142.14.56 ("Racial Episcopate" file); *JGC* (1937): xii, 333–34; and Reimers, "Negro Bishops," 238.

42. *JGC* (1940): 499 (quotation); and Reimers, "Negro Bishops," 238–39.

43. R. Bland Mitchell to Middleton S. Barnwell, [from Little Rock, Ark.], Feb. 16, 1940; [Charles C.J. Carpenter] to Barnwell, [from Birmingham], Mar. 11, 1940; Barnwell to Carpenter, from Savannah, Ga., July 24, 1940, in CCJC, folder 241.2.142.14.56 ("Racial Episcopate" file); *JGC* (1940): 342–43, 498–501; and Elizabeth McCracken, "Racial Missionary District Plan Causes Impassioned Debate," *LC* 102 (Nov. 13, 1940): 6–8 (Taitt quotation on 8).

44. Middleton S. Barnwell to [Charles] C.J. Carpenter, from Savannah, Ga., Dec. 7, 1939, in CCJC, folder 241.2.142.14.56 ("Racial Episcopate" file); and McCracken, "Racial Missionary District Plan," 8 (Barnwell quotation).

## 2. Negro Work and the Decline of the Jim Crow Church

1. Benjamin Elijah Mays and Joseph William Nicholson, *The Negro's Church* (1933; reprint, New York: Russell and Russell, 1969), v–vi; Benjamin Elijah Mays, *The Negro's God As Reflected in His Literature* (Boston: Chapman and Grimes, 1938), 21–25, 248–49; Walter A. Jackson, *Gunnar Myrdal and America's Conscience: Social Engineering and Racial Liberalism, 1938–1987* (Chapel Hill: Univ. of North Carolina Press, 1990), 223–24; Peter J. Paris, *The Social Teaching of the Black Churches* (Philadelphia: Fortress, 1985), 108–9; and Sernett, *Bound for the Promised Land,* 226–31. Nicholson later joined the Episcopal Church and was ordained a priest in 1947.

2. Mays and Nicholson, *Negro's Church,* 210–14, 222, 230–36, 251, 312–13; John Henry Edwards, *The Negro Churchman's Upward Climb* (Hartford, Conn.: Church Missions Publishing, 1937), 36–38; Theodore DuBose Bratton, *Wanted—Leaders! A Study of Negro Development* (New York: Presiding Bishop and Council, 1922), 208–9; Patton, *Inspiring Record,* 8–10; Bragg, *History of the Afro-American Group,* 215–18; and Lewis, *Yet with a Steady Beat,* 86–89.

3. "Evaluation Committee: Report of Sub-Committee on Work among Negroes,"

[1940], 3–7, in ECBM, folder 159-1-27; *JGC* (1937): 333–34; (1940): 342, 382, 495–501 (quotations on 497); and Lewis, *Yet with a Steady Beat*, 72–76, 137–40.

4. *JGC* (1898): 79–80; Frank S. Loescher, *The Protestant Church and the Negro: A Pattern of Segregation* (New York: Association, 1948), 55–56; Kenneth K. Bailey, *Southern White Protestantism in the Twentieth Century* (New York: Harper, 1964), 137–42; Alvis, *Religion and Race*, 13–17; John Lee Eighmy, *Churches in Cultural Captivity: A History of the Social Attitudes of Southern Baptists* (1972; reprint, Knoxville: Univ. of Tennessee Press, 1987), 30–40, 115–17; and David W. Wills, "An Enduring Distance: Black Americans and the Establishment," in William R. Hutchison, ed., *Between the Times: The Travail of the Protestant Establishment in America, 1900–1960* (Cambridge: Cambridge Univ. Press, 1989), 180–84.

5. NCEC, Oct. 13–15, 1942, 96–98; "Action of General Convention regarding Negro Work," [1943], 1–7, in TLCP, "Bravid W. Harris" folder; "Opinions and Counsel of Bishops regarding Program for Negro Work," [1943], 41–52, in TLCP, "Secretary for Negro Work" folder; and McCracken, "Racial Missionary District Plan," 6–8. For a listing of parishes that were designated as "colored" at this time, see *Living Church Annual* (1943).

6. Division of Domestic Missions of the National Council, "The Church and the Negro," [1944?], 10–11, in ECBM, folder 159-1-14; "Dr. Wieland's Address before General Convention, Cleveland, Ohio, Oct. 1943," 3–4, in TLCP, "George A. Wieland" folder; NCEC, Feb. 9–11, 1943, 4–9, 144–45; May 4–6, 1943, 65; BRC, Nov. 30, 1943, 1; "National Council Starts Enlarged Negro Program," *Forth* 108 (July 1943): 8–9, 31; and Lewis, *Yet with a Steady Beat*, 139–41. The original members of the Bi-Racial Committee were John M. Burgess, Gardiner M. Day, Hubert T. Delany (Henry Beard Delany's son), Luther H. Foster, John L. Jackson, John H. Johnson, Robert I. Johnson, B.B. Comer Lile, William A. McClenthen, George M. Plaskett, Mrs. W.L. Torrance, and William Turpin.

7. NCEC, Feb. 9–11, 1943, 160; Weston, *Social Policy*, 148–49; and Heather A. Warren, *Theologians of a New World Order: Reinhold Niebuhr and the Christian Realists, 1920–1948* (New York: Oxford Univ. Press, 1997), 76–83.

8. Shelton Hale Bishop, "Bishop of Liberia Consecrated in Southern Virginia," *W* 28 (Apr. 26, 1945): 3–4; "Urges Northerners Stop Meddling," *W* 28 (May 10, 1945): 5–6; W.B. Spofford, editorial comment in "Backfire," *W* 28 (May 31, 1945): 19; and D. Elwood Dunn, *A History of the Episcopal Church in Liberia, 1821–1980* (Metuchen, N.J.: Scarecrow, 1992), 214–17, 233–39. For a discussion of the importance of the "National Cathedral" idea to Episcopal leaders, see Douglas, *Fling Out the Banner!* 89–90. And for a discussion of the link between racial liberalism, civil religion, and cultural nationalism in the midtwentieth century, see Scott A. Sandage, "A Marble House Divided: The Lincoln Memorial, the Civil Rights Movement, and the Politics of Memory, 1939–1963," *Journal of American History* 80 (1993): 135–55.

9. Myrdal, *American Dilemma*, lxix–lxxi; Southern, *Gunnar Myrdal*, 49–54; Gerald L. Sittser, *A Cautious Patriotism: The American Churches and the Second World War* (Chapel Hill: Univ. of North Carolina Press, 1997), 178–85; Grantham, *South in Modern America*, 188–93; Robert A. Schneider, "Voice of Many Waters: Church Federation in the Twentieth Century," in Hutchison, *Between the Times*, 117 (Sherrill quotation); James T. Patterson, *Grand Expectations: The United States, 1945–1974* (New York: Oxford Univ. Press, 1996), 61–70; James Hudnut-Beumler, *Looking for God in the Suburbs: The Religion of the American Dream and Its Critics, 1945–1965* (New Brunswick, N.J.: Rutgers Univ. Press, 1994), 18–21; and Prichard, *History*, 229–34.

10. *JGC* (1943): 465–69 (source of quotations); (1952): 583; and Jacob Henry Dorn, *Washington Gladden: Prophet of the Social Gospel* ([Columbus]: Ohio State Univ. Press, 1967), 442.

11. William Scarlett, ed., *Christianity Takes a Stand: An Approach to the Issues of Today* (New York: Penguin, 1946), 1–8 (quotation on 6). The presence of Charles Carpenter of Alabama as one of the six bishops on Scarlett's commission proved to be a significant factor in the group's refusal to condemn segregation outright. S. Jonathan Bass, "Bishop C.C.J. Carpenter: From Segregation to Integration," *Alabama Review* 45 (1992): 184–89. For a black priest's criticism of the cautious approach of Scarlett's commission to racial prejudice, see Kenneth Hughes, "Negro-White Relationships," *W* 30 (Mar. 27, 1947): 9–11.

12. NCEC, Feb. 9–11, 1943, 6–8; BRC, Nov. 30, 1943, 2; *JGC* (1940): 497–98; (1946): 459–60; Douglas, *Story of the Program,* 208–9; Odell Greenleaf Harris, *It Can Be Done: The Autobiography of a Black Priest of the Protestant Episcopal Church,* ed. Robert W. Prichard (Alexandria: Protestant Episcopal Theological Seminary in Virginia, 1985), 40–41; and Harris, *Bishop Payne Divinity School,* 10–11, 25–30.

13. Author's interview of Quintin E. Primo Jr., Oct. 4, 1996, Hockessin, Del.; R.A. Goodwin to "My dear Brother," from Petersburg, Va., [Jan. 1945], 1–2; E. Sydnor Thomas to the Presiding Bishop and the National Council, from Germantown, Pa., Apr. 4, 1945; the Clericus, "Resolution," [Mar. 1945]; [Henry St. George Tucker] to Thomas, [from New York], Apr. 11, 1945, 1–2, in BPDS, folder 6:22; *The Church and the Negro: An Appeal* (Petersburg, Va.: Bishop Payne Divinity School, 1944), 1–16; Wills, "Enduring Distance," 172; and Weston, *Social Policy,* 153–56.

14. John H. Johnson to Cyril E. Bentley, from New York, Jan. 3, 1947; [Bentley] to Johnson, [from New York], Jan. 7, 1947; F. Ricksford Meyers to Bentley, from Detroit, Mich., Jan. 10, 1947, 1–2, in ACIN, folder 61–2–26; Elizabeth McCracken, "National Council," *LC* 113 (Dec. 29, 1946): 5–7; and Kenneth deP. Hughes, letter in "Backfire," *W* 30 (Jan. 23, 1947): 19.

15. Elizabeth McCracken, "National Council," *LC* 114 (Feb. 23, 1947): 6–8 (Barnwell and Penick quotations on 7).

16. Cyril E. Bentley to Joseph Holton Jones, [from New York], Mar. 25, 1947; [Bentley] to M[iddleton] S. Barnwell, [from New York], Mar. 25, 1947 (Bentley quotation), in ACIN, folder 61–2–26; Middleton S. Barnwell, "The Race Problem," *LC* 114 (Mar. 9, 1947): 2–3; John H. Johnson, "Racial Justice," *LC* 114 (Apr. 27, 1947): 2–3; and "Segregation," *LC* 114 (Apr. 27, 1947): 12–13.

17. BRC, Apr. 16–17, 1947, 2-4 (quotation on 4).

18. BRC, Jan. 19–20, 1954, 2; Bishop Payne Divinity School, *Catalogue* (1948), 2; Board of Trustees of Bishop Payne Divinity School, "Minutes of the Annual Meeting," May 21, 1948, 1–4, in ACIN, folder 61–5–6 ; Board of Trustees of Bishop Payne Divinity School, "Minutes of the Meeting," June 3, 1953, in BPDS, folder 6:15A; "Report of the Secretary for Negro Work to the Bi-Racial Committee on Negro Work, Jan. 4–5, 1950," 13 in TLCP; VTS Board of Trustees, "Minutes of the Meeting," June 4, 1947, 2:128–29; June 4, 1952, 2:212G; Nov. 4, 1953, 3:22–23, in VTSA; "Report of the Joint Committee Created for the Study of the Proposed Merger of the Virginia Theological Seminary and the Bishop Payne Divinity School," 2, in VTS Faculty, Minutes of the Meeting, Jan. 28, 1952, in VTSA; Jesse M. Trotter to David C. Lord from Alexandria, Va., Sept. 30, 1963, in Correspondence of the Dean, VTSA; John N. McCormick to Charles C.J. Carpenter, from Alexandria, Mar. 3, 1960, in CCJC, folder 241.2.129.14.33 ("Negro Postulants" file); Elizabeth McCracken, "National Council," *LC* 114 (May 4, 1947): 6–7; Andrew Van Dyke, "General Convention to Con-

sider Greatly Increased Budget," *W* 32 (May 5, 1949): 4–5; Harris, *Bishop Payne Divinity School,* 26–29; and Booty, *Mission and Ministry,* 131, 279–81.

19. VTS Board of Trustees, "Minutes of the Meeting," Apr. 4, 1949, 2:161; Nov. 16, 1949, 2:170–71; June 7, 28, 1950, 2:187; Nov. 8, 1950, 2:190–92, in VTSA; "Seminaries: On an Isolated Domain," *LC* 124 (June 29, 1952): 19; J.Y. Smith, "Washington Episcopal Bishop Dies," *Washington Post,* Oct. 1, 1989, A1, A14; John Thomas Walker, "Guest Lecture . . . Nov. 20, 1984," *Virginia Seminary Journal* 37 (Dec. 1995): 33–39 (quotation on 37); and Booty, *Mission and Ministry,* 279–80. After his ordination in 1954, Walker rose quickly to prominence in the church, and in 1971 he was elected suffragan bishop of the diocese of Washington (D.C.).

20. Jessie Ball duPont to Edward McCrady, from Wilmington, Del., July 1, 1952, 1–2, in RVC, "Negro File (D–I)" folder; "DuPont Gift," *LC* 126 (June 14, 1953): 6; "Education Notes: South—Major Gift," *NYT,* Nov. 7, 1954, sec. 4, p. 11; and Richard Greening Hewlett, *Jessie Ball duPont* (Gainesville: Univ. Press of Florida, 1992), xiii–xv, 150–52, 173–79, 188–93, 203–7, 320.

21. Author's interview of John E. Hines, Sept. 27, 1993, Austin, Tex.; Diocese of Texas, *Journal of the Annual Council* (1947), 39, 47, 77–78; (1948), 122–23; Carter Wesley, "Texas Editor Writes of Race Relations in Church," *W* 40 (Oct. 16, 1952): 3–4; Loescher, *Protestant Church and the Negro,* 53–55, 82–84; Reimers, *White Protestantism and the Negro,* 186–87; and Kenneth Kesselus, *John E. Hines: Granite on Fire* (Austin, Tex.: Episcopal Theological Seminary of the Southwest, 1995), 153–55.

22. *JGC* (1952): 277–81 (quotation on 279); "Stand against Exploitation Is Urged by Bishops," *W* 40 (Oct. 2, 1952): 3–6; "Houston: Convention City," *W* 40 (Oct. 16, 1952): 9; "Race Relations: General Convention and Houston," *LC* 126 (Feb. 8, 1953): 6–7; "Bishops Back Houston for Convention," *W* 41 (Nov. 25, 1953): 5; and Kesselus, *John E. Hines,* 156.

23. "Upper S.C.: Negro Delegates Seated," *LC* 114 (Mar. 23, 1947): 17–18; Thomas, *Historical Account,* 465, 472, 476, 630–34 (quotations on 633–34); and Reimers, "Negro Bishops," 240.

24. Diocese of Southern Virginia, *Journal of the Annual Council* (1947), 167; (1948), 43, 48; (1953), 183; (1954), 45, 63 (Martin quotation on 63); "Diocesan," *LC* 121 (July 2, 1950): 10; "Southern Virginia: No Colored Convocation," *LC* 128 (Feb. 28, 1954): 16; and Harris, *It Can Be Done,* 59–65.

25. "Georgia: Negro Representation Voted," *LC* 114 (June 1, 1947): 24; Peter Day, "Sorts and Conditions," *LC* 122 (Apr. 15, 1951): 5; [W. Leigh Ribble], "Racial Strife and Racial Peace," *Southern Churchman* 117 (July 21, 1951): 3; "Mississippi," *LC* 126 (Feb. 8, 1953): 19; "Mississippi: Higher Figure," *LC* 128 (Feb. 14, 1954): 19; Racial Study Commission of the Diocese of Virginia, *The Race Problem and the Church* ([Leesburg, Va.: Potomac Press], 1960–61), 1:22–23; and Reimers, "Negro Bishops," 240.

26. William M. Polk, *Leonidas Polk: Bishop and General,* new ed. (New York: Longmans, Green, 1915), 1:219–35 (quotations on 225, 227); Fairbanks, *History of the University of the South,* 228–31; and Joseph H. Parks, *General Leonidas Polk, C.S.A.: The Fighting Bishop* (Baton Rouge: Louisiana State Univ. Press, 1962), 117–33, 146–52.

27. Author's interview of Scott Bates, Sept. 13, 1994, Sewanee, Tenn.; author's interview of R. Emmet Gribbin Jr., Sept. 28, 1994, Northport, Ala.; Hodding Carter, "The Amazing Gentleman from Sewanee," *Saturday Evening Post,* Mar. 28, 1953, 28–29; Will D. Campbell, *And Also with You: Duncan Gray and the American Dilemma* (Franklin, Tenn.: Providence House, 1997), 71–72; Ely Green, *Ely: An Autobiography*

(1966; reprint, Athens: Univ. of Georgia Press, 1990), 21–23, 73; and Charles Reagan Wilson, *Baptized in Blood: The Religion of the Lost Cause, 1865–1920* (Athens: Univ. of Georgia Press, 1980), 145–51.

28. G.R. Madson, "Recommendation from Fourth Province Synod to Board of Trustees," Nov. 10, 1951, in IBS, "Integration—School of Theology" folder, box 1; Arthur [Ben Chitty] to Hinton F. Longino, [from Sewanee, Tenn.], Dec. 1, 1952, 1–3, in IBS, "Later Correspondence Involving Integration: Background and History" folder, box 3; Board of Trustees of the Univ. of the South, *Journal of Proceedings* (1952): 13–14 (quotation on 14); Harris, *It Can Be Done*, 79–80; Hewlett, *Jessie Ball duPont*, 203–8; Donald Smith Armentrout, *The Quest for the Informed Priest: A History of the School of Theology* (Sewanee, Tenn.: School of Theology, Univ. of the South, 1979), 279–82; Pauli Murray, ed., *States' Laws on Race and Color* (1951; reprint, Athens: Univ. of Georgia Press, 1997), 429; Richard Kluger, *Simple Justice: The History of* Brown v. Board of Education *and Black America's Struggle for Equality* (New York: Random House, 1977), 274–84; and Numan V. Bartley, *The New South, 1945–1980* (Baton Rouge: Louisiana State Univ. Press, 1995), 154–59.

29. Robert R. Parks to F. Craighill Brown, [from Quincy, Fla.], July 8, 1952, 1–2, in RVC, "Negro File (N–R)" folder; *JGC* (1952): 277–79; Hodding Carter, "Eight Courageous Men of God," *LC* 124 (June 29, 1952): 12; "Reconsider!" *EC* 118 (June 29, 1952): 10; "Sewanee and Christian Principle," *LC* 125 (Nov. 20, 1952): 15–16; "Statement on Sewanee Issue Made by Seminary Deans," *W* 40 (Jan. 29, 1953): 3; and Armentrout, *Quest for the Informed Priest,* 282–96 (quotations on 282). Richard Wilmer was the great-grandson of Richard Hooker Wilmer, the sole dissenter at the Sewanee conference of 1883.

30. Armentrout, *Quest for the Informed Priest,* 284–85.

31. Author's interview of John M. Allin, Aug. 6, 1994, Kennebunkport, Maine; Eugene M. Kayden to "Eight Members of the Faculty," from Sewanee, Tenn., June 18, 1952, 1–5 (Kayden quotations), in IBS, "Integration—School of Theology" folder, box 1; Arthur Ben Chitty, "Misfortune on the Mountain," *Sewanee Alumni News* 18 (Nov. 15, 1952): 12–13; and Armentrout, *Quest for the Informed Priest,* 282–96.

32. Author's interview of Austin M. Ford, June 21, 1994, Atlanta; author's interview of Arthur B. and Elizabeth N. Chitty, Sept. 15, 1994, Sewanee, Tenn.; author's interview of Duncan M. Gray Jr., Sept. 20, 1994, Jackson, Miss.; [Duncan M. Gray Jr. and Davis B. Carter], "On the Sewanee Situation," Oct. 31, 1952, [2–4], manuscript in the possession of Duncan Gray, Jackson, Miss.; [Charles C.J. Carpenter] to Edwin A. Penick, from Birmingham, Ala., Dec. 1, 1952, 1–2; [Carpenter] to R. Bland Mitchell, [from Birmingham, Ala.], Dec. 8, 1952, in CCJC, folder 241.2.159.15.32–33 ("Sewanee Faculty Resignation" file); Bayard H. Jones to [Edward] McCrady, from Sewanee, Tenn., Aug. 19, 1952, 1–2; Jones, "Memorandum," Nov. 20, 1952, 2–3 (quotation on 2); Jones to [Middleton S.] Barnwell, from Sewanee, May 2, 1953, 1, in RVC, "Negro File (J–L)" folder; Edward McCrady to John L. Cobbs Jr., [from Sewanee], Mar. 2, 1953, in RVC, "Negro File (A–C)" folder; [Mitchell] to F. Craighill Brown, [from Little Rock, Ark., Oct. 1952], 1–2, in RVC, "Negro File (M)" folder; Chitty, "Misfortune on the Mountain," 4–6; "What's Going On Here?" *W* 40 (Nov. 20, 1952): 6; "Students Favor Admitting Negroes," *LC* 125 (Nov. 23, 1952): 19–20; Campbell, *And Also with You,* 91–98; Hewlett, *Jessie Ball duPont,* 205–6; and Armentrout, *Quest for the Informed Priest,* 296–306.

33. Carter, "Amazing Gentleman," 197, 200.

34. Edward McCrady to Charles Clingman, [from Sewanee, Tenn.], Feb. 2, 1953, 1–2, in RVC, "Negro File (A–C)" folder; Murray M. Howard to McCrady, from Atlanta, Feb. 9, 1953; McCrady to Howard, [from Sewanee], Feb. 11, 1953, in RVC,

"Negro File (D–I)" folder; and McCrady to Mrs. George Stiger, [from Sewanee], June 20, 1953, in RVC, "Negro File (S–Z)" folder.

35. "Discrimination Fair, Just in Sewanee Issue: McCrady," *EC* 120 (Dec. 7, 1952): 8–9.

36. Ford interview; "Bishop Dandridge Accepts Deanship at Sewanee Seminary," *W* 40 (Feb. 12, 1953): 14; John M. Krumm, letter in "Backfire," *W* 40 (Feb. 19, 1953): 15; Campbell, *And Also with You,* 89–90; and Armentrout, *Quest for the Informed Priest,* 296–306.

37. Thomas M. Trabue to Edward B. McCrady, from Nashville, Tenn., Nov. 13, 1951, and attached "Resolution," Nov. 12, 1951, in RVC, "Negro File (S–Z)" folder; Albion W. Knight to Board of Regents of the Univ. of the South, from Jacksonville, Fla., Nov. 23, 1951, in RVC, "Negro File (J–L)" folder (Knight quotation); [Undergraduates of the College of Arts and Sciences of the Univ. of the South] to McCrady, [from Sewanee, Tenn.], Feb. 17, 1953, in RVC, "Negro File—Official and Miscellaneous" folder ("characteristic . . . gentleman" quotation); Albert S. Thomas, "Sewanee," *LC* 126 (Feb. 1, 1953): 3 (Thomas quotation); and "Praise for Dr. McCrady," *LC* 126 (Apr. 5, 1953): 20.

38. Ford interview; James A. Pike to [Edward] McCrady, from Wellfleet, Mass., July 14, [1952], 2–3; Pike to McCrady, from New York, Feb. 10, 1953, 1–3 (Pike quotations), in IBS, "Edward McCrady—James Pike Correspondence" folder, box 3; [Gray and Carter], "On the Sewanee Situation," [1]; "Dean Pike Rejects a 'White Divinity,'" *NYT,* Feb. 13, 1953, 23; "Dean Pike Declines an Honorary Degree," *CCe* 70 (1953): 244; "No White Doctorate," *LC* 126 (Feb. 22, 1953): 19–21; and Armentrout, *Quest for the Informed Priest,* 306–7.

39. Author's interview of Kenneth R. Franklin, May 27, 1994, Warwick, R.I.; Ford interview; Chitty interview; VTS Faculty, "Minutes of the Meeting," Oct. 20, 1952, 1; Apr. 6, 1953, 1, in VTSA; E. Felix Kloman to F. Craighill Brown, from Alexandria, Va., Oct. 24, 1952, in Correspondence of the Dean, VTSA; [Edward McCrady] to James A. Pike, [from Sewanee, Tenn.], Feb. 20, 1953, 3–4, in IBS, "McCrady—Pike Correspondence" folder, box 3; [Charles C.J. Carpenter] to R. Bland Mitchell, [from Birmingham, Ala.], Dec. 8, 1952 (Carpenter quotation); Mitchell to Carpenter, from Little Rock, Ark., Feb. 24, 1953, 2, in CCJC, folder 241.2.159.15.32–33 ("Sewanee Faculty Resignation" file); Carpenter to Clifford Eldred McWhorter, from Birmingham, June 1, 1953, manuscript in the possession of Clifford E. McWhorter, Millington, Tenn.; McWhorter to the author, from Millington, Tenn., Aug. 24, 1994; M. George Henry to McCrady, from Asheville, N.C., June 13, 1952, 1–2, in RVC, "Negro File (D–I)" folder; "Students Leave Sewanee," *W* 40 (June 25, 1953): 17; Bass, "Bishop C.C.J. Carpenter," 189–90; and Armentrout, *Quest for the Informed Priest,* 307–8.

40. E.P. Dandridge to Edward G. McCrady, from Nashville, Tenn., Nov. 17, 1952; Augustus T. Graydon to R. Bland Mitchell, from Columbia, S.C., Nov. 17, 1952 (Graydon quotation); Mitchell to Graydon, [from Little Rock, Ark.], Nov. 22, 1952, 1, in RVC, "Negro File (D–I)" folder; and Mitchell to Edwin A. Penick, [from Little Rock], Nov. 25, 1952, 1, in RVC, "Negro File (M)" folder.

41. [Augustus T. Graydon], "Legal Aspects of the Admission of Qualified Negroes to the Theological Seminary at Sewanee," [1953], 3:1b, 5:1d–14d, in IBS, "Later Correspondence Involving Integration: Background and History" folder, box 3.

42. Board of Trustees of the Univ. of the South, *Journal of Proceedings* (1953): 11–18, 49–60; "Fourth Province Bishops Hit Sewanee Segregation," *EC* 120 (Nov. 30, 1952): 3–4; "Diocesan: North Carolina," *LC* 126 (May 31, 1953): 20; Richard Park, "Sewanee Votes: No Discrimination in Admissions," *LC* 126 (June 14, 1953): 8–10;

Davis B. Carter and Duncan M. Gray Jr., "Trustees of Sewanee Reverse Segregation Rule," W 40 (June 25, 1953): 3–4; and Armentrout, *Quest for the Informed Priest,* 308–9. John Moncrief, a graduate of General Theological Seminary in New York and the priest-in-charge of St. Paul's Church in Orangeburg, South Carolina, became the first African American student at Sewanee when he enrolled in the summer graduate school in 1953; and Merrick Collier of Savannah, Georgia, entered as the first black B.D. student in the fall of 1954. Arthur Ben Chitty to F. Craighill Brown, from Sewanee, Tenn., Aug. 30, 1955, 1–2, in IBS, "Later Correspondence" folder, box 3; John N. Popham, "Negro Considered for Sewanee Study," *NYT,* June 6, 1953, 19; and "Sewanee Admits Negro," *NYT,* Sept. 24, 1954, 50.

43. [Graydon], "Legal Aspects," 5:8d–14d; and R.A. Park, "Eventful Weekend," *LC* 126 (June 21, 1953): 7–8.

44. BRC, Jan. 13–14, 1953, 2; Jan. 19–20, 1954, 1; "Repentance First," W 30 (Feb. 6, 1947): 8; and "Great Lack of Negro Clergy Hampers Church Work," W 40 (Jan. 29, 1953): 4. For a discussion of a similar dilemma faced by black clergy and lay leaders in the African Methodist Episcopal Church, see Joan Louise Bryant, "Race Debates among Nineteenth-Century Colored Reformers and Churchmen," Ph.D. diss., Yale Univ., 1996.

45. [M.M. Millikan], "Report of the Secretary," Oct. 5, 1950, 1–7 (quotation on 6), in ACIN, folder 61–1–16.

46. Earl H. McClenney to M.M. Millikan, from Lawrenceville, Va., July 14, 1950, 1–2 (quotation on 2); Harold L. Trigg to Millikan, from Raleigh, N.C., July 26, 1950, in ACIN, folder 61–2–26; and Millikan, "Decisions Challenge Church," *Forth* 115 (Dec. 1950): 10–12, 29–30.

47. BRC, Jan. 8–9, 1952, 6; and [William B. Spofford], "Is This Segregation?" W 34 (July 12, 1951): 6.

48. Alger L. Adams, "Church Jim Crow," W 34 (Oct. 25, 1951): 10–13; Adams, "Church Practice of Segregation," W 34 (Nov. 1, 1951): 7–8; Adams, "Segregation: How It Works," W 34 (Nov. 8, 1951): 12–13; Adams, "Church Jim Crow: We Lag Far Behind," W 34 (Nov. 15, 1951): 13–14 (source of quotations); Adams, "Church Jim Crow: What Can Be Done," W 34 (Nov. 22, 1951): 10–11; "Race Prejudice in the Church," *LC* 123 (Dec. 2, 1951): 13; and "Council Negro Work Guide Blasted by Yonkers Rector," *EC* 118 (May 18, 1952): 7.

49. Tollie L. Caution, "A Decade of Progress in Negro Work, 1941–1951," 2–7, 11–18, 21, in CSR-85, folder 85–3–21; NCEC, Dec. 4–6, 1951, 99; Feb. 12–14, 1952, 65. For information about Caution's background, see "The Rev. T.L. Caution Begins New Work," *Forth* 110 (July–Aug. 1945): 24; and [Richard L. Tolliver], *Struggle, Strife and Salvation: Black Ministry in the Episcopal Church* (New York: Office of Black Ministries, [1983]), 13–14.

50. BRC, Jan. 8–9, 1952, 1, 6, 11; "Twenty-Ninth Annual Session, St. Paul's Summer School of Religious Education for Church Workers," 1954, n.p., in TLCP, "Summer School of Religious Education for Church Workers" folder; and *JGC* (1952): 309–10 (Milliken quotation on 310).

51. "A Resolution Passed by the Woman's Auxiliary . . . Sept. 5, 1952," n.p.(source of quotation), in TLCP; Margaret Marston Sherman, *True to Their Heritage: A Brief History of the Woman's Auxiliary, 1871–1958* (New York: National Council, [1959?]), 32–33; and David E. Sumner, "The Episcopal Church's Involvement in Civil Rights: 1943–1973," S.T.M. thesis, School of Theology, Univ. of the South, 1983, 5.

52. Executive Committee of the Girls' Friendly Society, U.S.A., "Minutes of the Meeting," Oct. 31–Nov. 1, 1949, 5; Oct. 11–12, 1950, 6; Board of Directors of the

Girls' Friendly Society, U.S.A., "Minutes of Meeting," Apr. 18–20, 1950, 6; "A Statement of Policy in Race Relations for the Girls' Friendly Society," [Apr. 1950], 1 (source of quotation), in AEC, Records of the Girls' Friendly Society of the U.S.A., record group 134, folder 134–1–8; "A Statement of Policy in Race Relations for the Girls' Friendly Society, U.S.A. (Adopted by the Board of Directors, Nov., 1955)," 1, in AEC, Records of the Girls' Friendly Society, folder 134–3–24; and "GFS: Segregation, but No Prejudice," *LC* 120 (June 18, 1950): 9;

53. BRC, May 5–6, 1952, 5; NCEC, Sept. 5–6, 1952, 1–2; *Living Church Annual* (1952): 37; and *Episcopal Church Annual* (1953): 41.

54. "Social Relations: Not Just a Watch-Dog," *LC* 128 (May 16, 1954): 6 (source of quotation); and Lewis, *Yet with a Steady Beat,* 143–44.

55. Diocese of South Carolina, *Journal of the Annual Convention* (1953), 27–28; (1954), 18, 35; "South Carolina: Negro Representation Voted," *LC* 114 (May 18, 1947): 19; "South Carolina," *EC* 119 (June 27, 1954): 8; Thomas, *Historical Account,* 159, 163; and Reimers, "Negro Bishops," 240. The other parishes admitted to the convention were Calvary Church, Charleston, and St. Paul's Church, Orangeburg.

# 3. The Impact of the *Brown* Decision

1. Elizabeth Waring to [Sarah Patton Boyle], from New York, Oct. 17, 1955, 3–4, in SPBP, box 8; Tinsley E. Yarbrough, *A Passion for Justice: J. Waties Waring and Civil Rights* (New York: Oxford Univ. Press, 1987), 4–5; Bertram Wyatt-Brown, "Introduction: The Mind of W.J. Cash," in W.J. Cash, *The Mind of the South* (1941; reprint, New York: Knopf, 1991), xvii–xxvi; Southern, *Gunnar Myrdal,* 139; and Kluger, *Simple Justice,* 295–98.

2. David R. Goldfield, *Black, White, and Southern: Race Relations and Southern Culture, 1940 to the Present* (Baton Rouge: Louisiana State Univ. Press, 1990), 60–61; Yarbrough, *Passion for Justice,* 102–6; and Kluger, *Simple Justice,* 298–301 (quotation on 299).

3. Mark V. Tushnet, *Making Civil Rights Law: Thurgood Marshall and the Supreme Court, 1936–1961* (New York: Oxford Univ. Press, 1994), 8–9, 27; and Kluger, *Simple Justice,* 173–86, 214–17, 280–84.

4. Goldfield, *Black, White, and Southern,* 60–62; Tushnet, *Making Civil Rights Law,* 156–57; Southern, *Gunnar Myrdal,* 138–39; Yarbrough, *Passion for Justice,* 195–96 (Waring quotations); and Kluger, *Simple Justice,* 301–5, 365–66.

5. [Kenneth B. Clark], "Protecting Children against Racial and Religious Prejudices," [ca. 1951], 1–12, manuscript in the possession of Kenneth B. Clark, Hastings-on-Hudson, N.Y.; Kenneth B. Clark, *Prejudice and Your Child,* 2d ed. (Boston: Beacon, 1963), ix–xi, 6–24; Yarbrough, *Passion for Justice,* 182–83; Jackson, *Gunnar Myrdal,* 292–93; and Kluger, *Simple Justice,* 315–21, 328–31, 353–56.

6. Kenneth B. Clark to Edward McCrady, from New York, Sept. 22, 1953, 1–2; McCrady to Clark, [from Sewanee, Tenn., Sept. 1953], in RVC, "Negro File (A–C)" folder; Kenneth B. Clark, "The Present Crisis in Race Relations," May 19, 1956, 6, 14–15, manuscript in the possession of Kenneth Clark; Kenneth B. Clark, "Desegregation: An Appraisal of the Evidence," *Journal of Social Issues* 9 (4) (1953): 1, 13; Clark, *Prejudice and Your Child,* 104–12; and Mary Harrington Hall, "A Conversation with Kenneth B. Clark," *Psychology Today,* June 1968, 20, 25.

7. Thurgood Marshall to Pauli Murray, from New York, Apr. 11, 1951; Murray to George S. Schuyler, from New York, July 31, 1942, 1–3, in Pauli Murray Papers,

Schlesinger Library, Radcliffe College, Cambridge, Mass., MC 412, folders 98:1753, 1752; Pauli Murray, "Negroes Are Fed Up," *Common Sense* 12 (Aug. 1943): 274–76; Pauli Murray, "An American Credo," *Common Ground* 5 (winter 1945): 23–24 (quotation source); Pauli Murray, *Proud Shoes: The Story of an American Family* (1956; reprint, New York: Harper, 1978), vii–viii; and Pauli Murray, *Pauli Murray: The Autobiography of a Black Activist, Feminist, Lawyer, Priest, and Poet* (1987; reprint, Knoxville: Univ. of Tennessee Press, 1989), 125–26, 138–49, 175–76, 201, 221–24, 255, 283–87, 299–302.

8. [Pauli Murray] to Juanita [Morrow Nelson, from New York], Nov. 15, 1948, 1–2, in Murray Papers, folder 98:1753; Murray, *States' Laws*, 5–20; Murray, *Pauli Murray*, 2–7, 19, 48–50, 57, 70, 283–89; Alice G. Knotts, "Methodist Women Integrate Schools and Housing, 1952–1959," in Vicki L. Crawford et al., eds., *Women in the Civil Rights Movement: Trailblazers and Torchbearers, 1941–1965* (Brooklyn, N.Y.: Carlson, 1990), 251–52; and Casey Miller and Kate Swift, "Pauli Murray," *Ms.*, Mar. 1980, 60–64. Murray later became the first African American woman to be ordained a priest in the Episcopal Church.

9. Clark, *Prejudice and Your Child*, 156–65; Yarbrough, *Passion for Justice*, 224–25; and Kluger, *Simple Justice*, 538–40, 563–64, 700–714.

10. Neil R. McMillen, *The Citizens' Council: Organized Resistance to the Second Reconstruction, 1954–64* (1971; reprint, Urbana: Univ. of Illinois Press, 1994), 9–40; Goldfield, *Black, White, and Southern*, 75–84; Numan V. Bartley, *The Rise of Massive Resistance: Race and Politics in the South during the 1950's* (Baton Rouge: Louisiana State Univ. Press, 1969), 58–60, 84–87; Bartley, *New South* 160–69; and Grantham, *South in Modern America*, 204–6.

11. "Resist Racist Appeals!" *CCe* 71 (1954): 1294–95; James A. Pike, "The Court Decision," *W* 41 (June 10, 1954): 13; Michael B. Friedland, *Lift Up Your Voice like a Trumpet: White Clergy and the Civil Rights and Antiwar Movements, 1954–1973* (Chapel Hill: Univ. of North Carolina Press, 1998), 18–22; Alvis, *Religion and Race*, 57; Eighmy, *Churches in Cultural Captivity*, 189–90; James F. Findlay Jr., *Church People in the Struggle: The National Council of Churches and the Black Freedom Movement, 1950–1970* (New York: Oxford Univ. Press, 1993), 16–17; Andrew Michael Manis, *Southern Civil Religions in Conflict: Black and White Baptists and Civil Rights, 1947–1957* (Athens: Univ. of Georgia Press, 1987), 61–67; and Bailey, *Southern White Protestantism*, 142–47.

12. Gardiner M. Day to Tollie Caution, from Cambridge, Mass., Sept. 22, 1952, 1–4, in TLCP, "General Convention (1955)" folder; "The Church and the Churches," *Time*, Mar. 26, 1951, 70–75 (quotation on 70); "Houston: Convention City," *W* 40 (Oct. 16, 1952): 9; Murray, *States' Laws*, 452–56, 569–71, 662–64; Henry Knox Sherrill, *Among Friends* (Boston: Little, Brown, 1962), 225–27, 247, 257–59; Martin E. Marty, *Modern American Religion*, vol. 3. (Chicago: Univ. of Chicago Press, 1996), 267, 272–73; and David E. Sumner, *The Episcopal Church's History: 1945–1985* (Wilton, Conn.: Morehouse-Barlow, 1987), 36.

13. [Charles] A. Shaw to Henry K. Sherrill, [from Houston], Nov. 17, 1953, 1–2; [Kenneth deP. Hughes], "Summary of Remarks by Proposer of Resolution," [May 6, 1953], 1–2, in TLCP, "General Convention (1955)" folder; Diocese of Massachusetts, *Journal of the Convention* (1953), 69–70; "Washington: Segregatedly Unsegregated," *LC* 128 (May 16, 1954): 23–24; "New York: Mason, Dixon Line," *LC* 128 (May 30, 1954): 18–19; "Convention: Hospitality," *LC* 128 (June 6, 1954): 6–7; and Frank A. Rhea, "In Daring Spirit," letter in *LC* 128 (June 13, 1954): 2 (Rhea quotation). Rhea's position was somewhat understandable: he was white and a southerner by birth, and

at the beginning of his ministry he had served in parishes in Texas. See "Bishop Rhea," *LC* 147 (Nov. 10, 1963): 6.

14. "No Thunder, No Lightning, No Rain," *LC* 128 (June 20, 1954): 14.

15. John E. Hines, "Reminiscences," 168–80, in AEC, Columbia Univ. Oral History Research Office Collection; Diocese of Texas, *Journal of the Annual Council* (1955), 103–4; Russell Porter, "Episcopal Convention at Houston Canceled over Racial Segregation," *NYT*, June 9, 1954, 1, 31; "Houston Bishop Talks of Case," *NYT*, June 9, 1954, 31 (Quin quotation); "Episcopalians Choose Honolulu in Place of Houston for Triennial," *NYT*, June 18, 1954, 25; Sophie W. Wallace, "Houston Decision," letter in *LC* 129 (July 4, 1954): 2; J.L.C. McFaddin, "Houston Decision," letter in *LC* 129 (July 18, 1954): 3; "Convention at Honolulu," *W* 41 (July 22, 1954): 7; "Sherrill Hits Hard at Critics of Convention Change," *W* 41 (Oct. 28, 1954): 3; Charles G. Hamilton, "Keen Debate Plays Its Part in Synod of Sewanee," *W* 42 (Dec. 9, 1954): 6; Sherrill, *Among Friends*, 257–59; Lawrence L. Brown, *The Episcopal Church in Texas*, vol. 2 (Austin, Tex.: Eakin Press, 1985), 136; and Kesselus, *John E. Hines*, 156–57.

16. Gray interview; *The Church Considers the Supreme Court Decision* ([Jackson]: Department of Christian Social Relations, Diocese of Mississippi, 1954), 1–12 (quotations on 3, 6); "Race Relations: Light from Mississippi," *LC* 129 (Sept. 26, 1954): 10; and Campbell, *And Also with You*, 123–44. Gray's father, Duncan M. Gray, was the bishop of Mississippi at this time, and he quietly affirmed his son's commitment to racial equality; see Gray interview.

17. Gray interview; NCEC, Oct. 13–14, 1954, 102, 181–82, 197; Dec. 8–9, 1954, 28–30, 57–59, 72–74; Apr. 27–28, 1955, 131; Diocese of Mississippi, *Journal of the Annual Council* (1955), 111; *Just, Right, and Necessary: A Study of Reactions to the Supreme Court Decision on Segregation* (New York: National Council, 1955), 1–44 (quotations on 37); Elizabeth McCracken, ""National Council," *LC* 129 (Dec. 26, 1954): 8; "New Duties for New Occasions," *Forth* 120 (Feb. 1955): 12–13, 24–26, 28; and Campbell, *And Also with You*, 149. The Division of Christian Citizenship had been organized in 1953. Under the direction of Moran Weston, a black priest affiliated with St. Philip's Church in Harlem, it was given a mandate to educate church members about the relevance of the gospel to ordinary life and encourage "the application of Christian standards to social relations." "Two New Divisions," *LC* 126 (Mar. 1, 1953): 8; and Powel Mills Dawley, *The Episcopal Church and Its Work* (Greenwich, Conn.: Seabury, 1955), 234–37.

18. *Bridge Building in Race Relations: What the Episcopal Church Has Said and Done* (New York: National Council, 1957), 16–36; Robert S. Ellwood, *The Fifties Spiritual Marketplace: American Religion in a Decade of Conflict* (New Brunswick, N.J.: Rutgers Univ. Press, 1997), 123–24, 227–36; Woodward, *Strange Career*, 149–52; and Jackson, *Gunnar Myrdal*, 293–94.

19. *JGC* (1955): 258–59.

20. Diocese of Virginia, *Journal of the Annual Council* (1955), 59–60, 110–13 (quotation on 112).

21. "Social Relations: Leaven in the South," *LC* 128 (June 6, 1954): 7–8; "Supreme Court Ruling Weighed: Bishop Quin Speaks on Triennial," *EC* 119 (June 13, 1954): 7–8; "Segregation, Triennial Capture Synod Attention," *EC* 119 (Dec. 26, 1954): 9; Henry I. Louttit, *The Church and Segregation* (Cincinnati: Forward Movement, [1956]), 3–11 (Louttit quotation on 3); Carter and Carter, *So Great a Good*, 387–88 (Jones quotation on 387).

22. "Study Sees Episcopalians Lacking Social Education," *EC* 120 (Oct. 5, 1952): 4; "South Carolina: Injustices, Hardships," *LC* 128 (June 20, 1954): 16–17 (Guerry

quotations); Albert S. Thomas, "Development or Obliteration," letter in *LC* 129 (Oct. 24, 1954): 2–3 (Thomas quotation); and Thomas, *Historical Account*, 333–42. For further background on Guerry's views, see also Edward B. Guerry to "the Bishops and Chancellors of the Protestant Episcopal Church," from Charleston, S.C., May 30, 1955, 1–2 in AEWP; Guerry, "The Church and the Supreme Court Decision," *LC* 132 (Apr. 8, 1956): 4–6; and London and Lemmon, *Episcopal Church in North Carolina*, 414. Guerry was the son of William Alexander Guerry, a former bishop of South Carolina.

    23. NCEC, Feb. 21–23, 1956, 8.

    24. South Carolina, *Annual Convention* (1956), 17–23 (quotation on 17).

    25. Author's interview of John B. Morris, Oct. 23–25, 1993, Atlanta; John B. Morris and John T. Walker, "The Separation of God's People: The Problem of Racial Prejudice in the Episcopal Church," Jan. 1954, 1–5, 57–67, MM; "Diocese Votes Voluntary Segregation; Protests Use of 'un-Christian' Label," *EC* 121 (May 13, 1956): 5; B. Allston Moore, "No 'Gag Rule,'" letter in *LC* 132 (May 27, 1956): 3; Thomas N. Carruthers, "Convention Resolution," letter in *LC* 132 (June 3, 1956): 21; [G. Milton] Crum, "The Carolina Resolution," letter in *EC* 121 (June 24, 1956): 33 (Crum quotation); and Thomas, *Historical Account*, 163. For his later reflections on racial issues in the church, see G. Milton Crum, "Confessions of a Recovering Racist," *Virginia Seminary Journal*, Dec. 1997, 34–35.

    26. Grantham, *South in Modern America*, 209–11; Kluger, *Simple Justice*, 744–45; Bartley, *New South* 197–98; and Bartley, *Rise of Massive Resistance*, 60, 116–17, 128–31, 211–15.

    27. Hodding Carter, "Just Leave Us Alone," *Saturday Evening Post*, Jan. 14, 1950, 30, 90–92; Hodding Carter, "Segregation's Way in One Southern Town," *NYT Magazine*, Apr. 5, 1953, 11, 34–37; Hodding Carter, *Where Main Street Meets the River* (New York: Rinehart, 1953), 182–87, 228–44, 330–39; Hodding Carter, "The Court's Decision and the South," *Reader's Digest*, Sept. 1954, 51–56; Hodding Carter, "The Court and the Church," *EC* 119 (Oct. 3, 1954): 24, 39; Hodding Carter, "A Wave of Terror Threatens the South," *Look*, Mar. 22, 1955, 32–36; Morton Sosna, *In Search of the Silent South: Southern Liberals and the Race Issue* (New York: Columbia Univ. Press, 1977), vii–xi, 88–93, 198–208; John Egerton, *Speak Now Against the Day: The Generation Before the Civil Rights Movement in the South* (New York: Knopf, 1994), 253–58, 528; David L. Chappell, *Inside Agitators: White Southerners in the Civil Rights Movement* (Baltimore: Johns Hopkins Univ. Press, 1994), 4–49; James C. Cobb, *The Most Southern Place on Earth: The Mississippi Delta and the Roots of Regional Identity* (New York: Oxford Univ. Press, 1992), 320–22; and Grantham, *South in Modern America*, 149, 196, 213–16.

    28. Hodding Carter, *Southern Legacy* (Baton Rouge: Louisiana State Univ. Press, 1950), 27–37 (quotation on 30).

    29. Hodding Carter, "A Sign for Our Times," Feb. 9, 1949, 1–5 (quotations 2, 5); Carter to Wendell F. Kline, [from Greenville, Miss.], Mar. 24, 1953; Carter to James Fallon, [from Greenville], Apr. 5, 1955; Carter to F.X. Simcox, [from Greenville], June 16, 1955, in MSU, Hodding and Betty Werlein Carter Papers, boxes 55, 9, 13, 14; Hodding Carter, "The South and I," *Look*, June 28, 1955, 80; Ann Waldron, *Hodding Carter: The Reconstruction of a Racist* (Chapel Hill, N.C.: Algonquin, 1993), 175, 200, 228, 247–48; and John T. Kneebone, "Liberal on the Levee: Hodding Carter, 1944–1954," *Journal of Mississippi History* 49 (1987): 159–62.

    30. Sarah Patton Boyle to [Harold Fey], from Charlottesville, Va., Nov. 29, 1952; [Boyle] to Jim [Lawson, from Charlottesville], Jan. 14, 1953, 1–2 ("love of Negroes" quotation on 1), in SPBP, boxes 1, 4; Sarah Patton Boyle, *The Desegregated Heart: A*

*Virginian's Stand in Time of Transition* (New York: Morrow, 1962), xi, 3–21, 88–89, 117–25; Sarah Patton Boyle, "A Voice from the South," *CCe* 69 (1952): 1471–73 ("distasteful, ridiculous" quotation on 1471); Sarah Patton Boyle, "The Price of Brotherhood," *Ebony*, Sept. 1963, 79; Joanna Bowen Gillespie, "Sarah Patton Boyle's Desegregated Heart," in *Beyond Image and Convention: Explorations in Southern Women's History*, ed. Janet L. Coryell, Martha H. Swain, Sandra Gioia Treadway, and Elizabeth Hayes Turner (Columbia: Univ. of Missouri Press, 1998), 158–80.

31. Boyle, *Desegregated Heart*, 293.

32. [Sarah Patton Boyle] to Elizabeth [Waring, from Charlottesville], Jan. 24, 1958 in SPBP, box 8.

33. Boyle to Aubrey Williams, from Charlottesville, May 22, 1958; [Boyle] to Anne [Braden, from Charlottesville], Oct. 5, 1958, 1, in SPBP, box 7; Sarah Patton Boyle, "Southerners Will *Like* Integration," *Saturday Evening Post*, Feb. 19, 1955, 25, 133–34; Sarah Patton Boyle, "Spit in the Devil's Eye: A Southern Heretic Speaks," *Nation* 183 (1956): 327–29; Boyle, "Price of Brotherhood," 79–85; Dan Wakefield, "Charlottesville Battle: Symbol of the Divided South," *Nation* 183 (1956): 210–13; Boyle, *Desegregated Heart*, 252–54, 293–307, 324–33, 341–43, 350–64; and Kathleen Murphy Dierenfield, "One 'Desegregated Heart': Sarah Patton Boyle and the Crusade for Civil Rights in Virginia," *Virginia Magazine of History and Biography* 104 (1996): 251–80.

34. Author's interview of Anne Braden, Jan. 28, 1996, Louisville, Ky.; Braden to Sarah Patton Boyle, from Louisville, Ky., Dec. 7, 1957, 1, in SPBP, box 7; Anne Braden, "Church Leader in Kentucky Indicted for Sedition," *W* 42 (Feb. 17, 1955): 3–4; and Anne Braden, *The Wall Between* (New York: Monthly Review Press, 1958), 13–34, 229–30 (quotation on 22).

35. Braden interview; Walter Millis, "Louisville's Braden Case: A Test of Basic Rights," *Nation* 180 (1955): 393–98; Braden, "Church Leader in Kentucky," 3–6; "Braden Lawyers File Brief with Appeals Court," *W* 42 (Dec. 22, 1955): 6, 16; "Braden Case Dismissed," *W* 43 (Dec. 6, 1956): 17; Braden, *Wall Between*, 277–79; Emma Gelders Sterne, *They Took Their Stand* (New York: Crowell-Collier, 1968), 156–75; Sosna, *In Search of the Silent South*, 142–49; Frank T. Adams, *James A. Dombrowski: An American Heretic, 1897–1983* (Knoxville: Univ. of Tennessee Press, 1992), 240–44; and Linda Reed, *Simple Decency and Common Sense: The Southern Conference Movement, 1938–1963* (Bloomington: Indiana Univ. Press, 1991), 34, 161, 169, 172–79.

36. William Howard Melish, *When Christians Become "Subversive": A Sermon Preached . . . Sunday, Feb. 6, 1955* (Brooklyn, N.Y.: Episcopal League for Social Action, 1955), 3–11 (quotation on 11).

37. "Americans Must Defend Rights Declares Jurist," *W* 40 (Mar. 6, 1952): 3–4; "Equal Status and Opportunity for Racial Groups," advertisement in *W* 43 (May 24, 1956): 17; "Red Visitors Cause Rumpus," *Life*, Apr. 4, 1949, 42–43 (source of quotations); Melish Defense Committee, *The Melish Case: Challenge to the Church* ([Brooklyn, N.Y.]: Melish Defense Committee, [1949]), 30–31; Braden, *Wall Between*, 279; and Francis Henry Touchet, "The Social Gospel and the Cold War: The Melish Case," Ph.D. diss., New York Univ., 1981, 1–3, 510–13, 602–5, 670, 843–47.

38. Author's interview of Stiles B. Lines, Sept. 14–15, 1994, Sewanee, Tenn.; Morris interview; Stiles B. Lines, "'They Were Afraid to Ask Him': A Sermon Preached . . . on Dec. 30, 1956," n.p. ("climate of fear" quotation), manuscript in the author's possession, courtesy of Stiles Lines, Sewanee, Tenn.

39. Thomas P. Govan to John [Morris], from New York, Jan. 2, 1958, 2; [Morris]

to Tom [Govan, from Dillon, S.C.], Feb. 6, 1958, 2; [Morris], "A Prospectus," [1957], 1–3 (quotation on 3), in "34 Documents on *South Carolinians Speak*," MM; *South Carolinians Speak: A Moderate Approach to Race Relations* [Dillon, S.C.: n.p., 1957], iv–vi; Howard H. Quint, *Profile in Black and White: A Frank Portrait of South Carolina* (Washington, D.C.: Public Affairs Press, 1958), 170–71; and William Peters, *The Southern Temper* (Garden City, N.Y.: Doubleday, 1959), 28, 93–99.

40. Morris interview; John B. Morris, memorandum to "Persons Agreeing to Write for *South Carolinians Speak*," from Dillon, S.C., Apr. 3, 1957, 1–2 (Morris quotation on 2); John B. Morris, "A Final Report on 'South Carolinians Speak,'" July 12, 1958, 1–4, in "34 Documents on *South Carolinians Speak*," MM; *South Carolinians Speak*, iv–vi, 1–15, 69–73; Quint, *Profile in Black and White*, 171–75; and William Bagwell, *School Desegregation in the Carolinas: Two Case Studies* (Columbia: Univ. of South Carolina Press, 1972), 153. For background on James McBride Dabbs, see James McBride Dabbs, *The Southern Heritage* (New York: Knopf, 1958); and Alvis, *Religion and Race*, 58–60.

41. Will D. Campbell to John Morris, from Nashville, Tenn., Nov. 26, 1957; Campbell to Morris, from Nashville, Jan. 6, 1958, MM; Merrill M. Hawkins Jr., *Will Campbell: Radical Prophet of the South* (Macon, Ga.: Mercer Univ. Press, 1997), 40–44; and Findlay, *Church People*, 22–27.

42. John B. Morris to Thomas H. Wright, from Oyster Bay, N.Y., Sept. 20, 1958, 1–2, MM; Cornelius C. Tarplee, "Bridge Building in Areas of Racial Tension . . . Jan. 1–Feb. 18, 1957," 1–5 (quotations on 1, 3), in CSR-85, folder 85–3–22; Tarplee, "Initial Report to the Fund for the Republic on the Intergroup Education Project . . .," [Apr. 1957], 7–21; "Memorandum on the Intergroup Education Project: Department of Christian Social Relations, General Convention, 1958," [Sept. 23, 1958], 1, in CSR-31, folder 31–4–6; Tarplee, "Report on the Intergroup Cooperation Project," [1958], 1–2, in NCPC; NCEC, Dec. 11–13, 1956, 5, 100; Feb. 19–21, 1957, 148, 159–60; Apr. 30, May 1–2, 1957, 144; Apr. 28–30, 1959, 155–56; "South Carolina Clergy Publish Race Relations Book," *LC* 136 (Feb. 16, 1958): 12; and *Bridge Building in Race Relations*, 1, 14–15.

43. Gribbin interview; Robert E. Gribbin Jr., "Campus Crisis in Alabama," *EC* 121 (Mar. 3, 1956): 18–19, 34–35; "Chaplain Aided Negro Student," *W* 43 (Feb. 23, 1956): 5; Bartley, *New South*, 195; and E. Culpepper Clark, *The Schoolhouse Door: Segregation's Last Stand at the University of Alabama* (New York: Oxford Univ. Press, 1993), 59, 71–87, 123–24.

44. "The South: Attack on the Conscience," *Time*, Feb. 18, 1957, 17–20; Martin Luther King Jr., *Stride Toward Freedom: The Montgomery Story* (New York: Harper, 1958), 70; Chappell, *Inside Agitators*, 53; Robert Weisbrot, *Freedom Bound: A History of America's Civil Rights Movement* (New York: Penguin, 1990), 13–18; Taylor Branch, *Parting the Waters: America in the King Years, 1954–1963* (New York: Simon and Schuster, 1988), 128–42, 203–5; and Aldon D. Morris, *The Origins of the Civil Rights Movement: Black Communities Organizing for Change* (New York: Free Press, 1984), 17–25, 51–63.

45. Thomas R. Thrasher, "Jet-Propelled Gradualism," in *On the Battle Lines*, ed. Malcolm Boyd (New York: Morehouse-Barlow, 1964), 94–101; Virginia Foster Durr, *Outside the Magic Circle: The Autobiography of Virginia Foster Durr*, ed. Hollinger F. Barnard (Tuscaloosa: Univ. of Alabama Press, 1985), 245, 308–9; King, *Stride Toward Freedom*, 32–33, 108–9; Chappell, *Inside Agitators*, 56–58, 72–73, 244; and Friedland, *Lift Up Your Voice*, 27–30.

46. Gribbin interview; author's interview of Peggy H. Rupp, Aug. 24, 1995, Bir-

mingham, Ala.; author's interview of Francis X. Walter, Sept. 27, 1994, Birmingham; author's interview of William A. Yon, Sept. 30, 1994, Birmingham; [Charles C.J. Carpenter] to James T. Williams Jr., from Birmingham, Jan. 18, 1957, 1, in DAR; Diocese of Alabama, *Journal of the Annual Convention* (1955), 65–66 (Carpenter quotation on 66); (1958), 67; "Bishop Carpenter Deplores Breakdown," *W* 46 (Mar. 19, 1959): 16; Thrasher, "Jet-Propelled Gradualism," 98; and S. Jonathan Bass, "Not Time Yet: Alabama's Episcopal Bishop and the End of Segregation in the Deep South," *Anglican and Episcopal History* 53 (1994): 237–39.

    47. W.D. Workman Jr., "No Peace in Orangeburg," *LC* 132 (Jan. 1, 1956): 6–7; W.B. Spofford Sr., "South Carolina Case Raises Pulpit Freedom Issue," *W* 43 (May 3, 1956): 4–5; G. Ralph Madson, "Vicar of Negro Mission Asked to Leave by Bishop Carruthers," *LC* 132 (May 20, 1956): 7–9; "Bishop Carruthers Dismisses Deacon . . .," *EC* 121 (June 10, 1956): 13 (quotation source); Thomas, *Historical Account,* 159; and Morris, *Origins of the Civil Rights Movement,* 48.

    48. "Public Affairs: The Glass Wall," *LC* 127 (Nov. 15, 1953): 6–8; "Public Affairs: The Case of Two Priests," *LC* 128 (Jan. 31, 1954): 7–8; Kenneth Hughes, "Henry Parker Asked to Leave South Carolina Mission," *W* 43 (May 10, 1956): 3–6 (Hughes quotation on 5); Spofford, "South Carolina Case," 4–5; Madson, "Vicar of Negro Mission Asked to Leave," 7–9; and "Bishop Carruthers Dismisses Deacon . . . ," 13 (Parker quotation). For background on the tenuous position of the NAACP in the South at this time, see Grantham, *South in Modern America,* 210–11.

    49. BRC, Jan. 18–19, 1955, 2–3, 10–11; "The Bishop's Diocesan Committee to Study the Problem of Securing Young Negro Postulants for Holy Orders," Nov. 8, 1955, 2; William A. Clark to C.C.J. Carpenter, from Tuskegee, Ala., Jan. 13, 1956, 2, in CCJC, folder 241.2.129.14.32 ("Negro Postulants" file); Alabama, *Annual Convention* (1955), 61–65; (1956), 94–96; "No More Negro Churches," *LC* 129 (Dec. 26, 1954): 8–9; and Kenneth Hughes, "Perils of a Non-Integrated Church," *W* 42 (Feb. 17, 1955): 8–12.

    50. BRC, Jan. 18–19, 1955, 5; Jan. 17–18, 1956, 5–7 (quotations on 6–7); and NCEC, Feb. 9–11, 1943, 160.

    51. BRC, Jan. 17–18, 1956, 6–7.

    52. NCEC, Feb. 21–23, 1956, 60–63, 130 (quotations on 61); "Toward a Clearer Vision: A Bi-Racial Committee," *Forth* 121 (May 1956): 10–11, 24; and Elizabeth McCracken, "Records Are Broken as Dioceses, Districts Meet 97% of Quotas," *LC* 132 (Mar. 11, 1956): 12–13.

    53. BRC, Oct. 30, 1956, 2–4; and Jan. 22–23, 1957, 1, 5–6.

    54. NCEC, Feb. 19–21, 1957, 3–4. For an analysis of this issue in black churches generally, see Paris, *Social Teaching,* 79–80.

    55. NCEC, Feb. 19–21, 1957, 103–4, 113; Apr. 30, May 1–2, 1957, 121; Tollie L. Caution, "Memorandum to the Racial Minorities Committee," Apr. 1, 1957, in BRC, Jan. 22–23, 1957, n.p.; "The Division of Racial Minorities," [1959], 1–2, in TLCP, "Division of Racial Minorities" folder; "New Division of Racial Minorities Includes American Church Institute," *Forth* 122 (Sept. 1957): 24; Murray, *States' Laws,* 544–48; Gordon W. Allport, *The Nature of Prejudice* (1954; reprint, Reading, Mass.: Addison-Wesley, 1979), xvii–xviii, 512; Kenneth M. Stampp, *The Peculiar Institution: Slavery in the Ante-Bellum South* (New York: Knopf, 1956), vii, 9; Liston Pope, *The Kingdom beyond Caste* (New York: Friendship, 1957), 159–60; King, *Stride Toward Freedom,* 207; and Southern, *Gunnar Myrdal,* 199–204. As one bishop laconically remarked in this period, most southern dioceses were abandoning their "divisions of Negro work because we feel this in itself is a form of segregation or possibly of favoritism—we

cannot be sure which"; "The Southern Church Looks at Its Negro Work," *EC* 121 (Nov. 11, 1956): 11–13 (quotation on 12).

56. RMC, Sept. 24–25, 1957, 6; Friedland, *Lift Up Your Voice*, 32–36; Chappell, *Inside Agitators*, 100–121; and Bartley, *Rise of Massive Resistance*, 251–59.

57. Robert R. Brown, *Bigger than Little Rock* (Greenwich, Conn.: Seabury, 1958), 74–81, 103–7 (quotation on 75).

58. Robert R. Brown, Pastoral Letter to "the Churches in Little Rock," Sept. 23, 1957, in PB-22, folder 22–31–2; NCEC, Oct. 8–10, 1957, 74; Farnsworth Fowle, "40 Clergymen Bid Little Rock Pray," *NYT*, Oct. 4, 1957, 9; "Religion in Action: Little Rock's Clergy Leads the Way," *Time*, Oct. 14, 1957, 30; "Bishop Brown of Arkansas Takes a Stand on Integration," *LC* 135 (Oct. 6, 1957): 11–12; "Little Rock Churches Join in Prayer Asking Forgiveness, Understanding," *LC* 135 (Oct. 20, 1957): 12–13; "Little Rock Pauses to Pray for Peace," *LC* 135 (Oct. 27, 1957): 9; "Arkansas: No Uncertain Sound," *LC* 138 (Feb. 8, 1959): 13; and Friedland, *Lift Up Your Voice*, 34–35.

59. Author's telephone interview of Thomas F. Pettigrew, Nov. 2, 1995, Santa Cruz, Calif.; "Religion in Action," 30; Brown, *Bigger than Little Rock*, 87–103, 147–50; editorial, *Episcopal Church Annual* (1958): 4–5; "From Three to Zero," *LC* 139 (Aug. 16, 1959): 6; Ernest Q. Campbell and Thomas F. Pettigrew, "Men of God in Racial Crisis," *CCe* 75 (1958): 663–65; Ernest Q. Campbell and Thomas F. Pettigrew, *Christians in Racial Crisis: A Study of Little Rock's Ministry* (Washington, D.C.: Public Affairs Press, 1959), vii–ix, 11, 16–27, 40–41, 112–13, 121–26; Benjamin B. Ringer and Charles Y. Glock, "The Political Role of the Church as Defined by Its Parishioners," *Public Opinion Quarterly* 18 (1954): 337–47; and Bartley, *Rise of Massive Resistance*, 293–99. Brown later admitted how uncomfortable the situation in Little Rock had made him feel; he saw himself "as a mild-mannered, heaven-centered individual" and more than once during the crisis he had asked God, "How could this happen to a nice guy like me?" "Church Must Change with Times, Bishop Brown Says in Farewell," *W* 55 (1 May 1970): 4.

60. Edward B. Guerry to Henry Knox Sherrill, from Charleston, S.C., Oct. 11, 1957 (Guerry quotation), in PB-22, folder 22–31–2; and Jean Speiser, "Integration Inevitable in Church, Bishop Sherrill Tells Pressmen," *LC* 135 (Oct. 6, 1957): 8 (Sherrill quotation).

# 4. Theology, Social Activism, and the Founding of ESCRU

1. Das Kelley Barnett, "From Pronouncement to Practice in Christian Human Relations," Apr. 24, 1957, 1–11 (quotations on 4), in DAR, "Interracial Cooperation" folder; Charles Moss and Das Kelley Barnett, "Background and Proceedings of the Episcopal Conference on a Christian Strategy for Race Relations, . . . Apr. 25, 1957," 21–28, in John B. Morris Papers, Archives of the School of Theology of the Univ. of the South, Jessie Ball duPont Library, Sewanee, Tenn.; Leo Soroka, "Make Your Choice; Is It Jesus Christ or Jim Crow?" *LC* 134 (May 12, 1957): 8; Das Kelley Barnett, "Disciples of Christ, Texas Style," *CaC* 19 (1959–60): 55–58; Donahue, "Yearning for a Prophetic Southern Culture," 251–57; and Eighmy, *Churches in Cultural Captivity*, 155–56.

2. [Cornelius C. Tarplee], "The Episcopal Church and Race Relations in the South," [1958], 1–8, in CSR-31, folder 31–4–8; and [Tarplee], "The Episcopal Church: Officially Inclusive, Its Witness Has Been Stifled by Culturally-Conditioned Laymen,"

*CaC* 18 (1958–59): 18–20 (quotations on 18–19). For a similar analysis of the "culture religion" practiced by white southern Protestants during that period, see Samuel S. Hill Jr., *Southern Churches in Crisis* (Boston: Beacon Press, 1968), 3–31, 193–211.

3. John B. Morris to John M. Burgess, from North Haven, Maine, Aug. 8, 1959, 1; Francis X. Walter to Morris, from Savannah, Ga., [Aug. 24], 1961, 1–2, in ESCRU, folders 1:4, 5:37; "Progress in the South," EN, Sept. 17–29, 1961, 7; and Helga P. Sargent, "Law and Disobedience," letter in *LC* 140 (May 22, 1960): 2.

4. Dawley, *Episcopal Church and Its Work*, 234–36; Stephen F. Bayne, *Christian Living* (Greenwich, Conn.: Seabury, 1957), 169–82, 220–43; John Booty, *An American Apostle: The Life of Stephen Fielding Bayne, Jr.* (Valley Forge, Pa.: Trinity Press International, 1997), 79; Hood, *Social Teachings in the Episcopal Church*, 6–11; and Prichard, *History*, 229–32.

5. William Temple, *Christianity and Social Order* (New York: Penguin, 1942), 7–9, 15–17, 40–41; Charles K. Gilbert, *The Social Task of the Church as Set Forth by the Lambeth Conference of 1920* (New York: Department of Christian Social Service, [1921]), 6 (source of quotation); Douglas, *Fling Out the Banner!* 85–86; John L. Kater Jr., "Dwelling Together in Unity: Church, Theology, and Race, 1950–1965," *Anglican Theological Review* 58 (1976): 453–54; Paul T. Phillips, *A Kingdom on Earth: Anglo-American Social Christianity, 1880–1940* (University Park: Pennsylvania State Univ. Press, 1996), xvi–xvii, 1–4, 37–47, 280–83; and Bernard Kent Markwell, *The Anglican Left: Radical Social Reformers in the Church of England and the Protestant Episcopal Church, 1846–1954* (Brooklyn, N.Y.: Carlson, 1991), 223, 244–45.

6. Henry F. May, *Protestant Churches and Industrial America* (New York: Harper, 1949), 186; and William R. Hutchison, preface to Hutchison, *Between the Times*, viii.

7. Spencer Miller Jr. and Joseph F. Fletcher, *The Church and Industry* (New York: Longmans, Green, 1930), 52–56, 97–99 (quotation on 55).

8. Scudder, *Socialism and Character* (Boston: Houghton Mifflin, 1912), 349–55; Vida D. Scudder, *The Church and the Hour: Reflections of a Socialist Churchwoman* (New York: Dutton, 1917), 15–16, 37–39; *Episcopalians at Work in the World: A Study of Social Education and Community Action in the Protestant Episcopal Church* (New York: National Council, [1952]), 13; Donald Meyer, *The Protestant Search for Political Realism, 1919–1941*, 2d ed. (Middletown, Conn.: Wesleyan Univ. Press, 1988), 40–43; James Thayer Addison, *The Episcopal Church in the United States, 1789–1931* (New York: Scribner's, 1951), 328–29; Pamela W. Darling, *New Wine: The Story of Women Transforming Leadership and Power in the Episcopal Church* (Cambridge, Mass.: Cowley, 1994), 31–37; Holmes, *Brief History*, 126–31; and Markwell, *Anglican Left*, 218–23.

9. Department of Christian Social Relations, "Advance Projects for the Triennium, 1950–52," 3–4, in NCPC.

10. Gertrude Orr, "Ministry to Diversity," *LC* 137 (Dec. 7, 1958): 10; John C. Leffler, *Christian Social Relations: The National Program* (New York: National Council, 1959), 14–16; G. Paul Musselman, *The Church on the Urban Frontier* (Greenwich, Conn.: Seabury, 1960), 18–19, 34–43, 128–31; Bruce Kenrick, *Come Out the Wilderness* (New York: Harper, 1962), 29–35, 46, 65–72, 142–44; Mary V. Miree, "Churchmen in the News: Christianity and the Law," *Forth* 125 (Jan. 1960): 24–25; William Stringfellow, "Poverty, Piety, Charity and Mission," *CCe* 78 (1961): 584–86 (quotations on 584–85); William Stringfellow, *My People Is the Enemy: An Autobiographical Polemic* (New York: Holt, Rinehart, 1964) 3–32; William Stringfellow, "The Mission of the Church in the Decadent Society," *E.T.S. Journal* 7 (winter 1962): 3–8; and Patterson, *Grand Expectations*, 26–29, 70–76.

11. Ross W. Sanderson, *The Church Serves the Changing City* (New York: Harper, 1955), 89–101 (quotation on 90).

12. Paul Moore Jr., *The Church Reclaims the City* (New York: Seabury, 1964), 30–39, 47–57 (quotation on 32).

13. Author's interview of Paul Moore Jr., May 5, 1995, Stonington, Conn.; author's interview of James P. Morton, Oct. 3, 1995, New York; author's interview of William N. Penfield, Oct. 24, 1996, Hartford, Conn.; author's interview of Gerald W. Humphrey, Mar. 1, 1996, Little Compton, R.I.; "The New York Urban Priests' Group," [1957], in AEC, Records of the Home Department of the Episcopal Church, record group 32, folder 32-15-1; E.W. Southcott, *The Parish Comes Alive* (London: Mowbray, 1956), 17–21; Stephen Bayne, *The Optional God* (1953; reprint, Wilton, Conn.: Morehouse-Barlow, 1980), 115–16; Paul Moore Jr., "Resurrection in the City," *LC* 140 (Mar. 13, 1960): 12–13; Paul Moore Jr., *Presences: A Bishop's Life in the City* (New York: Farrar, Straus, 1997), 104–31; and Jenny Moore, *The People on Second Street* (New York: Morrow, 1968), 17–38, 100–104, 135–38 (quotation on 136). See also Georges Michonneau, *Revolution in a City Parish* (Westminster, Md.: Newman, 1949).

14. C. Kilmer Myers, *Light the Dark Streets* (Greenwich, Conn.: Seabury, 1957), 16–21, 147–53 (quotation on 152); and Harrison E. Salisbury, *The Shook-up Generation* (New York: Harper, 1958), 189–95.

15. Author's interview of Robert M. Muir, Feb. 24, 1995, Warwick, R.I.; author's interview of John J. Harmon, Sept. 29, 1996, Rochester, N.Y.; "Report of Annual Meeting," *Venite: The Episcopal League for Social Action* (Mar. 8, 1950): 1, in William M. Weber Collection, Watkinson Library, Trinity College, Hartford, Conn., "Episcopal League for Social Action" folder; Warren McKenna to the author, from Roadtown, Tortola, British Virgin Islands, May 23, 1995; "Too Much Peace?" *Time*, Sept. 4, 1950, 68; "New York's Trinity Parish Launches New Mission Work," *EC* 120 (Sept. 14, 1952): 13; John Harmon, "Revitalizing Roxbury," *E.T.S. Journal* 2 (May 1956): 4–9; John Harmon, "The Church and the Dispossessed," *E.T.S. Journal* 6 (winter 1961): 3–10 (quotation on 10); C. Kilmer Myers, "The Parish Church and Delinquency," *CaC* 18 (1958–59): 33–35; Warren McKenna, "Needed: A Christian Ideology," *W* 45 (Feb. 6, 1958): 9–11. For background on the Anglo-Catholic "slum priests" of the late nineteenth century, see John Shelton Reed, *Glorious Battle: The Cultural Politics of Victorian Anglo-Catholicism* (Nashville, Tenn.: Vanderbilt Univ. Press, 1996), 148–72; and Holmes, *Brief History*, 107, 112–15, 129. The Catholic Worker movement combined similar elements of traditional piety with a radical social critique; see Mel Piehl, *Breaking Bread: The Catholic Worker and the Origin of Catholic Radicalism in America* (Philadelphia: Temple Univ. Press, 1982), 64–73, 83–94. In addition, I am indebted to William A. Weber of Long Beach, California, for sharing materials on the views of his father, William M. Weber, about urban social ministry during this period.

16. Dietrich Bonhoeffer, *Prisoner for God: Letters and Papers from Prison*, ed. Eberhard Bethge (New York: Macmillan, 1953), 121–26, 156–60, 166–67, 179–81 (quotations on 156–57, 179); Dietrich Bonhoeffer, *Ethics*, ed. Eberhard Bethge (New York: Macmillan, 1955), 21, 62–72; Paul Tillich, *Theology of Culture*, ed. Robert C. Kimball (New York: Oxford Univ. Press, 1959), 3–9, 40–42; Harvey Cox, *The Secular City: Secularization and Urbanization in Theological Perspective*, rev. ed. (New York: Macmillan, 1966), 15–18, 91–98, 114–28; William Hamilton, *The New Essence of Christianity* (New York: Association, 1961), 104–11; John A.T. Robinson, *Honest to God* (Philadelphia: Westminster, 1963), 84–91; Martin E. Marty, "Bonhoeffer: Seminarians' Theologian," *CCe* 77 (1960): 467–69; Colin W. Williams, *Faith in a Secular Age* (New York: Harper, 1966), 54–61; and Robert S. Ellwood, *The Sixties Spiritual*

*Awakening: American Religion Moving from Modern to Postmodern* (New Brunswick, N.J.: Rutgers Univ. Press, 1994), 98–100, 124–33.

17. A. Roy Eckardt, *The Surge of Piety in America: An Appraisal* (New York: Association, 1958), 21–39, 169–77; Will Herberg, *Protestant—Catholic—Jew: An Essay in American Religious Sociology,* new ed. (Garden City, N.Y.: Doubleday, 1960), viii, 1–3, 46–50, 89, 258–72 (quotations on 89, 259); and "The Year the Revival Passed Crest," *CCe* 75 (1958): 1499–1501.

18. Gibson Winter, "The Church in Suburban Captivity," CCe 72 (1955): 1112–14 (quotations on 1113–14); Gibson Winter, *The Suburban Captivity of the Churches: An Analysis of Protestant Responsibility in the Expanding Metropolis* (Garden City, N.Y.: Doubleday, 1961), 76–78, 134–42, 163–64, 175–77; and "Last Train to Babylon," *Time,* Oct. 10, 1955, 73.

19. Paul Moore Jr., "Inner-City—Battle Line," W 45 (Mar. 31, 1960): 7–10. See also Hudnut-Beumler, *Looking for God in the Suburbs,* 107–45.

20. Author's interview of Arthur E. Walmsley, Nov. 3, 1994, Deering, N.H.; *Guiding Principles Pertaining to the Work of the Church among Negroes Adopted by the National Council, Feb. 21–23, 1956* (New York: National Council, [1956]), [1–3] (quotation on [3]), courtesy of Mary H. Miller, Washington, D.C.; "Christian Social Relations: Functions, Program, and Organization," Mar. 15, 1960, 1–3, in DAW, "Christian Social Relations" folder; and Arthur E. Walmsley, "Not Blueprints, but Wrestling," *LC* 139 (Nov. 22, 1959): 16–17 (Walmsley quotations on 17). Walmsley succeeded Moran Weston as director of the Division of Christian Citizenship after Weston became rector of St. Philip's Church, New York.

21. Arthur E. Walmsley and Cornelius C. Tarplee, "Report on Race Relations: A Study Document," Sept. 1958, 1–6 (quotations on 5–6), manuscript in the author's possession (courtesy of Mary Miller); and Arthur E. Walmsley to John Morris, from New York, July 14, 1958, MM. As Robert Ellwood argues, leaders in the mainline denominations in the 1950s "basked in the glow of their supposed special role in the shaping of American values" and thus were still sympathetic to the moral goals of the older Social Gospel movement. Ellwood, *Sixties Spiritual Awakening,* 37–38.

22. Author's interview of Will D. Campbell, Aug. 21, 1995, Mount Juliet, Tenn.; Walmsley interview; Morris interview; Willard S. Dillon to "Fellow Churchman," from New York, Sept. 17, 1958, 1–2; "Resolution," [Sept. 1958], in DAW, "Eaton Center Conference" folder; John B. Morris to F. Bland Tucker, from Miami Beach, Fla., Oct. 6, 1958, 1, MM; John H. Fenton, "Churchmen Urge a Stand on South," *NYT,* Sept. 18, 1958, 21; "Convention: 'An Abomination,'" *LC* 137 (Oct. 5, 1958): 8; and John L. Kater Jr., "The Episcopal Society for Cultural and Racial Unity and Its Role in the Episcopal Church, 1959–1970," Ph.D. diss., McGill Univ., 1973, 27–30. The idea for the Eaton Center gathering had first been proposed by David Works, a priest in nearby North Conway, New Hampshire, who was seeking to organize a meeting at which national leaders might discuss desegregation. Author's interview of David A. Works, Dec. 13, 1995, Charlottesville, Va.; David A. Works, telegram to Sherman Adams, from North Conway, N.H., Mar. 22, 1956; Works to Maxwell M. Rabb, [from North Conway, 1959], in DAW, "Outgoing Correspondence" box.

23. "House of Deputies Has Conflict over Resolutions on Race," W 45 (Oct. 16, 1958): 5.

24. *JGC* (1958): 48–50 (source of quotations); "A True Perspective to See God's Will: Pastoral Letter Issued by the House of Bishops, Oct., 1958," *Forth* 123 (Dec. 1958): 6–7, 22–23; John E. Culmer, "Integration in South Florida," letter in *LC* 136 (May 18, 1958): 5; Kenneth Hughes, "Problems of Minorities Discussed by Negro

Church Leaders," *W* 45 (Oct. 23, 1958): 6, 15–16; Charles D. Kean, "For Law and Integration," *CCe* 75 (1958): 1262–63; Milton E. Magruder, "Collins of Florida: He Dares to Be Different," *E* 125 (July 1960): 2–4, 32–33; LeRoy Collins, "Tolerance," *LC* 141 (Oct. 2, 1960): 12–13; and Bartley, *New South* 213–19.

25. Hughes, "Problems of Minorities," 6, 15–16 (quotation on 6).

26. John H. Johnson, *A Place of Adventure: Essays and Sermons* (Greenwich, Conn.: Seabury, 1955), 26–28; John H. Johnson, "St. Martin's Church in Harlem," *W* 46 (Apr. 30, 1959): 7–9 (quotation on 7); David Johnson, "Myths about Integration," *W* 49 (June 11, 1964): 8–10; and Lewis, *Yet with a Steady Beat,* 98–99, 142–44, 156–60, 205 n. 8, 226 n. 64. For a discussion of the important social role of black churches in urban areas, see also Morris, *Origins of the Civil Rights Movement,* 4–7, 115–26.

27. Morris to Tucker, Oct. 6, 1958, 2; *JGC* (1958): 317–20 (quotations on 319); "House of Deputies Has Conflict," 5; "Race Relations Agreement Reached after Long Debate by Deputies," *W* 45 (Oct. 30, 1958): 3–4; and Kean, "For Law and Integration," 1262.

28. Morris interview; Walmsley interview; Cornelius C. Tarplee and John B. Morris, "A Proposal: Formation in the Episcopal Church of a Church Society for Racial Unity," [1959], 1–2, in ESCRU, folder 1:1; Morris to Will D. Campbell, [from Dillon, S.C.], Apr. 18, 1958; Tarplee to Morris, from Lynchburg, Va., May 5, 1958, 1; Tarplee to Morris, from Lynchburg, Feb. 19, 1959, 2; Morris to [Tarplee, from Atlanta], Feb. 23, 1959, 1–2; Tarplee to Morris, from Lynchburg, Apr. 1, 1959, 1; [Morris] to [Govan], Feb. 6, 1958, 2; Morris to Wright, Sept. 20, 1958, 1, MM; Arthur Lichtenberger, "The Sermon at the Installation," *W* 45 (Jan. 22, 1959): 9–10; and Sumner, *Episcopal Church's History,* 37–38. At the Eaton Center meeting, Robert O. Kevin, who was a professor at Virginia Seminary, had suggested the idea of "an unofficial and independent society" similar to other single-issue organizations to which Episcopalians belonged, e.g., the low-church Evangelical Education Society, the Anglo-Catholic American Church Union, and the North Conway Institute (a ministry to the alcoholic). Works interview; and John Morris, "ESCRU: The Episcopal Society for Cultural and Racial Unity, 1959–1967," paper presented at the National Episcopal Historians and Archivists Conference, Austin, Tex., June 21–24, 1995, 7–8.

29. Goldfield, *Black, White, and Southern,* 104–6 (quotation on 105); and Morris, *Origins of the Civil Rights Movement,* 82–88.

30. John T. McGreevy, *Parish Boundaries: The Catholic Encounter with Race in the Twentieth-Century Urban North* (Chicago: Univ. of Chicago Press, 1996), 41–44, 85–91 (quotations on 86).

31. Morris interview; Morris to Richard H. Baker, from North Haven, Maine, Aug. 4, 1959, 1–3 (quotation on 2), in ESCRU, folder 1:4; Tarplee and Morris, "A Proposal," 1–2; and Patricia Carolyn Gloster, "A Critical Examination of the Educational Strategy of the Episcopal Society for Cultural and Racial Unity," M.R.E. thesis, Union Theological Seminary, [1962], 6.

32. [Sarah Patton Boyle] to Cornelius C. Tarplee, [from Charlottesville, Va.], Aug. 14, 1959 (Boyle quotation), in SPBP, box 16; [John B. Morris], "Churchmen Interested in Proposed Society," [Nov. 1959], 1–7, in ESCRU, folder 2:15; and Gloster, "Critical Examination," 6.

33. Morris interview; W. Russell Bowie to Morris, from Alexandria, Va., Oct. 27, 1959; Myron B. Bloy Jr. to Morris, from Cambridge, Mass., Oct. 22, 1959; William H. Baar to Morris, from Chicago, Sept. 16, 1959, in ESCRU, folder 1:4; William J. Chase to Morris, from New York, Sept. 10, 1959; Randolph R. Claiborne Jr. to Morris, from Atlanta, July 15, 1959, in ESCRU, folder 1:6; Rachel [Hosmer] to [Morris], from

Newburgh, N.Y., Sept. 25, 1959, 1–2, in ESCRU, folder 1:14; [Gerald] McAllister to Cornelius C. Tarplee, from Victoria, Tex., Oct. 19, 1959, 3, in ESCRU, folder 1:20; William H. Marmion to Tarplee, from Roanoke, Va., Aug. 14, 1959, in ESCRU, folder 1:19; Morris to R. Earl Dicus, from North Haven, Maine, Aug. 10, 1959, in ESCRU, folder 1:8; Tarplee to Thomas F. Pettigrew, from New York, Oct. 28, 1959, in ESCRU, folder 1:23; Morris to Walter [D. Dennis], from North Haven, July 23, 1959, 1, in ESCRU, folder 2:7; and Stephen F. Bayne Jr. to Tarplee, from Seattle, Wash., Nov. 13, 1959, MM.

34. [Elizabeth] Eddy to [Cornelius C. Tarplee, from New York], Aug. 26, 1959, in ESCRU, folder 1:9; Jesse F. Anderson to John B. Morris, from Philadelphia, Sept. 8, 1959, in ESCRU, folder 1:3; Helen B. Turnbull to Morris, from New York, Dec. 22, 1959, 1, in ESCRU, folder 2:5; [Merrill] O. Young to Morris, [from New York, Nov. 1959], 1; Walter D. Dennis, memorandum to Arthur Walmsley, [from New York], Nov. 9, 1959, 1–2, in ESCRU, folder 2:13; McRae Werth to [Morris], from Wilmington, Del., [July 15, 1959], 2, in ESCRU, folder 2:7; Thomas F. Pettigrew, "The Church Dilemma and Social Action," Dec. 29, 1959, 3, MM; and Gloster, "Critical Examination," 57.

35. Morris interview; "Founding Conference: The Episcopal Society for Cultural and Racial Unity," [Jan. 1960], 1–3, in ESCRU, folder 2:26; "The Episcopal Society for Cultural and Racial Unity: Statement of Purpose," [1960] (source of quotations), MM; George Dugan, "Protestants Aim for Racial Unity," NYT, Dec. 29, 1959, 10; Bill Andrews, "Society for Unity," LC 140 (Jan. 10, 1960): 6; John B. Morris, "Can We 'Interpret the Signs of the Times'?" Intercollegian 77 (Dec. 1959): 6–8; Gloster, "Critical Examination," 30, 65; and Kater, "Episcopal Society," 31–34.

36. Gray interview; Lines interview; Moultrie Guerry to John B. Morris, from Raleigh, N.C., Jan. 2, 1960, 1 (Guerry quotation [emphasis added]); Duncan M. Gray Jr. to Gerald Humphrey, from Oxford, Miss., Nov. 29, 1960, 1 (Gray quotation), in ESCRU, folder 27:3; James C. Fenhagen to Morris, from Columbia, S.C., June 16, 1960, in ESCRU, folder 27:2; Morris to "Conference Registrants and Members," from Atlanta, Feb. 3, 1960, MM; George Dugan, "Episcopal Church Is Called 'Racist,'" NYT, Dec. 30, 1959, 16 (Myers quotation); Dugan, "Churchmen Form Race Unity Panel," NYT, Dec. 31, 1959, 22; Andrews, "Society for Unity," 6 (Barnett quotation); "Perfect or Possible," LC 140 (Jan. 17, 1960): 20; Campbell, And Also with You, 186–87; and Gloster, "Critical Examination," 67.

37. Morris interview; EB, Feb. 24–25, 1960, 1–4; Sept. 23–24, 1960, 1; "Other Board Actions," EN, Mar. 25, 1960, 1–2; "Membership over a Thousand!" EN, Sept. 21, 1960, 1; John B. Morris to Arthur Walmsley, [from Atlanta], Apr. 5, 1961, 4, in ESCRU, folder 5:35; "The Placard on the Cathedral Grounds," LC 138 (Apr. 26, 1959): 11; "Wanted: Visible Objections," LC 140 (Mar. 13, 1960): 7–8; and Kater, "Episcopal Society," 34–36. The figure of Jesus as high priest, which had been used by the Catholic Worker movement, appeared on the stationery of St. Andrew's Church in Beacon, New York. The priest-in-charge of St. Andrew's, Gerald Humphrey, was one of the organizers of ESCRU and called the symbol to Morris's attention. Humphrey interview; Morris, "ESCRU," 11.

38. "Background Paper on the Student 'Sit-in' Protest Movement in the Light of the Church's Authoritative Statements," [Mar. 1960], 1, 4–9, 14–15 (quotation on 1), manuscript in the author's possession, courtesy of Mary Miller; C. Rankin Barnes to "Diocesan Bishops," from Greenwich, Conn., Apr. 27, 1960, in JHEP, "Christian Social Relations" folder; RMC, Mar. 15–16, 1960, 6, 12; ESCRU News Release, Mar. 6, 1960, 1–2, in ESCRU, folder 12:26; "Episcopal Group Backs Sitdowns," NYT, Mar. 6,

1960, 50; "Study by 2 Episcopalian Groups Voices Sympathy for Sitdowns," *NYT,* Mar. 31, 1960, 27; "Pro-Protest Paper," *LC* 140 (Apr. 10, 1960): 7–8; Christine Fleming Heffner, "National Council: Backgrounds," *LC* 140 (May 8, 1960): 7; "Episcopalians Back Negroes," *CCe* 77 (1960): 309; Clayborne Carson, *In Struggle: SNCC and the Black Awakening of the 1960s* (Cambridge, Mass.: Harvard Univ. Press, 1981), 9–18; and Morris, *Origins of the Civil Rights Movement,* 188–213.

39. B. Powell Harrison Jr. to Arthur Lichtenberger, from Leesburg, Va., Apr. 14, 1960, 5–6 (Harrison quotation); Charles C.J. Carpenter, "Memorandum to Officers and Members of the National Council," Apr. 7, 1960, 1–3 (Carpenter quotation on 2), in DCC, "Documents on Sit-In Demonstrations" folder; NCEC, Apr. 26–28, 1960, 8–11; Thomas A. Powell to Carpenter, from Carlowville, Ala., May 5, 1960; Edward B. Guerry to Lichtenberger, from [Charleston], S.C., July 18, 1960, 1 (Guerry quotation); Roger Winborne to "Dear Member of the Episcopal Church," from Lenoir, N.C., Oct. 20, 1960, in PB-22, folder 22–27–6; "Negro Protests Hit," *NYT,* Mar. 21, 1960, 37; George Dugan, "Bishop Criticizes Sitdown Support," *NYT,* Apr. 19, 1960, 20; Richard H. Parke, "Church Rebuffs Alabama Bishop," *NYT,* Apr. 29, 1960, 13; "Inadequate . . . Unfortunate," *LC* 140 (Apr. 24, 1960): 7–8; Dan Wakefield, *Revolt in the South* (New York: Grove, 1960), 105–6; and Bass, "Not Time Yet," 240–41.

40. John B. Morris, "Statement Given Press on Apr. 9, 1960, regarding Bishop Carpenter's Criticism . . ."(Morris quotation) in ESCRU, folder 12:26; "The Background Paper Matter," EN, May 26, 1960, 2; James W. Silver, *Confederate Morale and Church Propaganda* (1957; reprint, New York: Norton, 1967), [7–9], 93–101; Morris, "Centennial Observance Queried," *NYT,* June 7, 1959, sec. 4, p. 10; "Episcopal Bishop Scored on Sitdown," *NYT,* Apr. 11, 1960, 25; and Michael Kammen, *Mystic Chords of Memory: The Transformation of Tradition in American Culture* (New York: Knopf, 1991), 590–610. For similar observations on the continuing "Confederate" sympathies of white religious leaders in the South, see James W. Silver, "Mississippi: The Closed Society," *Journal of Southern History* 30 (1964): 3, 9, 33–34.

41. John B. Morris to [Thomas F. Pettigrew, from Atlanta], May 11, 1960, in ESCRU, folder 5:7; William S. Lea, "Christian Dilemma in the South," *E* 125 (May 1960): 35–37; John B. Morris, "*The Episcopalian:* To Be or Not to Be?" EN, May 26, 1960, 6–7; Thomas F. Pettigrew, "The Myth of the Moderates," *CCe* 78 (1961): 649–51 (Pettigrew quotations on 649–50); and Arthur E. Walmsley, "Racial Conflict: Crisis in the Soul," *W* 46 (Apr. 20, 1961): 13–16 (Walmsley quotation on 15).

42. Braden interview; John B. Morris to [Anne] Braden, [from Atlanta], July 7, 1960, 1–2 (quotations on 2); Anne Braden to Morris, from Little Compton, R.I., July 18, 1960, 1–2, in ESCRU, folder 8:2; Morris to Carl Braden, from Atlanta, Jan. 24, 1961, 1–2, in ESCRU, folder 8:3; Reed, *Simple Decency and Common Sense,* 161, 169–73; Michael Honey, "Anne and Carl Braden: Anti-Racists in a Hostile Southland," *W* 73 (Nov. 1990): 26–27; Patterson, *Grand Expectations,* 187–205; and Findlay, *Church People,* 86–87. Although Martin Luther King was similarly troubled by possible accusations of Communism against SCLC, he eventually added his name to a clemency petition on Carl Braden's behalf. David J. Garrow, *Bearing the Cross: Martin Luther King, Jr., and the Southern Christian Leadership Conference* (New York: Morrow, 1986), 155. For analysis of the ongoing conflict over churchmanship in the Episcopal Church, see E. Clowes Chorley, *Men and Movements in the Episcopal Church* (New York: Scribner's, 1950); Prichard, *History,* 118–23, 146–55; and Holmes, *Brief History,* 16–18, 151–54.

43. Morris interview; "Statements from the . . . First Annual Meeting, Williamsburg, Virginia, Jan. 8–11, 1961," 1–7, MM; George Dugan, "'Kneel-ins Held

Integration Key," *NYT,* Jan. 9, 1961, 28 (source of quotation); George Dugan, "Interracial Unit Meets First Test," *NYT,* Jan. 10, 1961, 22; George Dugan, "Episcopal Group Gets Race Study," *NYT,* Jan. 11, 1961, 16; and "Chain Reactions," *LC* 142 (Jan. 22, 1961): 8.

44. Author's telephone interview of McRae Werth, Mar. 10, 1995, Blue Hill, Maine; author's interview of William H. Marmion, Dec. 13, 1995, Roanoke, Va.; Morris interview; [McRae Werth], "A Journal of Disintegration in Southwestern Virginia Issued in Support of a Resolution," [1959], 15-19, 44-7, manuscript in the possession of McRae Werth, Blue Hill, Maine; Diocese of Southwestern Virginia, *Journal of the Annual Council* (1958), 53, 55, 61, 67-68; (1959), 55-57, 69-70; (1960), 57, 59-64, 69, 72-74, 80-82; (1961), 42, 49-51, 61; "Dioceses of Virginia Struggle over Integration Question," *W* 45 (June 12, 1958): 3-4; McRae Werth, "Southwestern Virginia: Challenge to Church," *W* 45 (Sept. 18, 1958): 7-10 (quotation on 9); William C. Turpin, letter in "Backfire," *W* 45 (Oct. 2, 1958): [19]; "Double Track or None," *LC* 140 (Feb. 28, 1960): 7; and William H. Marmion, "Appalachia and Race—One Diocese's Experience," *Saint Luke's Journal of Theology* 22 (1979): 112-16.

45. Werth interview; Marmion interview; EB, Feb. 10-11, 1961, 1-2; "Statements from the . . . First Annual Meeting," 2 (Worth quotation); George L. Cadigan to John B. Morris, from St. Louis, Mo., Jan. 20, 1961, 1 (Cadigan quotation) in ESCRU, folder 5:17; Anson Phelps Stokes Jr. to Morris, from Boston, Jan. 25, 1961, 1 (Stokes quotation), in ESCRU, folder 5:9; Albert R. Stuart to Morris, from Savannah, Ga., Jan. 17, 1961; Stuart to Morris, from Savannah, Jan. 28, 1961, 1-2, in ESCRU, folder 8:42; Henry I. Louttit to Morris, from Winter Park, Fla., Jan. 28, 1961, in ESCRU, folder 27:3; Angus Dun to Morris, from Washington, D.C., Feb. 16, 1961 (Dun quotation), in ESCRU, folder 27:25; Samuel J. Wylie to Morris, from Boston, Mar. 21, 1961 (Wylie quotation), in ESCRU, folder 28:4; John Turnbull to Morris, from Austin, Tex., Apr. 10, 1961, 1-2 (Turnbull quotation on 2), in ESCRU, folder 28:1; Barbara Kalif to Morris, from Richmond, Va., Oct. 15, 1961, 1 (Kalif quotation), in ESCRU, folder 17:7; and "Interracial Marriages Endorsed," *W* 46 (Feb. 2, 1961): 16.

46. "Opposed to Communism," *LC* 142 (Jan. 29, 1961): 6-7.

47. Morris interview; John B. Morris to Wilburn C. Campbell, from Atlanta, Jan. 16, 1961, 1-3; Ruth Whitaker to Morris, from Charleston, W.Va., [Jan. 1961]; "Statement Given to the Press Jointly," Jan. 19, 1961 (source of quotation), in ESCRU, folder 5:19; Morris, telegram to SCEF, from Atlanta, Jan. 23, [1961], in ESCRU, folder 8:3; "I Consider This Matter Closed," EN, Feb. 15, 1961, 8-9; Wilburn C. Campbell, "Blood Has One Color . . .," *LC* 127 (Nov. 8, 1953): 12; Campbell, "Blood Has One Color: III," *LC* 127 (Nov. 22, 1953): 12-13; and "Multiple Issues," *LC* 142 (Feb. 19, 1961): 10.

48. John B. Morris to [Frances B.] Cheney, [from Atlanta], Jan. 30, 1961, 1, in ESCRU, folder 3:6.

49. Morris to Carl Braden, from Atlanta, Jan. 24, 1961, 1-2 ("exploitative and self-aggrandizing" quotation on 2); Anne Braden to Morris, from Louisville, Ky., Jan. 26, 1961, 3-4, in ESCRU, folder 8:3; Carl Braden to Morris, from Louisville, Feb. 2, 1961, 1-2, in ESCRU, folder 8:4; and Morris to Samuel J. Wylie, [from Atlanta], Mar. 23, 1961 ("a militancy that is responsible" quotation), in ESCRU, folder 28:4; "Perfect or Possible," 20.

50. Morris interview; Braden interview; Morris to "Past and Present Board Members," from Atlanta, Jan. 23, 1961, MM; "So That Brothers May Dwell Together in Unity," EN, Feb. 15, 1961, 9-10 (quotation on 10); and John B. Morris, "Three Tall Men and a Personal Memoir," *Historiographer* 28 (spring 1996): 1, 13.

## 5. The Church's Response to the Civil Rights Crisis

1. Garrow, *Bearing the Cross*, 154–61; Goldfield, *Black, White, and Southern*, 124–30; Weisbrot, *Freedom Bound*, 55–63; and Bartley, *New South*, 306–12.

2. Walmsley interview; Kenneth B. Clark and Arthur E. Walmsley, "Memorandum to the Presiding Bishop," [from New York], June 19, 1961, 1–2 (quotation on 2), in CSR-85, folder 85–3–12.

3. Walmsley to Will D. Campbell, [from New York], June 22, 1961, in CSR-85, folder 85–4–7; "Politics and the Priest," *LC* 142 (June 4, 1961): 15; "Rider from California," *LC* 143 (July 9, 1961): 5; "'Proud of His Spirit,'" *LC* 143 (July 16, 1961): 4 (Muse quotation); "Out of Jail," *LC* 143 (July 23, 1961): 5; and *Book of Common Prayer* (1928), 44.

4. Morris interview; Walmsley interview; John B. Morris to "the Board and Key Personnel," [from Atlanta], June 14, 1961; Morris to "Clerical Members," from Atlanta, June 16, 1961, 1, 3; Morris to "Clerical Members," from Atlanta, June 30, 1961; Morris to "the Press," from Atlanta, July 21, 1961; Morris to "Pilgrimage Applicants," from Atlanta, Aug. 4, 1961, 1–4; Morris to "Pilgrimage Applicants," from Atlanta, Aug. 19, 1961, 1–4; Morris to "the Board and Key Personnel," from Atlanta, Sept. 6, 1961, in PP; C.K. Myers, telegram to Morris, [from New York], Sept. 10, 1961; Morris [to Myers, from Atlanta], Sept. 10, 1961, 1–2 (Morris quotation on 1); Myers to Morris, from New York, Dec. 12, 1961, in ESCRU, folder 5:30; "No Martyrs Need Apply," *LC* 143 (July 2, 1961): 5; "Mississippi Mission," *LC* 143 (July 30, 1961): 4; and Kater, "Episcopal Society," 45. Although the event gained little attention at the time, Martin Luther King and the SCLC had staged what they called a "Prayer Pilgrimage" rally in Washington, D.C., in May 1957. Adam Fairclough, *To Redeem the Soul of America: The Southern Christian Leadership Conference and Martin Luther King, Jr.* (Athens: Univ. of Georgia Press, 1987), 39–40. Besides Morris, the clergy who participated in the ESCRU prayer pilgrimage were Gilbert S. Avery III, Boston; Lee A. Belford, New York; Myron B. Bloy Jr., Cambridge, Mass.; Malcolm Boyd, Detroit; James P. Breeden, Boston; David H. Brooks, Tallahassee, Fla.; Robert C. Chapman, Hempstead, N.Y.; John Crocker Jr., Providence, R.I.; Joseph S. Dickson, Detroit; John Dorr Jr., Stillwater, Okla.; James W. Evans, St. Clair, Mo.; John M. Evans, Toledo, Ohio; Robert T. Fortna, New York; Quinland R. Gordon, Washington, D.C.; James B. Guinan, Farmington, Mich.; W. Robert Hampshire, Farmingdale, N.Y.; Cornelius DeWitt Hastie, Boston; James G. Jones, Chicago; Jack Malpas, Baltimore; Robert L. Pierson, Evanston, Ill.; Morris V. Samuel Jr., Long Beach, Calif.; Geoffrey S. Simpson, Pewaukee, Wis.; Robert Page Taylor, Chicago; William A. Wendt, Washington, D.C.; Vernon Powell Woodward, Cincinnati; Merrill Orne Young, Boston; and Layton P. Zimmer, Swarthmore, Pa.

5. Author's telephone interview of Malcolm Boyd, Nov. 3, 1995, Los Angeles; author's interview of James P. Breeden, Mar. 3, 1995, Hanover, N.H.; author's interview of John Crocker Jr., June 1, 1994, West Kingston, R.I.; author's interview of Cornelius deW. Hastie, Oct. 22, 1996, Boston; Morris, "For your information," [to the prayer pilgrims], from Atlanta, Sept. 9, 1961; [Morris], "Message to the Episcopal Church's 60th General Convention, Sept. 17–29 . . . (Second Draft)," 1–2 (quotation on 2, emphasis added), in PP; "The Prayer Pilgrimage," EN, Sept. 17–29, 1961, 2–3; Malcolm Boyd, "What Should the Church Be Doing? About Losing Her Life to Save It," *W* 46 (Feb. 23, 1961): 7–9; Malcolm Boyd, *Focus: Rethinking the Meaning of Our Evangelism* (New York: Morehouse-Barlow, 1960), 40–47; Malcolm Boyd, *The Hunger, The Thirst: The Questions of Students and Young Adults* (New York: Morehouse-

Barlow, 1964), 23–26; Merrill Orne Young, "For the Church's Sake," *CCe* 78 (1961): 1300–1301; and Morris, "ESCRU," 13–14. See also *Book of Common Prayer* (1928), 81.

6. Morris interview; Allin interview; Crocker interview; Hastie interview; Morris to George Mosley Murray, from Atlanta, Aug. 30, 1961; C.C.J. Carpenter and G.M. Murray to Morris, from Birmingham, Ala., Aug. 31, 1961 (Carpenter and Murray quotations); Morris to Alice Wallace, from Atlanta, Aug. 22, 1961; John M. Allin to Morris, from Vicksburg, Miss., Aug. 22, 1961, 1–2; Allin to Morris, from Vicksburg, Aug. 30, 1961, 1–2 (Allin quotation on 2), in PP; Mississippi, *Annual Council* (1956), 111; *The Episcopal Church in Mississippi, 1763–1992* (Jackson: Episcopal Diocese of Mississippi, 1992), 103–4; Hewlett, *Jessie Ball duPont*, 244–45; and Kater, "Episcopal Society," 47–48. Allin's remark about timing had a somewhat ironic quality: he had been elected bishop coadjutor of Mississippi just before the arrival of the prayer pilgrims. "Election Accepted," *LC* 143 (Sept. 24, 1961): 10.

7. Crocker interview; Morris interview; "Working Release No. 11: General Convention 1961," Sept. 16, 1961; "Working Release No. 13: General Convention 1961," Sept. 21, 1961; R.L. Pierson, "Statement to the People of Jackson, Mississippi," [Sept. 20, 1961], in PP; "Suit in Mississippi," EN, Sept. 2, 1962, 8; Claude Sitton, "Episcopal Group Held in Jackson," *NYT*, Sept. 14, 1961, 32; "15 Episcopal Clerics Convicted in South," *NYT*, Sept. 16, 1961, 1, 12; George Dugan, "Pilgrimage Gains Episcopal Favor," *NYT*, Sept. 18, 1961, 43; "13 Clerics Freed on Appeal Bonds," *NYT*, Sept. 20, 1961, 30; "God's Armor," *Newsweek*, Sept. 25, 1961, 101; Ray C. Wentworth, "It Happened in Jackson," *LC* 143 (Sept. 24, 1961): 8, 16; "Most Are Out—Two Are In," *LC* 143 (Oct. 1, 1961): 23; "Freedom at Last," *LC* 143 (Oct. 8, 1961): 17; William Stringfellow, "Race, the Church, and the Law," *E* 127 (Nov. 1962): 32; and *Book of Common Prayer* (1928), 610. "Breach of the peace" was the standard charge used against freedom riders, since as interstate travelers they were not subject to local segregation laws. ESCRU started a "Prayer Pilgrimage Appeal Fund" for the defense of the men arrested in Jackson, but when the case finally came to trial in May 1962, they were cleared of the charges. Later, four of the prayer pilgrims sued the police and the judge in Jackson for violating their civil rights. Morris to "Pilgrim Fathers," from Atlanta, Oct. 5, 1961, 2, in PP; "15 Clerics Facing Trial in Jackson," *NYT*, Apr. 11, 1962, 27; "15 Clerics Freed in Jackson Court," *NYT*, May 22, 1962, 34; John B. Morris, "A Report from Mississippi," EN, June 10, 1962, 3–4; and "ESCRU: Pilgrims to Court," *LC* 145 (Sept. 23, 1962): 6.

8. Bates interview; T.R. Waring to the editor of the *Boston Herald*, from Charleston, S.C., Dec. 20, 1952, 1–2, in RVC, "Negro File (S–Z)" folder; Ralph E. Cousins Jr., "News Release," May 15, 1961, in ESCRU, folder 12:27; "Editorial Reprints from *The News and Courier*," 1961, 1–8, MM; Massey H. Shepherd to Morris, from Berkeley, Calif., June 23, 1961, 1–2, in ESCRU, folder 27:38; Board of Trustees of the Univ. of the South, *Journal of Proceedings* (1961): 13–15, 23–25, 48–51; Thomas R. Waring, "The Southern Case against Desegregation," *Harper's*, Jan. 1956, 39–45; Arthur Ben Chitty, "Sewanee and Segregation," *Sewanee News*, May 1962, 22; "Immense Tragedy," *LC* 142 (Apr. 30, 1961): 23; "I Cannot Allow . . .," *LC* 142 (June 11, 1961): 6; "Sewanee Admits a Negro," *W* 46 (June 15, 1961): 5; "Sewanee Trustees Lift Race Ban," *W* 46 (June 29, 1961): 16; Yarbrough, *Passion for Justice*, 17, 64, 76–77, 190, 202–3, 233–35; Bartley, *Rise of Massive Resistance*, 175–77; Armentrout, *Quest for the Informed Priest*, 355–56; and Kater, "Episcopal Society," 48–50.

9. Bates interview; Chitty interview; Edward McCrady to S. Walter Martin, [from Sewanee, Tenn.], Mar. 27, 1961, 1–2, in RVC, "Segregation—Correspondence" folder;

Robert S. Lancaster to McCrady, from Sewanee, Aug. 14, 1961; McCrady to George
M. Murray, from Sewanee, Sept. 13, 1961; McCrady to Bertram Wyatt-Brown, from
Sewanee, Sept. 13, 1961, 1–2; Charles C.J. Carpenter to William G. Pollard, from
Birmingham, Ala., Oct. 3, 1961, 1–2; Pollard to Carpenter, from Oak Ridge, Tenn.,
Oct. 10, 1961, 1–3; Charles L. Winters Jr. and George M. Alexander, "Resolution to
the Board of Regents," [Oct. 1961]; Frank A. Juhan to McCrady, from Sewanee, Feb.
3, 1962, in RVC, "Negro Integration—Sewanee Inn" folder; W.R. Hampshire, "Prayer
Pilgrimage, 1961," newspaper clipping from the *Farmingdale (N.Y.) Observer,* Sept.
27, 1961, in PP; Massey H. Shepherd Jr. to John B. Morris, from Berkeley, Calif., May
19, 1962, in ESCRU, folder 48:8; "Sewanee Incident," *LC* 143 (Aug. 27, 1961): 5;
Boyd, *The Hunger, The Thirst,* 31–33; Hewlett, *Jessie Ball duPont,* 150–51, 203; Morris, "ESCRU," 15; and Kater, "Episcopal Society," 48–50. Juhan had enjoyed a long
and distinguished association with the University of the South; he not only received
his college and seminary education there, but he had also served as chaplain of the
military academy and as university chancellor. "Bishop Juhan Dies," *LC* 156 (Jan. 21,
1968): 4–5.

   10. Boyd, *The Hunger, The Thirst,* 35–37, 89–90, 116–27 (quotation on 35).

   11. Malcolm Boyd, "A Little Religion Is a Good Thing!" *W* 46 (Sept. 28, 1961):
11–14 (quotation on 14).

   12. Young, "For the Church's Sake," 1300–1301.

   13. "The Prayer Pilgrimage to the 60th General Convention of the Episcopal
Church, Sept. 1961," [1962], n.p., MM; Arthur Lichtenberger to Morris, from New
York, Sept. 12, 1961, in ESCRU, folder 5:27; Robert C. Chapman to James P. DeWolfe,
from Hempstead, N.Y., Sept. 7, 1961, 1–2, in ESCRU, folder 27:24; W.B. Spofford Sr.,
"Harmony Characterizes General Convention during First Week," *W* 46 (Sept. 28,
1961): 4; John M. Burgess, "Convention and Minority Groups," *W* 46 (Oct. 26, 1961):
10–11; "With Prayer Pilgrims," *E* 126 (Nov. 1961): 38, 40; and Ellen Naylor Bouton
and Thomas F. Pettigrew, "When a Priest Made a Pilgrimage," *CCe* 80 (1963): 363–
65.

   14. "Presiding Bishop Names Matters of Concern," *GCD,* Sept. 18, 1961, 1–2;
"Keynote Sermon Prepares Way for Convention Action," *GCD,* Sept. 18, 1961, 4
(Lichtenberger quotations); Charles Granville Hamilton, "A 20th Century General
Convention," *C* 175 (Nov. 1961): 6–9 (Bayne quotations on 6); Paul Moore Jr., "Do
You Mean What You Say?" *W* 46 (Oct. 5, 1961): 7–10 (Moore quotations on 7); *JGC*
(1961): 251, 419–20; *The Church Speaks: Christian Social Relations at General Con-
vention 1961* (New York: National Council, [1961]), 17, 43–44; David Steigerwald,
*The Sixties and the End of Modern America* (New York: St. Martin's, 1995), 5–12; and
Patterson, *Grand Expectations,* 438–41, 458–61. The New Testament term *kairos* (time
of opportunity) was frequently used by mainline Protestant leaders in the 1960s to
describe their sense that the churches were facing an era of unique opportunity. Findlay,
*Church People,* 4.

   15. Morris interview; Chitty interview; "Sewanee—an Editorial Report from the
Executive Director of the Society," EN, Jan. 6, 1962, 3 (Morris quotation); Board of
Regents of the Univ. of the South, "Resolution Adopted Unanimously . . . on Oct. 12,
1961," in PP; Board of Regents of the Univ. of the South, "Resolution Passed . . . on
Feb. 15, 1962"; Clara Shoemate to Edward McCrady, from Sewanee, Tenn., Feb. 16,
1962; Frank A. Juhan to McCrady, from Sewanee, Feb. 23, 1962; McCrady to Augustus
T. Graydon, from Sewanee, Mar. 29, 1962, in RVC, "Negro Integration—Sewanee
Inn" folder; John B. Morris, "A Call for Sit-Ins at Sewanee," Feb. 22, 1962, 1–2, in
ESCRU, folder 12:28; "Refusal at Claramont," *LC* 143 (Nov. 11, 1961): 9; "Let Them

Wait Patiently," *LC* 144 (Mar. 4, 1962): 9; "Sewanee Positions," *LC* 144 (Mar. 11, 1962): 10–11; and Kater, "Episcopal Society," 53–57.

16. Breeden interview; Robert C. Chapman, "We Went Up to Hell," [Apr. 1962], 2–4, in ESCRU, folder 48:7; "Sewanee Sit-Ins," [1962], n.p., manuscript in the author's possession, courtesy of Gerald W. Humphrey, Little Compton, R.I.; [Morris], "Memo to Pilgrims on Sewanee," May 12, 1962, 1–2, manuscript in the author's possession, courtesy of Humphrey; "Sewanee—an Editorial Report from the Executive Director of the Society," 2–4; "Sewanee Sit-Ins," EN, June 10, 1962, 2; "The University of the South and Race Relations," *Saint Luke's Journal of Theology* 5 (special issue [1962]): 1–3; "Fiery Cross for a Sit-In," *LC* 144 (Apr. 22, 1962): 6; "A Death on the Way," *LC* 144 (Apr. 29, 1962): 6; Ann Orlov, "Obvious Exception," letter in *LC* 144 (May 20, 1962): 2; Robert T. Fortna, "Sewanee and a Sit-in," *C* 176 (Sept. 1962): 7–8; and Boyd, *The Hunger, The Thirst*, 36–41.

17. John M. Gessell, "Test at Sewanee," *CCe* 79 (1962): 626–27 (quotations on 627); and Gessell, "What the Church Might Learn from Sewanee," *Saint Luke's Journal of Theology* 5 (commencement, 1962): 5–11 (quotations on 5, 8).

18. Alumni Council, "Minutes," Mar. 24, 1962, 2, 4, 7, in RVC; "Statement of Theological Faculty of Univ. of South, . . . Apr. 14, 1962," manuscript in the possession of John Crocker Jr., West Kingston, R.I.; [Thomas P. Govan] to [C. FitzSimons Allison, from New York], Apr. 19, 1962, 1–2, manuscript in the possession of John Crocker; Arthur E. Walmsley to John M. Gessell, from New York, Apr. 19, 1962, 2–3: Walmsley to Gessell, from New York, May 30, 1962, 1–2, in DCC, "University of the South" folder; Massey H. Shepherd Jr. to John [Morris], from Berkeley, Calif., May 3, 1963, in ESCRU, folder 48:9; "Sewanee Moves Ahead," EN, Aug. 6, 1963, 7; Board of Trustees of the Univ. of the South, *Journal of Proceedings* (1962): 36–42; and Fortna, "Sewanee and a Sit-in," 8.

19. Edward B. Guerry to Edward McCrady, from John's Island, S.C., Mar. 8, 1962; Jack N. Watts, "Vestry Resolution of St. Mark's Episcopal Church, Shreveport, La.," Mar. 15, 1962, in RVC, "Negro Integration—Sewanee Inn" folder; [Cornelius C. Tarplee], "Segregationist Organizations within Churches," Sept. 1959, 1–5, in CSR-31, folder 31–4–8; "Concerned Churchmen," *LC* 137 (Aug. 17, 1958): 7; and Charles D. Kean, "Pressures on Episcopalians," *CCe* 78 (1961): 1102–3.

20. T. Robert Ingram, ed., *Essays on Segregation* (Houston: St. Thomas Press, 1960), 19, 42–43, 78–80, 83–89, 92–93, 104–5 (quotations on 84); T. Robert Ingram, *Why Integration Is Un-Christian!* (Jackson, Miss.: Citizens' Council, [1962]), n.p.; Albert S. Thomas, letter in "Backfire," *W* 45 (Nov. 27, 1958): 18–19; and David L. Chappell, "Religious Ideas of the Segregationists," *Journal of American Studies* 32 (1998): 239–59.

21. John B. Morris to Henry Tobias Egger, from Dillon, S.C., Sept. 24, 1957, MM; "Integration Supported," *W* 44 (Oct. 10, 1957): 15; and Ingram, *Essays on Segregation*, 31–35, 66–71 (quotations on 33, 66).

22. James P. Dees, "Reply," letter in *LC* 138 (Mar. 15, 1959): 3–4; "No Church Endorsement," *LC* 139 (Sept. 27, 1959): 8; "Mr. Dees Leaves Church," *LC* 147 (Dec. 1, 1963): 7; "Followers for Mr. Dees," *LC* 148 (Feb. 16, 1964): 7; "Dees Consecrated," *LC* 148 (Apr. 19, 1964): 9–10; Ingram, *Essays on Segregation*, 39–46, (quotation on 40); Goldfield, *Black, White, and Southern*, 76–77; and McMillen, *Citizens' Council*, 114, 174–79.

23. Ralph McGill, "Let's Lead Where We Lag," *E* 127 (Mar. 1962): 40–42 (first quotation on 40); McGill, "The South Looks Ahead," *Ebony*, Sept. 1963, 99–102; McGill, "The Church in a Social Revolution," *CaR* 2 (Dec. 1964): 3–4 (second quota-

tion on 3); McGill, *The South and the Southerner* (Boston: Little, Brown, 1963), 225, 232–33, 276; "Kneel-ins," EN, Sept. 21, 1960, 5; Barbara Barksdale Clowse, *Ralph McGill: A Biography* (Macon, Ga.: Mercer Univ. Press, 1998), 11–12, 24, 74, 132–39, 157–59; and Egerton, *Speak Now Against the Day*, 256, 307–11, 492, 528, 549, 625–27.

24. Author's interview of Robert E. DuBose Jr., Oct. 8, 1996, Philadelphia; Rupp interview; Charles C.J. Carpenter to Vernon A. Jones, from Birmingham, Ala., Mar. 31, 1960, 1; Carpenter to Jones, from Birmingham, May 2, 1960, 1–2, in CCJC, folder 241.1.132.8.64 ("St. Andrew's, Tuskegee" file); Carpenter to William Scarlett, from Birmingham, Oct. 6, [1960], 1–2, in CCJC, folder 241.2.155.15.16 ("William Scarlett Correspondence" file); Claude Sitton, "Negroes Dispersed in Alabama March," *NYT,* Mar. 7, 1960, 1, 14; "Further Protests Forecast," *NYT,* Mar. 8, 1960, 23; and Fairclough, *To Redeem the Soul of America,* 60–61.

25. Walter interview; Franklin interview; author's telephone interview of Roberta Jones-Booker, Sept. 29, 1994, Talladega, Ala.; author's interview of Mona Davis, Sept. 30, 1994, Talladega, Ala.; Robert M. Man to Arthur Walmsley, from Bessemer, Ala., May 13, 1960, 1, in CSR-85, folder 85-3-12; Francis Walter to John [Morris], from Eufaula, Ala., May 4, 1960, 1–2, in ESCRU, folder 27:18; Charles C.J. Carpenter to M.M. DePass, from Birmingham, Ala., Apr. 26, 1962, 1–2, in CCJC, folder 241.1.122.8.41 ("St. Peter's, Talladega" file); "3 Negroes Jailed in Talladega Easter Mixing Attempt," newspaper clipping from the *Mobile Press,* Apr. 23, 1962, in ESCRU, folder 12:50; Thomas P. Govan to John P. Craine, [from New York], May 8, 1962, manuscript in the possession of John Crocker; and Maxine D. Jones and Joe M. Richardson, *Talladega College: The First Century* (Tuscaloosa: Univ. of Alabama Press, 1990), 181–84. I am also indebted to Robert H. Blackwell of Talladega, Ala., for his assistance in researching the 1962 incident at St. Peter's Church.

26. McGill, "Let's Lead Where We Lag," 40–41; "Mississippi Rector under Attack for Joining in Biracial Meeting," *NYT,* Apr. 14, 1961, 21; "A Troublesome Tape," *LC* 142 (Apr. 23, 1961): 7; "A Moderate," *LC* 142 (Apr. 30, 1961): 21–22; *Episcopal Church in Mississippi,* 118–20; and Sherwood Willing Wise, *The Cathedral Church of St. Andrew: A Sesquicentennial History, 1839–1989* (Jackson, Miss.: Cathedral Church of St. Andrew, 1989), 137–54.

27. Author's interview of Jane M. Schutt, Aug. 28, 1995, Florence, Miss.; John Jones and John Dittmer, "An Interview with Mrs. Jane Schutt, Feb. 2, 1981," 6–8, 28–30, manuscript in Mississippi Department of Archives and History, Jackson; Medgar W. Evers, memorandum to "Branch President," from Jackson, Miss., Dec. 31, 1959, in Mississippi State Advisory Committee of the United States Civil Rights Commission Subject File, Mississippi Department of Archives and History, Jackson; W.S. Curry to [Jane] Schutt, from Itta Bene, Miss., Dec. 8, 1959, in Jane M. Schutt Papers, DAT, "Correspondence (1959)" folder; [Jane] Schutt, "Testimony . . . before the Senate Subcommittee on Constitutional Rights," May 22, 1963, 1–8, in Schutt papers, DAT, "Correspondence (1963–64)" folder; Donald Cunnigen, "The Mississippi State Advisory Committee to the United States Commission on Civil Rights, 1960–1965," *Journal of Mississippi History* 53 (1991): 1–17; Donald Cunnigen, "Men and Women of Goodwill: Mississippi's White Liberals," Ph.D. diss., Harvard Univ., 1988, 221–29, 235–37, courtesy of Donald Cunnigen, Providence, R.I.; and John Dittmer, *Local People: The Struggle for Civil Rights in Mississippi* (Urbana: Univ. of Illinois Press, 1994), 195–96.

28. Gray interview; "Time for Decision," *LC* 145 (Oct. 7, 1962): 6; "Mobs in Mississippi," *LC* 145 (Oct. 14, 1962): 9–11; "Repentance and Redemption," *LC* 145

(Oct. 21, 1962): 7–8; "Duncan Gray Gets Roughed-up for Urging End of Violence," *W* 47 (Oct. 11, 1962): 3; Russell H. Barrett, *Integration at Ole Miss* (Chicago: Quadrangle, 1965), 97–98, 134–35, 155–56, 183, 225; James W. Silver, *Mississippi: The Closed Society,* new enl. ed. (New York: Harcourt, Brace, 1966), xxviii–xxix, 120, 282, 291; William H. Crook and Ross Coggins, *Seven Who Fought* (Waco, Tex.: Word, 1971), 9–25; Campbell, *And Also with You,* 17–21, 23–38, 41–43, 55–58; and Cunnigen, "Men and Women of Goodwill," 159, 605–9.

29. Alex D. Dickson Jr., "Sermon Preached in the Parish Church of St. Columb's on Oct. 14, 1962," 1, 5, in Schutt papers, DAT, "Newsletter, Brochures, Speeches" folder; NCEC, Oct. 9–11, 1962, 131–32, 228–29; "Recipe for Riot," *LC* 145 (Oct. 14, 1962): 18; Charles G. Hamilton, "The Church and Mississippi," *LC* 156 (May 12, 1968): 11, 13; "'We Have Failed' in Mississippi: Duncan Gray," *C* 176 (Nov. 1962): 16; "P.E. Council Backs Mississippi Clergy on Race," *C* 176 (Dec. 1962): 16; and "Gray Praised by the P.B.," *W* 47 (Oct. 11, 1962): 17. For background on the broad cultural impact of *To Kill a Mockingbird,* see Eric J. Sundquist, "Blues for Atticus Finch: Scottsboro, *Brown,* and Harper Lee," in *The South as an American Problem,* ed. Larry J. Griffin and Don H. Doyle (Athens: Univ. of Georgia Press, 1995), 181–206.

30. Although Will Campbell retained his status as a Southern Baptist minister, he was then in the midst of a brief "flirtation with Canterbury" and attended an Episcopal parish in the Nashville area. The rector not only supported Campbell's racial views but also allowed him to preach and serve as a "lay reader." Campbell interview; and Hawkins, *Will Campbell,* 159–61.

31. Cornelius C. Tarplee to Kenneth B. Clark, [from New York], Feb. 19, 1960, 1–2; Committee on Intergroup Relations, [Minutes, May 14–15, 1960], 1–3; Committee on Intergroup Relations, Minutes, July 16–17, 1960, 1–5; Thomas F. Pettigrew, "Proposed Committee Rationale," July 16–17, 1960, 1, in CSR-85, folder 85-3-12; American Church Institute for Negroes, Minutes of the Meeting of the Board of Trustees, Oct. 11, 1960, 2, in ACIN, folder 61-2-20; NCEC, Apr. 28–30, 1959, 155–56; Feb. 9–11, 1960, 84; Oct. 11–13, 1960, 10, 216–17, 226–27; RMC, Mar. 15–16, 1960, 6–8, 10–13; Sept. 6–8, 1960, 3–5, 9; Feb. 7–8, 1961, 2–3, 6; Morris [to Myers], Sept. 10, 1961, 1–2; "The Witness—On and Off," EN, June 10, 1962, 10; "Build Lunch Counters in Front of Church-Related Schools and Segregate Them," EN, Mar. 10, 1963, 6; "The Negro Episcopalian: A Special Report," *E* 127 (Mar. 1962): 19–42; and "Editorials: Let's Have a White Episcopalian Issue," *W* 47 (Apr. 26, 1962): 7.

32. Pettigrew interview; Walmsley interview; Campbell interview; Committee on Intergroup Relations, "Minutes," Apr. 29–30, 1961, 2; Dec. 8–9, 1961, 1, 5; Thomas F. Pettigrew, "Proposed Statement for Christian Social Relations Bulletin," May 2, 1961, 1–2; Charles C.J. Carpenter to Pettigrew, from Birmingham, Ala., Nov. 7, 1961, in CSR-85, folder 85-3-12; Almon R. Pepper to Pettigrew, from New York, Mar. 29, 1962; Pettigrew, ["Summary of the Work of the Advisory Committee on Intergroup Relations"], 1962, 1–2, in CSR-85, folder 85-3-13; Sarah Patton Boyle et al. to Arthur Lichtenberger, [from New York], Dec. 13, 1961 (source of quotation); Lichtenberger to Pettigrew, from New York, Dec. 19, 1961; Pettigrew to "Committee member," from Cambridge, Mass., Dec. 31, 1961, in SPBP, box 16; NCEC, May 1–3, 1962, 128; Oct. 9–11, 1962, 228; Nov. 29–30, Dec. 1, 1962, 77; "The House of Bishops and Little Rock," and "The House of Bishops' Statement on Race," EN, Nov. 30, 1962, 2, 5; and "Tactical Error?" *LC* 145 (Dec. 16, 1962): 7–8.

33. "Report of the Advisory Committee on Intergroup Relations to the Depart-

ment of Christian Social Relations of the National Council," Oct. 9, 1962, 1–10 (quotation on 8), in CSR-85, folder 85–3–13.

34. *Ibid.*, 11–15 ("brotherhood of man" on 11); and Sarah Patton Boyle to William B. Abbot, [from Charlottesville, Va.], Jan. 29, 1961 ("to be more executives" quotation), in SPBP, box 1.

35. "Report of the Advisory Committee on Intergroup Relations," 16–30 (quotation on 30).

36. *Ibid.*, 31–50 (quotations on 41, 47); and Gordon W. Allport, preface to Cornelius C. Tarplee, *Racial Prejudice* (New York: Seabury, 1962), 3. See also Sarah Patton Boyle to [Mamie] Clark, [from Charlottesville], May 2, 1961; Kenneth B. Clark to Boyle, from New York, Nov. 30, 1962, in SPBP, box 1; Thomas F. Pettigrew to Boyle, from Cambridge, Mass., June 25, 1962; [Boyle] to Pettigrew, [from Charlottesville], June 28, 1962, 2, in SPBP, box 16; Will D. Campbell, *Race and the Renewal of the Church* (Philadelphia: Westminster, 1962), 22–25, 41–45, 54–59; Boyle, "Price of Brotherhood," 85; Kenneth B. Clark, "A Relevant Celebration of the Emancipation Centennial," *Ebony*, Sept. 1963, 25; Thomas F. Pettigrew, "Wherein the Church Has Failed in Race," *Religious Education* 59 (1964): 64–72; "Reasons for Failure," *LC* 143 (Nov. 26, 1961): 22; Hawkins, *Will Campbell*, 87–101; and Findlay, *Church People,* 22–27.

37. [Cornelius] Tarplee et al., "Report of Staff Committee to the Department of Christian Social Relations concerning the Report of the Intergroup Advisory Committee," Nov. 29, [1962]; [Donald H. Wattley], "An Answer to Dr. Pettigrew," [Dec. 1962], 1–5, in CSR-85, folder 85–3–13 (quotations on 1, 3, 5); Frederick J. Warnecke to Almon R. Pepper, from Bethlehem, Pa., Jan. 15, 1963, 1–2, in CSR-85, folder 85–3–14; "Key Report Restricted," EN, Mar. 10, 1963, 3; and London and Lemmon, *Episcopal Church in North Carolina,* 417–18.

38. "The Chicago Conference," EN, Mar. 10, 1963, 5; "Time to Stand," *LC* 145 (Oct. 28, 1962): 7; William Stringfellow, "Care Enough To Weep," *W* 48 (Feb. 21, 1963): 13–15; Barbara G. Kremer, "For All of God's Children," *E* 128 (Mar. 1963): 36–39; Matthew Ahmann, ed., *Race: Challenge to Religion* (Chicago: Regnery, 1963), v–xi, 155–73 (quotations on 156, 171, 173); and Friedland, *Lift Up Your Voice,* 72–75.

39. Stringfellow, "Care Enough To Weep," 13 (Stringfellow quotation); Stringfellow, *My People Is the Enemy,* 135–36; "The Churches: 'That Awful Fatalism,'" *Time,* Jan. 25, 1963, 66; "Almost Abdication," *LC* 146 (May 12, 1963): 8; Benjamin E. Mays, *Born to Rebel: An Autobiography* (New York: Scribner's, 1971), 262–63; Arthur E. Walmsley, "A Theology for the Welfare State," *Bulletin: The Council for Social Service* 186 (May 1963): 12–16; Arthur E. Walmsley, "The Episcopal Church: Racism, the Civil Rights Struggle, and Christian Mission," paper presented at the National Episcopal Historians and Archivists Conference, Austin, Tex., June 21–24, 1995, 12; and Friedland, *Lift Up Your Voice,* 72–75.

40. Dan T. Carter, *The Politics of Rage: George Wallace, the Origins of the New Conservatism, and the Transformation of American Politics* (New York: Simon and Schuster, 1995), 108–9.

41. "11 Religious Leaders Appeal for 'Sanity' in Desegregation Issue," clipping from the *Birmingham News,* Jan. 17, 1963, in CCJC, folder 241.2.65.12.30 ("Eleven Leading Ministers' Resolution" file); George Mosley Murray, "In Truth and Love," *LC* 141 (Oct. 23, 1960): 10; and Friedland, *Lift Up Your Voice,* 77–79.

42. Breeden interview; Rupp interview; Yon interview; [George M. Murray] to Myron B. Bloy Jr., from Birmingham, Ala., Apr. 30, 1962, 2–3, manuscript in the

possession of John Crocker; "Birmingham Jails 6 More Negroes," *NYT,* Apr. 14, 1963, 46; Martin Luther King Jr., "Letter from Birmingham Jail," *CCe* 80 (1963): 767–73; Martin Luther King Jr., *Why We Can't Wait* (New York: Harper, 1964), 77–100; George M. Murray, letter in "Backfire," *W* 48 (June 27, 1963): [19]; "Distressed City," *LC* 146 (May 19, 1963): 9–10; Branch, *Parting the Waters,* 725–45; Bass, "Not Time Yet," 244–52; and Glenn T. Eskew, *But for Birmingham: The Local and National Movements in the Civil Rights Struggle* (Chapel Hill: Univ. of North Carolina Press, 1997), 174–75, 198–204, 235–36, 373 n. 11.

43. George M. Murray, "Letter from Alabama," *LC* 146 (May 26, 1963): 17; and Eskew, *But for Birmingham,* 235–36.

44. Walmsley interview; [Arthur Walmsley], handwritten note on "Full Text of Statement by the Presiding Bishop," July 30, 1963, 1, in AEWP, "Presiding Bishop's Whitsunday Statement (1963)" folder; "Time to Act! A Statement by the Presiding Bishop," *LC* 146 (June 2, 1963): 7–8; "Racial Plea Goes to Episcopalians," *NYT,* May 26, 1963, 59; "Race Relations: Birmingham and After," *E* 128 (July 1963): 33–35; and Walmsley, "Episcopal Church," 13–14. For responses to Lichtenberger's statement (mainly negative from the South and overwhelmingly positive from other parts of the country), see CSR-85, folder 85–4–31; AEWP, "Presiding Bishop's Whitsunday Statement (1963)" folder; and Arthur Walmsley, memorandum to [Arthur] Lichtenberger et al., June 27, 1963, in ECBM, folder 159–1–29.

45. Walmsley interview; John F. Kennedy, telegram to Clifford Morehouse, [from Washington, D.C.], June 12, 1963; Daniel Corrigan to "the President," from New York, June 13, 1963; "Joint Staff Committee on Race Relations," Apr. 28, 1964, 4, in ECBM, folder 159–1–29; Daniel Corrigan and Almon R. Pepper to "Dear Bishop," from New York, June 18, 1963, 1–2, in DCC; NCEC, Oct. 10–12, 1963, 73; Robert W. Spike, *The Freedom Revolution and the Churches* (New York: Association, 1965), 84–87; Walmsley, "Episcopal Church," 13–14; Findlay, *Church People,* 34–38; and Patterson, *Grand Expectations,* 478–81. As the Commission on Religion and Race was being organized, the contributions of J. Oscar Lee, the experienced black director of the Department of Racial and Cultural Relations of the National Council of Churches, were entirely overlooked. Like Tollie Caution, then the sole black officer at the headquarters of the Episcopal Church, Lee for many years had been the only African American on the National Council of Churches professional staff. By the early 1960s, however, his relatively cautious approach to racial affairs—a quality that once enabled him to succeed among white bureaucrats—was no longer deemed appropriate by the activists who designed the Commission on Religion and Race. Findlay, *Church People,* 17–19, 35–37.

46. Author's interview of John H. Snow, Oct. 26, 1995, Ashfield, Mass.; author's interview of David McI. Gracie, Nov. 16, 1995, Philadelphia; Gray interview; [Cornelius C. Tarplee, "Report on Visit to Jackson, Mississippi . . . ," June 1963], 5–6, 9, in CSR-31, folder 31–4–8; John B. Morris to Medgar Evers, [from Atlanta], June 10, 1963, in ESCRU, folder 59:4; Rowland Cox, "Memorandum on Trip to Jackson, Mississippi . . . June 15, 1963," 1–8 (quotation on 1, 7); Brian Kelley to John Morris, from Middlebury, Vt., Aug. 26, 1963, 1–2; David Gracie to [Morris], from Rogers City, Mich., June 19, 1963, 1–2; John H. Snow, "Taken from Letter about Trip to Jackson, . . . June 15, 1963," 1–2; John W.B. Thompson, "Taken from a Letter about the Trip to Jackson, . . . June 15, 1963," in ESCRU, folder 59:6; "Jackson Revisited a Month Later," EN, Aug. 6, 1963, 3; "Churchman Charged," *LC* 147 (July 7, 1963): 4; Malcolm Boyd, "The Funeral of Medgar Evers," *C* 177 (Sept. 1963): 6; Boyd, *The Hunger, The Thirst,* 50–53; Reed Massengill, *Portrait of a Racist: The Man Who Killed Medgar Evers?* (New

York: St. Martin's, 1994), 53, 83–84, 102–5, 113–14, 123, 162; and Branch, *Parting the Waters,* 824–31.

47. "Dr. Blake among 283 Held in Racial Rally in Maryland," *NYT,* July 5, 1963, 1, 44; "The National Council Takes Steps to Improve Its Racial Practices," *CaR* [1] (July 6, 1963): 2; "Around the Nation," *CaR* 1 (July 20, 1963): 11–12 (source of "to be where there is action" and "a higher law" quotations); "Episcopalians Take Leadership in Race Relations Crisis," *W* 48 (July 25, 1963): 6; "Trial by Jury," *LC* 147 (July 21, 1963): 4; Michael Allen, *This Time, This Place* (Indianapolis: Bobbs-Merrill, 1971), 74–75 (source of "go wherever his people go" quotation); and Friedland, *Lift Up Your Voice,* 82–84. For other examples of clerical activism in the South during the summer and fall of 1963, see "Raleigh Witness," *LC* 146 (June 23, 1963): 4; "Clergymen Turned Away at Restaurant in Raleigh . . .," *CaR* [1] (July 6, 1963): 12; "18 Ministers Stage March in Protest to Segregated Belair Development," *Washington Post,* Aug. 16, 1963, A10; and Wilfrid C. Rogers, "N.E. Ministers Jailed," *Boston Globe,* Nov. 15, 1963, 1–2.

48. "In Support of Protest," *CaR* [1] (July 6, 1963): 6–7; "Presiding Bishop Calls Special Meeting of the House of Bishops," *CaR* 1 (July 20, 1963): 14; "Plans Set for Aug. 28 March on Washington," *CaR* 1 (Aug. 6, 1963): 1–2; "March on Washington Special Issue," *CaR* 1 (Aug. 31, 1963): 1–2, 4–6, 13; "Bishop Warnecke Presents Report to House of Bishops," *CaR* 1 (Aug. 31, 1963): 14–20; Thomas LaBar, "A Summer of Significance," *E* 128 (Sept. 1963): 19–21, 46; "Support for Civil Rights," *LC* 147 (Aug. 25, 1963): 6; and William Griffith, "New York: Exodus," *LC* 147 (Sept. 15, 1963): 4 (Wetmore quotation); and Stringfellow, *My People Is the Enemy,* 139.

49. Walmsley interview; John B. Morris to "Churchmen Participating in the Washington March," Aug. 23, 1963, in ECBM, folder 159–1–29; "The House of Bishops of the Episcopal Church . . .," advertisement in *Washington Post,* Aug. 28, 1963, A7; "3 Faiths Join Hands to Demonstrate," *Washington Post,* Aug. 29, 1963, A17; Russell Baker, "Capital Is Occupied by a Gentle Army," *NYT,* Aug. 29, 1963, 17; "Three Faiths Join in Rights Demand," *NYT,* Aug. 29, 1963, 19; "Clerics at March See a Challenge," *NYT,* Aug. 30, 1963, 12; "Waking Up to Race," *Time,* Oct. 4, 1963, 79–80; "Special Report on the March," *E* 128 (Oct. 1963): 44–45; Robert A. MacGill, "United in the Cause," *LC* 147 (Sept. 8, 1963): 9; Martin Luther King Jr., "I Have a Dream," in *A Testament of Hope: The Essential Writings of Martin Luther King, Jr.,* ed. James Melvin Washington (San Francisco: HarperSanFrancisco, 1986), 217; Findlay, *Church People,* 50–51; and Friedland, *Lift Up Your Voice,* 85–91.

50. John E. Mandeville to Evans Dunn et al., from Mobile, Ala., Aug. 26, 1963 (Mandeville quotation); Dunn to Carroll Greene Jr., [from Birmingham], Aug. 29, 1963; Dunn to Arthur E. Walmsley, [from Birmingham], Sept. 7, 1963, in DAR, "Department of Christian Social Relations (NY), Correspondence, 1963" folder; C.C.J. Carpenter, memorandum to "the Presiding Bishop and Other Members of National Council," from Birmingham, Sept. 23, 1963, 1–3, in DCC; Warren H. Turner Jr. to Carpenter, from New York, Oct. 17, 1963, 1–2, in DCC, "Selma, Alabama—General" folder; NCEC, Oct. 10–12, 1963, 134–36; "The Question of Method," *LC* 147 (Aug. 25, 1963): 17–18 (Jones quotations); and Charles W. Arny, letter in *E* 128 (Oct. 1963): 9 (Arny quotation).

51. Spike, *Freedom Revolution and the Churches,* 106–8 (quotation on 107).

52. "Episcopalians Told Rights Drive Lags," *NYT,* Oct. 16, 1963, 28; George Dugan, "Religious Groups in the Capitol to Press for Civil Rights Bill," *NYT,* Nov. 15, 1963, 21; "Second Legislative Conference Held," *CaR* 1 (Oct. 1963): 1–2; Arthur Lichtenberger, "A Statement by the Presiding Bishop," *LC* 149 (July 12, 1964): 5;

"CapitalScene: Passing That Bill," *E* 129 (Apr. 1964): 44; "Civil Rights: Moral or Political," *E* 129 (July 1964): 32–33; James F. Findlay, "Religion and Politics in the Sixties: The Churches and the Civil Rights Act of 1964," *Journal of American History* 77 (1990): 66–92; Patterson, *Grand Expectations*, 542–47; and Taylor Branch, *Pillar of Fire: America in the King Years, 1963–65* (New York: Simon and Schuster, 1998), 387–88.

53. [Sarah Patton Boyle] to Arthur Walmsley, [from Charlottesville, Va.], Jan. 26, 1963, in SPBP, box 16.

## 6. Christian Witness and Racial Integration in the Deep South

1. Morris interview; "Albany: A Pivotal Symbol," EN, Sept. 2, 1962, 1; "The Lovett Situation," EN, Aug. 6, 1963, 5–6; Diocese of Atlanta, *Journal* (1963), 46, 51; "Atlanta: Out of Order," *LC* 146 (Feb. 10, 1963): 7; and "Church School Turns Down Negro Child," *LC* 146 (Mar. 24, 1963): 5–6. For information on the SCLC involvement in Albany, Georgia, see Fairclough, *To Redeem the Soul of America*, 85–109; and Garrow, *Bearing the Cross*, 173–219.

2. Ford interview; Morris interview; "Statement by the Rev. Joseph A. Pelham, President," June 7, 1963, 1–2; Randolph R. Claiborne Jr., "Pastoral Letter by the Bishop of Atlanta," [July 10, 1963], 1–4, in Walter H. Gray Papers, Archives of the Diocese of Connecticut, Hartford, "ESCRU" folder; "The Lovett Situation," 5–6; "Church School Turns Down Negro Child," 6; Roy Pettway, "Lovett School," letter in *LC* 146 (May 12, 1963): 5; "The Alternative," *LC* 146 (June 16, 1963): 7–8; "The Board's Instructions," *LC* 146 (June 30, 1963): 11; "No More Support," *LC* 147 (July 14, 1963): 4; Randolph R. Claiborne, letter in "Backfire," *W* 48 (Apr. 11, 1963): 18; "Racial Integrity through Free Choice," *CCe* 74 (1957): 1387; and Kater, "Episcopal Society," 61–67. Since Morris had chosen to remain "canonically resident" in the diocese of South Carolina after he moved to Atlanta, he was required to petition Bishop Claiborne every year for renewal of the license that allowed him to function as a priest in Claiborne's diocese.

3. "Episcopal Clergy Join Picket Line at Georgia Church-Related School," Oct. 19, 1963, 1–2, manuscript in the author's possession, courtesy of John J. Harmon, Rochester, N.Y.; J.A. Rabbe to "Dear Parents," from Atlanta, Aug. 8, 1963, MM; "March to Lovett," and "Statement of the Executive Committee . . . on the Lovett School Situation," EN, Oct. 13, 1963, 1, [6]; "The Lovett Situation," EN, Dec. 8, 1963, 7; "Lovett School Baccalaureate Service," EN, Aug. 6, 1964, 1; Claude Sitton, "'Hypocrisy Charge Censored by Atlanta Episcopal Newspaper," *NYT*, Oct. 3, 1963, 21; "Episcopalians: Faith and Prejudice in Georgia," *Time*, Nov. 15, 1963, 94; "Episcopal Diocese Censors McGill," *CCe* 80 (1963): 1260–61; "Atlanta: Scrapped Paper," *LC* 147 (Oct. 13, 1963): 10–11, 21–22; "Lovett Picketed," *LC* 147 (Oct. 27, 1963): 7–8; "Clergy Sign Protest," *LC* 147 (Nov. 3, 1963): 9; "Lovett Baccalaureate Protested," *LC* 148 (June 21, 1964): 6; Ralph McGill, *No Place to Hide: The South and Human Rights*, ed. Calvin M. Logue (Macon, Ga.: Mercer Univ. Press, 1984), 2:422–35; and Clowse, *Ralph McGill*, 206.

4. Ford interview; John B. Morris to Randolph R. Claiborne Jr., from Atlanta, Nov. 11, 1963, 13–14; Morris to "the Faculty and Staff of Lovett," from Atlanta, Jan. 10, 1964, MM; Morris to Claiborne, from Atlanta, Aug. 2, 1964; Morris to Claiborne, from Atlanta, July 19, 1966; Morris to "Member Bishops," from Atlanta, Oct. 4, 1966,

1–2; Morris to "National Episcopal Church Press Editors," from Atlanta, Feb. 8, 1967, MM, "Correspondence re: licensing" folder; ESCRU news release, May 30, 1965, in ESCRU, folder 12:31; "Lovett School: Church-Related or Not?" *CaR* 1 (Mar. 1964): 6–9; and Diocese of Atlanta, *Journal* (1965), 54–55. ESCRU protests continued until Lovett School finally desegregated in 1967. Bill Shipp, "Lovett School to Admit Negroes, Ending Dispute," EN, Sept. 29, 1966, 2; and "Policy Statement from Lovett," *LC* 153 (Sept. 25, 1966): 5.

5. Author's interview of Esther Burgess, June 7, 1995, Vineyard Haven, Mass.; author's interview of Hester H. Campbell, Mar. 2, 1995, Concord, N.H.; Breeden interview; Massachusetts, *Journal of the Convention* (1964), 53; "New York and Boston Churches Work for Integrated Schools," *W* 49 (Feb. 13, 1964): 6; Hester Hocking Campbell, "Day-by-Day Report on Happenings in St. Augustine Show-Down," *W* 49 (Apr. 23, 1964): 3–5; Hester H. Campbell, *Four for Freedom* (New York: Carlton, 1974), 8–11; "Bishop Burgess of Massachusetts," *Ebony*, Oct. 1969, 54–58; David R. Colburn, *Racial Change and Community Crisis: St. Augustine, Florida, 1877–1980* (New York: Columbia Univ. Press, 1985), 62–70; Fairclough, *To Redeem the Soul of America*, 180–81; and Branch, *Pillar of Fire*, 239.

6. Author's interview of Malcolm E. Peabody Jr., Dec. 4, 1995, Washington, D.C.; Burgess interview; Hester Campbell interview; National Council, press release, Apr. 6, [1964], 2, in JHEP, "Executive/National Council" folder; Martin Luther King Jr. to Hester H. Campbell, from Atlanta, June 16, 1964, manuscript in the possession of Hester Campbell, Concord, N.H.; "Mother of Massachusetts Governor Jailed in Florida," *NYT*, Apr. 1, 1964, 1, 27; Fred Powledge, "$450 Bond Posted by Mrs. Peabody," *NYT*, Apr. 3, 1964, 23; "Demonstrators in St. Augustine Joined by Bishops' Wives," *W* 49 (Apr. 9, 1964): 4–5; Hester H. Campbell, "Day-by-Day Report on Happenings in St. Augustine Show-Down," *W* 49 (Apr. 30, 1964): 3–6; Campbell, *Four for Freedom*, 73–82; Carroll E. Simcox, "From Suburbs to Jail," *LC* 148 (Apr. 12, 1964): 5–6; Esther J. Burgess, "Witness at St. Augustine, Florida," *Church Militant* 67 (May 1964): 2–3; Kay Longcope, ". . . To Do Something besides Talk," *CaR* 1 (Apr.–May 1964): 11–13; Robert K. Massie, "Don't Tread on Grandmother Peabody," *Saturday Evening Post*, May 16, 1964, 74–76 (quotation on 76); Colburn, *Racial Change and Community Crisis*, 163–65; Robert W. Hartley, "A Long Hot Summer: The St. Augustine Racial Disorders of 1964," in *St. Augustine, Florida, 1963–1964: Mass Protest and Racial Violence*, ed. David J. Garrow (Brooklyn, N.Y.: Carlson, 1989), 27–39; and Branch, *Pillar of Fire*, 277–85.

7. Snow interview; Morris interview; John B. Morris, memorandum to "Directors and Chapter Chairmen," from Atlanta, Apr. 6, 1964; Morris to C.M. Seymour Jr., from Atlanta, Apr. 6, 1964, in ESCRU, folder 56:10; Warren H. Turner Jr., memorandum to [Arthur] Walmsley, from New York, Apr. 14, 1964, in DCC, "St. Augustine Report" folder; "The Bishop of Florida and Thought Control," EN, May 28, 1961, 5; "Bishop West Again Stands in Rectory Door," EN, Mar. 1, 1964, 7; John Snow, "The Bishops' Wives, St. Augustine, and Trinity Church," EN, May 17, 1964, 3–4; "Bishop's Statement," *LC* 148 (Apr. 19, 1964): 10; and "Florida: Follow-up," *LC* 148 (May 3, 1964): 8.

8. John B. Morris, memorandum to "the Church Press," from Atlanta, June 23, 1964, in ESCRU, folder 56:10; Walter Robert Hampshire to Arthur Lichtenberger, from Atlanta, June 25, 1964, 1–2, in DCC, "St. Augustine Report" folder; Howard Schachern, "Duty before Comfort, Priest Takes Tough Job," EN, May 17, 1964, [9]; Henri A. Stines, "St. Augustine, Trinity Church and a Eucharist," EN, Aug. 6, 1964, 5; "Integrated Group Attends Services at Trinity Church," *LC* 149 (July 5, 1964): 4;

Dierenfield, "One 'Desegregated Heart,'" 283–84; Fairclough, *To Redeem the Soul of America,* 181–91; and Branch, *Pillar of Fire,* 375–83.

9. "Resolution by the Vestry of Trinity Episcopal Church, St. Augustine, Florida," [May 19, 1964], 1–2; John B. Morris to Charles M. Seymour, [from Atlanta], June 25, 1964; Hamilton West to Seymour, from Jacksonville, Fla., July 1, 1964, 1–2, in ESCRU, folder 56:11; Nancy Gregorik, "Jeers, Bruises, Hate—a Priest in Dixie," newspaper clipping from the *Detroit News,* July 4, 1964, in ESCRU, folder 56:14; West to the clergy of the Diocese of Florida, from Jacksonville, July 3, 1964, 1–2; Robert C. Martin Jr., memorandum to Muriel Webb and Arthur E. Walmsley, from New York, June 2, 1964; [Cornelius C. Tarplee], "Report on Mission to St. Augustine, June 27–July 1, 1964," 3–4, 8, in DCC, "St. Augustine Report" folder; "Rector in Florida Fights for Pulpit," *NYT,* July 1, 1964, 22; "Florida: Bishop West Supports Rector of Trinity," *LC* 149 (July 12, 1964): 4; and Colburn, *Racial Change and Community Crisis,* 166–72.

10. Author's interview of John M. Pratt, Mar. 3, 1995, Walpole, N.H.; Morris interview; John Morris, memorandum to "Directors and Chapter Chairmen," from Atlanta, Jan. 28, 1964, in ESCRU, folder 59:1; "Mission to Hattiesburg," EN, Mar. 1, 1964, 1–2; Hodding Carter, "Mississippi Now—Hate and Fear," *NYT Magazine,* June 23, 1963, 11, 28; Findlay, *Church People,* 78–84; Branch, *Pillar of Fire,* 128–29; Weisbrot, *Freedom Bound,* 94–97; and Carson, *In Struggle,* 108.

11. David Spain, "Mississippi Autopsy," *Ramparts Magazine* (special issue, 1964): 43–49; Doug McAdam, *Freedom Summer* (New York: Oxford Univ. Press, 1988), 12–15, 33, 48–51, 62; Carson, *In Struggle,* 96–121; and Bartley, *New South,* 344–47.

12. Author's interview of Earl A. Neil, Dec. 8, 1995, Washington, D.C.; Walmsley interview; Boyd interview; McKenna to the author, May 23, 1995; Arthur E. Walmsley, memorandum to "Bishops, CSR Chairmen and Executives, and Other Key Persons," from New York, May 5, 1964, in DCC, "1965 Recruiting—Civil Rights" folder; Arthur C. Thomas, memorandum to "Denominational Representatives," from New York [1964], 1, 4–5 in DMR, box 8 (courtesy of James F. Findlay Jr., Peace Dale, R.I.); "Recruitment for Confrontation," EN, May 17, 1964, 7; "Mississippi: Never Again the Same," EN, Sept. 6, 1964, 2; "Ministers Resume N.C. Hunger Strike," *Boston Globe,* Nov. 17, 1963, 1–2; "Program," *CaR* 2 (Oct. 1964): 11; Barbara G. Kremer, "Good News in Mississippi," *E* 129 (Sept. 1964): 42–47; "Rector and Bishop Give Views on Mississippi Situation," *W* 49 (Sept. 3, 1964): 3–4; "Message to McComb," *LC* 149 (Oct. 11, 1964): 10–11; "Mississippi: Discrimination," *LC* 149 (Oct. 18, 1964): 6–7; James F. Findlay, "In Keeping with the Prophets: The Mississippi Summer of 1964," *CCe* 105 (1988): 574–76; and Findlay, *Church People,* 88–100.

13. Author's interview of David B. Weden Jr., June 6, 1995, Truro, Mass.; author's interview of Gerald F. Gilmore, May 17, 1995, Falmouth, Mass.; author's interview of John C. Sanders, June 17, 1994, Atlanta; author's interview of Barbara C. Harris, Oct. 24, 1995, Boston; author's interview of John F. Stevens, July 5, 1994, Austin, Tex.; Neil interview; Boyd interview; [William M. Weber] to "Good People of St. James'," [from Columbus, Miss., July 1964], 1–2, in Weber Collection, "Weber's Trip to Mississippi (1964)" folder; Oliver B. Garver Jr. to ESCRU, from Los Angeles, Sept. 17, 1964, in ESCRU, folder 59:2; and Warren H. McKenna, "The National Council of Churches and Mississippi," *CaR* 2 (Oct. 1964): 30.

14. Harry J. Bowie to John [Morris], from McComb, Miss., Dec. 24, 1964, in ESCRU, folder 59:9; "Mississippi Denies Clerics Common Courtesy," *C* 178 (Nov. 1964): 18; Malcolm Boyd, "The Battle of McComb," *CCe* 81 (1964): 1400–1402; Malcolm Boyd, "We Are Just Captives," *W* 49 (Dec. 10, 1964): 12–13 (quotation on 13); Malcolm Boyd, "The Underground Church," *Commonweal* 88 (1968): 99; and

Leon Howell, *Freedom City: The Substance of Things Hoped For* (Richmond, Va.: John Knox, 1969), 96–111.

15. Author's interview of Colton M. Smith III, Dec. 27, 1994, Johns Island, S.C.; Moore interview; C. Kilmer Myers, "Stay Out of the Cathedral," *LC* 148 (Feb. 9, 1964): 10–11, 18; "Washington Bishop Visits MFDP," *LC* 149 (Sept. 6, 1964): 6; Kay Longcope, "Native Mississippi Family Driven from Their Home," *CaR* 2 (Oct. 1964): 3; Paul Moore Jr., "A Brief Rationale for the Mississippi Project," *CaR* 2 (Oct. 1964): 19–20; and Nicholas Von Hoffman, *Mississippi Notebook* (New York: David White, 1964), 48, 64–78. For a book-length discussion of the experiences of Red and Malva Heffner, see Hodding Carter, *So the Heffners Left McComb* (Garden City, N.Y.: Doubleday, 1965).

16. Smith interview; author's interview of Harry J. Bowie, Sept. 19, 1994, Jackson, Miss.; Paul Moore Jr., "A Long Hot Week," *W* 49 (Oct. 8, 1964): 8–11 ("The altar was an ironing board" quotation on 10); Paul Moore, "A Bishop Views the Underground Church," in *The Underground Church,* ed. Malcolm Boyd (Baltimore: Penguin, 1969), 221–37 ("presence of God" quotation on 231); and Moore, *Presences,* 176–80. For an understanding of the theological background that influenced Moore's ideas, see especially Colin W. Williams, *What in the World?* (New York: National Council of Churches, 1964), 29–47; Gayraud S. Wilmore, *The Secular Relevance of the Church* (Philadelphia: Westminster, 1962), 1–2, 19–31, 37–39; and Paul M. van Buren, *The Secular Meaning of the Gospel Based on an Analysis of Its Language* (New York: Macmillan, 1963), 190–200.

17. "Religion and Race: New Chairman," *LC* 148 (Mar. 1, 1964): 7; "Disability Forces Resignation," *LC* 148 (Apr. 12, 1964): 5; Arthur Lichtenberger, "And Make Thy Chosen People Joyful," *LC* 149 (Oct. 25, 1964): 10–12 (quotations on 10–11); and Margaret Frakes, "Episcopal Dichotomy," *CCe* 81 (1964): 1390–92.

18. William Stringfellow to Bill Spofford, from Aarhus, Denmark, Aug. 13, 1964, 1; Stringfellow, "A Statement of Conscience on Racism in the Presidential Campaign," Oct. 10–11, [1964], 1–2, in WSP, box 8; John B. Morris to Stringfellow, from Atlanta, Sept. 30, 1964, in ESCRU, folder 59:36; William Stringfellow, "God, Guilt and Goldwater," *CCe* 81 (1964): 1079–83; "Nomination of Barry Goldwater Stirs Comments by Churchmen," *W* 49 (Aug. 6, 1964): 3–5; "Christian Conscience and the Election," *W* 49 (Aug. 6, 1964): 7; "Candidate Denounced," *LC* 149 (Sept. 20, 1964): 4–5; Kater, "Episcopal Society," 67–70; and Weisbrot, *Freedom Bound,* 123–26.

19. John B. Morris to "Dear Friend," from Atlanta, Nov. 12, 1964; William Stringfellow to Vera Bollton, [from New York], Nov. 23, 1964, 1–2, in WSP, box 8; Morris to [Stringfellow], from Atlanta, Nov. 12, 1964, in WSP, box 9; *JGC* (1964): 144, 167, 372–73; Walter R. Hampshire, "Unofficial Action Causes Stir at General Convention," *CaR* 2 (Dec. 1964): 15–18; "National Council: In the Running," *LC* 144 (Apr. 22, 1962): 6; Fritzi Ryley, "Barry as a Christian," *LC* 149 (July 26, 1964): 4; "To Rectify a Charge," *LC* 149 (Nov. 8, 1964): 9; and Thomas LaBar, "General Convention 1964," *E* 129 (Dec. 1964): 4, 8.

20. Martin Luther King Jr., "Address . . . at the 61st General Convention," Oct. 12, 1964, 1–8 (quotation on 1), MM.

21. Grant M. Gallup, "Dr. King Addresses Deputies," *EN*, Nov. 8, 1964, 3; *JGC* (1964): x–xi (source of quotations); "P.B. Applauds King Award," *GCD,* Oct. 15, 1964, 1; "Christians Must Obey God, Not Man, Bishops Declare," *GCD,* Oct. 23, 1964, 1; "We Shall Overcome—Without the Lay Deputies?" *American Church News: General Convention Daily,* Oct. 21, 1964, 2; Walter R. Hampshire, "The General Convention on Race," *CaR* 2 (Dec. 1964): 19–21; "To Obey or Disobey," *LC* 149 (Nov. 1, 1964):

14; Robert L. Curry, "General Convention Warms Up after Getting a Slow Start," *W* 49 (Oct. 29, 1964): 3–6; "Convention Closes with Fireworks," *W* 49 (Oct. 29, 1964): 17–18; "Bishops Reaffirm Former Stand Upholding Civil Disobedience," *W* 49 (Nov. 5, 1964): 6; and Kean, "For Law and Integration," 1262. Thurgood Marshall was then a member of St. Philip's Church in Harlem. For an example of an Anglo-Catholic priest's application of clericalism and high-church ecclesiastical ideals to this question of civil disobedience, see also John R. Purnell, "Call for Civil and Social Disobedience," *LC* 46 (May 4, 1961): 9–12.

22. *JGC* (1964): 232–33, 359–60 (quotations on 233, 359); Hampshire, "General Convention on Race," 20–21; "Race Relations: No Barriers," *LC* 149 (Nov. 1, 1964): 14; "Conflict and Quiet Agents," *LC* 149 (Nov. 8, 1964): 10; Grant M. Gallup, "Racial Intermarriage Hearings Held: No Theological Objections Made," *American Church News: General Convention Daily,* Oct. 19, 1964, 4; "Theology Should End in Action, Bishops' Pastoral Stresses," *W* 49 (Nov. 5, 1964): 3–4; and [Barbara Kremer], *Agenda for Action* (New York: National Council, [1964]), n.p.

23. Author's interview of Paul M. Washington, Nov. 17, 1995, Philadelphia; Hines, "Reminiscences," 198, 226, 343–44; [John B. Morris], "Bishop Hines: A Godly Combination," *EN,* Nov. 8, 1964, 1; Diocese of Texas, *Journal of the Annual Council* (1957), 113–14, 228–30; (1958), 122–23, 301–2; (1959), 136–37, 252–54; (1960), 127, 235, 282; "John Hines of Texas Named P.B. to Succeed Bishop Lichtenberger," *GCD,* Oct. 19, 1964, 1; "The New P.B.—What Manner of Man?" *GCD,* Oct. 20, 1964, 1; "Texas— the Big Way," *LC* 136 (Feb. 9, 1958): 7; John Knoble, "For a Blunted Witness, Sharp Debate," *LC* 138 (Feb. 8, 1959): 13, 27; Clyde C. Hall, "Presiding Bishop: 'By Divine Providence . . . ,'" *LC* 150 (Feb. 14, 1965): 4–5; James L. Considine Jr., "Where There Is Smoke," *LC* 142 (Feb. 12, 1961): 7; "Texas: Arena of Life," *LC* 144 (Feb. 25, 1962): 9–10; "The New Presiding Bishop Looks at the Church," *E* 130 (Mar. 1965): 35; "Episcopalians: Holiness through Actions," *Time,* Feb. 5, 1965, 61 (Hines quotation); and Kesselus, *John E. Hines,* 156–85, 194–206.

24. *JGC* (1964): 393–94.

25. Boyd interview; Naomi M.L. Long and Malcolm Boyd, "Faculty Protest at a Church College," ESCRU: Special Report, July 1964, 1–7, MM; "Church Accuses a Negro College," *NYT,* July 8, 1964, 18 (source of quotation); and Naomi Long, "Away from the Hubbub," *LC* 146 (June 23, 1963): 5.

26. Daniel Corrigan to Malcolm Boyd, from New York, July 21, 1964; Boyd to Corrigan, [from Detroit], July 24, 1964, 1–2, in MBP, folder 17:1; Marvin C. Josephson, "Director's Report to the Board of Trustees . . . ," Dec. 7, 1964, 5, in ACIN, folder 61–1–17; and Tollie L. Caution et al. to John Morris, from New York, July 17, 1964, 1–2 (quotation on 2), in ESCRU, folder 3:15.

27. News release, "Episcopal Negro College Balks at Integration," July 8, 1964, in ESCRU, folder 12:30; [ESCRU], "Special Report: The Racial Status of Camps and Conference Centers in Southern Dioceses of the Episcopal Church," Apr. 1, 1964, 5 (quotation source), MM; and "ESCRU Special Report: Racial Status of Church Camps in the South," EN, May 17, 1964, 6.

28. [John B. Morris], "Faculty Protest at a Church College," EN, Aug. 6, 1964, 6.

29. Bowie interview; Paul Moore Jr., "A Total Ministry"(Feb. 4, 1966), 1 (quotation source), in Delta Ministry Papers, MSU, folder 8:82; "National Council, Protestant Episcopal Church: Projected Projects on Race, 1964," Feb. 17, 1964, 6, in ECBM, folder 159–1–29; "Delta and Metropolis," *LC* 149 (Dec. 20, 1964): 7; Bardwell L. Smith, "McComb—Divided down the Middle," *W* 50 (May 20, 1965): 9–12; and

Findlay, *Church People*, 111–68. For a full discussion of the Delta Ministry by a participant, see Bruce Hilton, *The Delta Ministry* (New York: Macmillan, 1969).

30. Pratt interview; Owen Brooks, interview, Aug. 18, 1978, in DAT, Tom Dent Mississippi Oral History Tapes; Braden, "A View from the Fringes," *Southern Exposure* 9 (spring 1981): 70–71; Branch, *Pillar of Fire*, 273; Dittmer, *Local People*, 230–32, 300–301, 336–37; Findlay, *Church People*, 86–87, 133 n. 12; and Adams, *James A. Dombrowski*, 254–55.

31. Bowie interview; Allin interview; John M. Allin to John B. Morris, from Jackson, Miss., July 16, 1964 (Allin quotation), in ESCRU, folder 29:15; Allin to Arthur Walmsley, from Jackson, Apr. 13, 1964, 1; David R. Hunter to Allin, from New York, Oct. 30, 1964, 1; Ross Flanagan, "A Report on Friends Visitation among the Burned Churches of Mississippi," Oct. 1964, 10; Allin to Hunter, from Jackson, Nov. 4, 1964, 1–2, in DCC, "Delta Ministry" folder; McKenna to the author, May 23, 1995; Mississippi, *Annual Council* (1965), 37–40; "Mississippi: Bishop Allin Speaks Plainly on Church, Race Relations," *C* 177 (Apr. 1963): 19–20; "Mississippi: Help to Reconstruct," *LC* 149 (Oct. 4, 1964): 15–16; "Mississippi: Pastoral Address," *LC* 150 (Feb. 21, 1965): 5–6; Allin, "Rebuilding Churches in Mississippi," *CaR* 2 (Dec. 1964): 5–7; "Reparation," *Church News: Episcopal Diocese of Mississippi* (Oct. 1964): 2; Malcolm Boyd, "Official Christian Leadership Not Doing Job in Mississippi," *W* 50 (Feb. 18, 1965): 4–5; "NCC Delta Ministry Workers Explain What It's About," *W* 50 (Mar. 4, 1965): 4–5; William J. Jacobs, "Notebook on Our Own Congo," *Ave Maria* 101 (Jan. 23, 1965): 8; "Churches: Beauty for Ashes," *Time*, Feb. 5, 1965, 61; Hilton, *Delta Ministry*, 165–77; Joel L. Alvis Jr., "Racial Turmoil and Religious Reaction: The Rt. Rev. John M. Allin," *HMPEC* 50 (1981): 83–96; Cunnigen, "Men and Women of Goodwill," 182–84; and Findlay, *Church People*, 143. Although Allin, as bishop coadjutor, would ordinarily have been the assistant to the diocesan bishop, Duncan Gray Sr., Gray was ill throughout this period; thus, responsibility for diocesan affairs belonged to Allin.

32. Arthur E. Walmsley to John M. Allin, from New York, Sept. 19, 1964, 1–2; Walmsley, memorandum to [Warren] Turner et al., from New York, Nov. 4, 1964; Policy and Strategy Committee, Division of Home Missions of the NCC, [Minutes], Nov. 9, 1964, 4, 7–9, 11, 17–18; Allin to David R. Hunter, from Jackson, Miss., Nov. 16, 1964, 1–2; Walmsley to Allin, from New York, Dec. 22, 1964, 1–4, in DCC, "Delta Ministry" folder; Peter Day, memorandum to Walmsley, from New York, Aug. 16, 1965, in DCC, "Commission on Delta Ministry (1965)" folder; Commission on the Delta Ministry, "Minutes of the Meeting," Apr. 2, 1965, 1; "About the Von Hoffman 'Interview,'" [Aug. 1965], 1–2, in DMR, box 1; Mississippi, *Annual Council* (1964), 22–23, 39–40; (1965), 34–35, 86, 116; (1967), 34–35; "The Episcopal Church and the National Council of Churches," *Church News: Episcopal Diocese of Mississippi* (May 1964): 5–6; "Question of NCCC Financial Support," *Church News: Episcopal Diocese of Mississippi* (Aug. 1964): 2; and Findlay, *Church People*, 143.

33. Almon R. Pepper, memorandum to "Bishops, CSR Chairmen and Executives," from New York, May 28, 1963; National Council, "Racial Appeal Facts," Jan. 7, 1964, in NCPC, "Race Relations: Church and Race Fund" folder; Joint Staff Committee on Race Relations, "Minutes," Jan. 8, 1964, 1–2, in ECBM, folder 159–1–29; NCEC, Dec. 10–12, 1963, 37–38; Feb. 18–20, 1964, 42–43, 108–9; "Bishop Warnecke Presents Report to House of Bishops," 16–20; "The 1964 Special Appeal," *CaR* 1 (Jan. 1964): 3–4; "Presiding Bishop Issues Special Appeal," *CaR* 1 (Jan. 1964): 5; "Statement of Policy with Regard to Race," *CaR* 1 (Jan. 1964): 11–16; "The Presiding Bishop

Calls for Aid," *LC* 148 (Feb. 9, 1964): 10; and Edward J. Mohr, "Money and What to Do with It Highlights Council Meeting," *W* 49 (Mar. 5, 1964): 5.

34. Bowie interview; Malcolm E. Peabody to John E. Hines, from Atlanta, Dec. 30, 1964, 1–2, in ESCRU, folder 3:17; Arthur E. Walmsley to William Stringfellow, from New York, Jan. 21, 1965, in WSP, box 9; John B. Morris to "Directors, Chapter Chairmen and Selected Key Members," from Atlanta, Jan. 8, 1965; Stringfellow to Hines, [from New York], Feb. 11, 1965, 2, in WSP, box 10; ECEC, Dec. 8–10, 1964, 84, 129; Feb. 16–18, 1965, 26–58; "Executive Council Retreats on Race," EN, Jan. 10, 1965, 1; Paul L. Montgomery, "Episcopal Clergy Curbed on Rights," *NYT*, Feb. 7, 1965, 49; "Episcopal Group Ends Rights Curb," *NYT*, Feb. 18, 1965, 26; Edward J. Mohr, "Executive Council Discusses Race behind Closed Doors," *W* 49 (Dec. 24, 1964): 3–4; Edward J. Mohr, "Executive Council Votes Funds for Race Projects of NCC," *W* 50 (Mar. 4, 1965): 3–4; "Executive Council Takes Significant Action," *W* 50 (Mar. 4, 1965): 7; "$100,000 Ain't Much," *W* 50 (Apr. 29, 1965): 7; "Executive Council: Special Order of Business," *LC* 150 (Feb. 21, 1965): 4; "Executive Council: Courtesy Policy," *LC* 150 (Feb. 28, 1965): 10–11; "The Church and Race: A Healthy Discussion," *E* 130 (Apr. 1965): 47; and advertisement in *E* 130 (May 1965): 5.

35. Gray interview; Moore interview; Daisuke Kitagawa, "On the Proposed Consultation on the Ministry in Areas of Acute Racial Tension," Dec. 22, 1962, 1–2, in ECBM, folder 159-1-29; Advisory Committee on Race Relations, "Minutes," Jan. 30–31, 1964, 2, 4, in CSR-85, folder 85-3-15; Officers of the National Council, memorandum to Jon Regier, from New York, Oct. 9, 1964, 1–2; Arthur Walmsley, memorandum to [Daniel] Corrigan, from New York, Jan. 14, 1965, 1–2: [Kitagawa] to Arthur Walmsley and Warren Turner, from Greenville, Miss., May 3, 1965; Patrick H. Sanders to John E. Hines, [from Greenville, Miss.], May 10, 1965; Kitagawa to Paul Moore, from New York, May 10, 1965; Kitagawa, "Report from a Tour in the Diocese of Mississippi, May 2–8, 1965," 1–4 (quotation on 3); Moore to Hines, from Washington, D.C., May 14, 1965, 1–2; Hines to Moore, from New York, May 17, 1965, in DCC, "Delta Ministry" folder; Daisuke Kitagawa, *Race Relations and Christian Mission* (New York: Friendship, 1964), 169–76, 188–90; Daisuke Kitagawa, *The Pastor and the Race Issue* (New York: Seabury, 1965), 58–74, 136–39; Duncan M. Gray Jr., "The Days Are Coming—A Sermon," in Boyd, *On the Battle Lines*, 109–14; Campbell, *Race and the Renewal of the Church*, 22–25, 42–47, 82–86; and Findlay, *Church People*, 142–47.

36. Moore, "A Bishop Views the Underground Church," 234 (quotation). For information on the backgrounds of Moore and Kitagawa, see Moore, *Presences*, 7–54; and Daisuke Kitagawa, *Issei and Nisei: The Internment Years* (New York: Seabury, 1967), 1–6, 167–71. During World War II Moore was severely wounded in combat at Guadalcanal; Kitagawa spent time in an internment camp for Japanese Americans.

37. Henri A. Stines, memorandum to "Key ESCRU Personnel and Other Concerned Churchmen," from Atlanta, Apr. 19, 1965; Stines to Albert R. Stuart, from Atlanta, Apr. 19, 1965, in ESCRU, folder 56:23; "Parish Seeks to Withdraw," EN, June 24, 1965, 2; Diocese of Georgia, *Journal of the Annual Convention* (1966), 34–35, 64–65; (1967), 95; "Georgia: Yes and No," *LC* 141 (Sept. 4, 1960): 7; "Georgia: Disassociation," *LC* 150 (May 9, 1965): 6; "Georgia: Status," *LC* 151 (Aug. 15, 1965): 7; "Canon Law and Discrimination," *E* 130 (June 1965): 49; "Savannah Parish Votes to Quit Church over Integration Canon," *W* 50 (May 6, 1965): 3–4; "Bishop Stuart Issues Statement Following Action of Parish," *W* 50 (May 27, 1965): 4–5; and "Secession in Savannah," *Time*, May 7, 1965, 70. By coincidence, Risley's predecessor at St. John's had been Charles Carpenter. "Bp. Carpenter Dies," *LC* 159 (July 27, 1969): 5.

38. Morris interview; Walmsley interview; "The Saga of Selma: A Tape Recording by ESCRU," Mar. 1965, MM; Morris to "All Bishops," from Atlanta, Mar. 27, 1965, in ESCRU, folder 3:24; James R. Gundrum to George M. Murray, [from Cedar Rapids, Iowa], Mar. 31, 1965, 1–3, in ESCRU, folder 47:36; Jonathan Myrick Daniels et al., "Statement," Apr. 29, 1965, in ESCRU, folder 56:26; Arthur E. Walmsley, memorandum to [John E. Hines, from New York], Mar. 17, 1965, 1–5, in DCC, "Selma (File Prepared for P.B.)" folder; C.C.J. Carpenter, undated statement, [Mar. 1965], in CCJC, folder 241.2.157.15.29 ("St. Paul's, Selma" file); Vernon A. Jones to Carpenter, from Tuskegee, Ala., Mar. 28, 1965 (Jones quotation), in CCJC, folder 241.1.132.8.67 ("St. Andrew's, Tuskegee" file); [Morris], "The Siege of Selma," EN, Mar. 14, 1965, 5; "Selma," LC 150 (Mar. 21, 1965): 8; Clyde Hall, "Engagement in Washington," LC 150 (Mar. 21, 1965): 8–9; "Alabama: 'Terrible Events,'" LC 150 (Mar. 28, 1965): 6; "Episcopal Bishop Calls Rights March 'Foolish,'" NYT, Mar. 20, 1965, 13 (Carpenter quotation); "500 Episcopal Clergymen Took Part in Alabama Drive," NYT, Mar. 29, 1965, 36; "Wolf or Shepherd," Newsweek, Apr. 12, 1965, 66–67; Allen, This Time, This Place, 84–85; and Morris, "ESCRU," 20–21. For further discussion of the Selma-Montgomery March and its background, see [Kenneth L. Woodward], "Selma, Civil Rights, and the Church Militant," Newsweek, Mar. 29, 1965, 75–78; Nan Robertson, "Clergymen in Capital to Hold White House Rally over Selma," NYT, Mar. 12, 1965, 18; Friedland, Lift Up Your Voice, 113–39; Garrow, Bearing the Cross, 369–413; and Fairclough, To Redeem the Soul of America, 225–51.

39. Carroll E. Simcox, "Selma Episcopalians Speak: An Editorial Report," LC 150 (June 27, 1965): 7, 11–12 (quotation on 7).

40. "Saga of Selma" tape.

41. Morris interview; Gribbin interview; author's interview of G.H. (Jack) Woodard, Dec. 7, 1995, Springfield, Va.; Arthur E. Walmsley, memorandum to [John E. Hines, from New York], Mar. 18, 1965, 1–2; [Walmsley], "Notes on Service of Witness Planned by ESCRU for Saturday, Mar. 20," Mar. 18, 1965; [Walmsley], "Resume of Conversation with the Rev. Henri Stines (ESCRU)," Mar. 18, 1965; Walmsley, memorandum to [Hines, from New York], Mar. 22, 1965, 1–2; Mar. 23, 1965, in DCC, "Selma (File Prepared for P.B.)" folder; C.K. [Myers], telegram to Charles C.J. Carpenter, from Detroit, Mar. 18, 1965; Malcolm E. Peabody Jr. to Carpenter, from Atlanta, Mar. 18, 1965, 1–2; Carpenter to Myers, from Birmingham, Ala., Mar. 19, 1965; Mar. 24, 1965, 1–3; Carpenter to [Richard S.] Emrich, from Birmingham, Mar. 25, 1965, in CCJC, folder 241.2.157.15.28 ("St. Paul's, Selma" file); [Ralph E. Smeltzer], "Interview with Rev. Frank T. Mathews," Nov. 27, 1963; [Smeltzer], "Mathews Interview," Apr. 2, 1965, in Ralph E. Smeltzer Manuscript Notes and Correspondence (microfilm), Harvard Univ. Library, Cambridge, Mass.; John B. Morris to David King, from Atlanta, Sept. 10, 1965, 1–2, in ESCRU, folder 30:27; "Bishops: Esse or Bene Esse?" EN, Jan. 10, 1965, 7; "St. Paul's, Selma: Seating from the Rear," EN, June 24, 1965, 1; "Eucharist Celebrated on Church Sidewalk in Selma," CIM 5 (spring 1965): 24 (source of quotation); "Letter to a Bishop," LC 150 (Apr. 11, 1965): 6; Edward G. McGrath, "Selma Church Bars Malcolm Peabody, Negroes," Boston Globe, Mar. 14, 1965, 1–2; Roy Reed, "Selma Protestant Church Integrated for First Time," NYT, Mar. 29, 1965, 1, 29; Walter C. Whitaker, History of the Protestant Episcopal Church in Alabama, 1763–1891 (Birmingham, Ala.: Roberts and Son, 1898), 80–83; Charles V. Willie, Church Action in the World: Studies in Sociology and Religion (New York: Morehouse-Barlow, 1969), 101–9; and Bass, "Not Time Yet," 254–55.

42. "Churchmen in Selma," EN, Apr. 4, 1965, 1; John B. Tillson, "Thirty Thousand in Montgomery," EN, Apr. 4, 1965, 41–43; Robert Healy, "Wallace Silent as

Marchers Enter City," *Boston Globe,* Mar. 25, 1965, 1–2; F. Goldthwaite Sherrill, "I've Seen Alabama—It's True," *Boston Globe,* Mar. 28, 1965, 1, 3, courtesy of F. Goldthwaite Sherrill, Center Harbor, N.H.; Martin Luther King Jr., "Our God Is Marching On!" in King, *Testament of Hope,* 227–30 (quotations on 228); Weisbrot, *Freedom Bound,* 143–53; and Patterson, *Grand Expectations,* 579–84.

43. Author's interview of Roberta C. Walmsley, Nov. 3, 1994, Deering, N.H.; John Morris, "The Role of the Church in Social Change," [May 1965], 1–15, MM; [Morris], "The Frontier beyond Civil Rights: Danger and Opportunity," EN, Mar. 14, 1965, 1–2 (Morris quotation on 2); "Selma and Montgomery—The Cathedral Was There," *Cathedral Age* 40 (summer 1965): 12–13, 39 (Workman quotation on 13); William Stringfellow, "Moved Not by Wrath but Despair," *C* 179 (July 1965): 10–11; William Stringfellow, "The Case against Christendom and the Case against Pierre Berton," in *The Restless Church: A Response to the Comfortable Pew,* ed. William Kilbourn (Toronto: McClelland and Stewart, 1966), 15–18; and [Woodward], "Selma, Civil Rights," 75, 78.

44. Woodard interview; Walmsley interview; Charles C.J. Carpenter to G.H. (Jack) Woodard, from Birmingham, Ala., Mar. 24, 1965; Carpenter to Almon R. Pepper, from Birmingham, Mar. 25, 1965, 1–2, in CCJC, folder 241.2.157.15.28 ("St. Paul's, Selma" file); Woodard to Carpenter, from New York, Apr. 2, 1965; [George M. Murray] to Richard S. Emrich, from Birmingham, May 24, 1965, 1–2, in CCJC, folder 241.2.157.15.29 ("St. Paul's, Selma" file); [John E. Hines], memorandum to the Executive Council, [from New York, Mar. 1965], 1–3, in ECBM, folder 159–1–29; Warren H. Turner Jr., memorandum to "All Executive Council Personnel," [from New York], Apr. 5, 1965, [2], in JHEP, "Executive/National Council" folder; Perry Laukhuff to Arthur E. Walmsley, from Norwalk, Conn., Mar. 12, 1965, in DCC, "Selma, Alabama—General" folder; Daniel Corrigan and Almon R. Pepper, memorandum to [Hines, from New York], Mar. 31, 1965, 1–3; George Lee to Carpenter, from New York, Apr. 2, 1965; Carpenter to "Members of the Executive Council," from Birmingham, May 13, 1965, 1–2, in DCC, "Selma (Prepared for P.B.)" folder; John B. Morris to R. Emmett Gribbin Jr., from Atlanta, Dec. 20, 1965, in ESCRU, folder 30:23; ECEC, May 18–20, 1965, 3; "Church 'Breakthrough' at Selma," *E* 130 (May 1965): 40; Woodard, "A Walk in Montgomery: Questions for the Church," *CIM* 5 (spring 1965): 20–23; "Breaking the Ties," *LC* 150 (June 6, 1965): 7; and Charles W. Eagles, *Outside Agitator: Jon Daniels and the Civil Rights Movement in Alabama* (Chapel Hill: Univ. of North Carolina Press, 1993), 36–37, 44–51.

45. Author's interview of Judith E. Upham, Dec. 6, 1995, Fort Washington, Md.; Jonathan Myrick Daniels and Judith Elizabeth Upham to C.C.J. Carpenter, from Selma, Ala., Apr. 21, 1965, 1–2, in WSP, box 10; Arthur E. Walmsley to Daniels, from New York, Apr. 23, 1965, in Jonathan M. Daniels Papers, Archives of the Diocese of Connecticut, Hartford; "ESCRU in Selma: A Continued Ministry of Presence," EN, June 24, 1965, 2; Jonathan M. Daniels and Judith E. Upham, "Report from Selma—Apr. 1965," *E.T.S. Journal* 10 (supplement, Jan. 1966): 2–11; Judith E. Upham, "Jonathan Daniels—A Recollection," *E.T.S. Journal* 10 (supplement, Jan. 1966): 15–22; Gloria House Manana, "Witness to Murder," *W* 77 (Jan.–Feb. 1994): 26–27; Sheyann Webb and Rachel West Nelson, *Selma, Lord, Selma: Girlhood Memories of the Civil-Rights Days* (University: Univ. of Alabama Press, 1980), 51–53, 132–33; William J. Schneider, *American Martyr: The Jon Daniels Story* (1967; reprint, Harrisburg, Pa.: Morehouse, 1992), 74–77 (quotations on 77); Bass, "Not Time Yet," 255–57; and Eagles, *Outside Agitator,* 38–59.

46. Author's telephone interview of Marc R. Oliver, Dec. 2, 1995, Ketchum, Idaho;

author's interview of Edward W. Rodman, May 10, 1995, Boston; Upham interview; John E. Hines, "Statement . . . on the Acquittal of Thomas Coleman in Hayneville, Alabama," Oct. 4, 1965, 2, in DCC; Roy Reed, "White Seminarian Slain in Alabama: Deputy Is Charged," *NYT,* Aug. 21, 1965, 1; "Hayneville Verdict Assailed," *LC* 151 (Oct. 17, 1965): 5–6; John B. Coburn, *The Jonathan Daniels Story: A Modern-Day Martyrdom* ([Cambridge, Mass.]: Cowley, [1992]), audio tape; Schneider, *American Martyr,* 38–50, 84–91, 104–11; and Eagles, *Outside Agitator,* 79–87, 163–80, 224–49. Thirty years later, Ruby Sales enrolled as a student at Daniels's seminary in order "to complete the process" of studying for the priesthood that he had begun but never finished. Bob Hohler, "Seminary Student Honors '65 Sacrifice," *Boston Globe,* Aug. 24, 1997, A1, A19.

47. Morris interview; William Stringfellow, "A Plenary Requiem," 6–7 (Stringfellow quotation on 7), in WSP, box 9; Upham, "Jonathan Daniels—A Recollection," 22 (source of Upham quotation); "Slain Seminarian Lauded for Work," *NYT,* Aug. 23, 1965, 34; "Jonathan Daniels: Services in Keene," *LC* 151 (Sept. 5, 1965): 4–5; Carroll E. Simcox, "Alabama: Dean's Visit," *LC* 151 (Sept. 12, 1965): 10; Malcolm Boyd, *As I Live and Breathe: Stages of an Autobiography* (New York: Random House, 1969), 155–56 (Carmichael quotation on 156); Schneider, *American Martyr,* 110 (source of Daniels quotation); and Eagles, *Outside Agitator,* 127–30, 182–84.

48. C.C.J. Carpenter and George M. Murray, "Statement," *Bulletin* 1 (Oct. 1965), in CCJC, folder 241.1.119.8.30 ("St. Paul's, Selma—Racial Problems" file); Alabama, *Annual Convention* (1966), 2 (source of Carpenter quotation); George Murray, "Ministry of Reconciliation," *E.T.S. Journal* 10 (supplement, Jan. 1966): 26–35 (Murray quotations on 34); and author's conversation with Guy F. Lytle, Mar. 12, 1999, Sewanee, Tenn.

## 7. Black Power and the Urban Crisis in the North

1. Kenneth B. Clark, "'The Wonder Is There Have Been So Few Riots,'" *NYT Magazine,* Sept. 5, 1965, 38, 48 (quotation on 38).

2. Kenneth B. Clark, "The New Negro in the North," in *The New Negro,* ed. Mathew H. Ahmann (Notre Dame, Ind.: Fides, 1961), 36–37; Kenneth B. Clark, "Introduction: The Dilemma of Power," in *The Negro American,* ed. Talcott Parsons and Kenneth B. Clark (Boston: Beacon, 1967), xi–xviii; "Liberalism and the Negro: A Round-Table Discussion," *Commentary* 37 (Mar. 1964): 39; Vincent Harding, "Other Roads from Selma," *CCe* 82 (1965): 580–81; and Weisbrot, *Freedom Bound,* 169 (source of quotation). For further background on the period after the signing of the 1965 Voting Rights Act, see also Weisbrot, *Freedom Bound,* 154–68; Jackson, *Gunnar Myrdal,* 302–11; and Patterson, *Grand Expectations,* 648–55.

3. Michael Harrington, *The Other America: Poverty in the United States* (New York: Macmillan, 1962), 9–24, 63–82; Arthur E. Walmsley, "Why the Controversy about Mr. Moynihan's Paper?" *Motive* 26 (Apr. 1966): 25–27 (Walmsley quotation on 27); Thomas F. Pettigrew, *A Profile of the Negro American* (Princeton, N.J.: Van Nostrand, 1964); 197–98; Patterson, *Grand Expectations,* 533–42; and Steigerwald, *Sixties and the End of Modern America,* 200–206.

4. [Daniel Patrick Moynihan], *The Negro Family: The Case for National Action* ([Washington, D.C.]: Office of Policy Planning and Research, U.S. Department of Labor, 1965), 5–14, 29–31, 47–48 (quotation on 30).

5. "The Negro Family: Visceral Reaction," *Newsweek,* Dec. 6, 1965, 38–40; "The

Moynihan Report," *CCe* 82 (1965): 1531–32; Lee Rainwater and William L. Yancey, *The Moynihan Report and the Politics of Controversy* (Cambridge, Mass.: MIT Press, 1967), 1–8, 25–32; Albert Murray, *The Omni-Americans: New Perspectives on Black Experience and American Culture* (New York: Outerbridge and Dienstfrey, 1970), 46–52; Willie, *Church Action in the World,* 125–27; Southern, *Gunnar Myrdal,* 255, 266–68; Nicholas Lemann, *The Promised Land: The Great Black Migration and How It Changed America* (New York: Knopf, 1991), 170–76 (quotation on 176); and Weisbrot, *Freedom Bound,* 161–70, 245–46.

6. Elkins, *Slavery,* 81–139.

7. Kenneth B. Clark, *Dark Ghetto: Dilemmas of Social Power,* 2d ed. (1965; reprint, Hanover, N.H.: Wesleyan Univ. Press, 1989), 70–110 (quotations on 70, 81).

8. "Light on the Ghetto," *Newsweek,* May 31, 1965, 78, 81; "The Negro Family," 40 (Clark quotation); Ben Keppel, *The Work of Democracy: Ralph Bunche, Kenneth B. Clark, Lorraine Hansberry, and the Cultural Politics of Race* (Cambridge, Mass.: Harvard Univ. Press, 1995), 151–67; and Southern, *Gunnar Myrdal,* 215–16, 267–68.

9. Kwame Ture [Stokely Carmichael] and Charles V. Hamilton, *Black Power: The Politics of Liberation in America* (1967; reprint, New York: Vintage, 1992), 3–56 (quotation on 37); Weisbrot, *Freedom Bound,* 193–206; Carson, *In Struggle,* 191–228; and Patterson, *Grand Expectations,* 655–59.

10. Quinland Gordon, "Position Paper on Black Power," [Dec. 1966], 3–4, in NCPC, "Race Relations: Conferences and Meetings" folder; ECEC, Oct. 4–6, 1966, 23–27, 43–44; "'Black Power': Statement by National Committee of Negro Churchmen," *NYT,* July 31, 1966, sec. 4, p. 5; Alex Poinsett, "The Black Revolt in White Churches," *Ebony,* Sept. 1968, 63–68; Nathan Wright Jr., *Black Power and Urban Unrest: Creative Possibilities* (New York: Hawthorn, 1967), 3–9; Harold Cruse, *The Crisis of the Negro Intellectual* (New York: Morrow, 1967), 12, 85, 90–91, 111; Gayraud S. Wilmore, *Black Religion and Black Radicalism: An Interpretation of the Religious History of Afro-American People,* 2d ed. (Maryknoll, N.Y.: Orbis, 1983), 195–98; Findlay, *Church People,* 183–86; and Paris, *Social Teaching,* 6–10, 74–80, 86–88, 121–23. Besides Gordon, who served on the Division of Christian Citizenship staff, the Episcopalians who signed the NCBC statement were John Burgess, suffragan bishop of Massachusetts; Robert E. Hood, rector of St. Augustine's Church, Gary, Ind.; Kenneth Hughes, rector of St. Bartholomew's Church, Cambridge, Mass.; Leon Modeste, a staff member of the Division of Community Services of the Executive Council; David Nickerson, an ESCRU staff member; Henri Stines, rector of the Church of the Atonement, Washington, D.C.; Paul M. Washington, rector of the Church of the Advocate, Philadelphia; and Nathan Wright Jr., director of the Department of Urban Work of the diocese of Newark.

11. Author's interview of John M. Burgess, June 7, 1995, Vineyard Haven, Mass.; [Tollie L. Caution], "Statistics on Negro Work: 1965" in ECBM, folder 159–1–26; RMC, Mar. 3–4, 1959, 5–6; Nov. 4–5, 1959, 5–6; Kenneth Clark, "De Facto Segregation (Transcript of a Speech) . . . Apr. 1965," 12–13, manuscript in the possession of Kenneth Clark; Clark, *Dark Ghetto,* 174–82; "The Negro in the Episcopal Church," *Ebony,* Nov. 1958, 72–78; Thomas LaBar and Mary S. Wright, "The New Citizen: A Progress Report on the Negro and the Episcopal Church," *E* 127 (Mar. 1962): 21, 26; and Lewis, *Yet with a Steady Beat,* 148–52.

12. Author's interview of Jesse F. Anderson Jr., Oct. 7, 1996, Philadelphia; Neil interview; Breeden interview; Washington interview; "A Letter to the Black Episcopal Churches from the Union of Black Clergy and Laymen, . . . Nov. 16, 1968," in ESCRU, folder 49:15; James P. Breeden to Philip F. McNairy, from New York, Mar. 2,

1967, 1–3, in PB-113, folder 113–5–12; Quintin E. Primo Jr. and Jesse F. Anderson Sr., "A Letter to the Black Episcopal Churches . . . Jan. 15, 1969," in MSU, Delta Ministry Papers, folder 11:28; "Episcopal Group Accuses Its Church of Denying Equal Opportunities to Negro Clerics," *NYT,* Sept. 11, 1967, 41; Henry I. Louttit, "Are 'Negro Churches' Necessary?" letter in *LC* 149 (Nov. 29, 1964): 3, 28; "Church Charged with Discrimination," *LC* 155 (Sept. 24, 1967): 8; "Canon Law and Discrimination: Entrance," *E* 130 (June 1965): 49; Johnson, "Myths about Integration," 8–10; Thomas S. Logan, letter in "Backfire," *W* 49 (July 23, 1964): 15; Moore, *People on Second Street,* 214–18; Paris, *Social Teaching,* 42; and Steigerwald, *Sixties and the End of Modern America,* 190–93. For examples of the "integration" of black parishes into white parishes and the replacing of black leaders with white clergy during this period, see "Texas: Open Rectory," *LC* 130 (Jan. 30, 1955): 20; "Negro Mission Unites with Parent Church in Holyoke, Mass.," *LC* 132 (Jan. 15, 1956): 12; Untitled paragraph ("Segregated worship of white and Negro Episcopalians . . ."), *Forth* 121 (June 1956): 7; "Phillips in Charge of Negro Church," *W* 45 (Dec. 18, 1958): 16; "White Rector for Negro Parish," *W* 46 (May 28, 1959): 17; "Negro Congregation Is Merged," *W* 46 (Dec. 31, 1959): 15; and "Integration in Philadelphia," *W* 49 (Apr. 16, 1964): 6.

13. Author's interview of Junius F. Carter Jr., Oct. 17, 1996, Edison, N.J.; EB, Feb. 2–4, 1964, 3; "Questions and Answers on the Whitsunday Witness," EN, Mar. 1, 1964, 4; [John B. Morris], "Negro Neutrality," EN, Mar. 1, 1964, 13; [Henri A. Stines], "The Need for an ESCRU Group in Every Diocese," EN, Jan. 10, 1965, 3; George Dugan, "White Episcopalians Urged to Join Negro Parishes," *NYT,* Feb. 9, 1964, 53; "Parish-Hopping," *LC* 148 (Mar. 1, 1964): 15; "A Call to Witness: Whitsunday, 1964," advertisement in *LC* 148 (May 3, 1964): 19 (source of quotation); "'Fair Employment' in the Church," *LC* 152 (Apr. 24, 1966): 21; Joseph Nicholson, *What Is Happening to the Negro in the Protestant Episcopal Church?* [n.p.: Ad Hoc Clergy Committee, 1968], 1–8, 25–28; and Lewis, *Yet with a Steady Beat,* 151–53. For an analysis of the deleterious effects of interracial thinking on black clergy and laity in the Roman Catholic Church in the United States, see McGreevy, *Parish Boundaries,* 41–47; and Southern, *John LaFarge,* 132–39.

14. Joint Committee on Race, "Report," Nov. 5, 1962, 2–7, 15–16; "Report of Joint Race Relations Committee to the Joint Program Planning Committee," Jan. 7, 1963, 1–4, in ECBM, folder 159–1–29; Tollie L. Caution, "Memorandum to the Presiding Bishop et al.," [from New York], Feb. 28, 1966, in ECBM, folder 159–1–13; "Church's Stand on Segregation Implemented by Bishops," *W* 50 (Sept. 30, 1965): 5; Henry L. McCorkle, "House of Bishops, 1965," *E* 130 (Nov. 1965): 26–29; and Lewis, *Yet with a Steady Beat,* 152–53.

15. Author's interview of Austin R. Cooper, Oct. 2, 1996, Cleveland, Ohio; John Burgess interview; "Second Meeting of Negro Clergy with the Presiding Bishop," June 27, 1967, 4–6, in DCC, "Negro Clergy—General" folder; "A Declaration by Priests who are Negroes," *W* 52 (Feb. 23, 1967): 11–13; and Nicholson, *What Is Happening to the Negro,* 22–24.

16. Author's interview of D. Barry Menuez, Sept. 25, 1995, Poughkeepsie, N.Y.; Morton interview; Woodard interview; author's interview of Robert W. Castle Jr., Sept. 22, 1995, New York; D. Barry Menuez, "Empowerment of the Poor and Powerless as Church Mission," B.D. thesis, Divinity School of the Univ. of Chicago, 1971, 3–4, in AEC, D. Barry Menuez Papers, accession record 89.32; NCEC, Feb. 19–21, 1963, 191–92; *JGC* (1961): 545–50; "They Preach What They Practice," *E* 127 (Oct. 1962): 46–52; "Joint Urban Program: What It Is, What It Does, How It Began," *CIM* 1 (spring 1964): 4–6; "Urban Pilot Diocese Program," *CIM* 3 (fall 1964): 3–5; Daisuke Kitagawa,

untitled editorial in *CIM* 4 (winter 1964): 2 (source of quotation); "A Capsule History of the Church's Joint Urban Program," *CIM* 14 (fall 1967): 4–5; "Protestants: On the Battle Line," *Time* Apr. 5, 1963, 52–53; and John E. Hines, "The Indispensable Dialogue," in *New Occasions: Review of a Decade of Experimentation* (New York: [Executive Council, 1970]), 65–67.

17. Walmsley interview; Morton interview; Menuez interview; Carter interview; Leon E. Modeste, "Mission: Empowerment," 9–12, in GCSP, folder 87–1–6; "The Pilot Dioceses," *CIM* 7 (fall 1965): 16–18; John Heuss, "Opportunity on the Doorstep," *LC* 147 (Nov. 10, 1963): 12–13; M. Moran Weston, "The Crisis—in Black and White," *LC* 150 (May 23, 1965): 14–16; Allen, *This Time, This Place,* 41–42; and Steigerwald, *Sixties and the End of Modern America,* 6–15.

18. Gibson Winter, "The New Christendom in the Metropolis," *CaC* 22 (1962–63): 206–11 (quotation on 207); Winter, *The New Creation as Metropolis* (New York: Macmillan, 1963), 54–61; and Winter, "Theology of the Future," *CIM* 8 (winter 1966): 5–7.

19. James P. Morton, "The Church of the Future," *CIM* 8 (winter 1966): 8–12 (quotation on 8).

20. Morton interview; Woodard interview; "Beyond Cooperation," *LC* 147 (Sept. 22, 1963): 9–10; "Morton Succeeds Myers," *LC* 149 (Aug. 16, 1964): 4; C. Kilmer Myers, "Episcopalians: Muddling Through vs. Creative Outreach," *CCe* 80 (1963): 1459–62; C. Kilmer Myers, "To Go Where the Action Is . . .," *LC* 148 (May 24, 1964): 13–14; C. Kilmer Myers, "At the Core of the City," in Boyd, *On the Battle Lines,* 27–36; [Kenneth R.] Clark, letter in *CIM* 10 (summer 1966): 13–14; Peter L. Berger, *The Noise of Solemn Assemblies: Christian Commitment and the Religious Establishment in America* (Garden City, N.Y.: Doubleday, 1961), 157–71; and Hudnut-Beumler, *Looking for God in the Suburbs,* 163–64.

21. Author's interview of Franklin D. Turner, Nov. 20, 1995, Philadelphia; Woodard interview; Esther Burgess interview; W.E.B. Du Bois, *The Philadelphia Negro: A Social Study* (1899; reprint, Philadelphia: Univ. of Pennsylvania Press, 1996), 7, 310 (quotation on 310); E. Franklin Frazier, *The Negro Church in America* (New York: Schocken, 1963), 51–52, 76–79; E. Franklin Frazier, *The Negro Family in the United States* (Chicago: Univ. of Chicago Press, 1939), 265–67, 296, 393–94, 428, 436; E. Franklin Frazier, *Black Bourgeoisie* (1957; reprint, New York: Free Press, 1997), 112–19; Myrdal, *American Dilemma,* 182–97; Drake and Cayton, *Black Metropolis,* 73–75, 495–97, 500–506, 537, 558–63; Murray, *Omni-Americans,* 59–68, 127–42; Willard B. Gatewood, *Aristocrats of Color: The Black Elite, 1880–1920* (Bloomington: Indiana Univ. Press, 1990), 276–77, 341–48; Gaines, *Uplifting the Race,* 158–66; and Lewis, *Yet with a Steady Beat,* 3–4.

22. [John B. Morris], "Whew!" EN, June 24, 1965, 4.

23. John Burgess interview; McRae Werth, "Background Paper—1st Annual Meeting of ESCRU," [(1961), 5–7], MM; John Burgess, "The Role of ESCRU in the Life of the Church," June 22, 1962, 2–3, MM; Burgess to J.W. Nicholson, from Boston, Mar. 2, 1964, 1–2, MM; John B. Morris to Burgess, from Atlanta, Mar. 9, 1964, MM; John B. Morris, "Power: Black and White—Some Reflections," [1966], 1 (source of quotation), MM; Cornelius C. Tarplee to Morris, from New York, Mar. 8, 1966, in ESCRU, folder 32:7; EB, May 31, 1968, 4; John B. Morris, "The Way Ahead?" EN, Dec. 26, 1966, [2]; John B. Morris, book review in *Virginia Seminary Journal* 20 (Mar. 1968): 41; "ESCRU: 'Black Power,'" *LC* 153 (Aug. 14, 1966): 5; Lee A. Belford, "Black Power: A Few Questions," W 52 (Feb. 23, 1967): 8–9; Kater, "Episcopal Society," 107–9, 208–9; and Gloster, "Critical Examination," 42–43, 53–54.

24. Morris interview; Peabody interview; Penfield interview; EB, Nov. 13, 1966, 1–2; Jan. 6–7, 1967, 2–3; John Morris to "Directors and Chapter Chairmen," from Atlanta, Nov. 16, 1966, 2, MM; John B. Morris, "Responsible Militancy and the Way Ahead—Part II," Dec. 6, 1966, 1–8 (Morris quotation on 3), MM; Morris to Carl Sayers, from Atlanta, Feb. 6, 1967, in ESCRU, folder 32:26; [Albert R. Dreisbach Jr.] to Robert E. Hood, from Atlanta, [1967] (source of Dreisbach quotation), in ESCRU, folder 32:17; Jesse F. Anderson to Dreisbach, from Philadelphia, Oct. 16, 1967, in ESCRU, folder 69:33; Judy [Upham] to Francis [Walter, from Cambridge, Mass.], Nov. 16, 1966, 1–2 (Upham quotation on 2), in SIP, folder 1044.2.11 ("Walter House, O–Z, 1966" file); "Leave of Absence for Executive Director," EN, Mar. 19, 1967, 1; [John B. Morris], "Reflections from One Taking Leave," EN, Mar. 19, 1967, 5; and Kater, "Episcopal Society," 138–40.

25. "You Can't Run Away," Newsweek, July 31, 1967, 17–19 (quotation on 17); "Battlefield, U.S.A.," Newsweek, Aug. 7, 1967, cover; "An American Tragedy, 1967—Detroit," Newsweek, Aug. 7, 1967, 18–26; "Cities: The Fire This Time," Time, Aug. 4, 1967, 13–18; Weisbrot, Freedom Bound, 262–65; and Patterson, Grand Expectations, 662–63.

26. Peabody interview; Morris interview; Walmsley interview; Malcolm E. Peabody Jr. to John Morris, from Cambridge, Mass., May 4, 1965, in WSP, box 10; Peabody to Morris, [from Chestnut Hill, Mass.], Aug. 30, 1967, 1–2, MM; [Malcolm E. Peabody Jr.], "ESCRU: Role in the Years Ahead," [1967], 3–6 (Peabody quotation on 3), MM; John Morris to Peabody, from Atlanta, Sept. 7, 1967, 1–4 (Morris quotation on 3), MM; and "ESCRU at the Crossroads," CCe 84 (1967): 1181.

27. Morris interview; John B. Morris to Randolph R. Claiborne, from Atlanta, Mar. 3, 1967, MM, "Correspondence re: licensing" folder; Morris to Peabody, Sept. 7, 1967, 4, MM; Patsy and John Morris, "Epiphany and New Year's Greetings," Jan. 6, 1968, MM; Morris to Arthur E. Walmsley, [from Atlanta], Feb. 19, 1968, 1–4 (quotation on 1), MM; EB, Sept. 17, 1967, 1–2; Nov. 10–11, 1967, 1–2; "Anderson Is New President," EN, Oct. 22, 1967, 1; "Board Accepts Morris Resignation," EN, Oct. 22, 1967, 1; "Atlanta: Clergy in Politics," LC 157 (Sept. 15, 1968): 11, 30; and Kater, "Episcopal Society," 134–37, 144–47.

28. Neil Tarplee, memorandum to Arthur Walmsley and [Quinland] Gordon, [from New York], Sept. 19, 1966, 1, in DCC, "Church and Race Fund Appeal" folder; ECEC, Dec. 14–16, 1965, 39; Feb. 8–10, 1966, 36, 40, 44, 101–4; Dec. 14–16, 1966, 29–33, 133a–36; Jo-Ann Price, "Endorsement of Guidelines," LC 152 (Feb. 27, 1966): 5; "Financial Crisis," LC 154 (Jan. 1, 1967): 4; and "Executive Council: What Is Voluntary?" E 132 (Feb. 1967): 56.

29. James McBride Dabbs, "Episcopalians Consider Megabagdad," CCe 81 (1964): 303; John E. Hines, "The Church's Mission," CIM 12 (spring 1967): 1, 41 (quotations on 41); E. John Mohr, "Big Problems Face the Church, Bishop Hines Tells Council," W 51 (Oct. 20, 1966): 3–4; John E. Hines, "The Right of the Poor to Power," W 52 (Sept. 14, 1967): 9; Kesselus, John E. Hines, 61–63; and Holmes, Brief History, 130, 150.

30. Hines interview.

31. Modeste, "Mission: Empowerment," 15–17 (quotation on 15).

32. Woodard interview; Hines, "Reminiscences," 369–73 (Hines quotations on 372–73); Leon E. Modeste, "Black Power . . . An Idea Whose Day Has Come," 1–2, in NCPC, "Race Relations: Conferences and Meetings" folder; Modeste, interview in Anniversary Booklet: A Tribute to John Elbridge Hines on the Fiftieth Anniversary of His Ordination to the Priesthood [Newark, N.J.: Diocese of Newark, 1984], n.p.; Robert B.

Semple Jr., "Urban Coalition Urges U.S. Spur Jobs for Million," *NYT,* Aug. 25, 1967, 1, 20; "Urban Coalition Meets," *LC* 155 (Sept. 10, 1967): 6; and Hines, "Right of the Poor," 9–11. In this section I have relied on the chronology of events provided in Kesselus, *John E. Hines,* 240–71.

33. Author's interview of Mary H. Miller, Dec. 4, 1995, Washington, D.C.; author's interview of Charles M. Crump, Aug. 23, 1995, Memphis, Tenn.; Stevens interview; "The First Five Years: A History of the General Convention Special Program," 1972, 23–28, in GCSP, folder 87–1–1; "Advisory Committee to the Presiding Bishop on Cities," Aug. 23, 1967, in PB-113, folder 113–3–1; "Advisory Committee to the Presiding Bishop on Cities," Aug. 29, 1967, 1–8; "Panel of Advice," Aug. 30, 1967, 1–5 ("without strings" quotation on 2), in DCC; Arthur E. Walmsley to the author, from Hillsboro, N.H., Nov. 29, 1996, 2; Modeste, "Mission: Empowerment," 17–19; Hines, "Reminiscences," 369–76; Sterling Tucker, *Beyond the Burning: Life and Death of the Ghetto* (New York: Association, 1968), 12, 147–51 (Tucker quotation on 148); and Lyle E. Schaller, *The Churches' War on Poverty* (Nashville, Tenn.: Abingdon, 1967), 129–32.

34. Menuez interview; Stevens interview; Crump interview; Warren H. Turner Jr., memoranda to [John E. Hines], Aug. 12, 1967, in CSR-31, folder 31–5–6; Charles M. Crump to Turner, [from Memphis, Tenn.], Sept. 1, 1967, 1–2, in CMCP, folder 227–4–31; Clifford P. Morehouse to Hines, from New York, Sept. 5, 1967, 1–2, in DCC; Executive Council of the Episcopal Church, "The $9,000,000 Misunderstanding," Apr. 20, 1970, in GCSP, folder 87–4–19; Menuez, "Empowerment of the Poor and Powerless," 23, 44–45; ECEC, Sept. 15, 1967, 4–7, 8–11, 15–16 (quotation on 6); "Episcopal Council Backs Plan to Give Big Role to Negroes," *NYT,* Sept. 16, 1967, 52; "United Thank Offering: Special Grants for 1966," *E* 131 (June 1966): 12; "Executive Council: Recommend $2 Million for Minorities," *LC* 155 (Oct. 1, 1967): 6; and Kesselus, *John E. Hines,* 252–56. In September 1967 the General Board of the National Council of Churches launched its own "Crisis in the Nation" program, which urged its constituent denominations to formulate programs for the alleviation of poverty in the United States. Several Protestant denominations soon followed the lead of the Episcopal Church and pledged money to programs related to the urban crisis. "Real 'Riot Control,'" *CCe* 85 (1968): 187; and Findlay, *Church People,* 188.

35. John Booty, *The Episcopal Church in Crisis* (Cambridge, Mass.: Cowley, 1988), 51.

36. Hines, "Reminiscences," 361–62; *JGC* (1967): vii–viii, 303–7; "Text of Bishop Hines' Address," *GCD,* Sept. 18, 1967, 3–4 (Hines quotations); "Episcopalians: How to Carry Out a Conviction," *Time,* Sept. 29, 1967, 53–54; "The Opening Session," *LC* 155 (Oct. 1, 1967): 7–8; and Ellwood, *Sixties Spiritual Awakening,* 37–38, 46–48, 222–23.

37. "Minutes of the Triennial Meeting," Sept. 17–23, 1967, 58–64, in AEC, Records of the Triennial Meetings of the Women of the Episcopal Church, record group 161, folder 161–1–12; *JGC* (1967): 1–3, 240–42, 303–7, 430–31; *Summary of General Convention Actions, 1967* (New York: Secretary of the General Convention, 1967), 3–10, courtesy of Mary Miller; Frederick H. Sontag, "Black Ghetto Hearing Quiet," *American Church News: General Convention Daily* 4 (Sept. 22, 1967): 2–3; J. Caldwell McFaddin, "The Minority Report of the Program and Budget Committee," *CCh* 7 (Jan. 1968): 14–15 (quotation on 14); "Budgeting Revised," *LC* 155 (Oct. 8, 1967): 5–6; "Churchwomen: 'Different' Triennial," *LC* 155 (Oct. 15, 1967): 12; "Over Fourteen and Half Million Budget Approved in Seattle," *W* 52 (Oct. 5, 1967): 3–5; Judy Mathe, "From Convention . . . with Love," *E* 133 (Feb. 1968): 8–11; [Robert R. Hansel],

*Showdown at Seattle* (New York: Seabury, 1968), 47–50, 62; and Kesselus, *John E. Hines,* 152–53, 165, 169–71, 189, 266–70. For a full overview of the work of GCSP, see David L. Holmes, "Presiding Bishop John E. Hines and the General Convention Special Program," *Anglican and Episcopal History* 61 (1992): 393–417.

38. Nathan Wright Jr., "The Colonial Mind and the Urban Condition," *CIM* 12 (spring 1967): 19–23 (quotations on 21).

39. Author's interview of Nathan Wright Jr., Oct. 3, 1995, New York; Frederick Williams, interview in *Anniversary Booklet,* n.p.; Martin Arnold, "Newark Meeting on Black Power Attended by 400," *NYT,* July 21, 1967, 1, 34; "Negro Spokesman: Nathan Wright Jr.," *NYT,* July 22, 1967, 11; Earl Caldwell, "Black Power Parley Reports Aid by 50 Concerns," *NYT,* July 25, 1967, 21; "Black-Power Summit," *Newsweek,* July 31, 1967, 19–20; "A Black Schism," *Newsweek,* Mar. 4, 1968, 90; "Wright Wrangle," *LC* 155 (Oct. 8, 1967): 14 (Wright quotation); "Negro Clergy Urged to Back Program," *W* 52 (Oct. 5, 1967): 18; Nathan Wright Jr., *Let's Work Together* (New York: Hawthorn, 1968), 34–36, 83–93, 211; Nathan Wright Jr., "The Ethics of Power in the Black Revolution," in *The Black Man in America: Integration and Separation,* ed. James A. Moss (New York: Dell, 1971), 13–23; Wright, *Black Power and Urban Unrest,* 135–55; Mark L. Chapman, *Christianity on Trial: African-American Religious Thought Before and After Black Power* (Maryknoll, N.Y.: Orbis, 1996), 85–86; and Barbara Sue Kaplan Lewinson, "Three Conceptions of Black Education: A Study of the Educational Ideas of Benjamin Elijah Mays, Booker T. Washington, and Nathan Wright, Jr.," Ed.D. diss., Rutgers Univ., 1973, 121–26, 131–33.

40. Rodman interview; Hines interview; Woodard interview; Leon E. Modeste, "Church Strategy in Relation to Social Conflict: Buffalo, New York, Oct. 28th, 1968," 5–6, 9, in GCSP, folder 87–5–17; ECEC, Dec. 12–14, 1967, 20; Leon E. Modeste, "General Convention Special Program: Evaluative Insights," in ECEC, Sept. 24–26, 1968, 103–7; Leon E. Modeste, "Progress Report: General Convention Special Program," in ECEC, May 20–22, 1969, 154–57 (quotation on 155); Modeste, "Mission: Empowerment," 6; Marjorie Hyer, "GCSP Begins," *LC* 156 (Jan. 7, 1968): 4, 12–13; "GCSP Report," *LC* 158 (June 29, 1969): 6; "Special Program Team: Men and Meaning," *E* 133 (Feb. 1968): 10–11; Judy Mathe Foley, "Modeste in Motion," *E* 134 (Nov. 1969): 25; and Kesselus, *John E. Hines,* 276–80.

41. Author's interview of Philip T. Zabriskie, Sept. 20, 1995, New York; Primo interview; Turner interview; John Burgess interview; Richard B. Martin, interview in *Anniversary Booklet,* n.p.; Tollie L. Caution, draft of a form letter, Jan. 30, 1968, in PB-113, folder 113–2–11; Quinland R. Gordon, memorandum to Quintin E. Primo et al., from New York, July 25, 1968; John O'Neal, memorandum to Herbert Callender, from New York, Oct. 30, 1968, 2 ("an aggravation" quotation), in GCSP, folder 87–25–10; Hines, "Reminiscences," 168–78, 525; Robert C. Martin to the author, from Granville, Ohio, Sept. 1, 1995; ECEC, Dec. 12–14, 1967, 13; "T.L. Caution to Retire," *LC* 156 (Jan. 14, 1968): 7; Vine Deloria Jr., "GCSP: The Demons at Work," *HMPEC* 47 (1978): 83–92; Walter Decoster Dennis, "Tollie LeRoy Caution: Forerunner, Pathfinder, Prophet," *Linkage* 9 (June 1988): 8; Kesselus, *John E. Hines,* 276; and Lewis, *Yet with a Steady Beat,* 155–57, 223–24.

42. John Burgess interview; NCEC, Apr. 30, May 1–2, 1963, 94; ECEC, May 16–18, 1967, 36–37; Dec. 12–14, 1967, 108–9; [Marvin C. Josephson], "Report to the President and Board of Trustees . . . ," Sept. 1, 1960, 20–24, in ACIN, folder 61–1–17; American Church Institute, "Minutes of the Meeting of the Board of Trustees," Oct. 8, 1962, 6, in ACIN, folder 61–2–20; "Meeting of the Presidents of the American Church Institute Colleges," June 26, 1963, 2–4; American Church Institute, "Min-

utes of the Meeting of the Board of Trustees," Dec. 11, 1967, 2–8, in ACIN, folder 61–2–21; "Minutes: Special Committee on American Church Institute . . . June 1, 1965," 2–5, in ACIN, folder 61–3–9; Peter Day, "Matters of Principle," *LC* 142 (Mar. 12, 1961): 9 (quotation source); Tollie L. Caution, "The Protestant Episcopal Church: Policies and Rationale upon Which Support of Its Negro Colleges Is Predicated," *Journal of Negro Education* (summer 1960): 274–83; and William B. Spofford Jr., "Restructure and Tooling-Up Highlight Council Session," *W* 53 (Mar. 7, 1968): 3.

43. Kenneth Hughes to Daniel Corrigan, from Cambridge, Mass., Jan. 17, 1968 in PB-113, folder 113–2–11.

44. John M. Burgess to Daniel Corrigan, from Boston, Jan. 8, 1968, 1–2, in PB-113, folder 113–2–11.

45. Metropolitan Chapter of the Union of Black Clergy and Laity, memorandum to [John E. Hines, from New York, 1968], 1–2, in GCSP, folder 87–25–10.

46. Author's interview of Walter D. Dennis, Oct. 2, 1995, New York; author's interview of Frederick B. Williams, Oct. 9, 1996, New York; John Burgess interview; Anderson interview; Donald O. Wilson et al. to Hines, from Baltimore, Feb. 19, 1968, 1–2, in CMCP, folder 227–4–27; George Dugan, "18 Negro Priests in Antibias Move," *NYT*, July 28, 1968, 46; and "Black Churchmen Meet," *LC* 157 (July 7, 1968): 7 (source of Dennis quotation). For letters protesting Caution's forced retirement, see PB-113, folder 113–2–11, reference courtesy of Kenneth Kesselus, Bastrop, Tex.

47. Williams interview; Primo interview; Cooper interview; Cooper, "Concerning an Association of Negro Priests," Jan. 5, 1968, 1–4, manuscript in the possession of Quintin E. Primo Jr., Hockessin, Del.; George Dugan, "Negro Episcopal Priests Form Union," *NYT*, Feb. 9, 1968, 57 (quotation source); Nicholson, *What Is Happening to the Negro*, 2, 23, 29–34, 40; Edward Rodman, *Let There Be Peace among Us: A Story of the Union of Black Episcopalians* (Lawrenceville, Va.: Brunswick, 1990), 4–10, courtesy of Edward Rodman, Boston; and Lewis, *Yet with a Steady Beat*, 144, 157–61. Besides Primo (the first president), Weston, and Cooper, the other founders of the UBCL were Jesse Anderson Sr.; Tollie Caution; Walter Dennis; James Edden, rector of St. Thomas' Church, Chicago; Thomas Gibbs, a member of the presiding bishop's staff; Quinland Gordon; Kenneth Hughes; H. Irving Mayson, rector of St. Andrew's Church, Cleveland; Joseph Nicholson, coauthor of *The Negro's Church* and rector of All Saints' Church, St. Louis; Henry Parker, then a member of the Delta Ministry staff; Shelton Pollen, curate at St. Luke's Church, Washington, D.C.; St. Julian A. Simpkins Jr., rector of St. Simon of Cyrene Church, Rochester, N.Y.; William A. Van Croft, rector of St. Luke's, Washington; John Walker, then canon of the National Cathedral in Washington; Frederick Williams, rector of St. Clement's Church, Inkster, Mich.; and Harold Louis Wright, rector of the Church of the Resurrection, East Elmhurst, N.Y.

48. EB, Sept. 17, 1967, 2; and Nov. 10–11, 1967, 3–5 (quotation on 4).

49. [Albert R. Dreisbach Jr.], "New Statement of Purpose," EN, Mar. 31, 1968, 1; "Board Decides to Focus on Suburban Racism . . .," EN, June 16, 1968, 1; "ESCRU: New Statement of Purpose," *LC* 156 (June 2, 1968): 7–8 (quotation on 7); "The ESCRU Statement of Purpose," *LC* 156 (June 2, 1968): 11; and Kater, "Episcopal Society," 149–50.

50. [Kerner Commission], *Report of the National Advisory Commission on Civil Disorders* (New York: Dutton, 1968), 1–2; and Patterson, *Grand Expectations*, 664–65.

51. Washington interview; Harris interview; Penfield interview; EB, May 31–June 2, 1968, 1; Nov. 15–17, 1968, 3 (source of Anderson quotation); "A Letter to the

Black Episcopal Churches from the Union of Black Clergy and Laymen, . . . Nov. 16, 1968" (source of "'mouthed' integration"quotation) in ESCRU, folder 49:15; "Board Decides to Focus on Suburban Racism," 1; Paul M. Washington, *"Other Sheep I Have": The Autobiography of Father Paul M. Washington,* [ed.] David McI. Gracie (Philadelphia: Temple Univ. Press, 1994), 40–48, 70–85; and Kater, "Episcopal Society," 153–54.

    52. [Albert R. Dreisbach], "Revolution—Despair and Hope," EN, Sept. 22, 1968, 1. The biblical reference to the rabbi Gamaliel is Acts 5:33–39.

    53. Author's interview of Albert R. Dreisbach Jr., June 20, 1994, Atlanta; Alan C. Parker to "Friends at ESCRU," from Cleveland, Ohio, Jan. 14, 1969 (quotation source); Jane Van Meter to ESCRU, from Riverdale, N.Y., Feb. 24, 1969, in ESCRU, folder 3:32; and Alfred T.K. Zadig to "the Episcopal Society," from Fairfield, Conn., Mar. 2, 1968, in ESCRU, folder 33:11.

    54. Albert R. Dreisbach to William R. Brown, from Atlanta, Sept. 19, 1969, 1–2, in ESCRU, folder 33:14; and [Dreisbach] to Malcolm Boyd, from Atlanta, Oct. 31, 1969, 1–2, in MBP, folder 17:1.

## 8. Backlash and the End of the Civil Rights Era

    1. IFCO Press Release, Aug. 23, [1969], 1–2 (quotation on 1); "IFCO News," 1:1, Nov. 1968, 5–6, in GCSP, folder 87–2–5; R.C. Martin Jr., memorandum to John Coburn, [from New York], July 3, 1969, 1, in PB-113, folder 113–5–1; ECEC, Feb. 14–16, 1967, 51; Arnold Schuchter, *Reparations: The Black Manifesto and Its Challenge to White America* (Philadelphia: Lippincott, 1970), 2–27; and Findlay, *Church People,* 188–89.

    2. "The Black Manifesto," in *Black Manifesto: Religion, Racism, and Reparations,* ed. Robert S. Lecky and H. Elliott Wright (New York: Sheed and Ward, 1969), 114–26 (quotations on 119, 126); "Vote Seizure of Churches," LC 158 (May 25, 1969): 4; "The Manifesto," LC 158 (June 8, 1969): 6, 12–13; Findlay, *Church People,* 199–203; and Carson, *In Struggle,* 294–95.

    3. James Forman, J. Brooke Moseley, and Stephen Bayne, "Meeting at Episcopal Church Headquarters," New York, May 1, 1969 (source of quotations), SFBP, audio tape; Forman et al., "News Conference at Episcopal Church Headquarters," New York, May 13, 1969, SFBP, audio tape; Forman to John Hines, [from New York], May 13, 1969, in SFBP, "Forman, Correspondence and Clippings" folder; C. Gerald Fraser, "2 Episcopal Bishops Here Given Negro Demand for $500 Million," NYT, May 2, 1969, 46; Hines, "Reminiscences," 436–38; "Black Manifesto Presented at 815," LC 158 (June 1, 1969): 5; and Wilmore, *Black Religion and Black Radicalism,* 202–10.

    4. Perry Laukhuff to Stephen Bayne, from Norwalk, Conn., May 3, 1969 (source of Laukhuff quotation); Bayne to "the diocesan bishops," from New York, May 7, 1969, 1–2, in SFBP, "Response to Forman" folder; ECEC, Feb. 12–13, 1969, 8–9; "Virginia Clergy Issue Statement Opposing Segregationists," W 45 (Sept. 18, 1958): 4; "Executive Council: Summary of December Meeting," LC 158 (Jan. 12, 1969): 5–6; "Executive Council," LC 158 (Mar. 9, 1969): 6; Cornelia McCarthy, "Reparations," letter in LC 158 (June 15, 1969): 4 (source of McCarthy quote); "Reaction to NBEDC," LC 159 (July 13, 1969): 7; Peter R. Doyle, "Racial Heresy within the Church," CCh 8 (June 1969): 5–7 (Doyle quotation on 6); "The Churches and James Forman," *Christianity Today,* 13 (June 6, 1969): 27–28; Booty, *American Apostle,* 151–58; and Findlay, *Church People,* 206–7.

5. EB, June 20–21, 1969, 2; ECEC, May 20–22, 1969, 11–12 (source of quotations); "ESCRU Endorses Manifesto," *LC* 159 (Aug. 3, 1969): 6; "Reparations? No!" *LC* 159 (Aug. 3, 1969): 11; Lee A. Belford, "Questions about the Black Manifesto," *C* 183 (Nov. 1969): 6–7; William Stringfellow, "Reparations: Repentance as a Necessity to Reconciliation," in Lecky and Wright, *Black Manifesto,* 52–64; and Kesselus, *John E. Hines,* 307–8.

6. Author's interview of John B. Coburn, May 18, 1995, Brewster, Mass.; Roger Blanchard, "A Response to the Manifesto," Aug. 13, 1969, 2 (quotation source), in JBCP, box 26:1, "Coburn Committee Reports, Aug. 1969" folder; Charles M. Crump to John E. Hines, from Memphis, Tenn., Aug. 27, 1969, 3, in JBCP, box 26:2, folder 5; "Dean Coburn Resigns to Teach in New York," *E* 133 (July 1968): 19; and John B. Coburn, "View from Harlem," *E* 134 (June 1969): 24–26, 43. All references from JBCP are courtesy of John B. Coburn, Brewster, Mass.

7. Crump interview; "Black Militant," poem in *Real Thing* 8 (1) (May 14, [1969]): 1–2, in CMCP, folder 227–5–7; Charles M. Crump to Gordon E. Gillett, from Memphis, Tenn., May 26, 1969, 1–4, in CMCP, folder 227–4–30; ECEC, May 20–22, 1969, 24–28, 55–56, 180; and [Jo-Ann Price], "Executive Council," *LC* 158 (June 15, 1969): 12, 33–35.

8. Coburn interview; [John Coburn], "Informal Notes on the 'Implementation of the Spirit' Committee . . .," [Aug. 1969], 1–2, in JBCP, box 26:2, folder 2; Quinland R. Gordon to Coburn, from New York, July 7, 1969, 1–2 (quotation on 2), in JBCP, box 26:2, folder 3; Frederick B. Williams to John Hines, [from Inkster, Mich.], June 26, 1969, 1–2; Williams to Coburn, from Inkster, Aug. 13, 1969, in JBCP, box 26:2, "Coburn Committee Report—Appendices A–N, 1969" folder; and Sumner, *Episcopal Church's History,* 52–54.

9. Author's interview of Charles V. Willie, Feb. 7, 1996, Cambridge, Mass.; Coburn interview; Willie to Quinland R. Gordon, from Boston, Dec. 19, 1966, 1–6 (quotations on 3–4), in DCC; and James P. Breeden to Willie, [from New York], Dec. 27, 1966, 1–2, in DCC.

10. Charles V. Willie, *Oreo: Race and Marginal Men and Women* (Wakefield, Mass.: Parameter, 1975), 11–23 (quotation on 17).

11. Charles V. Willie, "The Black Manifesto: Prophetic or Preposterous," *E* 134 (Sept. 1969): 22–4.

12. "Conclusions and Recommendations of the . . . Executive Council's Response to the 'Black Manifesto,'" [Aug. 1969], 1–6; "Report of the Committee for the . . . Response to the Manifesto," Aug. 29, 1969, 3–12 (quotations on 12), in JBCP, box 26:1, "Coburn Committee Reports, Aug. 1969" folder; and ECEC, Aug. 29, 1969, 1–11.

13. [John E. Hines], "Opening Address—Special General Convention II," 1, in PB-113, folder 113–4–4; Hines, "Keep Up Your Hopes for the Church," *E* 134 (Oct. 1969): 40–42 (quotations on 41–42); Hines, "Reminiscences," 439–50; and Kesselus, *John E. Hines,* 310–22.

14. Rodman interview; Coburn interview; Washington interview; "Black and White Militants Disrupt Episcopal Parley," *NYT,* Sept. 1, 1969, 8; "An Act of Faith," *E* 134 (Oct. 1969): 8–17, 22–29, 32–38, 56; "James A. Pike: Death in Judea," *E* 134 (Oct. 1969): 50–51; John M. Krumm, "Miracle Convention of 1969," *W* 54 (11 Sept. 1969): 7; Washington, *"Other Sheep I Have,"* 86–96; and Rodman, *Let There Be Peace,* 14–17. For a discussion of the growing interest in the antiwar and women's movements in the churches during this period, see Friedland, *Lift Up Your Voice,* 213–52; and Darling, *New Wine,* 86–137.

15. Carter interview; Williams interview; Rodman interview; Frederick B. Williams and James E.P. Woodruff, "A Parting Word to Special General Convention . . .," [Sept. 1969], in JBCP, box 26:1, "The Black Manifesto and the Response of the Church" folder; [Albert R. Dreisbach], "South Bend: Trust, Not Treasure—The Basic Issue," EN, Sept. 14, 1969, 1–2 (Carter quotations on 1); Jesse F. Anderson, "An Open Letter from President Anderson," EN, Sept. 14, 1969, 4; JGC (1969): 201–11; "Channeling Funds for Black Development Met by Council," W 54 (1 Oct. 1969): 3–4; "An Act of Faith," 15, 24–6; "Money for Blacks," LC 159 (Sept. 28, 1969): 8–9; Issues at Notre Dame [Cambridge, Mass.: Church Society for College Work, 1969], 12–17; James E.P. Woodruff, "Black Power in the Church," in What the Religious Revolutionaries Are Saying, ed. Elwyn A. Smith (Philadelphia: Fortress, 1971), 34–39; Schuchter, Reparations, 14–16 (Burgess quotation on 15); Rodman, Let There Be Peace, 14–17; and Lewis, Yet with a Steady Beat, 155–56.

16. Coburn interview; John E. Hines to Thomas Kingsley, from New York, Sept. 30, 1969; Owen H. Page to Hines, from Savannah, Ga., Oct. 9, 1969; Helen Smith Shoemaker to Hines, from Stevenson, Md., Oct. 16, 1969, 1–2; Vestry of St. Paul's Church, Selma, Ala., "Resolution," Oct. 20, 1969; James M. Stoney Jr. to Hines, from Talladega, Ala., Nov. 25, 1969, 1, in PB-113, folder 113–4–6; ECEC, Sept. 23–25, 1969, 15–20, 37–40; Executive Council of the Episcopal Church, press release, Sept. 25, 1969, 1–2, in MSU, Delta Ministry Papers, folder 1:58; Seth S. King, "Episcopal Leaders Vote $200,000 in 'Reparations,'" NYT, Sept. 4, 1969, 1, 38; "Militants Hail Episcopal 'Reparations,'" NYT, Sept. 5, 1969, 27; "Strange Precedent," NYT, Sept. 6, 1969, 28; Hines and Coburn, "Church Gift Not Reparations," letter in NYT, Sept. 11, 1969, 46; and "Episcopal Panel Backs Negro Gift," NYT, Sept. 27, 1969, 36. Despite the controversy surrounding the creation of the grant, $220,000 was eventually raised through voluntary contributions, and that money was funneled to BEDC through NCBC. "BEDC Recipient of Episcopal Money," E 135 (Sept. 1970): 38.

17. "Foundation for Christian Theology Formed," LC 153 (Sept. 18, 1966): 6–7; and "Foundation for Christian Theology Meets," LC 156 (Feb. 11, 1968): 5.

18. "F.C.T. Calls for P.B.'s Resignation," LC 159 (Aug. 3, 1969): 6.

19. Charles M. Crump to Gordon E. Gillett, [from Memphis, Tenn.], July 25, 1969, 1, in CMCP, folder 227–5–5; Paul H. Kratzig, "Foundation President's Key Note Speech," CCh 7 (Feb. 1968): 3–6; Barry M. Goldwater, "America and His Church," CCh 7 (Feb. 1968): 7, 14–15; "From the Foundation President," CCh 9 (Nov. 1970): 1, 5–7; "PB Raps FCT," LC 159 (Nov. 16, 1969): 6; "FCT: Church Aids Divisive Groups," LC 159 (Nov. 16, 1969): 7; "More Critics Speak Out," E 134 (Dec. 1969): 39–40; Aubrey B. Haines, "Polarization within the Churches," CCe 87 (1970): 1039–41; The General Convention Special Program of the Episcopal Church: 1967–1970 ([Victoria, Tex.]: Foundation for Christian Theology, 1970), 1–3, 28; Philip Deemer, ed., Episcopal Year 1970 (New York: Jarrow, 1971), 57; and Patterson, Grand Expectations, 735 (source of Nixon quotation).

20. George M. Murray, "Problems, Answers, and the Ministry," LC 153 (Nov. 6, 1966): 10–11 (quotation on 10).

21. Crump interview; George M. Murray to William H. Marmion, from Birmingham, Ala., Dec. 29, 1964, 1–2, in CSR-85, folder 85–3–18; Murray to John A. Pinkney, from Birmingham, Jan. 27, 1969, 1–2, in PB-113, folder 113–4–6; Executive Council press release, Dec. 12, 1969, 6, in PB-113, folder 113–4–8; Alabama, Annual Convention (1969), 80; (1970), 81; and George M. Murray, "We Must Keep Our Priorities Clear," E 134 (Aug. 1969): 16–18 (quotations on 18).

22. "Fund Started for 'Democratic' Negro Groups," LC 159 (Dec. 14, 1969): 8.

23. Stephen Bayne to "all bishops," from New York, Nov. 14, 1969, 1, in JHEP, "Executive/National Council" folder; "Wilkins on Reparations," *LC* 159 (Nov. 30, 1969): 12 (source of Wilkins quotation); "Black Manifesto or White Manifestation?" advertisement in *LC* 160 (Mar. 29, 1970): 13; "EORSA Makes Grants," *LC* 160 (May 31, 1970): 5; "Support for Blacks: Other Voices," *E* 135 (Feb. 1970): 34; "EORSA Makes First Grants," *E* 135 (June 1970): 45; and "Out of Business: ESCRU and EORSA," *CCh* 9 (Nov. 1970): 29.

24. Hines interview; Menuez interview; Crump interview; Hines, "Reminiscences," 392, 505, 524; "Charter for the Screening and Review Committee," Feb. 2, 1968, IV.A.1, in GCSP, folder 87-2-13; John E. Hines to Stanley F. Hauser, from New York, June 17, 1969, 1-2, in PB-113, folder 113-4-9; "First Five Years," 74; ECEC, Sept. 23-25, 1969, 8-10; Feb. 17-19, 1970, 3; Oct. 8-9, 1970, 65-68; "Who Rules PECUSA?" *LC* 160 (May 3, 1970): 11; and Holmes, "Presiding Bishop John E. Hines," 401.

25. Walter interview; Charles C.J. Carpenter to Francis Walter, from Birmingham, Ala., Oct. 5, 1965; George M. Murray to Walter, from Birmingham, Oct. 12, 1965, 1-2, in ESCRU, folder 49:20; Bruce Hanson, memorandum to "Denominational Race Staff and Concerned Agencies," from New York, Dec. 13, 1965, 1-2, in SIP, folder 1044.2.5 ("Walter House, A-F, 1965" file); Hanson, memorandum to "Denominational Race Staff and Concerned Agencies," from New York, Feb. 9, 1966, 1-2, in SIP, folder 1044.2.6 ("Walter House, A-F, 1966" file); Walter to Murray, from Decatur, Ala., Oct. 4, 1965, [3-4], in SIP, folder 1044.2.8 ("Walter House, G-N, 1965" file); Cornelius C. Tarplee to Walter, from New York, May 31, 1966, 1-2; Tarplee to Walter, from New York, Aug. 24, 1966, in SIP, folder 1044.2.11 ("Walter House, O-Z, 1966" file); "Selma Interreligious Project," EN, Oct. 28, 1965, 2; [James F. Findlay Jr.], "The Selma March and Other Roads Taken: Thoughts on the Mainline Churches and Race Relations After 1965," unpublished paper, [1995], 7-20, courtesy of James Findlay; and Nancy Callahan, *The Freedom Quilting Bee* (Tuscaloosa: Univ. of Alabama Press, 1987), 8-16.

26. Walter interview; Francis X. Walter to Leon Modeste, [from Tuscaloosa, Ala.], Jan. 15, 1968, in SIP, folder 1044.2.11 ("Walter House, O-Z, 1966" file); "Selma Inter-Religious Project: Proposal for Work in Rural Southwest Alabama," [1969], 1-3, in GCSP, folder 87-7-2; George M. Murray to Charles L. Glenn, from Birmingham, Ala., May 15, 1968 in GCSP, folder 87-7-3; John O'Neal, memorandum to Herbert Callender, [from New York], June 24, 1970; "Selma Project," [1971]; and Walter to Modeste, from Tuscaloosa, Apr. 21, 1971, 1, in GCSP, folder 87-7-4.

27. ECEC, Sept. 23-25, 1969, 49-52, 103, 106; Dec. 9-11, 1969, 5; Diocese of North Carolina, *Journal of the Annual Convention* (1965), 134; (1968), 69-70; "The KKK, Black Power, and Excommunication," *LC* 153 (Sept. 25, 1966): 5-6; R.E. Hood, "Black Power and KKK," letter in *LC* 153 (Oct. 30, 1966): 9; Thomas A. Fraser, "Integration in Carolina," letter in *LC* 153 (Nov. 27, 1966): 29; and "Grant to 'Liberation U' Disputed," *LC* 159 (Nov. 30, 1969): 8.

28. Thomas A. Fraser to Leon Modeste, from Raleigh, N.C., Sept. 18, 1969, 1-3; Modeste to Fraser, from New York, Nov. 12, 1969, 2 (source of Modeste quotation); Fraser to Modeste, from Raleigh, Nov. 25, 1969, 1-2, in GCSP, folder 87-16-51; Screening and Review Committee, "Minutes," Sept. 7, 1972, in GCSP, folder 87-2-12; Modeste to Fraser, from New York, Mar. 26, 1970, in ECEC, May 19-21, 1970, 268; North Carolina, *Annual Convention* (1970), 73-78 (Fraser quotation on 74); "North Carolina: Diocese Faces Crisis over Grant," *LC* 160 (Feb. 22, 1970): 12; "Diocesan Conventions," *LC* 160 (Mar. 1, 1970): 9; and "North Carolina: Bishop Criticizes GCSP

Procedure," *LC* 165 (Oct. 15, 1972): 7; and Judy Mathe Foley, "Diary of a Grant," *E* 135 (July 1970): 16–18, 24–28.

29. Robert B. Hunter, report, [Mar. 1970], 5, in GCSP, folder 87–25–45; "Borrowed Bell, Two Chairs," *LC* 128 (June 13, 1954): 7; "Voorhees Hit by Disruption," *E* 134 (June 1969): 33; "Voorhees Closed, Campus Occupied," *LC* 160 (Mar. 29, 1970): 7; Homer Bigart, "Carolina Negro College, Shut in Protests, Is Guarded by Troops," *NYT,* Mar. 2, 1970, 29; Robert J. Blanton, *The Story of Voorhees College* (Denmark, S.C.: [Voorhees College], 1983), 4–9, 21–24, 159–60, 185–89; Cleveland Sellers, *The River of No Return: The Autobiography of a Black Militant and the Life and Death of SNCC* (1973; reprint, Jackson: Univ. Press of Mississippi, 1990), 206–19; and Charles Marsh, *God's Long Summer: Stories of Faith and Civil Rights* (Princeton, N.J.: Princeton Univ. Press, 1997), 152–57.

30. Modeste, "Mission: Empowerment," 35–36, 55–57; John O'Neal, memorandum to GCSP Central Staff, May 6, 1971, 1–2 (O'Neal quotation on 1), in GCSP, folder 87–24–44; ECEC, May 20–22, 1969, 51–54; Oct. 8–9, 1970, 47–49; Dec. 8–10, 1970, 22–24; Feb. 17–18, 1971, 16–17; May 19–20, 1971, 6–7, 141–42; Sept. 29–30, 1971, 204; "Executive Council Acts on Laity and Voorhees," *E* 134 (July 1969): 29; J. Kenneth Morris, "Voorhees College: For the Record," letter in *E* 134 (Aug. 1969): 5–6; "Executive Council Report," *LC* 161 (Nov. 1, 1970): 10; "GCSP: BACC Representatives Fail to Show," *LC* 162 (June 6, 1971): 6–7; "Executive Council Report," *LC* 162 (June 13, 1971): 9–10 ("live in different worlds" quotation on 9); and "Executive Council Report," *LC* 163 (Oct. 31, 1971): 6.

31. Stevens interview; Crump interview; "Summary of Alianza Federal de Pueblos Libre," [1969], 1, 3; C.J. Kinsolving III, memorandum to the Executive Council, from Santa Fe, N.M., Nov. 14, 1969, 1; Executive Council, "Press Release," Dec. 12, 1969, 1, 4, 6; [John Hines], "Statement by the Presiding Bishop on the Alianza Federal de Mercedes," Dec. 15, 1969, 1–4, in PB-113, folder 113–4–8; ECEC, Dec. 9–11, 1969, 36, 154–55; Lewis E. Thompson, "After Alianza," *E* 135 (Feb. 1970): 28–30; "Bishop Opposes GCSP Grant," *LC* 159 (Dec. 14, 1969): 7; "Executive Council," *LC* 160 (Jan. 4, 1970): 6–7; "Thanks Given for Alianza Grant," *LC* 160 (Jan. 11, 1970): 6; "Executive Council: Member Opposes Grant," *LC* 160 (Jan. 25, 1970): 7–8; "Alianza Leader Sentenced," *LC* 160 (Feb. 15, 1970): 13–14; "Executive Council Report," *LC* 160 (Mar. 15, 1970): 9, 20; "Conventions," *LC* 161 (July 5, 1970): 13; and Holmes, "Presiding Bishop John E. Hines," 405–6.

32. Edwin B. Thayer to John E. Hines, from Denver, Colo., Dec. 19, 1969, 1–2, in PB-113, folder 113–4–8; James L. Duncan to Leon E. Modeste, from Miami, Fla., Apr. 15, 1970, 1–2, in PB-113, folder 113–4–9; and John W. Ellison, "J'Accuse—*The Alianza,*" *LC* 160 (Feb. 1, 1970): 8–10, 12–13.

33. "Policy and G.C.S.P.," [Apr. 1970], 1–4 (quotation on 4), in GCSP, folder 87–4–12; ECEC, May 19–21, 1970, 20–22, 144–206; *JGC* (1970): 432–46; "GCSP Evaluation Begins This Month," *E* 135 (Mar. 1970): 41; "Too Much, Too Little," *E* 135 (July 1970): 15, 30; Jeannie Willis, "Jackson Previews Houston," *E* 135 (Aug. 1970): 13; "Preview Houston: GCSP," *E* 135 (Oct. 1970): 24; "Executive Council Report," *LC* 160 (June 14, 1970): 9; and "Minority Report on GCSP," *LC* 161 (Aug. 3, 1970): 6–7.

34. Author's interview of Gerald N. McAllister, July 7, 25, 1994, Austin, Tex.; Cooper interview; Harris interview; ECEC, Apr. 28–29, 1970, 12; "Down a Million," *E* 135 (Apr. 1970): 16; "GCSP in the Mind," *E* 135 (Dec. 1970): 23; Brown, *Episcopal Church in Texas,* 137; Sumner, *Episcopal Church's History,* 54–55; and Kesselus, *John E. Hines,* 344–54.

35. McAllister interview; Rodman interview; Williams interview; ECEC, Sept. 15, 1967, 5 (source of quotation); *JGC* (1970): 195, 301–6; George Dugan, "Black Churchmen Obtain a Hearing," *NYT,* Oct. 15, 1970, 29; George Dugan, "Episcopal Funds for Poor Backed," *NYT,* Oct. 16, 1970, 45; "Casson Protests Black Stand," *GCD,* Oct. 23, 1970, 4; "News from the Convention," *LC* 161 (Nov. 8, 1970): 5–9; "General Convention Closes," *LC* 161 (Nov. 15, 1970): 7–8; "Unspectacular—Good Show," editorial in *LC* 161 (Nov. 15, 1970): 19; "Special Program Has Fine Support Following a Stormy Start," *W* 55 (II Oct. 1970): 5–6; "GCSP in the Mind," 21–27; Holmes, "Presiding Bishop John E. Hines," 407–8; Rodman, *Let There Be Peace,* 17–26; and Lewis, *Yet with a Steady Beat,* 155–56.

36. Boyd interview; Dreisbach interview; Penfield interview; John B. Morris, memorandum to ESCRU Board Members and Chapter Chairmen, from Atlanta, Dec. 2, 1965, 1, in WSP, box 10; Jesse F. Anderson to "the Saints in ESCRU," [from Philadelphia], Apr. 2, 1969, 1–2, MM; Kim [Dreisbach] to Malcolm Boyd, from Atlanta, Oct. 31, 1969, in MBP, folder 17:1; William R. Brown to ESCRU, from Farmington, N.M., Sept. 5, 1969, in ESCRU, folder 33:14; Dreisbach to Sandra J. Paige, from Atlanta, Nov. 11, 1969, in ESCRU, folder 71:7; [Morris], "ESCRU and the Peace Movement," EN, Feb. 23, 1966, 2; "The 9th Annual Meeting—A Capsule Review," EN, Nov. 30, 1969, 1–2; [Dreisbach], "Confirmation, the Coalition and Convention," EN, June 7, 1970, 1; "Bishops Among 150 Arrested at Pentagon," *LC* 159 (Dec. 14, 1969): 7; Friedland, *Lift Up Your Voice,* 191–92, 218–19; and Kater, "Episcopal Society," 165–83.

37. Author's telephone interview of Mary Eunice Oliver, Nov. 2, 1995, San Diego, Calif.; Harris interview; Dreisbach interview; Albert R. Dreisbach Jr. to "Member(s)," [from Atlanta], Nov. 4, 1970 (source of quotations), MM; "End of ESCRU Group?" *GCD,* Oct. 22, 1970, 3; and Rodman, *Let There Be Peace,* 60–62. Harris was later ordained a priest, and in 1989 she became the first woman bishop in the Episcopal Church.

38. David R. King to John E. Hines, from Elizabeth, N.J., Aug. 21, 1972, in ECEC, Sept. 26–28, 1972, 347–48; "The Troubled American: A Special Report on the White Majority," *Newsweek,* Oct. 6, 1969, 29; "A Case of 'Benign Neglect,'" *Newsweek,* Mar. 16, 1970, 25–26 (Moynihan quotation on 25); J. Howard Pew, "The Mission of the Church," *Christianity Today,* July 3, 1964, 11–14 (Pew quotation on 14); J. Howard Pew, "Should the Church 'Meddle' in Civil Affairs?" *Reader's Digest,* May 1966, 49–54; Edward B. Guerry, "GCSP," letter in *LC* 160 (June 14, 1970): 6 (source of Guerry quotations); Helen Smith Shoemaker, "The Arrogance of Confrontation," *LC* 161 (Oct. 4, 1970): 25–26 (Shoemaker quotations on 26); Judy Mathe Foley, "10 Years Later," *E* 137 (Jan. 1972): 27–29; and Robert Wuthnow, *The Restructuring of American Religion: Society and Faith since World War II* (Princeton, N.J.: Princeton Univ. Press, 1988), 145–49, 153–65.

39. Dean M. Kelley, *Why Conservative Churches Are Growing: A Study in the Sociology of Religion* (1972; reprint, San Francisco: Harper, 1977), xviii–xx, 1–16, 20–46, 133–53; "Church Faces Problems in Poverty Drive," *W* 50 (Nov. 25, 1965): 4–5; "Why Churches Grow—or Don't," *LC* 165 (July 9, 1972): 11; Duncan M. Gray Jr., "In Defense of the Steeple," *Katallagete: Be Reconciled* 2 (winter 1968–69): 29–31; Will D. Campbell and James Y. Holloway, "Up To Our Steeple in Politics," *CaC* 29 (1969–70): 36–40; William Stringfellow, "The Shadow of Judas," *CaC* 29 (1969–70): 40–41 (Stringfellow quotation on 40); Jeffrey K. Hadden, *The Gathering Storm in the Churches* (Garden City, N.Y.: Doubleday, 1969), 104–41, 159, 211–35; Jeffrey K. Hadden and Raymond C. Rymph, "The Marching Ministers," in *Religion in Radical Transition,* ed. Jeffrey K. Hadden (Chicago: Aldine, 1971), 99–109; Mark A. Noll, *A History of Chris-*

tianity in the United States and Canada (Grand Rapids, Mich.: Eerdmans, 1992), 460–78; Hudnut-Beumler, Looking for God in the Suburbs, 31–55; and Wuthnow, Restructuring of American Religion, 20–37. A photograph of ESCRU members carrying the distinctive "Segregation / Separation" sign appears in a magazine article decrying the political activism of clergy. "'Church Lobby' in Spotlight—A Look at How It Operates," U.S. News and World Report, Nov. 22, 1971, 53.

40. Dorothy A. Faber, "Another Opinion," LC 156 (Jan. 21, 1968): 12 (source of Faber quotations); Dorothy A. Faber, "Menticide in the Churches—Part I," CCh 7 (Mar. 1968): 7–8; Dorothy A. Faber, "The Speech I Would Have Delivered in the House of Bishops . . .," CCh 8 (Oct. 1969): 9–10; Ilse S. Helmus, "UTO Budgets," letter in LC 156 (Feb. 11, 1968): 13; and [Hansel], Showdown at Seattle, 7–56.

41. D. Barry Menuez, memorandum to Philip T. Zabriskie, [from New York], Mar. 18, 1966, 1 (source of "separate but equal" quotation), in ECBM, folder 159–1–26; Jo-Ann Price, "Executive Council: Propose $700,000 for IFCO," LC 156 (Mar. 17, 1968): 24; [Jo-Ann Price], "Executive Council: Chicago Police Scored," LC 157 (Oct. 13, 1968): 22 (source of Sorg quotations); Cynthia Wedel, "The Church and Social Action," CCe 87 (1970): 959–62 (Wedel quotations on 961–962); Harvey Cox, "The 'New Breed' in American Churches: Sources of Social Activism in American Religion," Daedalus (winter 1967): 135–36; Mary Sudman Donovan, "Beyond the Parallel Church: Strategies of Separatism and Integration in the Governing Councils of the Episcopal Church," in Episcopal Women: Gender, Spirituality, and Commitment in an American Mainline Denomination, ed. Catherine M. Prelinger (New York: Oxford Univ. Press, 1992), 147–50; and Darling, New Wine, 86–98.

42. Author's interview of Charles L. Glenn Jr., Oct. 24, 1995, Boston; Menuez interview; Hines, "Reminiscences," 66, 226; Richard S. Emrich to Stephen F. Bayne, from Detroit, Mar. 24, 1970, 1–2, in SFBP, "G.C.S.P." folder; ECEC, Feb. 17–18, 1971, 60–62; May 1–3, 1973, 50–52; Edward R. Welles, "Bishop Welles Writes," letter in E 135 (Mar. 1970): 2; Arthur E. Walmsley, "Christians in Search of a Future," E 138 (Aug. 1973): 14–16; Kenneth E. Clarke, "Bucking the Trend," LC 160 (Mar. 8, 1970): 8–9; L. William Countryman, "Authority and Crisis in the Church," LC 160 (June 21, 1970): 8–10; McGreevy, Parish Boundaries, 215–18; and Ellwood, Sixties Spiritual Awakening, 46, 222–23, 331.

43. Cox, Secular City, 91–128; Moore, "A Bishop Views the Underground Church," 221–37; Paul Seabury, "Trendier Than Thou: The Many Temptations of the Episcopal Church," Harper's, Oct. 1978, 39–47, 50, 52; and Findlay, Church People, 121–22, 222–24 ("last hurrah" quotation on 224).

44. Paul M. van Buren to Malcolm Boyd, from Chicago, June 3, 1963, 1, in MBP, folder 19:1; and van Buren, Secular Meaning of the Gospel, 190–92.

45. Warren E. Shaw, "Christians and Pressure Tactics," LC 150 (Jan. 3, 1965): 14–15; Warren E. Shaw, "Mother, I'd Rather Do It Myself!" LC 163 (Oct. 31, 1971): 11–12 (source of Shaw quotations); John E. Hines, "The Presiding Bishop's Opening Address," LC 167 (Oct. 21, 1973): 11–12; and Countryman, "Authority and Crisis in the Church," 9–10.

46. McAllister interview; ECEC, Dec. 8–10, 1970, 7–8; Feb. 17–18, 1971, 60–62, 74; Feb. 22–24, 1972, 279; "Executive Council," LC 162 (Jan. 3, 1971): 12–13 (Allin quotation on 13); "Executive Council: Staff Cut Drastically," LC 162 (Jan. 17, 1971): 10; "Daily Opinion: Black Church Mind Misread by Whites," GCD, Oct. 5, 1973, 2; Judy M. Foley, "A New Era," E 136 (Feb. 1971): 26–28; "Executive Council: Reports and Actions," E 136 (Nov. 1971): 41; and "What We Learned from What You Said," E 138 (Apr. 1973): 25–40 (quotations from report on 29).

47. Turner interview; Rodman interview; Williams interview; Williams, interview, *Anniversary Booklet* (source of Williams quotation); [Franklin Turner] to Jesse F. Anderson Jr., from New York, Nov. 2, 1972, 3; Union of Black Episcopalians, "Draft Proposal: Black Desk and Commission at 815," [Feb. 1973], 1, in GCSP, folder 87–25–10; John Burgess, quotation, Nov. 8, 1972, inserted in a letter from Anderson to [Turner, from Philadelphia], Jan. 9, 1973, in ECBM, folder 159–1–39; ECEC, Sept. 26–28, 1972, 156–57; Feb. 20–22, 1973, 191–92; May 1–3, 1973, 35–40; "All in All, a Good, Constructive Council Meeting," *LC* 165 (Oct. 22, 1972): 7; "Executive Council Faces Several Problems," *LC* 166 (Jan. 7, 1973): 5–6; and "Bp. Burgess Says Church Plays It 'Safe,'" *LC* 166 (May 20, 1973): 6–7.

48. "Why Issues?" *Issues,* Oct. 1, 1973, 1 (quotation source); "What's New?" *Issues,* Oct. 2, 1973, 1; "Unhealthy Silence on Empowerment," *Issues,* Oct. 3, 1973, 1; and "Facing the World's Pain," *Issues,* Oct. 5, 1973, 1.

49. Cornish Rogers, "Episcopalian Convention: 'Thou Shalt Not Polarize,'" *CCe* 90 (1973): 1046–47; "General Convention Closes," *LC* 167 (Nov. 4, 1973): 7–8; "GCSP: Radical Reorganization Ends Program," *LC* 167 (Nov. 18, 1973): 6; "GCSP Liquidated—At Long Last," *LC* 167 (Nov. 18, 1973): 13 (quotation source); *JGC* (1973): 390; and William S. Lea, "What Louisville Said to Us," *E* 138 (Nov. 1973): 3.

50. "GCSP 'Tear-Sheet,'" 9, Nov. 1973, 1–2, 13, in GCSP, folder 87–4–16; Modeste, "Mission: Empowerment," 1–3, 66–67; and ECEC, Dec. 11–13, 1973, 8, 22.

51. Hines interview; and Hines, "Reminiscences," 515–21, 525–26 (quotation on 526).

52. ECEC, Dec. 11–13, 1973, 43–44; "Presiding Bishop to Resign in 1974," *E* 137 (Dec. 1972): 36; "The Presiding Bishop: Involvement 'Goes along with Ministry,'" *LC* 167 (July 22, 1973): 5–6; Hines, "Presiding Bishop's Opening Address," 9–12 (Hines quotations on 11–12); [Carroll E. Simcox], "Executive Council Report," *LC* 168 (Jan. 6, 1974): 5; "Bishop Hines Steps Down," *CCe* 90 (1973): 1021–22; and Kesselus, *John E. Hines,* 376–78.

53. Allin interview; Rodman interview; Turner interview; *JGC* (1973): 118, 122, 198, 309–12; "The Bishop Answered Some Questions," *GCD,* Oct. 5, 1973, 1; "Allin Accepts; Pledges Support to Minorities," *GCD,* Oct. 8, 1973, 1; "Black Leader Is Pleased after Meeting with Bp. Allin," *GCD,* Oct. 10, 1973, 3; "The Third John and the 23rd PB," *E* 138 (Nov. 1973): 19–20; "More News from Louisville," *LC* 167 (Oct. 28, 1973): 6; "John M. Allin—A Splendid Choice," *LC* 167 (Oct. 28, 1973): 15 (quotation source); "Executive Council Prepares for the Future," *E* 139 (Feb. 1974): 12; Rodman, *Let There Be Peace,* 37–42; and Lewis, *Yet with a Steady Beat,* 166–67.

54. Allin interview; Hines interview; "Third John and the 23rd PB," 19–20 (Allin quotations on 20); and "More News from Louisville," 6.

# Epilogue

1. Gerald Eskenazi, "Phoenix May Lose Super Bowl over King Holiday Rejection," *NYT,* Nov. 8, 1990, D23; Robert Reinhold, "Arizona Struggles Anew to Erase Its Negative Image," *NYT,* Nov. 16, 1990, A18; "King's Daughter Avoids Arizona," *NYT,* Dec. 10, 1990, A14; Paul Tagliabue, "The Super Bowl: Not a Political Football," *NYT,* Dec. 23, 1990, sec. 8, p. 10; and Thomas George, "N.F.L. Is Nearly Unanimous in Stand on Phoenix Super Bowl Issue," *NYT,* Mar. 21, 1991, B16.

2. Stephanie Strom, "Arizona Meeting Splits Episcopalians," *NYT,* Dec. 10, 1990, A1.

3. "Episcopal Meeting to Stay in Arizona," *NYT,* Jan. 7, 1991, A12; "Presiding

Bishop Calls Council to Special Meeting," *LC* 202 (Jan. 6, 1991): 10; "No to Phoenix in 1991," editorial in *W* 73 (Dec. 1990): 5 (quotation source); and Sumner, *Episcopal Church's History,* 177–78.

4. Strom, "Arizona Meeting Splits Episcopalians," A14; "Episcopal Meeting to Stay in Arizona," A12 (source of Browning quotation); "Arizona Not Giving Up on King Holiday," *LC* 201 (Dec. 2, 1990): 7, 13; David Kalvelage, "Council Affirms Phoenix as Convention Site," *LC* 202 (Jan. 27, 1991): 6 (source of Kimsey quotation); Constance Tyndall and James Waring McCrady, "First Requirement," letters in *LC* 203 (Aug. 4, 1991): 5; and Lewis, *Yet with a Steady Beat,* 167–69.

5. David Kalvelage, "Protest Greets Bishops and Deputies," *LC* 203 (July 28, 1991): 6 (source of quotation); Kalvelage, "Council Affirms Phoenix," 6; and Lewis, *Yet with a Steady Beat,* 170–72.

6. General Convention of the Episcopal Church, *The Blue Book* (1991), 144–47, 475 (quotation on 475); *JGC* (1991): 170–71, 249, 284, 371, 382–83, 585, 688, 698–701, 844; David Kalvelage, "Racism Audit Shows Many Desire Change," *LC* 203 (Aug. 4, 1991): 8; Emmet Gribbin, "Jonathan Daniels in Calendar: 'A Measure of Redemption' to a Tragic Time," *LC* 203 (Sept. 1, 1991): 7; and Susan Erdey, "Lots of Heat, Not Much Light," *W* 74 (July–Aug., 1991): 23–26.

# Index

Abernathy, Ralph D., 119

ACIN. *See* American Church Institute for Negroes (ACIN)

Adams, Alger L., 51–53

African American religion: disparaged, by black Episcopalians, 16; —, by Booker T. Washington, 18; —, by white southerners, 10–12, 14–16, 19; and freedom from white control, 8–9, 166; study of, 31. *See also* African Methodist Episcopal Church; African Methodist Episcopal Zion Church; Colored Methodist Episcopal Church; National Baptist Convention of the U.S.A., Inc.

African Methodist Episcopal Church, 8, 13

African Methodist Episcopal Zion Church, 8, 13

African Orthodox Church, 22, 182

Alabama, diocese of: and ESCRU, 99, 111, 119, 154–57; and GCSP, 198–99; impact of civil rights movement on, 77, 119–20, 127–29, 132–34, 154–57, 159, 191; position of African Americans in, 79, 119, 154

Albany, Ga.: civil rights activities in, 135

Alianza Federal de Mercedes, 201–3

Allen, Michael, 130–31

Allin, John M.: and All Saints' College, 111–12, ; as bishop of Mississippi, 122, 142, 149–53, 191, 212, 250n. 6, 263n. 31; and Executive Council, 210; as opponent of Delta Ministry, 149–53; as presiding bishop, 212–13, 215; and University of the South, 116

Allison, C. FitzSimons, 116

All Saints' Church (Waccamaw), Pawley's Island, S.C., 8

All Saints' Church, St. Louis, Mo., 96

All Saints' College, 111–12, 120

Allport, Gordon W., 81, 125

American Baptist Convention, 64

American Church Institute for Negroes (ACIN): and Bishop Payne Divinity School, 39; board of trustees of, 52; dissolution of, 181–82; racial paternalism of, 20, 32, 181, 200–201; organized, 20; as segregation, 38–39, 50–53 123, 125, 147

American Church Union, 145–46, 245n. 28

Anderson, Jesse F., Sr., 100, 168, 174, 184, 274n. 47

Anglican Church of South Africa, 102

Anglican Communion, 45, 67. *See also* Lambeth Conference

Anglicanism: establishmentarian ideas of, 3, 90; and social responsibility, 3, 89–90, 94; social teachings of, 89–90, 103. *See also* Anglican Communion; Lambeth Conference

Anglican Orthodox Church, 118

Anglo-Catholicism, 92, 145–46

antebellum period: slavery and race relations during, 1, 4, 7–9, 14, 19–20, 43–44, 115, 157, 165, 167

anti-Communism: impact on church and church members, 66, 73–74, 92, 96, 104–7, 118, 121, 149, 247n. 42

antiwar movement, 194, 204–5

Arizona: state of. *See* General Convention: 1991

Arkansas, diocese of, 24, 26, 43, 82–83

Arny, Charles, 132

Asian Americans: and Episcopal